LOCALIZING DEVELOPMENT

A World Bank Policy Research Report

LOCALIZING DEVELOPMENT

DOES PARTICIPATION WORK?

Ghazala Mansuri and Vijayendra Rao

THE WORLD BANK
Washington, D.C.

Contents

Figures

Foreword

Promoting participation through community development projects and local decentralization has become a central tenet of development policy. The World Bank alone has invested about $85 billion over the last decade on development assistance for participation.

However, some observers feel that policy making in the area is conceptually weak, that project design is informed more by slogans than careful analysis. There have also been questions about whether participatory development is effective in reducing poverty, improving service delivery, and building the capacity for collective action. Some observers also find that participatory projects are complex to implement and deeply affected by context, and are thus unsuited for large development institutions such as the World Bank.

This groundbreaking report carefully examines each of these concerns. It outlines a conceptual framework for participation that is centered on the concept of civil society failure and how it interacts with market and government failures. The authors use this framework to understand the key policy debates surrounding participatory development and to frame the key policy questions. The report conducts the most comprehensive review of the evidence on the impact of participatory projects to date, looking at more than 400 papers and books.

For me, an important lesson from this report is its recognition of the difference between "organic" and "induced" participation. Organic participation is organized by civic groups outside government, sometimes in opposition to it; induced participation attempts to promote civic action through bureaucratically managed development interventions. Inducing participation requires a fundamentally different approach to development, one that is long term, context sensitive, committed to developing a culture of learning by doing through honest monitoring and evaluation systems, and that has the capacity to learn from failure. The report argues that participatory development is most effective when it works within a "sandwich" formed by support from an effective central state and bottom-up civic action.

This report represents an important contribution. It has significant implications for how to improve participation in development interventions and for development policy more broadly.

Martin Ravallion
Acting Chief Economist and Senior Vice President
The World Bank
Washington, DC
September 20, 2012

Acknowledgments

WE ARE GRATEFUL TO MARTIN RAVALLION, THE DIRECTOR OF THE World Bank's Development Economics Research Group (DECRG), and our managers, Peter Lanjouw and Will Martin, for giving us the time and the freedom to write this report in the best way we knew how. It has been more than three years in preparation, and we know that their patience was often tested. We hope the effort was worth it. We would also like to thank them for their prodding and constructive comments and suggestions at every stage of the process. We are also grateful to Gershon Feder, who started us off on this journey 10 years ago, when he convinced us that writing a big-picture piece on participatory development could be valuable. We acknowledge financial support from the DEC-managed Knowledge for Change Program (KCP-TF090806).

Radu Ban and Catherine Gamper helped research the report. Radu assisted with gathering and summarizing some of the literature and, along with Monica Yanez-Pagans, helped maintain the bibliographic database. Catherine's primary contribution was the analysis of data from World Bank reports and the management of the survey of project managers that forms an important part of chapter 7. Maribel Flewitt and Pauline Kokila provided excellent and uncomplaining administrative support.

Several other people worked on various aspects of the report, either as summer interns or on a part-time basis. They include Shahana Chattaraj, Deborah Davis, Indrajit Roy, and Bhrigupati Singh. Kent Eaton; Jesse Ribot, J. F. Lund, and T. True; Rachel Riedl and Tyler Dickovick; and Catherine Benson and Arun Agrawal provided background papers that contributed to our understanding of the management of common property resources, and decentralization in Africa and Latin America.

The World Bank's Office of the Publisher has been immensely supportive in bringing this report to timely completion. We would particularly like to thank Barbara Karni, who copyedited the manuscript and worked on the margin callouts; Janice Tuten, the publication production manager; and Stephen McGroarty, the acquisitions editor. We are also grateful to Marina Galvani, the World Bank's art curator, who helped us locate a wonderful piece of artwork for our cover, by the South African artist Zwelethu Mthethwa, from the Bank's collection.

Helpful and critical comments from Shanta Devarajan and Brian Levy when this report was still a concept note led to a major reconceptualization. We believe the report is much better for it. We are deeply grateful for the thoughtful, constructive, and detailed written comments from our colleagues in DECRG: Varun Gauri, Karla Hoff, Phil Keefer, Stuti Khemani, and Berk Özler. Karla Hoff also helped us sharpen and clarify many points of theory. We benefited greatly from discussions with other DECRG colleagues during various stages of writing this report. In particular, we would like to thank Francisco Ferreira, Deon Filmer, Emanuella Galasso, and Michael Woolcock.

The first draft of this report was widely circulated within the Bank. We received useful written comments from people from various departments, including the Social Development Anchor, the Community Driven Development (CDD) Community of Practice, the Chief Economist's offices in Africa and South Asia, the Human Development Anchor, and the Africa Decentralization team. We also benefited greatly from discussions with and comments from Robert Chase, Scott Guggenheim, Janmejay Singh, and Susan Wong. Robert Zoellick's comments on a summary of the report helped us sharpen some of the points in the conclusion.

We received extremely insightful and detailed written comments on an early draft of the report from a distinguished roster of external academic reviewers, to whom we are deeply indebted: Pranab Bardhan, Patrick Heller, Macartan Humphries, Dilip Mookherjee, and Jean-Philippe Platteau.

Over the years, our work on this report has been influenced by discussions with, and support from, a variety of colleagues and friends. We would particularly like to thank Kamran Akbar, Kripa Ananthpur, Arjun Appadurai, Granville and Nancy Austin, Rachid Bajwa, Tim

Besley, Mary Breeding, Monica Das Gupta, Peter Evans, Ariel Fiszbein, Archon Fung, John Gaventa, Qazi Azmat Isa, Ahmad Jamal, Agha Jawad, Shahnaz Kapadia, Michael Lipton, Deepa Narayan, Rohini Pande, Drew Permut, Menno Pradhan, Jesse Ribot, Paromita Sanyal, Amartya Sen, Parmesh Shah, Shubha Shankaran, Brian Silver, J. P. Singh, Ann Swidler, Mike Walton, Susan Watkins, and members of the Successful Societies Program at the Canadian Institute for Advanced Research (CIFAR).

Finally, Ghazala Mansuri would like to thank her son, Omar Sheheryar Agha, whose enthusiasm and intellectual curiosity has been a constant source of nourishment and whose patience with the seemingly endless weekends and nights spent on this report has been extraordinary for one so young. Vijayendra Rao would like to thank his father, Surendra Rao, for his many stimulating discussions and for his unstinting encouragement throughout the process of writing this report. He also thanks his mother, Vasanthi Rao Lokkur, and his partner, Monica Biradavolu, for their steadfast support.

Ghazala Mansuri and Vijayendra Rao
Washington, DC
September 20, 2012

About the Authors

Ghazala Mansuri is a lead economist in the Poverty Reduction and Equity Group of the World Bank. Her research spans four broad areas: rural land, labor and credit markets, the economics of household behavior, and the political economy of participatory development and institutional and governance reforms for development. Her research on the political economy of local development includes a number of evaluations of participatory development programs. Dr. Mansuri has published extensively in leading journals in economics and development. She holds a Ph.D. in economics from Boston University.

Vijayendra Rao is lead economist in the Development Research Group of the World Bank. He integrates his training in economics with theories and methods from anthropology, sociology, and political science to study the social and political context of extreme poverty in developing countries. Dr. Rao has published widely in leading journals in economics and development studies on subjects that include the rise in dowries in India, domestic violence, the economics of public celebrations, sex work in Calcutta, deliberative democracy, and village democracy. He co-edited *Culture and Public Action* and *History, Historians, and Development Policy*. He serves on the editorial boards of *Economic Development and Cultural Change*, the *Journal of Development Studies*, and the *World Bank Economic Review* and is a member of the Advisory Committee of the Successful Societies Program at the Canadian Institute for Advanced Research (CIFAR). He holds a Ph.D. in economics from the University of Pennsylvania.

Abbreviations

AKRSP	Agha Khan Rural Support Program
BPL	Below Poverty Line
DFID	Department for International Development
DPIP	District Poverty Initiative Program
EDUCO	Educación con Participación de la Comunidad (Education with Community Participation)
GDP	gross domestic product
HIV/AIDS	human immunodeficiency virus/ acquired immune deficiency syndrome
IAT	Implicit Association Test
KALAHI–CIDSS	Kapit Bisig Laban Sa Kahirapan–Comprehensive and Integrated Delivery of Social Services
KDP	Kecamatan Development Program
M&E	monitoring and evaluation
MIS	management information system
NGO	nongovernmental organization
NRSP	National Rural Support Program
PSF	Programa Saude da Família (Family Health Program)
PT	Partido dos Trabalhadores (Workers' Party)
SC	Scheduled Caste
ST	Scheduled Tribe
TASAF	Tanzanian Social Action Fund
USAID	U.S. Agency for International Development
VP	*van panchayat* (local forest council)
ZAMSIF	Zambia Social Fund

All amounts are presented in U.S. dollars unless otherwise indicated.

Overview

OVER THE PAST DECADE, THE WORLD BANK HAS ALLOCATED almost $85 billion to local participatory development. Driving this massive injection of funding has been the underlying belief that involving communities in at least some aspects of project design and implementation creates a closer connection between development aid and its intended beneficiaries. Indeed, local participation is proposed as a method to achieve a variety of goals, including sharpening poverty targeting, improving service delivery, expanding livelihood opportunities, and strengthening demand for good governance.

In principle, a more engaged citizenry should be able to achieve a higher level of cooperation and make government more accountable. In practice, little is known about how best to foster such engagement. Can participation be induced through the type of large-scale government and donor-funded participatory programs that have become a leitmotif of development policy? It is this question that is at the heart of this Policy Research Report.

The two major modalities for inducing local participation are community development and decentralization of resources and authority to local governments. *Community development* supports efforts to bring villages, urban neighborhoods, or other household groupings into the process of managing development resources without relying on formally constituted local governments. Community development projects— variously labeled community-driven development, community-based development, community livelihood projects, and social funds— include efforts to expand community engagement in service delivery. Designs for this type of aid can range from community-based targeting, in which only the selection of beneficiaries is decentralized, to projects in which communities are also involved to varying degrees in the design and management of resources.

Decentralization refers to efforts to strengthen village and municipal governments on both the demand and supply sides. On the demand side, decentralization strengthens citizens' participation in local government by, for example, instituting regular elections, improving access to information, and fostering mechanisms for deliberative decision making. On the supply side, it enhances the ability of local governments to provide services by increasing their financial resources, strengthening the capacity of local officials, and streamlining and rationalizing their administrative functions.

This report focuses on assessing the impact of large-scale, policy-driven efforts to induce participation. It does not, as such, examine the literature on organic participation—participation spurred by civic groups, whether organized or not, acting independently of and sometimes even in opposition to government. Organic participation is important, but it has not been the focus of donor funding. The report does draw on lessons from efforts to scale up organic movements through induced policy interventions. In this context, it views nongovernment organizations (NGOs) that are largely dependent on donor or government funding through participatory interventions as part of the effort to induce participation.

The report focuses on the "demand-side" aspects of participatory development. Important "supply-side" aspects of governance (fiscal decentralization, taxation policy, local government procedures, and bureaucratic inefficiency) have been dealt with extensively elsewhere and were beyond the scope of this work.

Most of the findings reviewed derive from econometric analysis. However, the report draws on case studies to develop specific ideas and to illustrate the conceptual framework. It also draws on observational studies from large samples to illustrate key points.

The History of Participatory Development and Decentralization

Participatory development and decentralization have common intellectual origins. Deliberative decision making has been a central feature of most religious and cultural traditions. In Athenian democracy, for example, important decisions were made in public deliberative settings in which all citizens (a group that excluded all women, slaves, and children) were expected to participate. Modern notions of participation arguably derive from the 18th and 19th centuries, notably from the work of Rousseau and John Stuart Mill.

In the early postcolonial period, the 1950s and 1960s, the U.S. Agency for International Development (USAID) and other donors helped drive the first wave of interest in participatory development by funding and promoting cooperative institutions, community-based development, and decentralization. By the 1970s, however, interest in participatory development had waned with the realization that cooperatives had largely failed and government reform was difficult to implement or sustain. The focus of policy shifted to large-scale investments in agricultural and industrial growth. By the mid-1980s, however, activists and scholars attacked this approach, seeing it as "top-down" and inherently disempowering and biased against the interests of the poor. Economists such as Sen and Ostrom made a vigorous case for a more bottom-up and deliberative vision of development that allows the "common sense" and "social capital" of communities to play a central part in decisions that affect them. Their scholarship led to renewed interest in community-based development, decentralization, and participation by donors and governments. As the social costs of structural adjustment programs became evident by the early 1990s, donors began to actively fund such participatory approaches, with the aim of ensuring minimal levels of investment in public services and infrastructure and in social programs to protect the most vulnerable.

This renewed policy interest in participatory initiatives, along with the expansion in funding, has proceeded, in large part, with little systematic effort to understand the particular challenges entailed in inducing participation or to learn from the failures of past programs. As a result, the process is, arguably, still driven more by ideology and optimism than by systematic analysis, either theoretical or empirical.

The aim of this report is to fill some of these lacunae. It does so by first outlining a conceptual framework within which local participatory development interventions can be analyzed and then using the evidence to draw some broad lessons with this framework as a guide.

A Conceptual Framework for Participation

Market and government failures are now reasonably well understood. Policy makers are less likely than they once were to assume that markets work perfectly or that governments can always provide effective solutions to market failures. In contrast, the policy literature is rife with solutions to market and government failures that assume that groups of people—village communities, urban neighborhood associations, school councils, water user groups—will always work toward the common interest. Rarely is much thought given to the possibility of "civil society failure." In fact, organizing groups of people to solve market and government failures is itself subject to problems of coordination, asymmetric information, and pervasive inequality.

Civil society failure at the local level can be broadly thought of as a situation in which groups that live in geographic proximity are unable to act collectively to reach a feasible and preferable outcome. It includes coordinated actions that are inefficient—or efficient but welfare reducing on average—as well as the inability to undertake any coordinated action at all. Development policy that uses participatory processes needs to be informed by a thoughtful diagnosis of potential civil society failures, so that policy makers can clearly understand the tradeoffs involved in devolving decisions to local communities and can identify potential ways of repairing such failures.

Thinking of local development policy as occurring at the intersection of market, government, and civil society failures invariably increases appreciation of context. Such interactions are deeply conditioned by culture, politics, and social structure, and they vary from place to place. A policy that works in one country, or even one municipality, may fail miserably in another. Moreover, effective collective action is usually conditioned by a "cooperative infrastructure" that presupposes functional state institutions—and is likely to be far more challenging in its absence.

Empowering civic groups may lead to good outcomes. But it is not clear that inducing civic empowerment is always superior to a pure market-based strategy or a strategy that strengthens the role of central bureaucrats. Policy makers need to keep all of these considerations in mind as they consider how best to harness the power of communities.

Empirical Findings

This report reviews almost 500 studies on participatory development and decentralization. The findings shed light on three key issues.

How Important Is Capture?

The purpose of participatory programs is to enhance the involvement of the poor and the marginalized in community-level decision-making bodies in order to give citizens greater say in decisions that affect their lives. Do these programs result in choices that are better aligned with their preferences? Does fostering participation increase social cohesion? Does it produce more resilient and inclusive local institutions? Does it reduce capture and corruption?

On balance, the review of the literature finds that participants in civic activities tend to be wealthier, more educated, of higher social status (by caste and ethnicity), male, and more politically connected than nonparticipants. This picture may partly reflect the higher opportunity cost of participation for the poor. It also appears, however, that the poor often benefit less from participatory processes than do the better off, because resource allocation processes typically reflect the preferences of elite groups. Studies from a variety of countries show that communities in which inequality is high have worse outcomes, especially where political, economic, and social power are concentrated in the hands of a few. "Capture" also tends to be greater in communities that are remote from centers of power; have low literacy; are poor; or have significant caste, race, or gender disparities.

Policy design may also have unintended consequences. A large injection of resources for a participatory development project can, for example, attract the attention of the better off, making exclusion more likely. Participatory projects also often fail to build cohesive and resilient organizations. During the course of a project, cash or other material payoffs induce people to participate and build networks—but these mechanisms tend to dissolve when the incentives are withdrawn. Only when projects explicitly link community-based organizations with markets, or provide skills training, do they tend to improve group cohesiveness and collective action beyond the life of the project.

Spending decisions do seem to be better aligned with local needs under democratic decentralization, and resources are reallocated in favor of the less advantaged. But much depends on the nature of electoral incentives and the capacity of higher levels of government to provide oversight and ensure downward accountability.

Capacity also matters. The benefits of decentralization seem to be weaker in more remote, more isolated, and less literate localities. Such localities also tend to be more poorly served by mass media and other sources of information, and they are less likely to have adequate central oversight.

Does Participation Improve Development Outcomes?

On balance, greater community involvement seems to modestly improve resource sustainability and infrastructure quality. But the evidence suggests that people who benefit tend to be the most literate, the least geographically isolated, and the most connected to wealthy and powerful people. Participation thus appears to affect the distribution of benefits in ways that suggest that capture is often not "benevolent" or altruistic.

Project design and implementation rules play a critical role in determining whether participatory programs are captured. Demand-driven, competitive application processes can exclude the weakest communities and exacerbate horizontal inequities.

For many years, willingness to contribute to programs and projects has been seen as evidence of commitment and of the sustainability of programs or of infrastructure. But this belief has little basis in evidence. What little is known suggests that co-financing—the sine qua non of participatory projects—tends to exclude the poorest, particularly when individuals or communities self-select into a program. Evidence also suggests that co-financing requirements for local governments can widen horizontal inequities in targeted transfer programs, because poorer municipalities or counties have an incentive to reduce the poverty threshold for transfer eligibility in order to reduce their own co-payment burden.

The review of the evidence on community management of common-pool resources and community engagement in the creation and maintenance of small-scale infrastructure focuses on five main questions:

- What evidence is there for greater resource sustainability under decentralized or community management?

- What evidence is there of more inclusive management and greater equity in the distribution of benefits?
- To what extent do community characteristics such as wealth inequality, ethnic heterogeneity, and management experience affect the sustainability of resources or infrastructure?
- How much can local management systems help overcome adverse local characteristics—that is, can good design induce the right type and level of participation?
- How dependent is success on the role played by the central state?

Four main findings emerge from the literature:

- Inequality tends to worsen both efficiency and equity, and there can be important tradeoffs between resource sustainability and equity.
- Transferring management responsibilities to a resource or an infrastructure scheme does not usually involve handing over control to a cohesive organic entity with the requisite capacity; often it requires creating local management capacity. In the absence of deliberate efforts to create such capacity and provide resources for ongoing maintenance and management, investments in infrastructure are largely wasted and natural resources poorly managed.
- Clear mechanisms for downward accountability are critical. The literature is rife with cases in which decentralization is used to tighten central control and increase incentives for upward accountability rather than to increase local discretion. The absence of robust mechanisms for downward accountability tends to go hand in hand with complex reporting and planning requirements, which are usually beyond the capacity of local actors and become a tool for retaining control and assigning patronage. Most of these requirements are holdovers from past rules designed to extract resources from rather than benefit communities.
- Communities need to benefit from the resources they manage. For natural resources that create substantial externalities, the benefit should be commensurate with the size of the externality created by the resource and should at least compensate communities for the alternative uses to which they could put the resource for immediate gain.

Only a few studies compare community-managed infrastructure projects with similar projects delivered by governmental line departments using a more "top-down" delivery mechanism. These studies find that community engagement seems to improve both the quality of construction and the management of local infrastructure—implying lower levels of corruption relative to government provision.

This suggests that carefully designed projects have the potential to limit capture. Indeed, a key feature of the projects studied is that the implementing agencies provided significant oversight during construction, the maintenance and recurrent costs were explicitly budgeted for, and the implementing agency was available to provide training and support for maintenance. These concerns imply considerable engagement of higher-tier governments or implementing agencies in building local capacity, monitoring outcomes, and setting the broad parameters under which management is devolved—with a view to enhancing downward rather than upward accountability while leaving sufficient discretion at the local level.

Studies of community participation in health service and education find modestly positive results overall, although the causal link between participation and service delivery outcomes is often vague. Studies that are able to assess the impact of participation typically find that although inducing community engagement alone has little impact on outcomes, community engagement can substantially amplify the impact of investments in other health or education inputs. In the case of health service delivery, for example, the formation of community health groups appears to have virtually no effect on any health-related outcome when done in isolation but is effective when combined with inputs such as trained health personnel or the upgrading of health facilities. Community engagement leads to significantly larger reductions in maternal and infant mortality, larger improvements in health-related behaviors, and greater use of health facilities than investments in health inputs alone can deliver. Interestingly, successful programs are often located within larger government health delivery systems. This finding is encouraging, because government participation is usually central for scaling up health initiatives. The evidence also suggests that the most successful programs tend to be implemented by local governments that have some discretion and are downwardly accountable. Devolving the management of public programs to NGOs appears to work less well, although the evidence remains thin. Community engagement in education has somewhat similar but more muted effects, primarily because impacts on learning tend to be weak, at least over the time spans covered by evaluations, which may be too short to measure results. Overall, studies report an increase in school access, an improvement in retention rates and attendance, and a reduction in grade repetition.

Interventions that provide information to households and communities about the quality of services in their community as well as government standards of service tend to improve outcomes. Moreover, they do so even when no additional resources are expended.

Funding also matters. Increasing the fiscal burden on poor communities can reduce the quality of public service delivery. When projects do not cover maintenance and recurrent costs, communities are left with crumbling schools without teachers and clinics without medicines.

As with other interventions, however, poorer, more remote areas are less able to realize gains from decentralized service delivery. The benefits of decentralization are smaller when communities are less well administered and more embedded in an extractive equilibrium characterized by weak democratic practices and a politicized administration. Literacy is also an important constraint—an effect that is consistent across several studies.

The evidence suggests that community-based development efforts have had a limited impact on income poverty. Projects with significant microfinance components do show positive impacts on savings and assets, but these effects appear to be confined largely to the life cycle of the project. There is also some evidence that community-based development projects improve nutrition and diet quality, especially among children, although some of these studies find that larger benefits accrue to better-off households.

Does Participation Strengthen Civil Society?

There is little evidence that induced participation builds long-lasting cohesion, even at the community level. Group formation tends to be both parochial and unequal. Absent some kind of affirmative action program, groups that form under the aegis of interventions tend to systematically exclude disadvantaged and minority groups and women. Moreover, because similar types of people tend to form groups with one another, projects rarely promote cross-group cohesion—and may actually reinforce existing divisions.

An important question in this context is the role of facilitators who work with communities. The evidence on this issue is scant, but the few studies that have tried to measure their effects find that facilitators strongly influence the stated preferences of community members, who often tell facilitators what they think they want to hear.

Participation often tends to be driven by project-related incentives; people get together to derive benefits from project funds. It is very difficult to know whether these effects will last beyond the tenure of the project and the limited evidence indicates that it usually does not. There is some heartening evidence, though, that participation may have intrinsic value. Communities tend to express greater satisfaction with decisions in which they participate, even when participation does not change the outcome or when outcomes are not consistent with their expressed preferences.

The ballot box, though far from perfect, appears to provide a clearer mechanism for sanctioning unpopular policy choices or excessive rent-seeking by traditional or political elites than more informal forums for deliberation. In decentralized settings, credible and open elections help align the decisions of politicians with the demands of their constituents. When participatory and deliberative councils exist in such settings, they can foster a significant degree of civic engagement. It is less clear how citizens can collectively sanction negligent or corrupt officials or local leaders where such venues for the exercise of voice are not available.

Repairing civic failures requires that social inequalities be addressed. One way of trying to do so is to mandate the inclusion of disadvantaged groups in the participatory process. There is virtually no evidence from evaluations of community-driven development projects on whether such mandates work. However, a growing body of evidence from village democracies in India indicates broadly positive impacts. Quotas in village councils and presidencies for disadvantaged groups and women tend to change political incentives in favor of the interests of the group that is favored by the quota.

Mandated inclusion also appears to provide an incubator for new political leadership. Evidence indicates that women and other excluded groups are more likely to run for nonmandated seats once they have had some experience on a mandated seat. Quotas can also weaken prevailing stereotypes that assign low ability and poor performance to traditionally excluded groups. However, lasting change requires that the inclusion mandates remain in place for long enough to change perceptions and social norms.

Democratic decentralization works because village and municipal democracies incentivize local politicians to nurture their constituencies. Because decentralized programs usually come with a constitutional mandate or other legal sanction from the center, they are relatively permanent and can therefore change social and political dynamics over the long term. In contrast, community-based projects are usually ad hoc interventions that are unable to open political opportunities for real social change.

Participatory interventions have been used in postconflict settings as a quick way of getting funds to the ground. The limited evidence on their effectiveness suggests that such projects have made little headway in building social cohesion or rebuilding the state. However, evidence from Africa seems to suggest that people emerging from civic conflict have a strong desire to participate in their communities and that well-designed and implemented projects could draw on this need.

In sum, the evidence suggests that, although local actors may have an informational and locational advantage, they use it to the benefit of the disadvantaged only where institutions and mechanisms to ensure local accountability are robust. Local oversight is most effective when other, higher-level institutions of accountability function well and communities have the capacity to effectively monitor service providers and others in charge of public resources. Local participation appears to increase, rather than diminish, the need for functional and strong institutions at the center. It also implies that implementing agencies for donor-funded projects need to have the capacity to exercise adequate oversight. There is little evidence that they can substitute for a nonfunctional state as a higher-level accountability agent, however. Reforms that enhance judicial oversight, allow for independent audit agencies, and protect and promote the right to information and a free media appear to be necessary for effective local oversight.

Moving Beyond the Evidence

Three main lessons emerge from distilling the evidence and thinking about the broader challenges in inducing participation.

1. **Induced participatory interventions work best when they are supported by a responsive state.** The state does not necessarily have to

be democratic—though being democratic helps a great deal. But in the sphere in which the intervention is being conducted—at the level of the community or the neighborhood—the state has to be responsive to community demands.

Parachuting funds into communities without any monitoring by a supportive state can result in the capture of decision making by elites who control the local cooperative infrastructure, leading to a high risk of corruption. In the absence of a supportive state, participatory engagement may still be able to make a difference, but projects implemented in such environments face much greater challenges.

2. Context, both local and national, is extremely important. Outcomes from interventions are highly variable across communities; local inequality, history, geography, the nature of social interactions, networks, and political systems all have a strong influence. The variability of these contexts is sometimes so large, and their effect so unpredictable, that projects that function well usually do so because they have strong built-in systems of learning and great sensitivity and adaptability to variations in context.

3. Effective civic engagement does not develop within a predictable trajectory. Instead, it is likely to proceed along a "punctuated equilibrium," in which long periods of seeming quietude are followed by intense, and often turbulent, change. Donor-driven participatory projects often assume a far less contentious trajectory. Conditioned by bureaucratic imperatives, they often declare that clear, measurable, and usually wildly optimistic outcomes will be delivered within a specified timeframe. There is a danger that such projects set themselves up for failure that derives not from what they achieve on the ground but from their unrealistic expectations.

One important reason for this overly ambitious approach, especially at the World Bank, is that many donors' institutional structure continues to derive from a focus on capital-intensive development and reconstruction. Building dams, bridges, and roads, or even schools and clinics, is a much more predictable activity than changing social and political systems. Repairing civil society and political failure requires a shift in the social equilibrium that derives from a change in the nature of social interactions and from modifying norms and local cultures. These much more difficult tasks require a fundamentally different approach to development—one that is flexible, long term, self-critical, and strongly infused with the spirit of learning by doing.

The variability of local context and the unpredictable nature of change trajectories in participatory interventions underscore the need for effective systems of monitoring and assessing impact. Such projects require constant adjustment, learning in the field, and experimentation in order to be effective—none of which can be done without tailoring project design to the local context, carefully monitoring implementation, and designing robust evaluation systems.

As demonstrated in chapter 7 of this report, the World Bank falls far short on these measures—and other donors probably perform no better. The results are sobering—and instructive. Despite wide differences in contexts, the Project Assessment Documents of World Bank–funded projects (which lay out a project's design) are striking in their similarity, with language often simply cut and pasted from one project to another. A review of the monitoring and evaluation (M&E) systems in World Bank projects in which at least a third of the budget was allocated to local participation, as well as a survey of project managers, also reveals pervasive inattention to monitoring and evaluation systems. Only 40 percent of Project Assessment Documents included a monitoring system as an essential part of the project design, and a third failed to mention basic monitoring requirements such as a management information system (MIS). When monitoring was mentioned, it usually involved collecting extremely imprecise indicators, and even this data collection was done irregularly. Even less attention was paid to evaluating project effectiveness through a credible evaluation. The majority of project managers indicated that the Bank's operational policies do not provide adequate incentives for M&E and that M&E is not perceived to be a priority of senior management. M&E seems to be treated as a box to be checked to obtain a loan rather than as an instrument for improving project effectiveness.

Conclusion

Evaluations of participatory development efforts improved somewhat between 2007 and 2012, generating some new evidence. However, the evidence base for most questions relevant to policy remains thin, and far too little attention is still paid to monitoring and evaluation. Project design continues to show little appreciation of context, and inflexible institutional rules fail to internalize the complexity inherent in engaging with civic-led development. Unless these problems are addressed, participatory development projects will continue to struggle to make a difference.

Local participation tends to work well when it has teeth and when projects are based on well-thought-out and tested designs, facilitated by a responsive center, adequately and sustainably funded, and conditioned by a culture of learning by doing. To ensure that it supports projects with these characteristics, the World Bank and other donor agencies need to take several steps:

- Project structures need to change to allow for flexible, long-term engagement. Patience is a virtue.
- Project designs and impact evaluations need to be informed by political and social analyses, in addition to economic analysis.
- Monitoring needs to be taken far more seriously. The use of new, more cost-effective tools, such as short message service (SMS)–based reporting, could help enormously.
- Clear systems of facilitator feedback as well as participatory monitoring and redress systems need to be created.
- Most important, there needs to room for honest feedback to facilitate learning, instead of a tendency to rush to judgment coupled with a pervasive fear of failure. The complexity of participatory development requires a high tolerance for failure and clear incentives for project managers to report evidence of it. Failure is sometimes the best way to learn about what works. Only in an environment in which failure is tolerated can innovation take place and evidence-based policy decisions be made.

CHAPTER ONE

Why Does Participation Matter?

OVER THE PAST DECADE, THE WORLD BANK HAS ALLOCATED almost $85 billion to local participatory development.[1] Other development agencies—bilateral donors and regional development banks—have probably spent at least as much, as have the governments of most developing countries.[2]

The current wave of interest in participation began as a reaction to the highly centralized development strategies of the 1970s and 1980s, which created the widespread perception among activists and nongovernmental organization (NGOs) that "top-down" development aid was deeply disconnected from the needs of the poor, the marginalized, and the excluded. Underlying this shift was the belief that giving the poor a greater say in decisions that affected their lives by involving them in at least some aspects of project design and implementation would result in a closer connection between development aid and its intended beneficiaries.

Local participation has acquired a life of its own over the past decade. It is now proposed as a way to achieve a variety of goals, including improving poverty targeting, building community-level social capital, and increasing the demand for good governance.

One of the key objectives of participation is to incorporate local knowledge and preferences into the decision-making processes of governments, private providers, and donor agencies. When potential beneficiaries are able to make key decisions, participation becomes self-initiated action—what is known as the "exercise of voice and choice," or "empowerment." Participation is expected to lead to better-designed development projects, more effective service delivery, and improvements in the targeting of benefits. Ultimately, it is expected to lead to a more

Local participation has been proposed as a way to improve poverty targeting, build social capital, and increase demand for good governance.

15

equitable allocation of public resources and to reductions in corruption and rent-seeking.

The two major modalities for fostering local participation are community development and decentralization of resources and authority to local governments. *Community development* supports efforts to bring villages, urban neighborhoods, and other household groupings into the process of managing development resources, without relying on formally constituted local governments. Community development projects are labeled as community-driven development, community-based development, community livelihood projects, and social funds. In recent years, the effort to expand community engagement in service delivery has also introduced participatory education and health projects, which have some of the same features as community-driven and community-based development projects. Designs for this type of aid can range from community-based targeting, in which only the selection of beneficiaries is decentralized, to projects in which communities are also involved to varying degrees in project design, project management, and the management of resources.

Decentralization refers to efforts to strengthen village and municipal governments on both the demand and supply sides. On the demand side, it strengthens citizens' participation in local government—by, for example, instituting regular elections, improving access to information, and fostering mechanisms for deliberative decision making. On the supply side, it enhances the ability of local governments to provide services by increasing their financial resources, strengthening the capacity of local officials, and streamlining and rationalizing administrative functions.

Community development and decentralization share a common intellectual pedigree, firmly rooted in historical notions of participatory government. Proponents of participation hold that it has intrinsic value because it enhances pro-social thinking, strengthens citizenship, and enables more inclusive civic engagement. Insofar as taking part in community decision making also builds capacity for self-reliance and collective action (what is sometimes called "social capital"), participation also has instrumental value. When successful, participation can transform passive residents into effective public citizens, who use it as a tool to hold states and markets accountable and influence decisions that affect their lives.

Advocates of community development view it as a mechanism for enhancing sustainability, improving efficiency and effectiveness, scaling up poverty reduction programs, making development more inclusive, empowering poor people, building social capital, strengthening governance, and complementing market and public sector activities (see, for example, Dongier and others 2001). They argue that community-driven development in particular is able to achieve these results by aligning development priorities with community goals; enhancing communication between aid agencies and beneficiaries; expanding the resources available to the poor (through microcredit, social funds, and occupational training); and strengthening the capacity of community-based organizations to represent and advocate for their communities. Community-driven development has the explicit objective of reversing power relations in a manner that creates agency and voice for poor people and gives them more control over development assistance. It also strengthens their capacity to undertake and manage self-initiated development activities.

Advocates for local decentralization are motivated by a closely related logic that argues that reducing the distance between government and citizens allows governments to be closely observed. Citizens can communicate their preferences and needs to elected officials and closely monitor their performance, which improves both transparency and accountability; they are more likely to notice when local government officials steal money from a construction project, engage in nepotism, or spend their budgets without taking the views of citizens into account. Enhanced visibility is coupled with a greater capacity for citizens to mobilize and demand better services and hold local governments "socially accountable" by activating the local capacity for collective action. Decentralization, it is argued, also improves electoral accountability, because better-informed citizens are more capable of making more informed electoral choices. Furthermore, local governments "hear" citizens better through direct interactions or deliberative forums, which increase the voice of citizens. Thus, according to advocates, decentralization improves voice, accountability, and transparency, making governments more responsive to the needs of citizens.

Advocates of both community development and decentralization also argue that these forms of participatory development can be a training ground for citizenship. Local democracies teach citizens how to

Community development and decentralization share a common intellectual pedigree, firmly rooted in historical notions of participatory government.

engage in democratic politics and to engage, deliberate, and mobilize in ways that strengthen civil society.

This vision is not universally shared. Some skeptics have misgivings about the basic precepts of the approach; others are concerned about the practical challenges of implementing large participatory projects on tight timelines (Cooke and Kothari 2001; Harriss 2001; Li 2007; Mosse 2002). Particularly when the incentives they face are poorly aligned with the needs of the project, implementers may gloss over differences within target groups and local power structures or evade the difficult task of institution building in favor of more easily deliverable and measurable outcomes. Community development may also be inherently subject to elite capture because of the entrenched influence of local elites (Abraham and Platteau 2004).

The capacity of donor-led participation to educate and transform communities has been challenged on several grounds. First, some researchers argue that the exercise of voice and choice can be costly (Mansuri and Rao 2004). It may involve financial losses for beneficiaries, because of the time required to ensure adequate participation. Participation may also lead to psychological or physical duress for the most socially and economically disadvantaged, because it may require that they take positions that are in conflict with the interests of powerful groups. The premise of participatory approaches is that its potential benefits outweigh such costs, but critics argue that this is by no means certain.

Second, as participation has become mainstreamed, it has often been used to promote pragmatic policy interests, such as cost-effective delivery or low-cost maintenance rather than as a vehicle for radical social transformation, by shifting some of the costs of service delivery to potential beneficiaries. Indeed, in both Asia (Bowen 1986) and Africa (Ribot 1995), participation has been described as a form of forced or *corvée* labor, with the poor pressured into making far more substantial contributions than the rich.

Third, critics argue that the belief that participatory experiences will transform the attitudes and implementation styles of authoritarian bureaucracies (governments or donors) may be naive. The routinization of participatory planning exercises into the work of public sector agencies creates additional pressure on resources while leaving implementers unclear about the implications of this new accountability. An examination of several participatory projects finds that even in projects

> The capacity of donor-led participation to educate and transform communities has been challenged on several grounds.

with high levels of participation, "local knowledge" was often a construct of the planning context and concealed the underlying politics of knowledge production and use (Mosse 2002). Four potential pitfalls were identified:

- Participatory exercises are often public events that are open ended regarding target groups and program activities. Thus, such events are inherently political, and the resulting project design is often shaped by local power and gender relations.
- Outside agendas are often expressed as local knowledge. Project facilitators shape and direct participatory exercises, and the "needs" of beneficiaries are often shaped by perceptions of what the project can deliver.
- Participants may concur in the process of problem definition and planning in order to manipulate the program to serve their own interests. Although their concurrence can benefit both project staff and beneficiaries, it places consensus and action above detailed planning.
- Participatory processes can be used to legitimize a project that has previously established priorities and little real support from the community.

Fourth, critics argue that local governments in developing countries are not necessarily more accountable and transparent than central governments because of the absence of prerequisites for local accountability to work (Bardhan and Mookherjee 2006). These prerequisites include an educated and aware citizenry, relative social and economic equality, law and order, the ability to run free and fair elections within a constitutional setting, reliable and trustworthy information channels, and oversight by an active and effective civil society.

This report thus appears in the midst of a raging debate over the effectiveness of participatory development. Does it work? Does it increase accountability? Is it captured by elites? Does it increase voice and choice? Is it "empowering"? Is the money directed toward participatory development well spent? Sparked by concerns that the expansion in funding has not been accompanied by careful evaluations and independent analysis (Mansuri and Rao 2004), in recent years there has been a sharp increase in research, particularly impact evaluations, of community-based development. Scholars from a variety of disciplines have also substantially increased the understanding of the political

> Critics argue that local governments in developing countries are not necessarily more accountable and transparent than central governments.

economy of decentralization. The goal of this report is to place this research within an integrated conceptual framework, to summarize its conclusions, and to draw implications for policy.

The History of Participatory Development

> The idea of civic participation is as old as the idea of democracy.

The idea of civic participation is as old as the idea of democracy (Elster 1998); it has existed in many different cultures throughout history. In ancient Athens, policy decisions were made deliberatively, in public settings, with every male citizen given the opportunity to state his point of view. In Hinduism and Buddhism, public debate and deliberation have long been seen as a superior form of discourse (Sen 2005). Local deliberative institutions in South Asia, where these religions predominate, have been documented dating back to about the fifth century BC (Altekar 1949). The Quran requires that communal affairs be decided by mutual consultation (*shura*) (Ayish 2008). In Islam, the community (*umma*) uses *shura* to not only deliberate but also provide inputs into public policy, which the ruler (*khalifa*) must consider.

In pre-European Africa, Zulu chiefs could not make decisions without first consulting their councils (*chila ya njama*). Although the chiefs exercised ritual power, their influence depended on their ability to persuade and convince, not coerce. Among the Akan people in West Africa, the authority of the chief was greatly circumscribed. He was required to act in concurrence with counselors; an attempt to act on his own was legitimate grounds for dethronement.

> Local decentralization has an even longer history than participation.

Local decentralization has an even longer history than participation. Archaeological evidence shows that small city-states in Mesopotamia and districts in Egypt ruled for many hundreds of years before being unified (around 3200 BC) into centrally ruled nations. Through conquest, these nations formed even greater empires, but cities and districts within the conquered territories, although obliged to pay tribute and contribute soldiers to their overlords' armies, essentially enjoyed home rule. In addition, as soon as the hold of the conqueror faltered, local hegemony grew strong (Gardiner 1961; Kramer 1971).

Around 1200 BC, for instance, when the great powers of Egypt and Mesopotamia faced internal problems and invasion from the north, Phoenician vassal cities seized the opportunity to declare their independence. Although each city continued to rule itself, the cities agreed to form a loose geopolitical alliance. For the next 600 years, even during periods of foreign rule, ships from the Phoenician alliance plied the Mediterranean and traded throughout their vast economic empire (Mann 1986). When Phoenicia was later conquered—first by the Greeks, then by the Romans—its cities were forced to levy, collect, and send back revenues to the central power, but their municipal life continued to thrive. Rome actually encouraged (nonsubversive) civic activity, contributing handsomely to public buildings and activities across the empire (Abbot and Johnson 1968).

Decentralized but loosely affiliated structures were also the rule in South Asia during the Mauryan (321–185 BC) and Mughal (1526–1857) eras. Village governments had considerable authority and power over practical affairs; the center was seen largely as a place of moral and symbolic authority that extracted taxes and tribute. In Africa, vassals used collective decision making to hold chieftains in check, and community members used consultations and popular assemblies to hold vassal governments accountable to the public at large.

The modern theory of participation was first coherently articulated in the 18th century by Jean-Jacques Rousseau, author of *The Social Contract*. Rousseau outlined a vision of democracy in which equal citizens assemble to make decisions in an interdependent, deliberative manner, to uncover the "general will"—that is, to forge a policy in which benefits and burdens are equally shared (Pateman 1976). Rousseau was searching for a vision of human progress in which communities and connectedness could complement the Enlightenment's notions of individual liberty, and in which the human soul was more important than science (Damrosch 2007). To Rousseau, participation was more than a method of decision making. It was a process by which an individual developed empathy for another's point of view and learned to take account of the public interest in order to gain cooperation. Participation therefore served an important educative function: the individual learned how to become a public citizen, and community members developed a sense of belonging. Rousseau intimately linked the notion of participation with the development of civic life—an idea that has had a profound influence on subsequent political thought.

Among the many 19th century philosophers who built on these ideas, perhaps the most notable was John Stuart Mill (1859, 1879),

> Rousseau first articulated the modern theory of participation in the 18th century.

21

who also emphasized the educative value of participation. Influenced by Alexis de Tocqueville's laudatory descriptions in *Democracy in America* (1838) of local political institutions in the United States and the spirit of participatory democracy they fostered, Mill became deeply skeptical of centralized forms of government. His fears led him to argue that universal suffrage and participation in national government are of little use if citizens have not been prepared for participation at the local level. Mill applied this logic to notions of participation in industry, where, he argued, collective management would lead to individuals valuing public over individual interests.

Mill's vision of a participatory society was taken forward by G. D. H. Cole, Henry Maine, and other philosophers (known as the English Pluralists), who rejected the idea of a centralized state and argued that "individual freedom would best be realized in the groups and associations that made up the fabric of modern civil society" (Mantena 2009). Henry Maine is of particular relevance to contemporary development thought. Sent to India in the 1860s to advise the British government on legal matters, he came across several accounts by British administrators of thriving indigenous systems of autonomous village governments that had many characteristics of participatory democracies. These "data" led him to articulate a theory of the village community as an alternative to the centralized state (Maine 1876). In Maine's view, village communities, led by a council of elders (*panchayat*), were not subject to a set of laws articulated from above but had more fluid legal and governance structures that adapted to changing conditions while maintaining strict adherence to traditional customs (Mantena 2009).

Support for participation stems from a belief that it has both intrinsic and instrumental value.

Community development and government decentralization thus have a common intellectual history, stemming from a belief that participation has both intrinsic and instrumental value. Participation in decision making, Maine believed, makes individuals into public citizens by training them to think in terms of the public good rather than merely private interests; it builds the capacity for collective action and what modern social theorists would call "agency." Participation also has instrumental value in developing the ability of citizens to hold the state and markets accountable and to influence decisions that affect their lives. As the concept evolved, two distinct forms of participation emerged: participation in Rousseau's sense of building a collective identity and participation in the sense of electing a representative government.

Participation in Asia, Africa, and Latin America

Rousseau, Mill, and Maine had a deep influence on colonial thought. In India, which became fertile territory for colonial experiments in governance, the liberal British Viceroy Lord Ripon instituted local government reforms in 1882 for the primary purpose of providing "political education" and reviving and extending India's indigenous system of government (Tinker 1967).

Maine's description of autonomously governed and self-reliant Indian village communities also influenced Mohandas Gandhi, who made it a central tenet of his philosophy of decentralized economic and political power, as articulated in his writings on village self-reliance, collected in his book *Village Swaraj* (Gandhi 1962). Gandhi saw the self-reliant village as the cornerstone of a system of government and of economic life. The village was to be "a complete republic, independent of its neighbors for its own vital wants, and yet interdependent for many others where dependence is a necessity." Gandhi's village-republic would be emblematic of a "perfect democracy," ensuring equality across castes and religions and self-sufficiency in all needs; it would be driven by cooperation and nonviolence. Gandhi remains a central figure in the participatory and decentralization movements in both India and the development community at large, particularly among people who see participation as an antidote to the community-corroding effects of economic growth and modernization.

Decentralization in colonial anglophone Africa followed a similar trajectory, as the colonial powers adopted a policy of "decentralized despotism" (Mamdani 1996). The principal colonizers established administrative systems to efficiently govern and extract revenues from the conquered territories. The British established "indirect rule" that was, according to Mamdani, based on the lessons they had learned in India from the innovations in local self-government initiated by Ripon. The British converted traditional chiefs into "administrative chiefs" responsible for several functions at the lowest level of the civil administration, granting them fiscal and functional autonomy as long as they did not challenge the colonial state. Decentralization in colonial India and Africa was as much an effort at streamlining colonial power as it was an effort at good governance.

In the French colonies, by contrast, decentralization involved the direct application of French administrative structures, culture,

Autonomously governed and self-reliant Indian village communities were a central tenet of Gandhi's philosophy of decentralized economic and political power.

civil law, and education to the colonies. The early colonies, such as Senegal, were organized according to the French local government model, based on urban communes represented by municipal councils. Citizens of the "four communes" of Senegal (Dakar, Gorée, St. Louis, and Rufisque) even elected representatives to the French parliament in Paris. Developments in Senegalese communes mirrored political developments in France: when, in 1831, French communes were given legal status and the principle of elected municipal councils was established, these changes applied to the communes in Senegal.

As the French acquired more territory and extended their control over larger populations, they reversed their policies and began to rule their new African colonies indirectly, through Africans. They established a *code de l'indigénat*, which outlined the legal system under which indigenous populations were to be governed (Levine 2004). This law provided for the establishment of administrative *cercles* ruled by appointed indigenous authorities, religious courts, and the native police. *Cercles* comprised cantons, and cantons comprised villages. Villages were governed by *chefs du village*, cantons by *chefs de canton,* and *cercles* by *cercle commandeurs,* each of whom was appointed by and responsible to the French authorities. The administrators who supervised these chiefs were recruited, trained, and fielded by the central state. Ribot (2009) points out that in "all these decentralized systems, the colonial rulers used local 'customary' chiefs to administer the rural world—that is, maintain law and order, collect taxes, and conscript labor. The systems were created to manage Africans under local administrative rule."

In Latin America, Spanish and Portuguese rule left a centralized legacy (Selee and Tulchin 2004; Grindle 2007; Eaton 2008). Colonial systems were based on the extraction of wealth and required highly centralized structures to coordinate the process. In Mexico, for example, the conquistadores appointed local councils tasked with maintaining law and order and overseeing food and water supplies (Grindle 2007); the councils were supervised and held in check by district agents, who were also responsible for tax collection.

After independence, countries in Latin America modified these structures to conform with the more federalist notions from France and the United States. In Brazil, for instance, the First Republic (which followed the centralized empire established immediately after independence) had pronounced federal features but provided little or no support for local governments or municipalities. With its collapse, in

After independence, countries in Latin America modified their centralized structures to conform with the more federalist notions from France and the United States.

1930, decentralization gave way to centralized institutions (Melo and Rezende 2004) and, paradoxically, "municipalism" became a hallmark of the more centralized developmentalist period.

History of Policy in Participatory Development

By the end of World War II, the disintegration of colonial regimes made reconstruction and development the central endeavors in Africa and Asia. Driven by the Bretton Woods institutions, development was viewed as a "big" undertaking, influenced by structural theories and planning models. "Small" development also had proponents, particularly among policy makers at the United Nations and the U.S. Agency for International Development (USAID), who tended toward a communitarian vision of human progress. Their influence led to a first wave of participatory development in the 1950s that by 1960 had spread to more than 60 countries in Africa, Asia, and Latin America (White 1999; Arizpe 2004).[3] By 1959, USAID had pumped more than $50 million into community development projects in about 30 countries. In the context of the Cold War, community development was seen as a means of protecting newly independent states against the dual threats of external military aggression and internal subversion. Perhaps the most important motive was to provide a democratic alternative to Communism (White 1999; Arizpe 2004).

In the 1950s, the communitarian approach was also promoted in India, primarily by the U.S. government and the Ford Foundation, where it resonated because of its compatibility with Gandhian ideals. The Ford Foundation approach drew on ideas from regional planners in the United States who were concerned about the erosion of communities with the onset of modernization and urbanization, as well as on Gandhi's ideas about sustainable village communities (Immerwahr 2010). In 1952, a Ford Foundation–supported program based on participatory models of community development was launched in 16,500 villages; the government of India soon expanded the program to cover the entire country.

Funding for community development programs began to dry up in the early 1960s, because of their perceived failures and because the specter of famine in Asia made the more top-down, technical approaches to development seem more urgent. White (1999) argues that community development programs during this period were undermined

In the 1950s, the U.S. government and the Ford Foundation promoted the communitarian approach to development in India.

Funding for community development programs began to dry up in the early 1960s.

25

by the inability of donors to incorporate the lessons learned about elite capture or to engage in genuine partnerships with beneficiaries. As a consequence, community development programs were widely perceived, whether correctly or not, as having failed to achieve their stated objectives. They were more or less completely abandoned by the end of the 1960s.

As donor interest in local participatory development waned, there was a revival of interest among radical thinkers. Particularly influential were Frantz Fanon's *The Wretched of the Earth* (1961) and Paulo Freire's *Pedagogy of the Oppressed* (1970). Fanon's work, which was sometimes accused of exhorting readers to violence, was born out of frustration with the racism, torture, and vindictiveness of the colonial administration in Algeria. In *The Wretched of the Earth*, he critiques both imperialism and nationalism and calls for the redistribution of wealth and technology that orient effective power in favor of the poorest people.

Freire was influenced by Fanon and by liberation theologists in Brazil. His lifelong commitment to adult education helped him explore the ways in which the oppressed could overcome powerlessness and "unfreedom." In *Pedagogy of the Oppressed*, he stresses the need to develop an educational system that is more "dialogic," is rooted in students' lived experiences, and values local and diverse kinds of knowledge. This kind of education becomes a tool for "conscientizing" illiterate (and oppressed) populations. In effect, Freire argues for a model of education that does not consider students' minds a *tabula rasa*. Instead, the role of education is to make students more self-aware and sensitive to their position and to that of others—a theme very similar to Rousseau's notion of the "general will."

During the 1960s and 1970s, policy makers began to shift their focus to agricultural and industrial growth. This shift was given intellectual support from the apparent success of industrializing planning models of Soviet Russia and from early neoclassical growth models. The McNamara era at the World Bank focused first on large infrastructure projects and later on the centralized provision of housing, education, and health. Politically, centralized polities appeared to be viable and desirable. Even in the established democracies, mainstream democratic theories emphasized the representative rather than participatory features of democracy and the desirability of stability rather than the involvement of the lower classes. Democracy came to be thought of as merely a method of aggregating preferences by choosing leaders,

During the 1960s and 1970s, policy makers began to shift their focus to agricultural and industrial growth . . .

and the deliberation and civic empowerment aspects of the concept were deemphasized (see Schumpeter 1942 and Dahl 1963 for typical formulations).

Also during this period, economists, who had long been skeptical of community-centered development, began to have a profound influence on development policy. The early literature on development policy was strongly influenced by the work of Mancur Olson (1965, 2), who argued that without coercion or some other special device to make individuals act in their common interest "rational self-interested individuals will not act to achieve their common or group interests." Olson was concerned with "exploitation of the great by the small," because people with smaller interests in a public good would tend to free-ride on the efforts of people with greater interests.

Hardin's (1968) powerful idea of the "tragedy of the commons" had even broader implications for a range of economic issues, including the domain of the public and the private, decentralization of power to local governments, and the provision and management of common-pool resources. Like Hardin, property rights theorists such as Demsetz (1970) and North (1990) argued that common property resources would be overexploited as demand rose unless the commons were enclosed or protected by strong state regulation. This view generated a great deal of pessimism in multilateral development institutions about the viability of local provision or management of public goods or the commons. It created a strong impetus for centralized state provision of public goods, central regulation of common-pool resources, and an emphasis on private property rights.

At the same time, there was strong support among economic theorists for decentralized government with electoral democracy. Economists approached this problem in several ways. Tiebout's (1956) work on the theory of local government expenditures emphasized the efficiency of decentralized governance. He argued that in a community context, if mobility were relatively costless, individuals would reveal their true preferences for levels and combinations of public goods provision by "voting with their feet"—moving to the locality that offered their preferred tax-benefit mix. Competition among jurisdictions supplying different combinations of local public goods would thus lead to an efficient supply of such goods.

The Tiebout hypothesis later came under heavy attack on the grounds that its assumptions—full information about community

... and economists, who had long been skeptical of community-centered development, began to have a profound influence on development policy.

characteristics, costless mobility, no externalities, no economies of scale, and static preferences—were untenable in developing countries, and indeed in many developed countries as well. Nevertheless, Tiebout continues to be widely invoked to support the view that competition among local jurisdictions in the provision of public goods increases allocative efficiency—and consequently to justify a push toward decentralization.

By the mid-1980s, critics of the top-down approach began to complain that many large-scale, centralized, government-initiated development programs—from schooling to health to credit to irrigation systems—were performing poorly while rapidly degrading common-pool resources and having significant negative environmental and poverty impacts. These complaints reawakened interest in local decision making and the local management of resources. Led by Chambers (1983) and others, a new participatory development movement applied these ideas to small-scale projects in ways that allowed the poor to act as informed participants, with external agents serving mainly as facilitators and sources of funds. Further support came from the increasingly strong critique of development from academic social scientists such as Escobar (1995) and Scott (1999), who argued that top-down perspectives were both disempowering and ineffective. Meanwhile, highly successful community-driven development initiatives—such as the Self-Employed Women's Association in India, the Orangi Slum Improvement Project in Pakistan, and the Iringa Nutrition Project in Tanzania—were providing important lessons for large donors (Krishna, Uphoff, and Esman 1997).

Thinking in mainstream development circles was also significantly affected by the work of Hirschman (1970, 1984); Cernea (1985); and Ostrom (1990). Hirschman's (1970) notions of "voice" and "exit" helped development practitioners understand how collective agency could improve well-being. Hirschman's (1984) own attempts to apply these ideas to participatory development helped confirm his theories. Cernea (1985) showed how large organizations such as the World Bank could "put people first" by working systematically at the local level. Ostrom's (1990) work on the management of common-pool resources shifted perceptions about the potential for collective action in poor communities. She argued that what made Olson's and Hardin's work most powerful also made it dangerous as a foundation for policy making, as their results depended on a set of constraints imposed for purposes of analysis. The relevance of their theories for policy making, she contended, was an open question rather than a foregone conclusion. In the real

By the mid-1980s, critics of the top-down approach began to complain that many large-scale, centralized, government-initiated development programs were performing poorly.

world, the capabilities of the people involved can be changed, altering the constraints. Ostrom and others assembled considerable evidence from case studies showing that endogenous institutions often managed common-pool resources successfully. Thus, Hardin's "remorseless tragedies" were not an inevitable outcome of community management.

Sen's (1985, 1999) effort to shift the focus of development from material well-being to a broad-based "capability" approach also deeply influenced the development community. Central to this approach were strategies to "empower" poor people—an agenda taken on by the World Bank and other donors as part of their response to criticism of top-down development. Arguments for "participatory development," as advocated by Chambers (1983) and others, led to the inclusion of participation as a crucial means of allowing the poor to have some control over decisions that affected them.

These intellectual developments paralleled the rise of pro-democracy movements, which led to the breakdown of authoritarian regimes in many parts of the world (Leftwich 1993; O'Donnell 1993). The 1980s and 1990s witnessed the collapse of totalitarian systems in Eastern Europe, the former Soviet Union, and Indonesia and the radical redistribution of power and authority in Brazil and the Philippines. The rise of democratic movements and the conviction that centralized state institutions were corrupt, unaccountable, and unable to deliver public services led to a growing belief in the value of decentralized government. Mexico is a typical example. By 1982, international donors had begun to advise the country's central government to both initiate structural adjustment and share administrative and fiscal responsibilities with lower tiers of government (Mizrahi 2004; Grindle 2007).

USAID was among the earliest donors to extend explicit support to democratic decentralization. In the late 1980s, with the fall of Communism in Eastern Europe, the agency spelled out its agenda to support democratic local governance. It viewed decentralization as a "means to empower citizens locally and to disperse power from the central government to localities" (USAID 2000, 4). By the early 1990s, the British and French governments, the Development Assistance Committee, the European Council, the Heads of State and Government of the Organization of African Unity, and the Commonwealth Heads of Government had all (re)committed to strengthening democracy, participation, and accountability through the mechanism of decentralization. The United Nations Development Programme began to explicitly

USAID was among the earliest donors to extend explicit support to democratic decentralization.

The World Bank was instrumental in popularizing the concept of decentralization.

extend assistance to decentralization in 1992; by 1999, it had spent more than $138 million on decentralization projects.

The World Bank was perhaps most instrumental in popularizing the concept of decentralization, by articulating the pressing significance of governance issues, especially in Africa. Its focus on governance was motivated by the difficult economic climate of the 1980s, coupled with the realization that investment lending required an appropriate policy framework to achieve its objectives. Its influential publication, *Governance and Development,* summed up the benefits of local decentralization as resulting in significant improvements in efficiency and effectiveness (World Bank 1992).

Support for decentralization was by no means unqualified: some observers noted that the "pure decentralization of fiscal federalism theory" (Prud'homme 1995, 202) could jeopardize macroeconomic stability and increase regional disparities within countries. Nonetheless, by 1996, the Bank recognized the role of citizen participation in holding state structures accountable as key to effective local government.

If the move toward local decentralization was driven largely by a desire for better governance, community development was driven by the belief that investing in the "social capital" of communities would lead to their empowerment and give them a sustainable capacity to fashion development in their own terms. The inclusion of participatory elements in large-scale development assistance came quickly at the World Bank, in social investment funds (Narayan and Ebbe 1997) and other forms of assistance. Initially focused on targeting poverty, these projects moved toward a more holistic effort to encourage participation through institutions that organize the poor and build their capabilities to act collectively in their own interest (Narayan 2002). The World Bank's (2001) *World Development Report 2000/2001: Attacking Poverty* focused on empowerment as a key priority of development policy. Its publication led to a broad-based effort at the Bank to scale up community-based development. The *World Development Report 2004: Making Services Work for Poor People* identified local accountability and local decentralization as important elements of programs that seek to improve the delivery of public services (World Bank 2004). More recently, donors have recognized that strengthening governance is key to effective development and that improving civic participation, or the "demand side" of governance, should be an important object of community development and decentralization. With this second wave of interest in participatory approaches to development, participatory notions have, once again, been absorbed into the mainstream of development thought and practice.[4]

Thus, the two types of local participation—community development and local decentralization—have common goals and intellectual origins. They became distinct modalities promoted by distinct ideological camps in the second half of the 20th century. In the current (21st century) wave of interest in local participation, policy does not distinguish clearly between the two interpretations. Many decentralization programs with local electoral democracy place local deliberative forums at the heart of decision making (examples include participatory budgeting and *gram sabhas* [village assemblies]), and many community-driven projects build electoral accountability into their leadership selection process. Thus, lessons from the evidence on village democracy could have implications for the design of community-driven projects, and lessons from participatory forums in community-driven projects could have implications for the design of decentralization programs. For this reason, both are treated here within the common framework of local participatory development.

Organic versus Induced Participation

Achieving participatory governance and building civic capacity has historically been an organic rather than a state-led process—a process spurred by civic groups acting independently of, and often in opposition to, government. Organic participation is usually driven by social movements aimed at confronting powerful individuals and institutions within industries and government and improving the functioning of these spheres through a process of conflict, confrontation, and accommodation.

Such processes are often effective because they arise endogenously, within a country's trajectory of change, and are directed by highly motivated, charismatic leaders who mobilize citizens to give voice to their interests (grievances, rights, and concerns) and exploit political opportunities. Social movements demand change by confronting situations they find untenable; they ultimately achieve their goals when they are able to influence the political process or obtain political power. They engage in a process of creative destruction. First, they imagine a world in which social and political relationships are more equitably arranged—or

> Organic participation is spurred by civic groups acting independently of, and often in opposition to, government.

at least restructured in a manner congruent with the interests of the movement—they articulate their vision of this world to expand their influence. Then, they mobilize citizens who believe in this vision to fight for the cause, often at considerable personal cost.

Organic participation is a broad term that covers a variety of civic activities. It has historically been the norm for civic expression. It includes social movements that fight for greater democratic expression and for the rights of the underprivileged, such as the civil rights movement in the United States and the anti-apartheid movement in South Africa. It also includes attempts to build membership-based organizations to improve livelihoods and living standards, such as the Grameen Bank in Bangladesh or the Self-Employed Women's Association in India. Organic participation may also include labor movements that form unions to protect workers and trade associations formed to represent the interests of a particular industry.

Induced participation, by contrast, refers to participation promoted through policy actions of the state and implemented by bureaucracies (the "state" can include external governments working through bilateral and multilateral agencies, which usually operate with the consent of the sovereign state). Induced participation comes in two forms: decentralization and community-driven development.

The important difference between induced and organic participation is that powerful institutions extrinsically promote inducted participation, usually in a manner that affects a large number of communities at the same time. In contrast, intrinsically motivated local actors drive organic participation.

There is often some overlap between organic and induced participation. Governments may decentralize because of the efforts of social movements, and the designs of induced participatory programs are often built on organic models. A government may decide to scale up the efforts of small-scale organic initiatives and thus turn them into induced initiatives. An important question is whether efforts initiated by organic participation can be scaled up by policy interventions in the form of projects. Rather than wait for the slow process of the endogenous development of civic capacity, can policy interventions harness the capacity of citizens to help themselves and improve the quality of government and the functioning of markets?

The organic development of civic capacity is a complex process that is deeply imbedded in a country's history, its internal conflicts,

Induced participation refers to participation promoted through policy actions of the state and implemented by bureaucracies.

its conception of nationalism, its levels of education and literacy, the distribution of education and wealth, the nature of the state, the nature of economic and political markets, and a variety of other conditions. Organic participation is driven by self-motivated leaders who work tirelessly, with little compensation, often at a high opportunity cost. They are constantly innovating, networking, and organizing to get the movement to succeed. When this complex process of organic change, driven by intrinsically motivated people, is turned into policy—projects and interventions to induce participation—it has to be transformed into manageable, bureaucratically defined entities, with budgets, targets, and extrinsically motivated salaried staff as agents of change. This transformation is common to all large-scale, state-led policy initiatives; it has been famously characterized by Scott (1999) as "seeing like a state." But participatory interventions are different from other types of policy initiatives, because they are based on an inherent irony: the government is creating institutions structured to resist failures in government. When government induces participation by means of projects, its agents often must act against their self-interest by promoting institutions whose purpose is to upset the equilibrium that gives them considerable personal advantage. Moreover, by devolving power to the local level, higher levels of government cede power, authority, and finances to communities over which they may have little control.

Despite these challenges, in recent years, some countries have successfully induced participation by actively promoting participatory spaces within decentralized systems of governance. One of the best-known cases involves participatory budgeting in Porto Alegre, Brazil. Baiocchi (2005) reviews the history of Brazil's transition from dictatorship to democracy in 1985, placing the Porto Alegre experiment within the context of this shift. By 1988, decentralization to the local level was codified in the new Brazilian constitution, and municipal elections were held. Two years later, a candidate from the Workers Party, which had become a leader in the citizens' rights movement during the dictatorship, was elected mayor of Porto Alegre.[5] The new mayor introduced participatory budgeting. After some years of experimentation, by the year 2000 participatory budgeting assemblies were drawing more than 14,000 participants from the city's poorer classes and achieving substantial success in improving a range of development outcomes. About 9–21 percent of the city's annual budget was dedicated to pro-poor investments, leading to almost full sewerage and

Some countries have induced participation by actively promoting participatory spaces within decentralized systems of governance.

water coverage, a threefold increase in municipal school enrollment, and a significant increase in housing for poor families.

Another important, if less than ideal, example of an entire country trying to introduce empowered participatory governance is the *panchayat* (rural governance) reform in India. Before the enactment of the 73rd amendment to the constitution, in 1992, village democracy in India was extremely uneven, despite the fact that most state constitutions mandated regular village elections and gave village governments some degree of fiscal authority. The amendment addressed these problems in several ways:

- It set up a three-tiered *panchayat* system consisting of *gram panchayats* (village councils), *block panchayats* (block councils), and *zila panchayats* (district councils).
- It systematized *panchayat* elections to all three levels, established independent election commissions, and gave the *panchayat*s more fiscal authority and political power.
- It mandated that *gram sabhas* (village meetings) be held at regular intervals throughout the year, to allow anyone in the village to discuss budgets, development plans, and the selection of beneficiaries and to interrogate *gram panchayat* and local administrative officials on any issue.
- It reserved a proportion of seats on *gram panchayat*s, including the position of *gram panchayat* president, for members of disadvantaged castes (according to their share of the village population) and women (who are allocated a third of all seats in the *gram panchayat* and a third of *gram panchayat* presidencies on a rotating basis).

By making deliberative processes through the *gram sabha* a cornerstone of village government, the central authorities in India created a civic sphere that was not organically derived but, rather, sponsored by the state—in effect, blurring the boundary between the state and civil society and between organic and induced participation. By reducing its monopoly on power and altering its relationship with citizens, the government changed the terms of citizens' engagement with the power structure. However, although a constitutional amendment sparked reforms in village democracy, responsibility for implementing those reforms remained with state governments, which has made the quality of the implementation variable, and dependent on local state politics.

Village democracy in China is another example of a centrally driven policy change toward decentralization and participation. Through much of China's long history, the central state has ruled the countryside only indirectly. In fact, during the Ming (1468–1644) and Qing (1644–1911) dynasties, the imperial bureaucracy extended only to the *xian* (county) level, leaving control of the countryside largely in the hands of the local gentry and elites. It was not until the modern era (comprising the Republican Period [1911–49] and the People's Republic of China [1949–present]) that the central government consolidated its control of the countryside. Beginning with land reforms in 1949 and accelerating with the collectivization of agriculture in the mid-1950s, the state established official bureaucracies at the county, township, and (through the Communist Party Secretariat and branches) village levels. Despite tight governmental control for state purposes, however, rural citizens remained marginalized when it came to social services, and the vast majority of national resources went to build cities and industry. It was not until the 1970s that administrative power was decentralized to rural communes, which were converted into townships and villages. In these new entities, the more entrepreneurial officials soon began using their newfound authority and discretion to take advantage of opportunities opened up by market liberalization. Within a few years, China's countryside became a dynamic new source of economic growth.

Politically and administratively, however, decollectivization and the break-up of the communes left a vacuum in governance below the township level. To fill this gap, China enacted the Draft Village Organic Law (1987) and the Village Organic Law (1998), which reaffirmed villagers' right to self-government, the popular election of local officials, and the central Communist Party's role in village rule. These reforms recognized the village as the most important funder and provider of local public goods and services for the rural population. They vested land ownership rights in the village or collective and allocated use rights to households on terms regulated by national law. Electoral democracy at the local level now coexists with nominated or appointed Communist Party rule at the apex. Since 1998, China has held direct elections for village committees, the organizational blocks of rural life that are responsible for public services at the local level. The electoral process, enshrined in Article 14 of the Organic Law on Villagers Committees, combines a process of public nomination with secret ballots. The design of this process was based on a series of pilots encouraged by the

In China, the introduction of local democracy was entirely the result of a technocratic decision by the center.

government in as many as 24 provinces (Zhenyao 2007), making China one of the few countries in the world where popular deliberations have been organized to determine electoral mechanisms.

In Brazil and India, participatory innovations were the culmination of long periods of engagement by social movements that exploited political opportunities at the center to slowly move the case for participatory democracy forward. This was not the case in China, where the introduction of local democracy was entirely the result of a technocratic decision by the center. As such, local democracy is more an administrative mandate, which could be withdrawn.

Unlike participatory innovations in decentralized local governments, community-driven development interventions are usually packaged as "projects" and designed as grants or loans that work within, and are often implemented by, existing government institutions. They are consequently greatly influenced by the institutional structures and incentives of donors and bound by their time frames (usually three to five years). At their best, these projects attempt to speed up the rate of institutional change by nudging reforms in a direction to which national governments are already committed. More typically, community-driven development projects work in parallel with local governments, often bypassing them by setting up competing sources of authority within communities. Some projects have very ambitious goals ("reduce poverty by 20 percent," "rebuild trust," "enhance civic capacity"). Others have more circumscribed objectives, such as the introduction of a participatory mechanism into particular arenas (schools with parent-teacher associations, rural clinics with village health committees). Many projects that are not classified as community driven also use deliberative and participatory processes for limited objectives, such as selecting deserving beneficiaries for targeted programs, forming village committees to manage the construction of a village infrastructure project, or establishing microcredit groups.

Figure 1.1 illustrates the difficult task of characterizing the different modalities of induced participation. The nature of participation is influenced not just by the social and political context in which it is situated but also by the way in which it is designed. Both the context and the design have a strong influence on incentives for implementers and beneficiaries and, consequently, on accountability and the sustainability of the intervention.

A country's political system matters a great deal. In democracies, electoral incentives shape participatory interventions. Participatory

Figure 1.1 A typology of induced participation

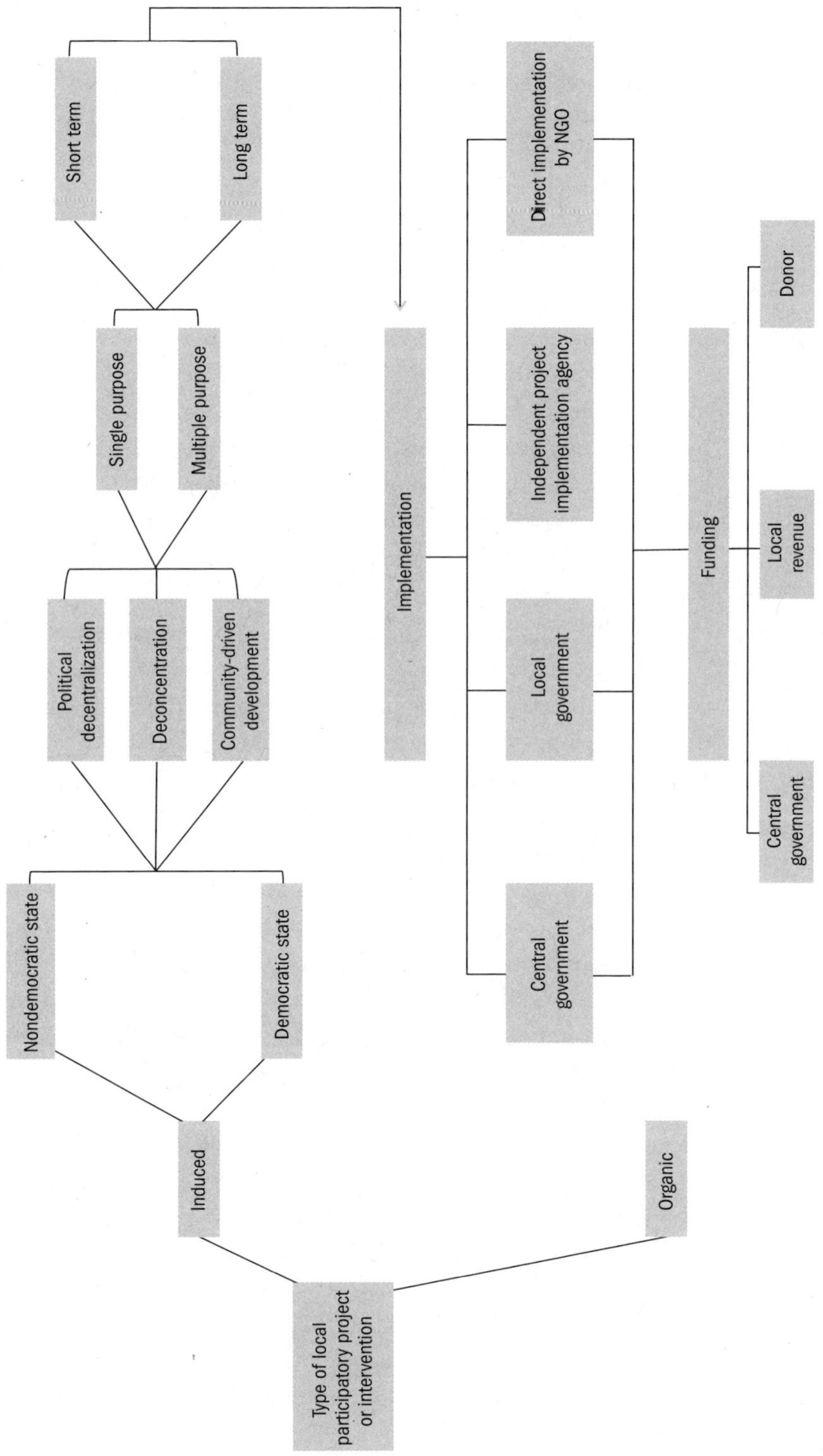

In democracies, electoral incentives shape participatory interventions.

projects are often pushed through just before elections as an easy way to dole out money to voters. There is a constant tension between central and local governments, with central governments attempting to reclaim powers that have been locally devolved. Stable democracies also allow for more stable trajectories of decentralization. They have an affinity for empowered participation functioning in the presence of strong civic institutions, which can play an important role in local empowerment.

Nondemocratic countries, particularly countries that have a history of careening between democracy and dictatorship, have more unstable polities. As a result, citizens cannot always act in ways that are consistent with the expectation of long-term change. This uncertainty, in turn, reduces their confidence that the increase in local power brought about by a project will result in lasting change, making them more fearful of eventual retaliation by local elites. Even nondemocratic countries that have stable, technocratically driven administrations can demonstrate a commitment to local decentralization, motivated by allocative efficiency. Thus, there can be situations in which democratic participation at the local level is coupled with a more authoritarian structure at the center.

The next node in figure 1.1 categorizes participation into three modalities: political decentralization, deconcentration, and community-driven development. In politically decentralized systems, community leaders are democratically elected through credible and competitive elections. At the same time, power and finances are devolved to local governments. Administrative decentralization occurs when central authorities allocate some functions of government to lower-level administrators, who generally report to the central state. Community-based and community-driven development refer to projects in which communities, functioning outside a formal system of government, are given funds that they manage to implement subinterventions. In practice, these modalities often overlap, or exist in parallel, with a variety of submodalities. For instance, some community-driven development projects are designed to strengthen local democratically elected governments or create alternative power structures to counter the power of nonelected local administrators.

The stability of political decentralization depends on the extent to which the center is committed to local democracy.

The stability of political decentralization depends on the extent to which the center is committed to local democracy; decentralization is most stable when village and municipal democracies have been granted constitutional sanction. Political decentralization sharply increases the incentives for electoral accountability and therefore for the sustained empowerment of citizens, but it can be influenced by clientelistic politics. In deconcentrated systems, local administrators tend to face incentives driven by the center; they are therefore usually characterized by upward rather than downward accountability. Effective deconcentration, which is technocratically driven, can also result in the efficient allocation of tasks. It is, however, not generally conducive to the development of sustained local participation.

The effectiveness of community-driven interventions at the local level is highly conditioned by local capacity, in particular the capacity for collective action. Local social structures and levels of elite control can play a strong role in its functioning. In such interventions, the challenge is for state agencies responsible for projects to internalize the intrinsic and instrumental values of participation and to ensure that projects are implemented in a manner that meets their stated intentions. If participation is introduced to solve a principal-agent problem in a situation in which the central managers of an agency lack the information and the capacity to monitor the quality of services in local communities, participation will likely be seen as a complement to their objectives. In contrast, if central agencies are enmeshed in a nexus of accommodation and capture with local elites, which would be jeopardized by effective participation, central government officials will more likely see participation as a threat.

In its early stages, the process of participation may be more noisy than useful; changing this dynamic requires sustained engagement and a strong commitment from the center. The nature of the state thus affects the quality of participation. A state that is reasonably effective and seeks to improve its ability to deliver local public goods and services could provide an enabling environment for participation. A weak state that is dominated by elites and enmeshed in structures of expropriation and that introduces participation only in response to external donor pressure probably would not provide such an environment.

The next node in figure 1.1 indicates that participatory interventions that focus on a single objective (such as parental control over schools) are fundamentally different from interventions with multiple purposes (such as devolution of a set of powers to village governments or livelihoods projects that provide everything from credit and jobs to nutrition and sanitation). The structure of incentives in each is different. It affects the extent and nature of community participation and the involvement of higher levels of government.

The effectiveness of community-driven interventions at the local level is highly conditioned by local capacity, in particular the capacity for collective action.

An important concern, depicted in the next node in figure 1.1, is whether the intervention has a long or short horizon. Interventions with long-term horizons—say, an effort to introduce local democracy at the local level that has constitutional sanction—fundamentally improve the incentives of citizens to confront local elites and fight for their interests. Interventions with short-term horizons will incentivize individuals to extract all the rents that they can from the project during its tenure.

The top half of figure 1.1 maps some of the permutations within which participatory interventions can be designed. Each permutation results in different incentives, which influence the effectiveness and sustainability of the project. It suggests that a community-based effort to manage village schools run within a political decentralized system within a democratic country is more likely to lead to a sustainable and equitable improvement in welfare than a well-funded community-driven development project with a three-year horizon that is run by a deconcentrated administration within an unstable authoritarian country.

The bottom half of figure 1.1 shows how project implementation matters. Central governments, local governments, NGOs, and independent project implementation agencies can all run induced participatory projects. Typically, some combination of these bodies runs projects (for instance, the central government or the project agency may hire an NGO to implement a project at the local level). Who manages project implementation has implications for accountability and the quality of implementation. If democratically elected, local governments can be the most downwardly accountable. NGOs and project implementation agencies are deeply affected by the incentives of their organizations; unless their organizational incentives are set up in a way that encourages them to do so, they may not be accountable to the demands of communities.

Funding matters. Funding also matters. Is funding derived entirely from central allocations to local communities? Is it dependent on local revenue generation through taxes and community participation, or is it entirely dependent on donor funds? Each situation is affected by a different political economy and incentives for community participation. If, for example, a community-based effort to manage schools is managed exclusively by NGOs and dependent on donor funds, it might be well funded and well managed in the short term but it would be subject to the risk of failure in the long term. In contrast, if the intervention is managed by local governments and funded by local taxes, implementation may be ineffective in the short term, because of clientelism and the inability of local governments to collect taxes. However, the project could become more effective over the long term as communities become more politically mature.

Scope of the Report and Roadmap

The scope of this report is broad. The report focuses on the impact of efforts to induce participation. It therefore does not review the large body of literature on organic participation, although it draws on several lessons from efforts to scale-up organic movements through induced policy interventions.

The focus is on participatory development; much less attention is paid to the important "supply-side" aspects of governance (fiscal decentralization, taxation policy, local government procedures, and bureaucratic inefficiency). The literature on this issue has been the subject of other reports and reviews by the World Bank, in particular the series of books edited by Anwar Shah (2006a, 2006b, 2006c, 2006d).

"Local" development does not mean decentralization to subnational bodies, such as state or district governments. Decentralization of this kind is the subject of a large body of literature related to fiscal federalism and its variants. The focus here is on local participatory development. Attention is therefore confined to the lowest level of government, typically the municipal and village levels, and to community organizations, village committees, and neighborhood associations.

The report examines large-scale participatory projects that have been evaluated based on representative samples of target populations with adequate counterfactuals (alternate scenarios of what would have happened to the targeted communities in the absence of the intervention). The ideal counterfactual would be the same community in the absence of the intervention—a situation that cannot be observed. Econometricians and statisticians have therefore devised various methods that attempt to approximate this ideal by finding methods of selecting "control" groups. These methods include randomized trials, regression discontinuity designs, well-designed methods of matching, and natural experiments.

A limitation of the counterfactuals used by evaluations of participatory projects is that they generally compare communities with the intervention to control communities in which the status quo is maintained. Few compare the participatory intervention to an alternate type of intervention (or "arm") that could help inform design. For example, very few studies compare outcomes delivered by participatory interventions with top-down interventions, limiting the ability to determine whether participatory methods work better or worse than alternate designs. Examining the impact of a participatory intervention with respect to the status quo remains extremely useful, however, because it allows researchers to credibly assess the impact of the intervention. Several useful lessons emerge from the review of a large body of such evidence. Most of the findings, therefore, derive from econometric analysis, although case studies are used to develop ideas and illustrate the conceptual framework. Several observational studies are also summarized to illustrate key points throughout the report.

Another criterion used to select studies for review is that they were published in a peer-reviewed journal or written by scholars with a track record of peer-reviewed publication. Some studies that do not satisfy these criteria were included because of thinness in the literature on a particular topic or some other compelling reason. In such cases, potential problems with the study are clearly identified before conclusions are drawn from it. (Throughout the report, the strengths and weaknesses in the methodology used by the researchers is assessed and conclusions are drawn only from studies whose methodology can be defended.)

The rest of this report is organized as follows. Chapter 2 provides a conceptual framework for participatory development. It develops the notion of civil society failure and explores the interactions among civil society failure, government failure, and market failure as key to diagnosing problems in local development. The chapter also examines the implications of civil society failure and how such failure relates to the size of groups and elite control and capture.

Chapter 3 focuses on the challenge of inducing participation by developing some of the policy implications of this "failure triangle." It develops a set of criteria for diagnosing civil society failures and understanding how the intersection of market, government, and civil society failure affects the dynamics of local development. This framework is used to examine the challenges of implementation, including the role of donors and facilitators, and of working within the multiple uncertainties of highly variant contexts and unknown trajectories of change. A set of hypotheses is derived from the conceptual framework.

Chapters 4, 5, and 6 present the evidence in support of and at odds with the hypotheses. Chapter 4 focuses on the evidence on elite capture and its importance within the broader context of leadership and representation within communities. It also examines the role of political and electoral incentives in determining the quality of leadership and the local prevalence of corruption, investigating whether corruption can be countered by better accountability mechanisms. The chapter attempts to answer a series of questions: How does inequality in communities affect the process of resource allocation? To what extent do elites dominate the process of decision making? To what extent does introducing local democracy make government more accountable? To what extent does it change political incentives? Does devolving the allocation of funds to communities make them more susceptible to corruption and theft? Under what conditions does participation empower citizens to act in their own interests?

Chapter 5 examines the claim that participation improves the delivery of public goods and services, the management of common property resources, and living standards. It begins by examining the effectiveness of community-based approaches in targeting the poor. It tries to determine whether localized projects outperform centrally driven projects in targeted private transfers to the poor and whether local projects allocate public goods in a manner that better matches the needs of the poor. The chapter then looks at the impact of participation on common-pool resources, local infrastructure, schooling, and health. Does involving communities in managing local public facilities improve maintenance? Are common-property resources more sustainable when communities manage them? Does involving parents in the management of schools improve learning outcomes? Does oversight of local public clinics and hospitals by individuals who come within their scope of operation improve health outcomes? When citizens participate in decisions on local public goods and services, are they more satisfied with how the agents of government provide these services? More generally, are participatory projects effective in expanding livelihood options for the poor and generating wealth?

Chapter 6 assesses the evidence on whether participatory development can build civil society. The evidence is examined to answer some fundamental questions: How do deliberative processes actually work in developing countries? Is deliberation equitable? Is it sustainable? Under what conditions does it build the capacity to engage? Can local inequalities in power and social structure be remedied by mandating the inclusion of women and discriminated against minorities in leadership positions? Does improving, and equalizing, access to information result in better outcomes? Does participation build social capital? Does it improve the community's capacity to monitor and sanction government? How well do participatory projects work in postconflict settings in particularly dysfunctional states?

Chapter 7 poses some remaining open questions and suggests some directions for future research on participatory development. It then assesses the World Bank's approach to participatory development, reviewing the extent to which it reflects some of the principles that are essential to effective implementation. The chapter reviews design documents from a large sample of World Bank participatory projects and reports findings from a survey of project managers. It offers some policy recommendations for the World Bank and other agencies engaged in designing and implementing induced participatory projects.

Notes

1. Lack of data availability and problems with definitions make it difficult to find accurate estimates of total World Bank lending for these sectors. According to the Bank's Social Development Department, total lending for community-based and community-drive development was $54 billion over the 1999–2011 period, with $7.8 billion allocated in fiscal 2010 alone. Between 1990 and 2007, another $31.6 billion was allocated to lending for projects with decentralization components, raising the total allocation for local participatory development to about $85 billion.
2. Reliable figures are hard to come by because of the large numbers of such organizations and the diverse ways in which they report their data.
3. Community development programs were also in vogue in francophone Africa as *animation rurale,* since at least 1945 (White 1999).
4. White (1999) identifies a second wave in the 1970s and 1980s, initiated by the UN system. In fact, it seems more a ripple than a wave, as it had little influence on large lending agencies. White calls the current interest in community-driven development a third wave, "with the added impetus given by the conversion of the World Bank to the cause" (109).
5. The left-leaning Workers Party was founded in 1980 as a party where "social movements can speak."

References

Abbot, F. F., and C. Johnson. 1968. *Municipal Administration in the Roman Empire*. New York: Russell and Russell.

Abraham, A., and J.-P. Platteau. 2004. "Participatory Development: When Culture Creeps." In *Culture and Public Action*, ed. V. Rao and M. Walton, 210–33. Stanford, CA: Stanford University Press.

Altekar, A. S. 1949. *State and Government in Ancient India: From Earliest Times till 1200 A.D.* New Delhi: Motilal Banarsidass.

Arizpe, L. 2004. "The Intellectual History of Culture and Development Institutions." In *Culture and Public Action*, ed. V. Rao and M. Walton, 163–84. Stanford, CA: Stanford University Press.

Ayish, M. I. 2008. *The New Arab Public Sphere*. Berlin: Frank and Timme GmbH Verlag.

Baiocchi, G. 2005. *Militants and Citizens: The Politics of Participatory Democracy in Porto Alegre*. Stanford, CA: Stanford University Press.

Bardhan, P., and D. Mookherjee. 2006. "The Rise of Local Governments: An Overview." In *Decentralization and Governance in Developing Countries*, ed. P. Bardhan and D. Mookherhee, 1–52. Cambridge, MA: MIT Press.

Bowen, J. R. 1986. "On the Political Construction of Tradition: Gotong Royong in Indonesia." *Journal of Asian Studies* 45(3): 545–61.

Cernea, M. M. 1985. *Putting People First: Sociological Variables in Rural Development*. New York: Oxford University Press.

Chambers, R. 1983. *Rural Development: Putting the Last First*. Harlow, U.K.: Pearson Education.

Cooke, B., and U. Kothari. 2001. *Participation: The New Tyranny?* London: Zed Books.

Dahl, R. 1963. *A Preface to Democratic Theory*. Chicago: University of Chicago Press.

Damrosch, L. 2007. *Jean-Jacques Rousseau: Restless Genius*. New York: Mariner Books.

Demsetz, H. 1970. "The Private Production of Public Goods." *Journal of Law and Economics* 13(2): 293–306.

de Tocqueville, Alexis. 1838. *Democracy in America*. New York: George Dearborn and Company.

Dongier, P., J. V. Domelen, E. Ostrom, A. Ryan, W. Wakeman, A. Bebbington, S. Alkire, T. Esmail, and M. Polski. 2001. "Community Driven Development." In *A Sourcebook for Poverty Reduction Strategies*, ed. Jeni Klugman, 301–31. Washington, DC: World Bank.

Eaton, K. 2008. "Decentralization and Governance: Lessons from Latin America." Background paper for World Bank Policy Research Report, Washington, DC.

Elster, J. 1998. "Introduction." In *Deliberative Democracy*. ed. J. Elster, 1–18, Cambridge, U.K.: Cambridge University Press.

Escobar, A. 1995. *Encountering Development: The Making and Unmaking of the Third World*. Princeton, NJ: Princeton University Press.

Fanon, F. 1961. *Les damnés de la terre*. Paris: François Maspero.

Freire, P. 1970. *Pedagogy of the Oppressed*. New York: Herder and Herder.

Gandhi, M. 1962. *Village Swaraj*. Ahmedabad, India: Navjivan Press.

Gardiner, A. 1961. *Egypt of the Pharaohs: An Introduction*. New York: Oxford University Press.

Grindle, M. 2007. *Going Local: Decentralization, Democratization, and the Promise of Good Governance*. Princeton, NJ: Princeton University Press.

Hardin, G. 1968. "The Tragedy of the Commons." *Science* 162(3859): 1243–48.

Harriss, J. 2001. *Depoliticizing Development: The World Bank and Social Capital*. New Delhi: LeftWord Books.

Hirschman, A. O. 1970. *Exit Voice and Loyalty: Responses to Decline in Firms, Organizations and States*. Cambridge, MA: Harvard University Press.

———. 1984. *Getting Ahead Collectively: Grassroots Experiences in Latin America*. New York: Pergamon.

Immerwahr, D. 2010. *Community Development in India*. Working Paper, Department of History, University of California, Berkeley.

Kramer, S.N. 1971, *The Sumerians: Their History, Culture and Character*. Chicago: University of Chicago Press.

Krishna, A., N. T. Uphoff, and M. J. Esman. 1997. *Reasons for Hope: Instructive Experiences in Rural Development*. West Hartford, CT: Kumarian.

Leftwich, A. 1993. "Governance, Democracy and Development in the Third World." *Third World Quarterly* 14(3): 605–24.

Levine, V. T. 2004. *Politics in Francophone Africa*. Boulder, CO: Lynne Rienner.

Li, T. 2007. *The Will to Improve*. Durham, NC: Duke University Press.

Maine, H. 1876. *Village Communities in the East and West*. London: John Murray.

Mamdani, M. 1996. *Citizen and Subject: Contemporary Africa and the Legacy of Late Colonialism*. Princeton, NJ: Princeton University Press.

Mann, M. 1986. *The Sources of Social Power: A History of Power from the Beginning to A.D 1760,* vol. I. Cambridge, U.K.: Cambridge University Press.

Mansuri, G., and V. Rao. 2004. "Community-Based and -Driven Development: A Critical Review." *World Bank Research Observer* 19(1): 1–39.

Mantena, K. 2009. *Alibis of Empire*. Princeton, NJ: Princeton University Press.

Melo, M., and F. Rezende. 2004. "Decentralism and Governance in Brazil." In *Decentralization and Governance in Latin America*, ed. J. S. Tulchin and A. Selee, 37–66. Washington, DC: Woodrow Wilson Center Press.

Mill, J. S. 1859. *On Liberty*. London: John W. Parker and Son.

———. 1879. "Chapters on Socialism." *Fortnightly Review* 25(February): 217–37; March: 373–82; April: 513–30.

Mizrahi, Y. 2004. "Twenty Years of Decentralization in Mexico: A Top-Down Process." In *Decentralization, Democratic Governance, and Civil Society in Comparative Perspective: Africa, Asia and Latin America*, ed. P. Oxhorn, J. S. Tulchin, and A. D. Selee, 33–58. Washington, DC: Woodrow Wilson Center Press.

Mosse, D. 2002. "People's Knowledge, Participation and Patronage: Operations and Representations in Rural Development." In *Empowerment and Poverty Reduction: A Sourcebook*, ed. D. Narayan. Washington, DC: World Bank.

Narayan, D. 2002. *Empowerment and Poverty Reduction: A Sourcebook*. Washington, DC: World Bank.

Narayan, D., and K. Ebbe. 1997. "Design of Social Funds: Participation, Demand Orientation, and Local Organizational Capacity." World Bank Discussion Paper 375, World Bank, Washington, DC.

North, D. C. 1990. *Institutions, Institutional Change, and Economic Performance*. Cambridge, U.K.: Cambridge University Press.

O'Donnell, G. 1993. "On the State, Democratization and Some Conceptual Problems (A Latin American View with Glances at Some Post-Communist Countries)." *World Development* 21(8): 1355–70.

Olson, M. 1965. *The Logic of Collective Action: Public Goods and the Theory of Groups*. Cambridge, MA: Harvard University Press.

Ostrom, E. 1990. *Governing the Commons: The Evolution of Institutions for Collective Action*. New York: Cambridge University Press.

Pateman, C. 1976. *Participation and Democratic Theory*. Cambridge, U.K.: Cambridge University Press.

Prud'homme, R. 1995. "The Dangers of Decentralization." *World Bank Research Observer* 10(2): 201–20.

Ribot, J. C. 1995. "From Exclusion to Participation: Turning Senegal's Forestry Policy Around?" *World Development* 23(9): 1587–99.

———. 2009. "Forestry and Democratic Decentralization in Sub-Saharan Africa: A Review." In *Governing Africa's Forests in a Globalized World*, ed. L. A. German, A. Karsenty, and A. Tiani, 29–55. London: Earthscan.

Schumpeter, J. 1942. *Capitalism, Socialism and Democracy*. New York: Harper and Brothers.

Scott, J. 1999. *Seeing Like a State: How Certain Schemes to Improve the Human Condition Have Failed*. New Haven, CT: Yale University Press.

Selee, A. D., and J. S. Tulchin. 2004. "Decentralization and Democratic Governance: Lessons and Challenges." In *Decentralization, Democratic Governance, and Civil Society in Comparative Perspective: Africa, Asia and Latin America*, ed. P. Oxhorn, J. S. Tulchin, and A. D. Selee, 295–319. Washington, DC: Woodrow Wilson Center Press.

Sen, A. 1985. *Commodities and Capabilities*. Amsterdam: Elsevier.

———. 1999. *Development as Freedom*. New York: Knopf.

———. 2005. *Argumentative Indian*. London: Allen Lane.

Shah, A., ed. 2006a. *Local Budgeting*. Public Sector Governance and Accountability Series. Washington, DC: World Bank.

———. 2006b. *Local Governance in Developing Countries*. Public Sector Governance and Accountability Series. Washington, DC: World Bank.

———. 2006c. *Local Governance in Industrial Countries*. Public Sector Governance and Accountability Series. Washington, DC: World Bank.

———. 2006d. *Local Public Financial Management*. Public Sector Governance and Accountability Series. Washington, DC: World Bank.

Tiebout, C. 1956. "A Pure Theory of Local Expenditures." *Journal of Political Economy* 64(5): 416–24.

Tinker, H. 1967. *The Foundations of Local Self-Government in India, Pakistan and Burma.* Bombay: Lalvani.

USAID. 2000. *USAID's Experience in Decentralization and Local Governance.* Washington, DC: Center for Democracy and Governance, USAID.

White, H. 1999. "Politicising Development? The Role of Participation in the Activities of Aid Agencies." In *Foreign Aid: New Perspectives,* ed. K. Gupta, 109–25. Boston: Kluwer Academic Press.

World Bank. 1992. *Governance and Development.* Washington, DC: World Bank.

———. 2001. *World Development Report 2000/2001: Attacking Poverty.* Washington, DC: World Bank.

———. 2004. *World Development Report 2004: Making Services Work for Poor People.* Washington, DC: World Bank.

Zhenyao, W. 2007. "The Process of Establishing and Extending Direct Elections in Rural China." In *Narratives of Chinese Economic Reforms: How Does China Cross the River?* ed. X. Zhang, S. Fan, and A. de Haan. Singapore: World Scientific.

CHAPTER TWO

A Conceptual Framework for Participatory Development

DESPITE THE RECENT UPSURGE IN INTEREST, PARTICIPATORY DE-velopment policy is beset with a lack of conceptual clarity. Allocations of many millions of dollars are justified by little more than slogans, such as "empowering the poor," "improving accountability," "building social capital," and "improving the demand side of governance." Part of the conceptual challenge lies in understanding what these notions mean, how they fit within broader conceptions of development policy, and how they differ across diverse contexts and over time. This chapter presents a framework within which to think about some of these issues. The goal is to understand participatory interventions as a response to a development failure, much as other development interventions are viewed as responses to market or government failures.

The chapter begins by briefly reviewing the concept of market fail-ure, the key construct used to justify development policy. It then reviews the extension of the basic notion of failure to the state before introduc-ing the concept of civil society failure. The section on civil society failures discusses how a vibrant civil society can help mitigate market and government failures and illustrates how the interaction of markets, government, and civil society failures affect local development. The chapter argues that participatory development interventions should, for the most part, be understood as an attempt to repair civil society failure. This framework leads to an extended discussion of the various elements of civil society failure—the roles of coordination and cooperation, cul-ture, inequality and elite domination, and group heterogeneity—and discusses some consequent challenges and concerns.

Participatory development policy is beset with a lack of conceptual clarity . . .

. . . with many millions of dollars justified by little more than buzzwords.

Market Failure

Markets fail when they are unable to allocate resources efficiently. They fail for a variety of reasons: one party to a transaction may have more information than the other; a firm may monopolize control over a market by restricting the entry of competitors; failures in information or coordination may cause a common need to not be provided by the market mechanism, resulting in a missing market.

Although inequality and poverty can coexist with both efficient and inefficient markets, market failures tend to deepen poverty traps and inhibit growth. Therefore, in theory, correcting or repairing market failures can help economies produce larger pies, and—in situations where the market failure disproportionately affects the poor—allocate larger shares of the pie to the poor. Correcting market failures is thought of as one of the central challenges of development (Hoff and Stiglitz 2001; Devarajan and Kanbur 2005). The other main challenge is distributing resources equitably—in particular ensuring that the poor benefit from development.

Many market failures are caused by externalities—situations in which an act produces a cost (or benefit) that is borne (enjoyed) by a party that was not involved in it. Externalities exist in the marketplace when the exchange of goods and services between two individuals has consequences, positive or negative, for people who were not involved in the decision.

A negative externality occurs when an individual or firm does not bear the full cost of its decisions. In this case, the cost to society is greater than the cost borne by the individual or firm. Examples include companies that pollute the environment without having to pay for cleaning it up. Negative externalities lead to the overproduction of goods and services, because sellers are not charged the full costs their goods and services impose.

A positive externality exists when an individual or firm does not receive the full benefit of its decisions. In this case, the benefit to society is greater than the benefit reaped by the individual or firm. Examples of positive externalities are spillovers from research and development or the pollination of crops by bees. Positive externalities lead to the underproduction of goods and services, because sellers are not compensated for the full benefits of the goods and services they create.

Coordination failures are a special case of externalities in which the failure of individuals "to coordinate complementary changes in

> Although inequality and poverty can coexist with both efficient and inefficient markets, market failures tend to deepen poverty traps and inhibit growth.

their actions leads to a state of affairs that is worse for everyone than an alternate state of affairs that is also an equilibrium" (Hoff 2000, 145). When parties to a transaction are unable to reliably connect and coordinate with one another, they are often forced into situations that make at least one of them worse off without making the other better off. The market is not always able to solve this problem, for a variety of reasons. Formal and informal institutions to enforce contracts may not exist or may be unreliable, for example, making transactions unpredictable and subject to manipulation and rent-seeking.

Another important cause of market failure is the existence of constraints in the distribution of information. Information is asymmetric when some firms or individuals have more information than others. Poor households typically have very little access to formal credit markets, for example, and rely largely on informal lenders partly because it is difficult for commercial banks to collect reliable information on their ability to repay loans.

Poverty and inequality exist in the absence of market failures, and market failures exist in the absence of poverty and inequality. But a highly unequal distribution of resources can amplify the effects of market failures such as failures of credit and labor markets. Market failures can also lead to highly skewed distributions of power or social status that are resistant to change, leading to poverty traps.

A poverty trap is a situation in which a group of people and their descendants remain in a perpetual state of poverty because of mechanisms such as credit market imperfections, corruption, dysfunctional institutions, or decreasing returns from investments in health, education, or physical capital. In an inequality trap, the entire distribution is stable, because—as noted in the *World Development Report 2006: Equity and Development*—the various dimensions of inequality (wealth, power, social status) interact to protect the rich from downward mobility and obstruct upward mobility by the poor (World Bank 2006; Rao 2006). The unequal distribution of power between the rich and the poor—between dominant and subservient groups—helps elites maintain control over resources and reduces the potential productivity of the poor. Credit and capital market failures tend to have a disproportionate impact on the poor, and asymmetries in information can both be caused by and perpetuate inequalities in income and power.

Consider, for instance, agricultural laborers working for a large landholder. Illiteracy, malnourishment, and indebtedness are likely to make it very difficult for such workers to break out of the cycle of poverty.

Important causes of market failure include externalities, of which coordination failures are a special case, and constraints in the distribution of information.

Even if laws were in place making it possible to challenge the land-holder's dictates, illiterate workers would have great difficulty navigating the political and judicial institutions that might help them assert their rights. In many parts of the world, entrenched social structures widen this distance between landholders and laborers: landholders typically belong to a dominant group defined by race or caste, whereas tenants belong to a subservient group. Such group-based inequalities are more likely to be intergenerationally perpetuated when social norms and networks prevent intermarriage across groups.

Inequity, which can exist even in perfectly functioning markets is, thus, a concern in its own right. In addition, it can combine with market failures to magnify inefficiencies and can result in situations in which the aggregate loss in welfare is disproportionately borne by the poor. These factors provide a rationale for government intervention where it can intervene in ways that improve outcomes—by, for example, providing services such as health, education, credit, or insurance to communities in which markets are unwilling or unable to do so or by implementing land reform or other equalizing interventions to correct for poverty and inequality traps.

> Inequity can combine with market failures to magnify inefficiencies and can result in situations in which the aggregate loss in welfare is disproportionately borne by the poor.

Government Failure

The concern with looking to government to solve market failures is that problems of coordination, information asymmetry, and inequality also characterize the government. Government failure occurs when a policy or political intervention makes resource allocation less efficient than the outcome produced by the market (Besley 2006).

It is useful to distinguish government failures, which are common to all political systems, from political failures, which are government failures within a democratic framework. Like market failures, government and political failures are related to failures in information and coordination.

Information failures. The classic information failure in governance is ignorance—the inability of a government to know the preferences of its citizens. Ignorance results in the misallocation of resources—providing schools where clinics are needed, building roads that head off in untraveled directions while septic tanks fester. Decentralization is often seen as a solution to this problem, because bringing government closer to the

> Looking to government to solve market failures is problematic . . .

people increases the public's access to information and the government's knowledge of citizens' preferences.

Another cause of government failure is information asymmetries—situations in which one set of agents in a transaction has more relevant information than another. Governments keep vast amounts of information that citizens cannot access—details about contracts for public projects, budgetary allocations, and lists of people under detention.

Coordination failures. Governments are continually subject to various types of coordination failures, which result in some people being unable to influence decision making while others have undue access to state favors as a result of lobbying, corruption, or both. Coordination failures can also arise when incentives in the political system prevent good candidates from running for office, resulting in societies being managed by ineffective leaders, or when polarized sets of preferences result in inaction (a failure of collective action). Coordination failures can create endemic problems such as absenteeism among public servants, which disproportionately affects schools and clinics in poor and isolated communities (World Bank 2004). They can also result in a "loss of the monopoly over the means of coercion" (Bates 2008), leaving countries vulnerable to civil war and ethnic strife.

Inequity. Just as in the case of market failure, the burden of government failure frequently falls disproportionately on the poor. Poor and illiterate people tend to suffer from vast gaps in information about laws and government procedures. In relatively stable societies with deep-seated inequalities, the rich are likely to use their influence to control the reins of power; in cases of complete state failure, politicians can use their power to extract resources from the poor and powerless, thereby transforming the state into an instrument of predation (Bates 2008).

One of the challenges of development is to understand where, when, and how to balance the power of the state against the freedom of markets. Can governments solve market failures and redress inequities in a manner that does not weaken market efficiency? Can markets take over the provision of services such as water supply, health, and education when a government is unable to do so? Can governments provide credit and insurance in underserved areas that the private sector will not enter? What level of government regulation will optimally solve information and coordination problems while not impeding the potential for sustainable growth?

. . . because it, too, suffers from problems of coordination, information asymmetry, and inequality.

Just as in the case of market failure, the burden of government failure frequently falls disproportionately on the poor.

One of the challenges of policy making is to understand where, when, and how to balance the power of the state against the freedom of markets.

As markets and governments are fundamentally interconnected, the challenges of information and coordination influence not just failures within markets and governments but also the links between them. Institutional economists have demonstrated that development occurs when institutions are able to resolve market failures and address inequality in a manner that is conducive to long-run inclusive growth (World Bank 2005; Acemoglu and Robinson 2006).

Civil Society Failure

The fundamental goal of local participatory development is to build an effective local civic sphere. The philosopher Jurgen Habermas (1991) argues that civil society is activated by a "public sphere" in which citizens, collectively and publicly, create a "third space" that engages with states and markets. Thus, civil society is symbiotically linked to the effective functioning of markets and governments.

An effective civil society is the social arena in which citizens participate, voluntarily organizing to work toward their collective benefit. It is the space in which individuals turn into citizens. The terms *civil society* and *nongovernmental organization* (NGO) are often used interchangeably, but civil society is much more than a collection of NGOs. As defined by the sociologist Jeffrey Alexander (2006, 4), ideally, civil society is

> "a world of values and institutions that generates the capacity for social criticism and democratic integration at the same time. Such a sphere relies on solidarity, on feelings for others whom we do not know but whom we respect out of principle, not experience, because of our putative commitment to a common secular faith."

Any collective effort to voluntarily mobilize citizens with shared values toward a common goal—consumer cooperatives, credit groups, neighborhood associations, religious organizations, social movements of various kinds, producer cooperatives, and a variety of formal and informal associations and advocacy organizations—is arguably a civil society activity.[1]

Historians have increasingly recognized how fundamental civic action is to the development process.

Following Habermas, contemporary historians have increasingly recognized how fundamental civic action is to the development process. Bayly (2004, 2008) shows that poorer countries that have had high rates of growth in recent years, such as India and China, did not simply borrow Western ideas and technologies. Instead, groups of highly educated elites who served as peer educators and activated the civic sphere indigenized those ideas and ideologies. In India, for instance, beginning in the early 19th century, liberal leaders created an *ecumene* (public sphere) that laid the foundation for the vibrant civic and democratic life of the country today. McCloskey (2006) and Mokyr (2010) argue that the creation of an entrepreneurial class requires the development of networks and discourse that foster "bourgeois virtues," which in turn facilitate the development of innovation and capitalism. An active and effective civil society thus allows citizens to engage with governments and markets, hold them accountable, and generate a culture that facilitates economic and democratic activity.

In their ideal state, the three spheres, while complementary in their functions, have competing ideological bases: civil society involves collective action, with justice, fairness, and other social norms as core goals; ideally, it is based on the principles of reciprocity, open criticism, and debate.[2] In contrast, markets involve individual actors following individual goals of maximizing profits and generating wealth.

Firms tend to depend on a hierarchically organized division of labor, rather than equality, to meet their goals. Governments tend to be organized around politics, the goal of which is the reproduction of power; they depend on authority and loyalty to function. In contrast, civil society tends to be mobilized around common interests and the principle of equality (Alexander 2006). All three spheres are needed to balance one another—and create a virtuous cycle. Market and government failures and inequity thrive in the absence of an active and engaged civil society, and civil society failures can exacerbate market and government failures. When the three spheres are equally healthy, they work in concert; the unequal tendencies of the market are balanced by the equalizing valance of the civic sphere, and the tendency of governments to monopolize power is balanced by pressures for accountability and openness that come from civil society.

Civil Society Interaction with Markets and Governments

Civic interaction with markets and governments is often conflictual: being held accountable, answering uncomfortable questions, and responding to requests from mobilized groups of citizens are often costly and unpleasant for government officials and private sector actors.

To be effective, civic action often has to force agents of government and the market to act against their private interests and in the interest of citizens.

In its interaction with markets, a well-functioning civil society acts first as a watchdog.

Absent appropriate regulation, markets would be motivated solely by profit maximization. In many cases, the short-term interests of a firm or industry do not coincide with the best interests of citizens. Similarly, in the absence of civic accountability, the interests of political leaders would be to hold on to power, capture rents, and preserve the existing hierarchy. Civic action is thus almost never smooth; to be effective, it has to introduce constraints into the decision-making processes of governments and markets that cannot be ignored and that often force them to act against their private interests (by reducing profit margins or limiting power).

In its interaction with markets, a well-functioning civil society acts first as a watchdog—through consumer groups, for instance, that highlight firm behaviors that are detrimental to consumers. These behaviors include practices that endanger people's lives (such as food and drug adulteration) as well as practices that are unethical, inefficient, and inequitable, such as collusion and price fixing. Pressure from civil society groups has been responsible, in many parts of the world, for the establishment of agencies to regulate drugs, food, automobiles, and corporate behavior. When they function well, civil society groups also watch out for egregious inequities, such as discrimination in hiring practices or price discrimination against particular groups or communities. The civil rights movement in the United States, the Arab Spring in Tunisia and the Arab Republic of Egypt, the Solidarity movement in Poland, and pro-democracy rallies in the Islamic Republic of Iran are archetypal examples of civil society activity. Civil society can be a source of countervailing power that acts as a check on government. Such a check is usually a good thing, but it can sometimes be socially detrimental—as it is, for example, when vigilante groups attempt to impose unpopular points of view through a reign of terror or when extremists capture the state.

In addition to their watchdog function, civil society groups play a direct role in generating economic activity (microfinance organizations are a prime example). Moreover, an active civic sphere can help create an enabling environment for the rise of an entrepreneurial class, by facilitating social networks that transmit information and creating collectives to help with credit and insurance. Trade groups such as farmers cooperatives, industry federations, and ethnic networks that help migrants with credit and jobs are all examples of civil society activity.

An engaged civil sphere is even more critical to good government. If government is transparent and accountable, it is transparent to and held accountable by civil society. Civil society works much more effectively when it is cohesive—when it has a high capacity for collective action, which is central to the functioning of an effective state—because cohesion gives citizens the capability of engaging effectively with the state. Some scholars follow Putnam (1993) and others in calling this capacity "social capital." This term dilutes the idea of an engaged public sphere into something conceptually much weaker, making it overly simplistic and therefore less effective as a guide for policy (Mansuri and Rao 2004).

An engaged civil sphere makes a critical contribution to good government by keeping it transparent and accountable.

Markets interact with civil society in various ways—by providing information on products and services, for example, or by funding the creation of civil society organizations that are consistent with their interests. Governments engage with civil society in similar ways, providing it with information and attempting to influence and control it, including through rules that prohibit rallies and political organizing. Governments also attempt to nurture, and even create, civil society activity in order to jump-start a participatory development process.[3]

Markets, Government, and Civil Society at the Local Level

Civil society, markets, and governments interact at various levels—global, national, subnational (state/district), and local (city/village/neighborhood). Each level has a unique set of challenges, modes of operation, and incentive structures.

Market failures work differently at each level. Market failures in the global sphere require global coordination and regulation to correct—a role that, for instance, the World Trade Organization (WTO) attempts to perform. Market failures at the national level are the concern of governments and central banks. Market failures at the local level may be addressed by local approaches such as microcredit and microinsurance. The appropriate level of action may depend on the type of market failure. The management of river basin issues that affect multiple countries requires regional action, for example; the creation of a collective response to global warming requires global action.

Government also operates at different levels. Concerns about global governance are addressed by the United Nations system and by negotiations between and among governments. The functions of government should be allocated to the levels most competent to handle them. Some functions, such as national defense, foreign policy, and interstate relations, cannot be sensibly decentralized. In allocating other functions to local levels, a few trade-offs need to be considered (Bardhan and

Mookherjee 2006). Local governments can be better informed about citizen preferences, and they are better able to respond to the needs of citizens because of better information and lower transactions costs. But they may have difficulty coordinating decision making across communities (because of intercommunity externalities or spillovers). Moreover, decentralization leads to a potential loss in scale economies.

The optimal design of decentralization requires trading off the advantages of better-aligned incentives against the disadvantages of more challenging coordination problems.

Thus, the optimal design of decentralization requires trading off the advantages of better-aligned incentives against the disadvantages of more challenging coordination problems. In general, the provision of local public goods is best decentralized when preferences and needs for the goods are heterogeneous, vary with time, and require a high degree of responsiveness to community needs or local knowledge and when there are few intercommunity spillovers or economies of scale. Public goods and services that typically fall into these categories include sanitation and drainage, local irrigation canals, and village roads. Often common-pool resources such as water bodies and forests can also be locally managed. Conversely, if a public good is homogenous; has significant economies of scale, perhaps because of technical complexity; or requires central coordination, it should usually be managed centrally (examples include national vaccination campaigns and national highways).

The decentralization of government functions could, however, merely result in the decentralization of government failure. Local governments fail for a number of reasons, including the absence of democratic mechanisms by which voters can communicate preferences, lack of effective political competition, and lack of civic capacity. When this is the case, policies tend to reflect the views of the people in power, there is a general lack of accountability to citizens, and the decentralization of resource allocation decisions can actually exacerbate rent-seeking and corruption (Bardhan and Mookherjee 2006; Besley 2006). In making decisions about decentralization in developing countries, it is thus important to understand the nature and degree of potential government failure at different levels of government, as well as the potential for civil society failure, and to balance these considerations with policy prescriptions that rely on politics-free economic theory.

Just as markets and governments operate at different levels, so does civil society. Most political theorists generally think about civil society as operating at the level of nation-states, in the context of national politics (Alexander 2006). But in recent years there has been increasing recognition of a global public sphere and global civil society (examples include the movement to combat climate change (or the protests against "neoliberal" development institutions that promote "market fundamentalism"). A vibrant civil society at the national level is important not just for its own sake—to make effective citizens—but also for repairing market and government failures. Social movements have made markets accountable by exposing systematic failures in particular industries (an example is Ralph Nader's highly successful effort to improve automobile safety). They have equalized the rights and welfare of excluded social groups (including indigenous people in Latin America and nonwhites in South Africa) and pushed for greater democracy (in Indonesia) and openness in government (in India). The larger development challenge is to build a virtuous cycle of checks and balances among markets, governments, and civil society that compensates and corrects for the weaknesses in each sphere.

The concern here is with the local civil sphere—groups of citizens who organize themselves into collectives to hold the local state accountable; assist with the functions of government (school committees, public village meetings); remedy market failures such as lack of access to credit or insurance (microcredit and microinsurance groups); and directly manage common resources (forest management groups, water users groups). If government functions are decentralized to the local level, it is important to have citizen groups that watch out and correct for local government failures through a process of active engagement.

Local civil society can also have important linkages with a national civic sphere. Following Rousseau and Mill, local governments, community organizations, and local civic groups are thought to be a training ground for civic activity. If several small local *ecumenes* develop that connect with and learn from one another by exchanging ideas and methods and providing mutual support, they may have the capacity to shift civic culture at the national level.

Defining Civil Society Failure

Civil society failure can be broadly thought of as a situation in which civic action is either absent or operates in a way that results in a net reduction in efficiency.[4] It can occur because a group is unable to act collectively. For example, a group of individuals may be unable to coordinate their actions and make collective decisions that would leave all members of the group better off over the long run because individuals

> Just as markets and governments operate at different levels, so does civil society.

> Civil society failure can be broadly thought of as a situation in which civic action is either absent or operates in a way that results in a net reduction in efficiency.

act in their own short-run best interest (the "tragedy of the commons"). It can also occur when one subgroup is able to mobilize collectively to further its interests while other subgroups, with different interests, are unable to do so, with the potential result that the welfare of the average citizen is reduced.

How does participation occur? Collective participation occurs in two stages. Individuals first have to decide to participate in civic groups; the groups then have to be able to resolve the challenges of collective action and act with a common purpose. Failure can affect both individual incentives for participation and the group's capacity for collective action. There can also be varying degrees of institutional receptivity to participatory activity. For instance, receptivity to participation increases when a country transitions from dictatorship to democracy. It is low in an authoritarian country that functions by suppressing voice and dissent. Even in authoritarian societies, however, there may be some nascent vulnerabilities in the political structure that change activists can exploit—as they did in the Arab Spring and South Africa; if those vulnerabilities increase (say, because of international pressure), the receptivity for participation could increase as well. In the literature on social movements, these vulnerabilities are referred to as the "political opportunity structure" (Kriesi 2007). Such structures can be either "open" (allowing easy access to the political system) or "closed" (making such access difficult). Effective civic action requires that groups have enough information to identify and gauge political opportunities and are then able to mobilize citizens in a manner that takes advantage of them.

Participation is a broad term that covers a variety of activities, including the following:

- participation in decision making through consultative processes or deliberative bodies without the authority to make or veto resource allocation decisions
- the contribution of cash, material goods, or physical labor to construct public goods or provide public services
- the monitoring and sanctioning of public and private service providers
- the provision of information and involvement in awareness-raising activities
- the formation of neighborhood committees (for instance, to reduce crime or resolve local conflicts)
- the selection or election of local representatives.

Instrumental, ideological, and identity-based motives induce individuals to participate in civic activities. Instrumental motives have to do with the economic and political benefits an individual may reap by participating. For instance, if a community development project comes into a village with funds for building local infrastructure, an individual may participate in meetings associated with the project in order to gain access to the funds to repair a road outside her house; he or she may vote in a local council election in order to help remove a corrupt politician from office. Ideological motives have to do with adhering to a shared belief. In some countries, for instance, nationalism is strongly tinged with the ideology of communitarianism, making participation in community projects an expression of patriotism. Identity-based motives have to do with social or religious identity. Examples include helping build a mosque or church or mobilizing a caste group to fight for greater dignity within a village.

Participation entails some costs. The most obvious is the opportunity cost of time, which depends on an individual's economic position, employment status, and family obligations, among other factors. Participation also involves a range of social costs, which can be prohibitively high for individuals or groups that are otherwise proscribed from free engagement in communal public life, as is often the case for women and members of disadvantaged castes, ethnic groups, or tribes. There may also be psychic costs. Years of oppression may have caused low-caste groups to have internalized discriminatory ideologies, making it particularly challenging to mobilize them for development activity. Communities that have grown accustomed to receiving free benefits from the state may be find it troubling to be asked to exert physical effort to obtain those benefits. Individuals, embedded in their particular social groups and networks, will balance all these costs and benefits before deciding to participate.

The decision to participate is not merely an individual decision, however, as civic activity is most effective—perhaps only effective—when engaged in collectively. Although an individual may want to participate, the group to which he or she belongs may be unable to come to a collective decision. Participation by groups—the classic challenge of collective action—thus needs to be distinguished from participation by individuals. Furthermore, an individual's decision to participate is deeply connected to the group's ability to cooperate; if individuals believe that the group will be ineffective or unable to reach consensus, they will be less inclined to participate.

Instrumental, ideological, and identity-based motives induce individuals to participate in civic activities.

Participation entails some costs. The most obvious is the opportunity cost of time, which is higher for the poor.

61

Mancur Olson (1965) theorized almost 50 years ago that without coercion or some other special device to make individuals act in their common interest, "rational self-interested individuals will not act to achieve their common or group interests." Olson was concerned with "exploitation of the great by the small," noting that people with smaller interests in a public good would tend to free ride on the efforts of people with greater interests.

Under what conditions will a group of people cooperate? Under what conditions will they trust one another enough to believe that the promises they have made are credible? Ostrom (1990) emphasizes the role of social institutions that generate norms, impose sanctions, and improve the incentives for collective action, basing her analysis on field observations that demonstrate the success of collective action in management of commons. Arguing against a general theory of collective action, she contends that particularities matter a great deal but postulates a set of "design principles" that may serve as a guide. These principles include clearly defined boundaries to the commons, with a defined community associated with the resource; rules to manage the commons that are appropriate to local conditions; arrangements to manage collective decisions, which are themselves subject to collective negotiations; graduated sanctions, with heavier sanctions for repeated or more egregious violators of rules; low-cost and widely accepted mechanisms to resolve conflict; and the absence of excessive government interference. In deriving these conditions, Ostrom was thinking specifically about common-pool resource management; her arguments do not necessarily apply to the wider issue of local participatory development.

Incorporating these insights and summarizing work by game theorists on collective action over the last four decades, Dasgupta (2009) identifies two necessary conditions for cooperation:

1. At every stage in the agreed course of action, it is in the interest of every party to plan to keep its word if every other party also does so.
2. At every stage of the agreed course of action, every party believes that all parties will keep their word.

The first condition self-enforces promises by ensuring that promises made by one person are expected to be reciprocated by others. This condition is not sufficient, however, because even if it is met, it is still possible that every agent believes that everyone else will act opportunistically.

> Under what conditions will a group of people cooperate? Under what conditions will they trust one another enough to believe that the promises they have made are credible?

If this is the case, then all parties will think that it is in their best interest not to cooperate. The second condition is needed to generate trust, by ensuring that all parties believe that everyone else will keep his or her word. Together, the two conditions generate a system of self-enforcing beliefs that facilitate collective action.

What, then, are the conditions and the social environments that ensure that both conditions are met? When are promises that people make to one another credible, hence ensuring cooperation?

People may belong to "cultures"—relational environments that generate ideologies and preferences that are conducive to collective action. People from the same "culture" share the following characteristics:

1. *Mutual affection.* Coordination is facilitated when parties care about one another sufficiently and recognize that others feel the same way.

2. *Pro-social disposition.* If people trust one another enough to know that any promises made are credible, then even in the absence of mutual affection, a group can have strong ties that generate loyalty. Loyalty of this kind can be shaped by group-specific culture and upbringing; members of a community internalize norms of cooperation to the extent that they feel shame or guilt when not cooperating. Loyalty can also arise because of the presence of social norms that prescribe punishment for people who do not have a pro-social disposition toward the group.

Incentives can also help ensure cooperation. People are more likely to keep agreements if a "cooperative infrastructure"—a set of institutions that ensures that keeping promises is in the interest of each party if everyone else keeps them—is in place. Three types of cooperative infrastructure can be identified:

3. *External enforcement.* External enforcement of agreements made within the group requires an explicit contract enforced by an established structure of power and authority, such as the state and its legal institutions or, in the absence of a formal state, a traditional leader (such as a chief, warlord, or head of a traditional *panchayat* [village council]). The external enforcer does not have to act: the very fact that such enforcement exists will lead people to make credible commitments to one another, and promises will be reinforced by the belief that they will be kept. Collective action can be more successful in the presence of a successful state, and

People are more likely to keep agreements if a "cooperative infrastructure"—a set of institutions that ensures that keeping promises is in the interest of every party if everyone else keeps them—is in place.

state failure can reinforce failures in civic action, just as civil society failure can reinforce state failure. When the external enforcer cannot be trusted to enforce agreements, the parties will not trust one another enough to enter into collective agreements, which could result in noncooperation.

4. *Reputation as a capital asset.* Even in the absence of external enforcement, people will keep their promises if they value their reputation enough. Reputation becomes a capital asset because individuals want to maintain status, uphold an ethical code, or preserve long-term relationships.

5. *Long-term relationships.* In a long-term relationship, reputation becomes a capital asset after a transaction is completed, because it enables individuals to enter into other credible contracts. Agreements, therefore, are mutually enforced. To achieve functioning social relationships, the community might impose stiff sanctions on anyone who breaks an agreement.

In practice, characteristics 3, 4, and 5 could blend with one another, as all of these solutions impose collective sanctions on people who intentionally fail to comply with agreements. However, as Dasgupta (2009) points out, "a credible threat of punishment for misdemeanors would be an effective deterrent only if future costs and benefits are not discounted at too high a rate relative to other parameters of the social environment." In situations in which individuals are forced to become myopic—in periods of civil conflict or social disruption, for instance—such self-reinforcing norms may be rendered ineffective, leading to civic failure (Coate and Ravallion 1993).

Capacity for cooperation can be enhanced where individuals are bound together in multiple social, economic, and political relationships.

Where individuals are bound together in multiple social, economic, and political relationships, the capacity for cooperation can be enhanced. If, for instance, the mutual provision of credit and insurance depends on norms of obligation and cooperation, which in turn depend on commitments for marriage or political support, the violation of one interaction would result in a collapse of all the others. Thus, interlinked agreements make cooperation robust.

They may, however, also make them deeply inequitable. Highly hierarchical societies, such as societies in rural India and West Africa, which depend on elites enforcing norms and "taking care" of others lower in the social hierarchy, may make such societies both highly cooperative and deeply ridden with inequality traps.

Coordination failures in civic action. What makes civic participation effective in some contexts and ineffective in others? What are the challenges local communities face in activating their capacity for collective action?

The most important source of civil society failure is probably coordination failure. An important reason to devolve decisions to the local level is to reduce coordination problems—by allowing the people most affected by projects to manage them directly.

Such devolution by no means implies that coordination failures will disappear. Coordination failures at the local level have two main causes: the lack of a cooperative infrastructure (institutions that make individuals' promises to the collective credible) and the absence of a mechanism to help ensure that individuals in a group have altruistic, or common, preferences (that is, "pro-social dispositions").

Consider the challenges of setting up a project that encourages a community to sustainably manage a local forest. For the project to work, individuals in the community have to agree to restrict their harvesting of trees from the forest. They also have to participate in activities, such as planting and nurturing trees and policing forest grounds to prevent outsiders from poaching. If all individuals were left to their own devices and did not engage in collective action, a tragedy of the commons would occur, leading rapidly to deforestation and the destruction of local livelihoods. In practice, many forest communities around the world have, over centuries, evolved strong norms of collective action to manage common resources, setting up an effective cooperative infrastructure.

The presence of a cooperative infrastructure affects the outcomes of development projects. Say a project wants to improve the collective management of a forest by setting up a community-managed fund that provides financial incentives for individuals to cooperate by compensating them for income lost by limiting their harvest. The fund would be far more effective if a traditional leader was present who was in complete agreement with the aims of the project, was considered honest and beyond reproach, and had the authority to enforce agreements made between individuals and the fund. The fund would also be more likely to succeed if the community had evolved a method by which promises were rendered credible because each individual believed the promises made by every other individual, based on long-term ties and a strong belief that violating promises would result in ostracism from the community. Ideally, the fund would introduce enough additional

> The most important source of civil society failure is probably coordination failure.

> The presence, or absence, of a cooperative infrastructure affects the outcomes of development projects.

incentives within this favorable cooperative environment to sustain cooperation during periods of change and vulnerability. In the absence of an authority figure or strong long-term ties within the community, the fund would degenerate into a haven for rent-seekers, creating a failure. Thus, an authority figure and the long-term ties that come from repeated interactions among individuals in the community are both examples of effective cooperative infrastructure.

Consider another example, a decentralized program in which a village council is given the authority to select beneficiaries for a centrally managed poverty reduction program. As part of the program, it is mandated that beneficiary selection should be vetted in open village meetings, where anyone in the village can question the choices of the village council. This mandate is an attempt to use local participation and local knowledge to improve poverty targeting, create links between villagers and the central government, and hold local governments publically accountable. If the central government were weak and its functionaries corrupt, decisions made in the village meeting would not be enforced. If this were the case, villagers would decide not to waste their time participating in such meetings, because the benefits would not be worth the cost. The project's attempt to foster participatory, community-based targeting would fail because of a weak state's inability to enforce collectively made decisions.

State enforcement can matter in the management of common-pool goods as well. If communities are required to follow laws and regulations passed by the state and these laws and regulations are poorly enforced, there is no incentive for the community to follow the law. If the community had strong norms of collective action, it would revert to traditional forms of resource management. If it did not, the common resources would be privatized and allocated in a way that reflected the interests of the most powerful.

An interesting example of how cooperative infrastructure helps facilitate participation in the decentralization process comes from Tsai's (2007) work on China.[5] Tsai asks a simple question: How can variations in the provision of public goods be explained in the absence of formal institutions of accountability? The Chinese state has decentralized to local governments primary responsibility for the provision of basic public goods and services (road construction, drainage systems, irrigation works, primary school facilities, sanitation). Some village governments provide outstanding public goods and services, whereas others provide

barely anything at all. According to Tsai, the explanation for this variation is the presence in some villages of local "solidary" groups, which
provide informal institutions of accountability. A solidary group is a
collection of individuals who share moral obligations and interests.
Of the three types of groups Tsai delineates—village temple groups,
village churches, and lineage groups—only temple groups and some
lineage groups have the two structural characteristics crucial to Tsai's
argument—namely, the group must be encompassing (open to everyone under the jurisdiction of the local government), and it must be
embedding (incorporating local officials into the group as members).[6]
"When the boundaries of a solidary group overlap with the administrative boundaries of the local government, embedded officials have a
strong social obligation to contribute to the good of the group," writes
Tsai (2007, 356). In groups with embedded officials, the incentive for
accountability is an amorphous sense of moral standing or prestige for
the provision of public goods.

This thesis is quite different from the idea of civic "social capital."
Whatever "social capital" such groups may have, groups that do not
meet the "embedding" criteria (such as church groups) are not able
to hold village officials accountable for the provision of public goods,
as Communist Party members are prohibited from membership.[7] In
contrast, village temple groups can be both encompassing and embedded; they are thus able to serve effectively as informal institutions of
accountability. Lineage groups play this role only marginally, because
their segmentation makes them less cohesive.

A more daring claim made by Tsai is that neither bureaucratic institutions of top-down control nor democratic institutions seem to have
a significant positive effect on the provision of public goods by village
governments. "Implementation of elections does not guarantee good
governmental performance, especially when other democratic institutions are weak" (Tsai 2007, 370).

In countries with strong traditions of electoral democracy, externally
induced improvements in the cooperative infrastructure that come
from the state, such as improved enforcement of laws or decentralization programs with strong participatory elements, can substantially
improve the quality of participation. Consider the case of the South
Indian state of Kerala. Kerala has a long history of egalitarian social
programs emphasizing education, health, and women's equality, but
until 1996 these efforts were mainly top-down programs directed from

In countries with strong
traditions of electoral
democracy, externally
induced improvements in the
cooperative infrastructure
that come from the state can
substantially improve the
quality of participation.

the state capital. Although Kerala is blessed with a literate and engaged electorate, participation was restricted to the political sphere and to membership in unions.

Following passage of a constitutional amendment in 1993, which mandated that state governments devolve resources and powers to democratically elected village councils (*gram panchayats*), Kerala began to plan and initiate a radical and deeply participatory program of decentralization (Heller and Issac 2003). The program rested on three pillars. It devolved 40 percent of the state's development budget to village councils, devolved substantial powers to these councils, and instituted an extensive people's campaign—a grassroots training and awareness-raising effort to inform citizens about and energize them to participate in the *panchayat* system.

The campaign instituted a planning process based on a set of nested piecemeal stages (for example, working committees meetings and development seminars held in conjunction with the village meetings, which are structured to facilitate participation). Instead of open deliberation, attendees (members of the public) are divided into resource-themed groups or committees. The discussions within each group yield consensual decisions regarding the designated resource. This structure, which operates uniformly in all districts in Kerala, is geared toward increasing the efficiency of consensual decision making about public resource demands and prioritizing individual beneficiaries for the allocation of government-subsidized private benefits. The process has been facilitated by various training programs to instruct citizens on deliberative planning and village functionaries on methods for turning plans into actions that result in more effective public service delivery.

In Kerala, direct intervention by the democratic state increased demand for participation not only by creating greater opportunities of participatory planning but also by providing resources to make that planning meaningful while embedding it within a decentralized system of government with enforcement authority. The state thus created mechanisms that strengthened its links with civil society.

Literacy in Kerala was almost 100 percent—much higher than the Indian average at the time of 66 percent; the state also has a long history of civic mobilization because of strong labor unions associated with the communist movement. Local participation in Kerala thus did not start from scratch; it was fostered by channeling democratically and politically aware citizens into participatory avenues that resulted in better

In Kerala, India, the state created mechanisms that strengthened its links with civil society.

local government. In the absence of Kerala's well-developed democratic and participatory traditions, it is unlikely that the people's campaign would have worked.

To fully understand the nature of a failure of collective action, it is thus important to understand how context, history, and culture shape the nature of cooperative infrastructure. The local history of a community shapes the norms that have evolved to facilitate collective action, the extent to which such norms exclude women or disadvantaged groups, and whether those norms are transferrable. Local collective action norms may be effective enough to manage water resources, for instance, but not school management. Similarly, the history and evolution of the national government—the extent to which it supports an active civic culture and has an effective legal system and democratic systems—has deep implications for the success of efforts to foster local participation.

Culture and civic identity. Coordinating civic action at the local level is also affected by the formation of collective identity—which, in many societies, has been consciously shaped to facilitate cooperation. In a small, ethnically homogenous community, intermarriage may have forged strong ties across families.[8] In some instances, such ties could result in common preferences and strong deference to the views of traditional authority figures. More generally, a common cultural identity helps individuals anticipate how others in the group will react to their actions, greatly facilitating collective action.

State policy can forge a common cultural identity and common preferences. For instance, the state can actively create a communitarian national identity by introducing notions of cooperation into the constitution; symbols of the state, such as the flag or pledges of allegiance; and school curricula.

One way of thinking about how culture and civic identity affect the capacity for collective action is by thinking about the formation of what Rao (2008) calls "symbolic public goods." Rao builds on the work of Chwe (1999, 2001), who demonstrates how collective action needs to distinguish between structure and strategy. Chwe's basic argument goes as follows. Most models of collective action assume, implicitly, some preexisting "common knowledge." When a group of individuals plays a collective action game, whether static or dynamic, it is assumed that individual A knows the payoffs, information sets, costs, incentives, possible moves, and so forth faced by individual B. Individual B, in

To fully understand the nature of a failure of collective action, it is important to understand how context, history, and culture shape the nature of cooperative infrastructure.

turn, knows all of this about individual A and knows that individual A knows everything about individual B. Individual A, in turn, knows that individual B knows that individual A knows, and so on. This common knowledge assumption permits games of strategy to be played with a common understanding of the rules of the game: everyone knows how everyone else is playing.

In contrast, a cricket player persuaded to play baseball will be quickly confused—enough to be unable to understand or appreciate the skill, strategy, and actions of the other players. It is this aspect of coordination and common understanding that common knowledge attempts to capture. It plays a coordinating function that is a precondition for collective activity, which cannot occur in its absence. Common knowledge is arguably the core concept behind such amorphous notions as "trust" and "social capital," which figure prominently in the discourse on collective action.[9]

In order to understand collective action, therefore, it is crucial to understand its social context through the symbolic public goods that facilitate it. Yet symbolic public goods are themselves the product of strategy and contestation. They can take a variety of forms, including intangible processes of identity formation such as nationalism; physical entities, such as mosques and temples; and periodic ritual events, such as festivals. All of these forms share characteristics of public goods, in the sense that they can be simultaneously "nonrival" (consumption by one person does not reduce the ability of others to consume the same good) and sometimes "nonexcludable" (it is not possible to deny anyone access to the good).

Symbolic public goods facilitate the social basis for collective action.

Indonesia has constructed symbolic public goods to facilitate cooperative behavior. Postcolonial Indonesia was dominated by upper-class Muslims from Java. The country's history in the decades following independence can be seen primarily as the "Javanization" of the country (Ricklefs 2002). The ideological basis of Javanese belief is that social interaction is "collective, consensual and cooperative" (Bowen 1986, 545). Bowen argues that much of this belief is expressed in the term *gotong royong* (mutual assistance), which has become the framework for Indonesian nationalism and the basis for construction of a national tradition. Sukarno, the "father" of Indonesia, attempted to use the notion to unify the diverse (Islamic, non-Islamic, nationalist, Communist) groups in the new country by calling for a spirit of *ke gotong royong* (*gotong royong*-ness). *Gotong royong* provided a form of cultural legitimacy for state control.

When Sukarno was ousted, in a coup in 1967, his successor, Suharto, introduced a "New Order" economic policy. Especially in its initial phases, the new policy adopted the two-pronged strategy of putting policies in place to enable high rates of growth and passing on the benefits of that growth to the rural poor. An important element in this strategy was to dictatorially force the spirit of *gotong royong* into hamlets and villages around the country. *Gotong royong* became a key element in development strategies in rural areas, particularly in the mobilization of rural labor. In order to protect the political and cultural unity of the Indonesian state, Suharto believed that it had to be strongly authoritarian and that development had to proceed in a cooperative and collaborative manner. By the early 1970s, the Sanskrit word *svadaya* (self-help) started to be used in combination with *gotong royong*, and *svadaya gotong royong* (mobilizing) became central to the implementation of development policy (Bowen 1986).

In a detailed ethnography of local development in a Javanese community, Sullivan (1992) demonstrates that the combination of an autocratic state and the principle of *svadaya* resulted in a form of forced labor. To be a good Indonesian, one had to contribute labor and cash for development projects. Collective action was the norm, not the exception. Mobilizing communities was straightforward: grants received by the village headman (*kepala desa*) were small, because donors assumed that the gap between the expected cost of the proposed project and the funds allocated would be provided locally. In fact, ward leaders actively mobilized contributions from the community. Everyone was expected to contribute free labor; individuals who failed to do so could be labeled unpatriotic or uncooperative and face social, political, material, and even physical sanctions.

In this manner, Indonesian political leaders constructed the symbolic public good of nationalism, deploying "imagined" traditional beliefs that made the individual subservient to the community. As most of this effort was undertaken in the context of a military dictatorship, the approach was successful in coordinating public action.

Suharto's two-pronged strategy yielded good results for more than two decades, with high rates of growth and substantial improvements in the living standards of the poor. These improvements were achieved in a cost-effective way by, in effect, taxing the poor in the name of community participation. Suharto suppressed freedom and imposed an implicitly regressive tax structure, but he also achieved excellent poverty reduction and human development outcomes.

> Indonesia consciously built symbolic goods by establishing a communitarian ethic (*gotong royong*) as state policy via school curricula and public education campaigns.

In the past decade, with the rise of a robust democratic order and a concerted effort to decentralize the political and fiscal authority of state and district governments, the authority of village leaders in Indonesia has been increasingly questioned. But, as recent survey data demonstrate, the spirit of *gotong royong* has by no means disappeared. It has been so deeply institutionalized that not abiding by it is seen as a violation of a communitarian ethic, which remains part of the foundation of what it means to be a good Indonesian. A 2004 survey of the Second Urban Poverty Project evaluation (Pradhan, Rao, and Rosemberg 2010) shows that levels of participation in public goods construction remain high, at 47 percent, with 59 percent of those respondents saying they participate primarily because of "tradition" or "obligation." This high level of participation has real consequences: communities in Indonesia contribute 37 percent of the cost of village public goods. Indonesia has thus successfully introduced a communitarian ideology that facilitates the spirit of cooperation at the local level, improving the capacity for collective action.

Rather than build symbolic public goods, the state can attempt to manipulate preferences to induce behaviors that are in line with its policy objectives. Agrawal (2005) provides an example of this phenomenon in India, where, he argues, the state explicitly attempted to shift the preferences of forest communities toward a more collective purpose in order to facilitate community-based forest management. Based on a variety of archival and survey data, Agrawal seeks to understand how villagers in the Kumaon region shifted from violently protesting the government's efforts to regulate forests in the 1920s to using active community-managed forest conservation methods by the 1990s. He finds that the shift was achieved by the decentralization of decision making to the local level and by explicit efforts to induce community members to value forests as a public good and to build trust between government officials and local forest councils.

Villages with forest councils and active council headmen made greater attempts at regulation and the desire for forest protection grew stronger in villages that were most closely involved in actual monitoring (Agrawal 2005). Efforts to change the way villagers thought about the forests were so successful that council members and headmen often acted against their own material and family interests in enforcing rules of forest protection.

> The state can also attempt to directly manipulate preferences to induce behaviors that are in line with its policy objectives.

Inequality and the role of elites. One of the purported advantages of local participation is its capacity to improve the match between beneficiaries' preferences and the allocation of public goods and benefits. The principle of subsidiarity states that when preferences of communities are heterogeneous or vary with time, decentralizing decision making and project management results in more efficient outcomes and a better preference match.

Local communities in many developing countries tend to be not only very heterogeneous but also highly unequal. It is therefore also important to understand how both inequality and heterogeneity affect local civic failure.

The seminal insight on the role of inequality in collective action comes from Olson (1965), who theorized that if the rich have a strong interest in the provision of a public good, inequality could facilitate collective action because it would be in the interest of the wealthy to provide the good, allowing the poor to free ride. Economists have extended this basic insight in several ways (Baland and Platteau 2006; Bardhan, Ghatak, and Karaivanov 2006).

Baland, Bardhan, and Bowles (2006) summarize these extensions. They note that inequality can have ambiguous and contradictory effects on collective action, for a variety of reasons:

- Higher income may increase rich people's demand for a public good but also increase the opportunity cost of their time, meaning they may be less able to devote time to its provision. If the opportunity cost of the rich is high enough, it may discourage collective action. It could also result in situations in which the collective objective is achieved by the rich providing money and the poor providing labor.
- Poor participants' lower assets may reduce both their demand for the resource and their ability to extract large amounts of it. Thus, poorer people may choose not to participate in setting up a committee to manage a high school—but they would also be less likely to send their children to the school.
- Inequality may increase the propensity of the rich to contribute toward a public good, but it may also discourage poorer people from participating at all, as Olson (1965) notes.
- Collective provision of public goods may be easier in situations of both very high inequality and almost perfectly equality,

One of the purported advantages of local participation is its capacity to improve the match between beneficiaries' preferences and the allocation of public goods and benefits.

Olson's seminal insight was that if the rich have a strong interest in the provision of a public good, inequality can facilitate collective action . . .

. . . later theorists have demonstrated that the link between inequality and collective action is more ambiguous.

where everyone has an equal interest in the good. Inequality could therefore have a *U*-shaped effect on collective action.

These results are derived in the context of static collective action problems, where communities are not engaged in repeated interactions. Where community members have lived together for a long time and expect to continue to engage in social and economic relations over the long term—situations that are very common in developing countries— the relationship between equity and the cooperative infrastructure becomes much more salient. Rural communities are often characterized by inequality in income and wealth, which is usually highly correlated with inequality in power and social status. These communities are trapped in an "inequality trap," in which the same families have been rich, and poor, for generations. The same rich families maintain a tight hold over power relations in the village and rule with dictatorial authority. In such situations, high inequality is combined with a strong cooperative infrastructure; if the local feudal leader believes that collective action is in his best interest, he will ensure that it occurs.

> Inequality traps can create situations in which successful collective action exploits the poor.

In such situations, successful collective action comes with high inequality, as in the Olson model. But, as Dasgupta (2009) demonstrates in models with repeated games, rather than allowing the poor to free ride on the contributions of the rich, inequality traps can harbor exploitation. The reason, in intuitive terms, is that the poor who refuse to cooperate could face sanctions that would push them to accept outcomes that would make them worse off than they would have been in the absence of collective action. If they discount their future payoffs at a low enough rate, they may be forced to enter into cooperative situations whose outcomes make them better off than they would have been with sanctions, but worse off than they would have been acting on their own. Consequently, a cooperative equilibrium could be sustained in which the poor would be exploited over the long term.

Anthropologists have long noted that in such situations the poor tend to internalize such unequal norms: a disadvantaged group may view its status within the hierarchy as correct and appropriate and therefore be subject to what Rao and Walton (2004) call "constraining preferences." For instance, preferences derived from the Hindu caste system may create an acceptance of hierarchy and constrain the motivation for mobility. These beliefs are also simultaneously external constraints; individuals from lower castes who engage in class struggle may face severe social sanctions. For people at the top of the hierarchy, both types of constraints provide the means to maintain their high position; for people at the bottom, these internal and external constraints can limit aspirations, create discrimination and exploitation, and block mobility. Inequality can thus result in the systematic exclusion of disadvantaged groups and women.

An important aspect of the relationship between inequality and collective action is the role elites play in local development. An influential strand of the literature on elites focuses on "capture," arguing that elite domination sharply increases the risk that elites gain control over community development resources provided to benefit local communities (see, for example, Abraham and Platteau 2004). In contrast, studies of organic collective action emphasize that the leaders of such social movements usually emerge from the educated middle and upper classes (Morris and Staggenborg 2004).

One problem in understanding the role of elites in development is that the term refers to a large and heterogeneous set of people. Elites can be the most educated or the most experienced members of a community, or they can be the wealthiest and most powerful. *Elite* can also refer to men or to people who belong to a dominant ethnic, religious, or caste group. None of these characteristics is mutually exclusive; an elite individual may possess many of these attributes simultaneously. The relevant question is the purpose to which elites direct the dominance and influence they possess.

When power is used to facilitate collective action toward the public good—because of an ethic of public service, a communitarian norm, or another reason that results in altruistic behavior—elite control can be an effective part of the cooperative infrastructure: elites can help mobilize communities, persuade others, and shepherd them toward collectively driven, welfare-enhancing behavior. Local development projects demand fairly sophisticated leaders; educated elites are in a position to negotiate with bureaucrats, read and interpret project documents, manage accounts, and engage in other important activities that are part of the everyday business of local projects. This type of control can be described as a form of "benevolent capture" (Rao and Ibanez 2005; Beard and Dasgupta 2006).

However, even benevolent elites have social networks and work within them to facilitate change. Thus, beneficiaries of local projects are likely to be people who are more closely linked to the leadership. In developing countries in particular, younger generations tend to be better

> Elite control can be an effective part of the cooperative infrastructure when power is used to facilitate collective action toward the public good.

Control becomes malevolent capture when elites extract public resources for their private benefit.

It is important to distinguish capture from clientelism.

educated than older generations, so any form of participation is likely to be led by younger people, creating a degree of intergenerational conflict.

Control becomes malevolent capture when elites extract public resources for their private benefit. Capture can manifest itself in various ways, including theft, corruption, and the distribution of benefits to close relatives.

It is important to distinguish capture from another practice that is, generally, inimical to the public good—clientelism. Clientelism occurs when leaders allocate public resources to feed and nurture their networks and relationships in an effort to consolidate social status and power.

In nondemocratic settings, within which many communities in the developing world function, whether capture is benevolent or malevolent is a function of the particularities of the community: whether leaders are hereditary or appointed by higher levels of government; the degree to which communitarian norms or "symbolic public goods" have developed in those communities; and, as in Tsai's example from China, whether nondemocratic forms of accountability exist. In nondemocratic settings, clientelism is largely a consequence of social norms and alignments. Benefits are doled out to individuals and groups to whom the leader has a social obligation, or to build alliances, or sustain a potlatch.

The local context also determines the nature of elite capture in the presence of democratic decentralization. Bardhan and Mookherjee (1999, 2000) construct a model of elite capture with electoral competition. They find that the level of capture depends on the nature and extent of political participation, the political awareness of different groups in the population, and the evenness of competition between local political parties representing different interests. Wealthy groups can make contributions to the finances of politicians, who can then use the funds to recruit "unaware" voters. Aware voters vote on the basis of their interests. Levels of political participation and awareness depend on the distribution of literacy, socioeconomic status, and exposure to media. Democratic decentralization will result in a greater dispersion in the quality of governance, increasing the gap between more and less advanced regions. It will also tend to highlight local inequalities and the distribution of interests, making the extent of capture much more specific to the local context.

Clientelism in democratic settings occurs when relationships between citizens and politicians are predicated on a material transaction, "the direct exchange of a citizen's vote in return for direct payments or continuing access to employment, goods and services" (Kitschelt and Wilkinson 2007, 2). As Bardhan and Mookherjee (2011) point out, (democratic) clientelism has several important negative consequences for development. First, resources are directed toward short-term benefits with quick political gains—cash payments and private goods (housing, subsidized food) rather than goods that contribute to development in the long term (education, health). Private transfers, moreover, tend to be directed toward swing voters at the expense of voters who are not amenable to switching votes. Voters who are more easily monitored by the political party (to ensure that the transfers result in clear political gains) benefit at the expense of voters who are more difficult to monitor. The consequence is that allocations are unequally distributed even among deserving beneficiaries. Clientelism can thus reduce efficiency and exacerbate inequality even in the absence of explicit capture.

When initiating a local development project, it is therefore important to understand the role of elites and to distinguish between elite control, which often contributes to effective participation at the local level; clientelism; and outright capture. Understanding local structures of inequality and local social and political relationships insulates against the naïve and potentially disempowering belief that participation will necessarily benefit the poor. Explicitly recognizing structures of power and dominance could result in designs to address such inequalities with affirmative action programs, such as the mandated inclusion of women and minorities in village councils, the adoption of programs that exclusively target certain groups, or the use of monitoring and audit systems to reduce the prevalence of capture.

Group composition and collective action. The number of groups in a community makes a difference, particularly if each group has a distinct identity and preferences. Groups tend to care more for their own members than for the members of other groups. Consequently, individuals may balance their individual incentives to participate with the interest that derives from their group identity.

The fact that larger communities have more groups within them would suggest that collective action is more difficult to achieve in more populous communities. However, as Alesina and La Ferrara (2005) point out, more heterogeneous societies may be more productive, because diversity may allow different skills to play complementary roles in the production process. The presence of groups that are interlinked

Clientelism in democratic settings occurs when relationships between citizens and politicians are predicated on a material transaction.

The number of groups in a community can make a difference, particularly if each group has a distinct identity and preferences.

77

in production processes may increase incentives to avoid disagreement and conflict.

The relationship between the size of a community and its capacity for collective action goes beyond the issue of heterogeneity. As Olson (1965) argues, larger communities also have more free riders, because the impact of each individual defector is smaller. Moreover, if the public good generated is not "pure" (not nonexcludable), an individual's share in the public good declines in larger groups, reducing the incentive for collective action. This phenomenon is known in the literature as the *group-size paradox.* However, in the case of pure (nonexcludable) public goods, Olson's result is reversed, as larger groups are able to produce more of them. Moreover, Esteban and Ray (2000) show that when the marginal cost of participation rises sufficiently, larger groups have a greater capacity to come to agreement even if the good is excludable (that is, it has characteristics of a private good).

To understand what this means, consider a situation in which poor people need to mobilize to counter a powerful and exploitative local leader. The marginal cost of participation of a poor person in this case is extremely high, both because, being poor, the opportunity cost of her time is high and because the more she participates, the more visible she becomes and the more she risks becoming a target of the leader. Consequently, mobilization against the leader is unlikely to happen unless a large enough number of poor people would benefit from doing so.

It is therefore not necessarily true that larger communities, more unequal communities, or more heterogeneous communities are more prone to collective action failure. The impact of these factors is complex and highly dependent on the purpose underlying the collective action, the extent of interdependence within the community, the nature of the cooperative infrastructure, the opportunity cost of participation, the level of poverty, and the extent of literacy and political awareness.

Information failures. A purported advantage of decentralization is that it solves an important information failure—the inability of distant central governments to observe the preferences of people who are socially, administratively, or geographically far away from central decision makers. This lack of information becomes particularly acute when preferences are highly variable, either across heterogeneous populations or over time. Decentralization promises to make governments more responsive to the needs of citizens by making it more proximate to citizens. Whether decentralization actually solves the information problem

> Larger, more unequal, or more heterogeneous communities are not necessarily more prone to collective action failure.

by improving the match between policy decisions and the preferences of beneficiaries is an empirical question.

Information failures in the civic arena are largely failures in the links between civil society, the state, and markets. Such failures are widely prevalent and highly correlated with inequality and heterogeneity. They include imperfections in the availability of information about such basic issues as transparency in village budgets, citizens' knowledge of legal and bureaucratic procedures, and opportunities for credit and insurance. Greater inequality contributes greatly to asymmetric information; richer and more powerful people are likely to have better connected networks, better access to powerful people in government, more education (and therefore greater awareness), and greater capacity to influence decision making. Lack of information and transparency greatly hampers efforts at political and social accountability (Khemani 2007). The rectification of information failures (by mass media, information campaigns, or "report cards" in a credible manner and on a regular basis) has the potential to improve the ability of citizens to mobilize themselves to hold states and markets more accountable. With better information, citizens become more aware and better able to make more informed electoral decisions, which results in greater electoral accountability. Even in the absence of electoral accountability, better information may enable citizens to engage in a more informed version of "rude" accountability—that is, confronting public officials directly and forcing them to be more responsive to their needs (Hossain 2009).

In confronting the government, lobbying for resources, and making demands on the state, unequal communities face a problem in that the interests of the rich differ from the interests of the poor and the rich have more voice. Even if the poor mobilize, inequality may create distortions in linking civic groups to the state (Esteban and Ray 2006). More unequal communities will have more polarized lobbies, which have distorting effects when governments lack information about the preferences of different types of citizens. More polarized lobbies may also be more effective in voicing their interests. Consequently, governments may be more influenced by the preferences of extreme groups and end up making inefficient decisions. Thus, in the Esteban-Ray model, inequality creates a particular type of civil society failure.

Solving imperfections in the provision of information is relatively straightforward, in that it is less likely to involve a reversal in local power relations. However, solving information asymmetries—equalizing

> Information failures in the civic arena are largely failures in the links between civil society, the state, and markets.

Equalizing access to information is relatively straightforward . . .

access to information between the rich and the poor—is often not enough. Direct confrontation with structures of power may be necessary to create more accountable and responsive policies. Whether the provision of information improves the functioning of states and markets and the capacity of citizens to mobilize remains an empirical question.

Conclusions

. . . but citizens may need to confront the structures of power directly to use that information to make governments more responsive to them.

Fads, rather than analysis, tend to drive policy decisions on participatory development. Passionate advocates spark a wave of interest, followed in a few years by disillusionment, which gives ammunition to centralizers, who engineer a sharp reversal. In time, excessive centralization generates negative fallout, which reinvigorates the climate for local participation.

There have been at least two such waves in the post–World War II period (as shown in chapter 1). If current trends are extrapolated, another centralizing shift may have begun. Advocates and the vicissitudes of fashion are perhaps unavoidable in the aid allocation process, but they need to be supplemented by a thoughtful diagnosis of market, government, and civil society failures; inequality; and a contextual understanding of the best ways to rectify them.

Participatory development policy needs to be driven by a thoughtful diagnosis of the interaction between market, government, and civil society failures.

These spheres do not operate independently; well-being is enhanced by both improving the functioning of each sphere and enhancing the links among them. The problems of information asymmetry and coordination that affect markets and governments also affect civil society. Decisions about whether, when, and how to promote local participation are therefore never easy. They need to be made with an understanding of the cooperative infrastructure; the role of elites; and the economic, political, and social costs and benefits associated with localizing decision making in a given country at a given time.

Notes

1. Effective civic action can also have harmful consequences for the average citizen, particularly when multiple groups with competing interests coexist within the same society—when, for instance, a fringe group is able to impose its beliefs on society at large by effectively mobilizing its members and cowering the majority into submission (Kuran 2004). This

situation represents a case of civil society failure that is, arguably, not a sustainable equilibrium in the long run.

2. These notions of justice and fairness may vary from society to society and group to group. But every social group has norms that determine what is fair and just, and civic action is mobilized based on these norms.

3. See Bardhan (2005) for an elaboration of this point. Another way of looking at the connection among governments, markets, and civil society is to examine them within the frame of accountability relationships (see figure 3.2 in World Bank 2004). When citizens/clients organize collectively, they engage with the state by participating in politics and finding various other ways of expressing voice. The state consists of politicians and policy makers who engage in a compact with service providers. The compact can be managerial, with the state directly managing the service providers through a government bureaucracy, or the government can delegate the provision of services to the market by having private providers deliver public services to citizens. The 2004 *World Development Report* specifies two routes by which a group of citizens can hold service providers accountable. The "long route" involves electoral accountability; citizens reward governments that are responsible for service provision by reelecting them or removing them from office by voting for their opponents. The "short route" decentralizes service provisions to communities, so that frontline providers are under the direct control and management of citizens, who exercise "client power" to hold them directly accountable.

4. The standard benchmark for market and government failures is "constrained Pareto efficiency"—the failure of self-interested individuals to obtain a Pareto optimum subject to constraints of information, given fixed preferences and technology. In the civic sphere, preferences cannot be assumed to be fixed; deliberative processes are intended to change preferences. Furthermore, coordinated actions can change information and the possibilities for contracting. For these reasons, a tight definition of civil society failure is elusive at this stage. The authors are grateful to Karla Hoff for alerting them to this point. For discussions of the related concept of "community failure," see Hayami and Kikuchi (1981), Baland and Platteau (1996), Aoki (2001), and Bardhan (2005).

5. In the course of a year of research, Tsai surveyed 316 villages in four provinces in northern and southern China.

6. Village temple groups are organized around a village guardian deity, an aspect of Chinese popular religion attacked during the Cultural Revolution period but subsequently rehabilitated. Lineage groups are organized around village ancestral halls.

7. Village church groups cannot be embedded, because Party members are prohibited from taking part in church activities. By contrast, given the centrality of the village temple as a symbolic resource—and the fact that the temple council is a fulcrum on which moral standing and prestige are regulated—Party members are almost always members of the temple council and among the top donors to temple activities.

8. The focus here is on the role of culture in building collective identity. For more on how a cultural lens can help with development policy, see Rao and Walton (2004) and Lamont and Small (2008).

9. See Bouchard (2009) for an exposition of the related idea of "collective imaginaries."

References

Abraham, A., and J.-P. Platteau. 2004. "Participatory Development: When Culture Creeps." In *Culture and Public Action*, ed. V. Rao and M. Walton, 210–33. Stanford, CA: Stanford University Press.

Acemoglu, D., and J. A. Robinson. 2006. *Economic Origins of Dictatorship and Democracy*. New York: Cambridge University Press.

Agrawal, A. 2005. "Environmentality: Community, Intimate Government, and the Making of Environmental Subjects in Kumaon, India." *Current Anthropology* 46(2): 161–89.

Alesina, A., and E. La Ferrara. 2005. "Ethnic Diversity and Economic Performance." *Journal of Economic Literature* 43(3): 762–800.

Alexander, J. 2006. *The Civil Sphere*. New York: Oxford University Press.

Aoki, M. 2001. *Toward a Comparative Institutional Analysis*. Cambridge, MA: MIT Press.

Baland, J.-M., P. Bardhan, and S. Bowles. 2006. "Introduction." In *Inequality, Cooperation and Environmental Sustainability*, ed. J.-M. Baland, P. Bardhan, and S. Bowles, 1–9. Princeton, NJ: Princeton University Press.

Baland, J.-M., and J.P. Platteau. 1996. *Halting Degradation of Natural Resources: Is there a Role for Rural Communities?* Oxford, U.K.: Clarendon Press.

———. 2006. "Collective Action and the Commons." In *Inequality, Cooperation and Environmental Sustainability*, ed. J.-M. Baland, P. Bardhan, and S. Bowles, 10–35. Princeton, NJ: Princeton University Press.

Bardhan, P. 2005. *Scarcity, Conflict and Cooperation*. Cambridge, MA: MIT Press.

Bardhan, P., M. Ghatak, and A. Karaivanov. 2006. "Inequality and Collective Action." In *Inequality, Cooperation and Environmental Sustainability*, ed. J.-M. Baland, P. Bardhan, and S. Bowles, 36–59. Princeton, NJ: Princeton University Press.

Bardhan, P., and D. Mookherjee. 1999. "Relative Capture of Local and National Governments: An Essay in the Political Economy of Decentralization." Working Paper, Institute for Economic Development, Boston University, Boston.

———. 2000. "Capture and Governance at Local and National Levels." *American Economic Review* 90(2): 135–39.

———. 2006. "The Rise of Local Governments: An Overview." In *Decentralization and Governance in Developing Countries*, ed. P. Bardhan and D. Mookherjee, 1–52. Cambridge, MA: MIT Press.

———. 2011. "Political Clientelism and Capture: Theory and Evidence from West Bengal." Working Paper, Department of Economics, University of California, Berkeley.

Bates, R. H. 2008. "State Failure." *Annual Review of Political Science* 11(1): 1–12.

Bayly, C. A. 2004. *The Birth of the Modern World: 1780 1914*. Malden, MA: Blackwell.

———. 2008. "Indigenous and Colonial Origins of Comparative Development." World Bank Policy Research Working Paper 4474, World Bank, Washington, DC.

Beard, V. A., and A. Dasgupta. 2006. "Collective Action and Community-Driven Development in Rural and Urban Indonesia." *Urban Studies* 43(9): 1451–68.

Besley, T. 2006. *Principled Agents? The Political Economy of Good Government*. Oxford, U.K.: Oxford University Press.

Bouchard, G. 2009. "Collective Imaginaries and Population Health: How Health Data Can Highlight Cultural History." In *Successful Societies: How Institutions and Culture Affect Health*, ed. P. A. Hall and M. Lamont, 169–200. Cambridge, U.K.: Cambridge University Press.

Bowen, J. R. 1986. "On the Political Construction of Tradition: Gotong Royong in Indonesia." *Journal of Asian Studies* 45(3): 545–61.

Chwe, M. S.-Y. 1999. "Structure and Strategy in Collective Action." *American Journal of Sociology* 105(1): 128–56.

———. 2001. *Rational Ritual: Culture, Coordination, and Common Knowledge*. Princeton, NJ: Princeton University Press.

Coate, S., and M. Ravallion. 1993. "Reciprocity without Commitment: Characterization and Performance of Informal Insurance Arrangements." *Journal of Development Economics* 40(1): 1–24.

Dasgupta, P. 2009. "Trust and Cooperation among Economic Agents." *Philosophical Transactions of the Royal Society* 364(1533): 3301–9.

Devarajan, S., and R. Kanbur. 2005. "A Framework for Scaling-Up Poverty Reduction with Illustrations from South India." Working Paper, Department of Economics, Cornell University, Ithaca, NY.

Esteban, J., and D. Ray. 2000. "Collective Action and the Group-Size Paradox." *American Political Science Review* 95(3): 663–72.

———. 2006. "Inequality, Lobbying and Resource Allocation." *American Economic Review* (March): 257–79.

Habermas, J. 1991. *Structural Transformation of the Public Sphere*. Cambridge, MA: MIT Press.

Hayami, Y. and M. Kikuchi. 1981. *Asian Village Economy at the Crossroads: An Economic Approach to Institutional Change*. Tokyo: University of Tokyo Press.

Heller, P., and T. M. Thomas Issac. 2003. "Democracy and Development: Decentralized Planning in Kerala." In *Deepening Democracy*, ed. A. Fung and E. O. Wright, 77–110. London: Verso.

Hoff, K. 2000. "Beyond Rosenstein-Rodan: The Modern Theory of Coordination Problems in Development." In *Annual World Bank Conference on Development Economics*, ed. B. Pleskovic and N. Stern, 145–76. Washington, DC: World Bank.

Hoff, K., M. Kshetramade, and E. Fehr. 2011. "Caste and Punishment: The Legacy of Caste Culture in Norm Enforcement." *Economic Journal* 121(556): F449–F475.

Hoff, K., and J. E. Stiglitz. 2001. "Modern Economic Theory and Development." In *Frontiers of Development Economics*, ed. G. Meier and J. Stiglitz, 389–459. Oxford, U.K.: Oxford University Press.

Hossain, N. 2009. *Rude Accountability in the Unreformed State: Informal Pressures on Frontline Bureaucrats in Bangladesh*. Institute for Development Studies, Sussex, United Kingdom.

Khemani, S. 2007. "Can Information Campaigns Overcome Political Obstacles to Serving the Poor?" In *The Politics of Service Delivery in Democracies: Better Access for the Poor*, ed. S. Devarajan and I. Widlung, 56–69. Stockholm: Ministry of Foreign Affairs, Government of Sweden.

Kitschelt, H., and S. I. Wilkinson. 2007. "Citizen-Politician Linkages: An Introduction." In *Patrons, Clients and Policies: Patterns of Democratic Accountability and Political Competition*, ed. H. Kitschelt and S. I. Wilkinson, 1–49. Cambridge, U.K.: Cambridge University Press.

Kriesi, H. 2007. "Political Context and Opportunity." In *The Blackwell Companion to Social Movements*, ed. D. A. Snow, S. A. Soule, and H. Kriesi, 67–90. Oxford, U.K.: Blackwell.

Kuran, T. 2004. "Why the Middle East Is Economically Underdeveloped: Historical Mechanisms of Institutional Stagnation." *Journal of Economic Perspectives* 18(3): 71–90.

Lamont, M., and M. L. Small. 2008. "How Culture Matters: Enriching Our Understanding of Poverty." In *The Colors of Poverty*, ed. A. C. Lin and D. R. Harris, 76–102. New York: Russell Sage.

Mansuri, G., and V. Rao. 2004. "Community-Based and -Driven Development: A Critical Review." *World Bank Research Observer* 19(1): 1–39.

McCloskey, D. 2006. *The Bourgeois Virtues: Ethics for an Age of Commerce*. Chicago: University of Chicago Press.

Mokyr, J. 2010. *The Enlightened Economy: An Economic History of Britain 1700–1850*. London: Penguin Press.

Morris, A. D., and S. Staggenborg. 2004. "Leadership in Social Movements." In *The Blackwell Companion to Social Movements*, ed. D. A. Snow, S. A. Soule, and H. Kriese, 171–96. Oxford, U.K.: Blackwell.

Olson, M. 1965. *The Logic of Collective Action: Public Goods and the Theory of Groups*. Cambridge, MA: Harvard University Press.

Ostrom, E. 1990. *Governing the Commons: The Evolution of Institutions for Collective Action*. New York: Cambridge University Press.

Pradhan, M, V. Rao, and C. Rosemberg. 2010. "The Impact of Community Level Activities of the Second Urban Poverty Project (UPP)." Department of Economics, University of Amsterdam, Amsterdam.

Putnam, R. 1993. *Making Democracy Work: Civic Traditions in Modern Italy.* Princeton, NJ: Princeton University Press.

Rao, V. 2006. "On Inequality Traps and Development Policy." *Development Outreach* 8(1): 10–13.

———. 2008. "Symbolic Public Goods and the Coordination of Collective Action: A Comparison of Local Development in India and Indonesia." In *Contested Commons: Conversations Between Economists and Anthropologists,* ed. P. Bardhan and I. Ray, 46–65. Oxford, U.K.: Blackwell.

Rao, V., and A. M. Ibanez. 2005. "The Social Impact of Social Funds in Jamaica: A 'Participatory Econometric' Analysis of Targeting, Collective Action, and Participation in Community-Driven Development." *Journal of Development Studies* 41(5): 788–838.

Rao, V., and M. Walton, eds. 2004. *Culture and Public Action.* Palo Alto, CA: Stanford University Press.

Ricklefs, M . 2002. *A History of Modern Indonesia since c. 1200,* 3rd. ed. Palo Alto, CA: Stanford University Press.

Sullivan, J. 1992. *Local Government and Community in Java: An Urban Case-Study.* Singapore: Oxford University Press.

Tsai, L. 2007. *Accountability without Democracy: Solidarity Groups and Public Goods Provision in Rural China.* Cambridge, U.K.: Cambridge University Press.

World Bank. 2004. *World Development Report 2004: Making Services Work for Poor People.* Washington, DC: World Bank.

———. 2005. "The Effectiveness of World Bank Support for Community-Based and -Driven Development." Operations Evaluation Department, World Bank, Washington, DC.

———. 2006. *World Development Report 2006: Equity and Development.* Washington, DC: World Bank.

CHAPTER THREE

The Challenge of Inducing Participation

THIS CHAPTER APPLIES THE ANALYTICAL FRAMEWORK OUTLINED in chapter 2 in order to better understand the challenges faced in resolving civil society failures, improving the interaction of civil society with markets and governments, and implementing participatory projects. What can participatory development achieve, and under what conditions? What do the structures of failure at the local level say about options for policy? What are some of the challenges of using policy interventions to repair civic failures and induce participation? How do incentives within donor institutions and government bureaucracies affect the implementation of participatory projects? The chapter uses the analytical framework to derive a set of hypotheses that guide the analysis of the evidence in the subsequent chapters.

Under the right conditions, effective local participation can be a powerful force for change and the achievement of various development objectives. Local development moves from being "participatory" to "empowered" when decisions made by ordinary people through deliberation are tied to policy decisions and actions—what Fung and Wright (2003) call "empowered participatory governance." This process is characterized by three foundational principles:

- Participation must have a practical orientation.
- Participation must be "bottom up," in the sense that all of the people most affected by the problem and knowledgeable about solutions to it should be involved in decision making.
- Participation must be deliberative.

Fung and Wright define deliberation as a process of collective decision making in which a group reaches a consensus across diverse points

> Under the right conditions, effective local participation can be a powerful force for change and the achievement of various development objectives.

of view. It is an alternate to what economists call "preference aggregation" through electoral mechanisms. In electoral decision making, preferences are aggregated by counting votes. Deliberative decision making requires that participants listen to one another's positions and generate group choices after due consideration of other points of view, even if they do not necessarily endorse those choices or find them optimal.

After examining various successful cases of empowered participatory governance around the world, Fung and Wright conclude that in order to advance these foundational principles, governance institutions need to incorporate three design features:

- *Devolution.* Local decision-making units should have meaningful power and be downwardly accountable.
- *Centralized supervision and coordination.* Local decision-making units need to share information, learn from one another, and discover what works by trial and error while being monitored and held accountable by the center.
- *State-centered, not voluntary.* Empowered participation should remake state institutions to align with their foundational principles rather than develop parallel structures.

Ironically, empowered participation requires a strong, functioning state.

Ironically, empowered participation requires a strong, functioning state that has not only internalized the broad objective of deepening democracy and developed a much more astute view of citizens' role in shaping policy but has also actively promoted and supervised the process by which this process happens.

The premise underlying participatory development is the power of the group—the notion that individuals are far more effective when they work together toward a common objective than when they attempt to achieve the same objective on their own. By mobilizing citizens to work together for their collective well-being, participatory development has the potential to redress some failures of the state and some failures of markets while improving the capacity of individuals to bond and work together.

One reason participation can do so is that it can have intrinsic value. People may value the simple courtesy of having their opinions heard, of being listened to. If public decisions are determined deliberatively rather than dictatorially, in a manner that gives everyone—poor and rich, female and male, lower and upper caste—an equal voice, the process by which decisions are made has, in itself, the potential to enhance agency.

Political theorists contend that participation has the potential to lead to a process of positive self-transformation by catalyzing a set of desirable changes in individuals: enhanced facility for practical reasoning, greater tolerance of difference, more sensitivity about the need for reciprocity, enhanced ability to think and act with autonomy on the basis of their own preferences, and the ability to engage in moral discourse and make moral judgments (Warren 1995).

Much of the value of participation can be encapsulated in Hirschman's (1970) view that "voice" has both intrinsic and instrumental value. The anthropologist Arjun Appadurai (2004) goes farther, describing voice as a "cultural capacity." Voice, he contends, is a matter not just of people demanding democratic rights but of engaging with social, political, and economic issues in terms of metaphor, rhetoric, organization, and public performance, in order to negotiate and navigate their worlds. This "capacity to aspire" is not evenly distributed. In situations where the rich have consistently benefited from better social, political, and economic connections and have the cultural tools to navigate those worlds, they are "more likely . . . to be conscious of the links between the more and less immediate objects of aspiration." The rich are thus better able to navigate their way toward actualizing their aspirations. If participation is to build this navigational capacity, then voice and the capacity to aspire need to be "reciprocally linked, with each accelerating the nurture of the other" (Appadurai 2004).

> Participation can have intrinsic value: people may value the simple courtesy of being listened to.

Participatory interventions are, however, more often justified by their instrumental value—their potential to make states and markets more accountable to the needs of citizens, to help communities mobilize to improve credit and livelihood opportunities and manage common property resources. The accountability function of participation requires groups to mobilize in a manner that changes the incentives of the agents of the state so that they act in the interests of citizens. State failure often occurs because the incentives of the individuals who comprise the state, and function as its agents, are not aligned with the needs of citizens; instead, these agents seek to maximize their own interests. In the absence of adequate oversight, this tendency could result in a range of adverse outcomes, from absenteeism to corruption and theft of public resources. Furthermore, if oversight of officials is largely managerial (that is, from the top rather than the bottom), local officials are accountable only upward, motivating officials to fulfill the dictates of their bosses rather than meeting local needs. The consequences—phantom schools with crumbling buildings and absent teachers, nonfunctioning toilets that are used to store fodder, roads that crumble at the first sign of rain—are ubiquitous in the developing world.

Participation has the potential to force agents of the state to act against their private interests and for the public good.

Participation has the potential to force agents of the state to act against their private interests and for the public good. It makes accountability—whether it be electoral, social, or "rude"—inherently conflictual. How this conflict is managed and channeled depends on the nature of the state, the institutional incentives of its agents, the division of power and responsibility between political leadership and bureaucrats, the nature and extent of the decentralization of authority, and the receptivity of the state to the demands of citizens.

Participation is also used to enhance livelihood opportunities and credit for the poor. Microcredit programs mobilize groups of individuals to collectively enforce the repayment schedule of every member, in an attempt to resolve coordination problems and asymmetries in information on the creditworthiness of individuals, which prevent banks and other large credit suppliers from servicing such communities. Self-help groups have also been mobilized to help expand livelihood opportunities more generally—by providing training in handicrafts and agricultural techniques, for example, and assisting in small-scale entrepreneurial and other activities. The group provides peer education and technical and moral support, using the power of networks to diffuse information and knowledge.

Participation has been used to try to redress the underprovision of public goods and services . . .

Participation has been used to try to redress the underprovision of public goods and services such as roads, water tanks, schools, and health clinics, which local governments typically provide. In community-driven development interventions, such public goods and services may be handed over entirely to communities to manage. In times of unexpected crisis—when a typhoon or earthquake strikes and governments and markets are unable to respond quickly, for example—communities are mobilized to rebuild homes, roads, and bridges and manage emergency aid. When a country is emerging from a long war or civil strife, community-based aid is often used to lead postconflict efforts at reconstruction.

. . . and to reduce social, political, and economic inequality.

Participation has also been used to try to reduce social, political, and economic inequality. By reserving leadership positions in civic bodies for women or other disadvantaged groups, participatory interventions have explicitly attempted to redress discrimination by promoting more egalitarian notions of leadership and breaking the power of traditional elites. These interventions are inherently conflictual, in that they challenge the prerogatives of the people in authority.

Using civic groups to help reduce poverty usually involves far less conflict with elites, because it does not challenge the basis of their authority. In many countries, for instance, community-based participatory bodies select the beneficiaries of poverty reduction programs, an alternative method of targeting that even local elites may perceive as fair.

Participation and the Capacity to Engage

An important way in which participatory interventions can work is by changing the character of everyday interactions—a process that, over time, reshapes social relationships. In highly unequal environments, social status structures the way people talk to one another. Moving toward accountable government both requires and brings about a change in the tone and content of discourse. The conversation shifts from being embedded within existing power relationships and conditioned by social norms to one in which people confront authority, demand change, debate points of policy, and speak as citizens rather than as subjects. Such shifts in "recognition" can have important economic implications (Basu 2011).

To bring about this change, citizens must have access to a new toolkit of discursive strategies—conciliatory, confrontational, pleading, demanding, threatening—that they are able to strategically deploy. Even if these approaches do not have an immediate impact on the allocation of public resources, changes in the nature of speech can, over time, build what Gibson and Woolcock (2008) call the "capacity to engage." Having the tools for "deliberative contestation" gives marginalized groups a more equitable shot at negotiating, asserting, and making demands that are in line with their interests and life experience. With repeated interaction, more equality in the ability to articulate demands can help move communities toward a trajectory of better and more equitable governance. This expansion in their strategic toolkits can change not only how people are perceived within their communities but also how they perceive themselves.

Rao and Sanyal (2010) analyzed the transcripts of 300 *gram sabhas* (village meetings) from India. This excerpt—from an interaction between the upper-caste president of the *panchayat* (village council),

> Participatory interventions have the potential to change the character of everyday interactions—a process that, over time, reshapes social relationships.

> To bring about this change, citizens must have access to a new toolkit of discursive strategies that they are able to deploy strategically.

a poor upper-caste villager (Jayaraman), and a poor villager (Muniraj) from an untouchable (Dalit) caste—provides an example of deliberative contestation in which the Dalit villager asserts his rights as a citizen.

Jayaraman: There are 45 families in our village. None of us has any land. We work for meager daily wages. Whatever little we get we spend on our children's education. But it's impossible to educate our children up to high school because we don't have the money. . . . So we request that the government do something. . . . Our whole area is dirty. Even the water is muddy, and that's what we drink. . . . How many times we have requested a road near the cremation ground and for the supply for clean water?! We can only request and apply. The rest is up to you.

Panchayat president: If there are 20–25 houses in an area, a ward member should be appointed to represent the area. That ward member should listen to your problems and must do something to help you.

Muniraj: That way [if we have a ward member], we will have the guts to enter this room [where the *gram sabha* meeting is taking place]. If the required ward members are not with us, to whom can we voice our woes? Who will represent us? . . . If the ward member belongs to another community, he won't even listen to our problems. Earlier, there was a time when a backward caste person was not even allowed to sit in the same area with others! The officers and leaders who come here [to the *gram sabha* meeting] already have a preset plan about what to do and say. You come, sit on the chair, say something, decide among yourselves, and go away. What's there for us to do?! You've enjoyed power for all these years. Why don't you let us have a turn? . . . We don't want any problem at the communal level. For us, whether X comes or Y comes, it is the same. We vote, but what happens later? Whereas other people get water even before they ask for it, we have to ask endlessly, and even so, our demand is not fulfilled. . . . We don't want to fight with anyone. But at least there should be someone to listen to our problems. We've been without water supply for the past one month. Even the village president knows it. He has promised to send water. But the ward member is not allowing us to take water. The water is sent to all his relatives. We cannot do anything to stop it.

Panchayat president: In any competition, it's a rule that one should win and the other should lose. There's no community-based discrimination or problem. If all of you in booth number 1 join and vote for me, I become the president. On the other hand, if everyone in the other booths votes for another person, then he'll become the president. And then what will matter is what he can do for those booths that voted for him. Today, among youngsters, the level of public awareness is very high. Anyone can become a leader. . . . Even though there are problems between your two groups, I try to mediate. I don't encourage communal riots.

Muniraj: Everyone should be treated equally. No one should be treated as inferior to others. We should also be given a chance to sit on the dais [where the leaders sit]. Why should we be denied that right? Just because I talk like this, it doesn't mean that I fight with you or disrespect you. I am simply voicing my feeling.

Caste-based divisions have deep historical roots in India. They manifest themselves in practices such as physical distancing and symbolic deference. It is noteworthy that these traditional patterns of interaction are now being openly challenged in *gram sabha* meetings, as Muniraj's angry complaints indicate. Lower-caste challenges are not completely new; what makes the exchange excerpted above different is that it comes not from a member of the educated elite but from an ordinary villager embedded in everyday, local structures of inequality. Ordinary people from disadvantaged castes now have a stake in political participation, because the *gram sabha* allows them to momentarily discard the stigma of their ascriptive identity and low economic status and slip into their identity as citizens with equal rights in the eyes of the state. These public interactions have the potential to challenge entrenched social relations because they make overt the heretofore unseen "weapons of the weak"—the expression of dissatisfaction in private while presenting compliant demeanors in public, foot dragging in respond to the demands of elites. Such interactions expose "hidden transcripts" (Scott 1990) such as the feelings of oppression and domination felt by lower castes and provide a means to challenge them.

Minor as it may seem, the fact that poor people and people from lower castes are able to make demands and voice complaints gives them a sense of possessing equal recognition as citizens. When—and whether—such small-scale changes cascade into effective civic capacity depends on the community's level of literacy and numeracy, the level of inequality, and the extent to which inequality is embedded within durable social and power relationships.

Diagnosing Failure Triangles

Each type of participatory intervention can be associated with a different diagnosis of the failures it will confront—whether it is trying to generate an intrinsic or instrumental outcome, address a long-term development objective, or respond to a short-term crisis. Each type of intervention may employ a different definition of community (a microcredit group is very different from a group of households mobilized to reconstruct homes after a hurricane). Not only can these groups differ in their composition, they may also have different geographic and social boundaries and incentives for collective action. Consequently, they may be subject to different types of failures.

Potential spillovers from one civic objective to another also need to be thought through. Will building microcredit groups also result in the formation of groups that can fight village council corruption? Will starting a social fund to deal with postearthquake reconstruction result in a community-based institution that can act as a substitute for a failed local state?

Government intervention may be justified when markets fail or economic and social inequalities need to be narrowed (see chapter 2). Theory also indicates that "each public service should be provided by the jurisdiction having control over the minimum geographic area that would internalize [its] benefits and costs" (Oates 1972, 55). Local needs are difficult for central governments to ascertain, because of the huge information costs of doing so and because of heterogeneities in preferences and variations in the condition and composition of communities. For this reason, theory suggests that decisions on such issues as the provision of local public goods need to be decentralized.[1]

Justifications for government interventions are complicated by the fact that governments themselves are prone to failure, because of problems of coordination, commitment, and information asymmetries—locally as well as at the center. The power exercised by government can reflect and reproduce inequality. The degree to which community-based

Each type of participatory intervention needs to be associated with a different diagnosis of the failures it will confront.

bodies and local governments are embedded within structures of local inequality can be extremely heterogeneous, making central monitoring of local bodies very difficult. Consequently, local civic action (local participation) is seen as the most effective and sustainable way of redressing local government failure—dealing with corruption, giving the poor a greater say in policy decisions, and holding local governments more accountable.

There are, however, some omissions in this logic, which often tend to be ignored. First, civil society is subject to the same sorts of failures and inequalities as markets and states. Incorporating failures and inequalities in civil society makes the policy logic far more complicated and less prescriptive. Participation is usually not a substitute but a complement to the state. Civil society exists in a symbiotic relationship with the state: it both shapes and conditions the state and is shaped and conditioned by it.

Second, the development of civic capacity is not just a local challenge; civil society matters in checking the tendency of all levels of government—central and local—toward authoritarianism. In addition, civic groups play an important role in the development of markets, by creating an enabling environment for entrepreneurship; protecting the interests of workers; providing credit, and other functions that are important for inclusive economic growth. Thus, one challenge of development is to develop civic activity at both the micro and macro levels.

Third, civil society is not an abstract concept that exists outside local forms of knowledge, social structures, meaning and belief systems, and power relations. It is shaped by people, who are products as much of their social and cultural milieus as of economic and political systems. The manner in which people organize, the interests around which they mobilize, the styles and narratives of their discourse and resistance, and the objects of their resistance are hybrid products of local dynamics and national and global influences. Policy makers should therefore be careful not to impose conceptions of civil society that come from outside the local environment (for example, Western political theory). Instead, they should try to understand the meaning of terms such as "civil," "society," and "participation" from within indigenous frames. Indeed, policy makers should try to understand how history and the history of interventions—whether colonial or developmental—have shaped those frames (Comaroff and Comaroff 1999). Doing so calls for a less prescriptive and more adaptive approach to policy.

Local civic action is believed to be the most effective way of redressing local government failure . . .

. . . but civil society and government, which are subject to failure themselves, shape and condition each other, in a manner determined by the nature of the failure.

Developing civil society is not just a local challenge . . . doing so helps check the tendency of all levels of government—central and local—toward authoritarianism.

Civil society is not an abstract concept that exists outside local forms of knowledge, social structures, meaning and belief systems, and power relations . . .

. . . it is shaped by people, who are products as much of their social and cultural milieus as of economic and political systems.

Finally, when all three spheres—markets, governments, and civil society—are beset by failures and inequalities, which is typically the case almost everywhere, policy becomes murky, leading back to a variant of the old balanced and unbalanced growth debates of the 1950s (Levy and Fukuyama 2010). Should development policy be sequential—focusing first, for example, on building markets and spurring industrial growth—in the expectation that better government and civic capacity will follow, or should it focus on first developing an effective government or effective civic sphere? Should the strategy attempt to be more balanced by simultaneously improving the functioning of all three spheres? How do market, government, and civil society capacities at the macro level affect policy options at the local level? At the local level—where every village and neighborhood faces a different set of problems and is conditioned by different social structures, geographies, climates, and levels of connectivity—answers to these questions are perhaps best drawn deductively by examining the evidence, as chapters 4–6 do.

Local Government Failure and the Nexus of Accommodation

In most communities in the developing world, both the state and the market have failed. Local market failures—in the provision of public goods, such as schooling, health, and local infrastructure; in access to credit, markets, and so forth—are easy to identify. Local government failure can, however, be dispersed across a variety of local institutions and individuals. A local government typically consists of leaders and bureaucrats. Leaders can be members of village councils, neighborhood committees, mayors and municipal councils, city administrators, or chiefs and their advisers. They function within various systems of accountability. They may be elected in regular, independently supervised elections or in "endogenous" elections that are organized and supervised locally; they may be appointed by upper-level political leaders and thus free of local accountability; or they may be hereditary.

Even in formally constituted democracies, the theoretical logic of democratic accountability does not necessarily map into the real world logic of interactions between government and citizens. Locally organized elections can be manipulated by local leaders to their advantage; independent elections, although much more effective and important as accountability mechanisms, can be subject to clientelism and the appropriation of public funds to pay for electoral campaigns. Even if

Local government failure is dispersed across a variety of local institutions and individuals.

leaders appointed by upper levels of government are accountable only upward, the central government can be effective in requiring good local government. Hereditary leaders selected in democratic settings, although often authoritarian, can be subject to various long-term commitments, contracts, and symbolic functions that obligate them to act in the interests of their subjects.

All local leaders are placed in the difficult position of negotiating power with the central government, within the context of central regulations and political incentives. The degree of autonomy enjoyed by local leaders depends on their bargaining power with the center. At the lowest tier of government, leaders may have limited room to maneuver and be constantly in the position of having to beg for resources from higher levels. They may, however, have established fiefdoms that are politically important to the center, giving them a measure of power and autonomy. The authority of local leaders and bureaucrats depends on the extent to which they control the funds and functions of government and on their local capacity to raise revenues. The less they depend on the center for funds, the greater their autonomy. But local governments often function within the domain of local strongmen, such as large landowners or warlords, who wield considerable influence and whose own demands and interests need to be satisfied.

Local leaders also have to share power with local bureaucrats, who are also subject to the institutional structures of government. Local bureaucrats often come from the lowest rung of government service; their professional incentives are geared toward pleasing their central bosses and moving up in the hierarchy. They often perform important functions at the local level and control an array of public resources, which gives them considerable power within the village or municipality. These local bureaucrats can range from district administrators to "street-level" officials, such as extension officers and junior engineers, to employees of local governments, such as janitors and bill collectors.

In participatory projects, it is the street-level bureaucrats (usually known as "project facilitators") who have the most proximate impact on outcomes, because they are the people who deal with communities on a day-to-day basis. They are expected to mobilize communities; build the capacity for collective action; ensure adequate representation and participation; and, where necessary, break elite domination. These trainers, anthropologists, engineers, economists, and accountants must be culturally and politically sensitive charismatic leaders. It is ironic that

The theoretical logic of democratic accountability does not necessarily map into the real world logic of interactions between government and citizens.

In participatory projects, project facilitators have the most proximate impact on outcomes, because they are the people who deal with communities on a day-to-day basis.

Local politicians, bureaucrats, strongmen, and other elites often function in a "nexus of accommodation" that is hard to break.

this difficult role, on which participation can succeed or fail, is usually entrusted to the least experienced, worst-paid, and most junior staff.

All of these weaknesses of local government can lead to situations in which resources would have been allocated more efficiently had the government not intervened. Weaknesses are caused by accommodations made to the center, by the manipulation of accountability mechanisms, and by accommodations to local strongmen and between local bureaucrats and politicians (Migdal 1988). The concentration of power in any of these actors—a local strongman who also heads the village council, for example—can lead to a strong local state but one that tends to be dictatorial in its decisions. When all actors are equally powerful, power and authority can be diffused in a way that makes actions unpredictable, dilutes responsibility for action, and weakens the cooperative infrastructure.

It is difficult for central governments to monitor the work of local governments because of the very imperfections in information and coordination that caused power to be devolved in the first place.

It is difficult for central governments to monitor the work of local governments because of the very imperfections in information and coordination that caused power to be devolved in the first place. The nexus of social structures, power relations, the management of accommodations, the needs of citizens, and the quality of personnel vary greatly from jurisdiction to jurisdiction, causing communities to have a high degree of heterogeneity. These variations place an untenable burden of monitoring and supervision on the central government; if power is decentralized, they can produce an entirely new set of government failures. The constant process of accommodation among the center, local strongmen, local government leaders, and bureaucrats, often makes the interests of citizens the last priority—the residual element in a hierarchy of interests that must be accommodated.

Participation has the potential to move the actions of local governments toward the interests of citizens by adding their voice to the mix of necessary accommodations . . .

. . . but realizing this potential requires radical change, including confrontation with elites.

Participation has the potential to change this dynamic. It can move the actions of local governments toward the interests of citizens by adding their voice to the mix of necessary accommodations. If civic groups are sophisticated enough to understand the procedures of local governments and nimble enough to know how to exploit the political economy of accommodation, they can become a potent political force. If the cooperative infrastructure is strong and elite interests not dominant, citizens can be united, lobby effectively, and persuade local governments to listen to their points of view, furthering their interests by changing incentives within local governments.

Although participatory projects are packaged and promoted on the promise of "empowerment" or enhancing the "demand side of governance," they often downplay the fact that both outcomes require radical change—a confrontation with local elites and a shift, to use Migdal's language, in the "nexus of accommodation." If external donors and central and state governments have not completely internalized these radical goals and participation is instead nothing more than a donor-driven mandate, it is unlikely that interventions will be implemented in a manner that is truly empowering. Instead, the goals will be processed within the existing nexus of accommodation, and lasting change in outcomes will be unlikely—and may actually lead to elite capture. Participatory interventions then become archetypes of what Hoff and Stiglitz (2001) call "shallow interventions"—interventions that result in no sustainable and irreversible changes in political dynamics and therefore have a negligible impact on outcomes. To achieve a "deep intervention," the state has to commit to a long-term process of engineering; a more downwardly accountable cooperative infrastructure that is equity enhancing and empowering. Doing so requires strong monitoring to avoid elite backlash, subversion, or capture, and the ability to distinguish between benevolent and malevolent elite engagement with communities.

Lasting change is unlikely if the radical process of breaking the local nexus of accommodation is not internalized and supported by donors and the central state.

Participation and Political Opportunity

Effective participation requires the skillful exploitation of local political opportunities (Kreisi 2007). An individual's political opportunity set is determined by his or her interests (material, ideological, or identity based), as well as by the economic, social, political, or psychic constraints he or she faces. The decision to participate, however, depends largely on the actions of the other members of the group to which an individual belongs. A group's willingness to mobilize and act collectively depends on its shared opportunity set, the gains that accrue from acting collectively, and the costs and other constraints associated with coordinating collective activity. It is not just individual and collective interests that influence the set of opportunities—it is also the beliefs about those opportunities (Elster 1989). These beliefs are important because they may cause actors to underestimate or overestimate their capacity to effect change. Sociologists call this mix of individual and group political opportunities and beliefs the "political opportunity structure" (Kriesi 2007).

Effective participation requires the skillful exploitation of local political opportunities.

Indonesia provides an interesting example of how a village group was able to exploit political opportunities for change by developing its capacity to engage (Gibson and Woolcock 2008). An extended conflict over a leaky dam served as a flashpoint for organizing farmers and other villagers who depended on its shrinking reservoir supply for irrigation and drinking water. Initially, villagers used bureaucratic channels to request repairs to the dam. When their demands fell on deaf ears, they began expressing their anger through arguments and small-scale violence among themselves, including a hoe fight between two family members that resulted in head injuries.

As unrest peaked in 2001, the villagers changed their tactics and began to mobilize hundreds of teachers, police, civil servants, and rice paddy owners and workers through a broad array of social networks. This mass mobilization caught the attention of a candidate for the local council, who used it as an opportunity to confront the incumbent. As hundreds of villagers blockaded a key road to the dam, the candidates sat in chairs facing the dilapidated structure until the deputy head of the council arrived and promised to make the repairs—which were completed within a year.

This victory gave rise to a flurry of peaceful and fruitful engagement aimed at forcing the government to compensate farmers for lands inundated by the dam. In using the original conflict to develop their capacity to engage with local officials—and exploit the competition between them—the villagers developed new open political opportunity structures and beliefs about themselves that will have a lasting impact on local power relations.

An open political opportunity structure is one in which civic action can exploit changes in the political system—in the structure of the state, in leadership, or in dominance by a particular elite—to further the interests of a particular group. Localizing development—through decentralization or a community-driven development project, for example—can open up political opportunities by bringing the locus of decision making closer to citizens, which increases the benefits to participation while reducing its costs. Because of the nexus of accommodation between local and central politicians and between local and central bureaucrats, however, the effectiveness of local civic mobilization can be modest. Although civic mobilization can potentially change the incentives of the agents of the local state so that they act more in the interests of citizens, these agents will have to balance the demands of local citizens against the demands of central authorities and the

Localizing development can open up political opportunities by bringing the locus of decision making closer to citizens, increasing the benefits to participation while reducing its costs.

competing demands of other local actors. In the absence of a sharp and sustainable shift in the nexus of accommodation, therefore, expansion of civic opportunities at the local level may have limited impact.

Acemoglu and Robinson offer some important insights into the process of participatory democratic change in *Economic Origins of Dictatorship and Democracy*. They find that the conditions under which political opportunities for citizens are maximized and the manner in which citizens can effect change in a manner that progressively empowers them depends on whether a particular group believes it has the capacity "to obtain its favored policies against the resistance" of the people in power and can convince other groups that it can do so (Acemoglu and Robinson 2006, 21). Before they can act, citizens have to be persuaded that any move toward an open political opportunity structure will be durable and that old political institutions enmeshed with old economic and social arrangements will give way to more accountable structures. If change is seen as temporary, individuals will tend to use the opportunity to maximize their immediate personal gains. Citizens will participate in a manner that challenges powerful elites only if they feel they can "lock in" political power in a way that is not easily reversed.

Citizens' willingness to act is further complicated by uncertainty about decentralization, which could be recentralized during the next political cycle, as has happened in almost every developing country. Similarly, in the absence of durable shifts toward a more accountable state, participation in community-driven development projects may not lead to greater citizen mobilization on other issues, as the costs will exceed the benefits. In contrast, a genuine change in the political opportunity structure, accompanied by collective mobilization, can permanently increase the cost to elites of maintaining their domination.

Citizens thus make decisions about participation based on the likely success of a specific reform, their beliefs about how sustainable it is, and the potential for repression and backlash. Even with active participation, a small number of protagonists will lead the charge—spurred on by lower opportunity costs or greater altruism. Some people will prefer to have a free ride whereas others will play it safe, waiting to see how quickly the winds change before deciding to act. There will also be antagonists—people who actively oppose civic agents because those agents challenge their interests.

Elites who stand to lose under the new regime will include many local and central bureaucrats, local strongmen, and local and central politicians. Some elites may become protagonists, however, if they see a

> Before they can act, citizens have to be persuaded that any move toward an open political opportunity structure will be durable.

101

way that a change in policy could serve their own interests; there is, in fact, a risk of elite capture if gains from an intervention accrue mainly to these pro-reform elites and their supporters. A third category of elites—often better-educated citizens with high moral but low political authority, such as teachers, pastors, and imams—may help lead the process, either because they are altruistic and see doing so as a way of effecting positive change or because leadership gives them an opportunity to gain power and status. In this case, elite domination can facilitate an intervention and may even be essential to its success.

> In some societies, there is no recognizable conception of citizenship in the textbook sense of the term . . .

Part of the challenge of introducing decentralized and participatory government into societies with "traditional" authority structures is that traditional systems function with a different theory of governance, which the community generally accepts as just and legitimate. In some societies, there is no recognizable conception of citizenship in the textbook sense of the term; there are, instead, only leaders and subjects. The legitimacy of local leaders is based on a gift economy, a system of mutual obligation between leaders and subjects in which civic activity consists largely of subjects making requests to leaders. Leaders grant these requests if they are able to do so, expecting obedience in return. The resulting equilibrium creates elite dominance, authoritarian rule, and sharp inequalities in wealth, power, and social status.

> . . . instead, leaders and subjects relate to one another through systems of mutual obligation.

Development projects come with "modern" notions of governance and citizenship, which are predicated on the assumptions that government and citizens represent separate and equal spheres and separate loci of power and that "good governance" requires leaders to be accountable to citizens. This notion of governance is based on competition and negotiation for power rather than on mutual obligation.

> Shifting from a gift-based to a competition- and negotiation-based model of governance and citizenship is a highly contentious process.

Shifting from a gift-based to a competition- and negotiation-based model of governance and citizenship is a highly contentious process. During periods of what can be called "traditional equilibrium"—when social and political roles are well defined and everyone's actions and interactions are highly predictable—levels of conflict are low. Within this system, however, there may be few opportunities to break inequality traps or empower the poor. At best, the poor can employ Scott's (1990) "weapons of the weak" to express resentment without explicit confrontation. Participatory interventions—along with other efforts to reduce inequalities, such as land reform—seek to disrupt this equilibrium by changing the local cooperative infrastructure, replacing leadership legitimized by mutual obligation with a relationship between leaders and citizens based on democratic accountability. Unless traditional inequalities resting on inherited wealth, status, and identity are concurrently replaced by a system in which power and status reward ability and effort, however, the traditional order and existing power structures will subsume and subvert any nascent participatory institutions.

If, however, participatory interventions break down durable inequalities, collective well-being could well diminish in the short run, as elites resist, object to, and attempt to disrupt this challenge to their status. Some of their subjects will be left anchorless, not knowing how to navigate the new environment. Others will compete for power by using violence. The major challenge during this transition period is to channel conflicts into venues for deliberation and debate, in order to achieve a negotiated transition to a new regime. If the process is effective, it will lead to a new equilibrium in which leadership is legitimated by its ability to meet the needs of citizens and social status is based on achievement.

Implementation Challenges: The Role of Donors

Challenges in inducing participation lie not only in the power dynamics within communities; they are also deeply influenced by incentives within agencies tasked with funding and implementing participatory projects. In particular, donors—both multilateral and bilateral—have been key players in the spread of participatory innovations. They have been responsible for transferring ideas and techniques from one region of the world to another and actively scaling up interventions developed in a few communities to an entire country. Donors have tended to ignore the fact that context (historical trajectories, social and economic inequality, ethnic heterogeneity, and symbolic public goods) affects political and social institutions, especially at the community level, relying instead on "best practice" templates.

This tendency results in what Evans (2004) calls "institutional monocropping"—the "imposition of blueprints based on idealized versions of Anglo-American institutions, the applicability of which is presumed to transcend national circumstances and cultures." Other critics, including Harriss (2001) and Cooke and Kothari (2001), argue that in participatory projects, complex and contextual concepts such as community, empowerment, and capacity for collective action are applied to large development projects on tight timelines. Consequently, project implementers, whose incentives are often poorly aligned with

Challenges in inducing participation lie not only in the power dynamics within communities . . .

. . . they are also deeply influenced by incentives within agencies tasked with funding and implementing participatory projects.

103

the needs of the project, may gloss over differences within target groups that underscore local power structures and sidestep the difficult task of institution building in favor of more easily deliverable and measurable outcomes.

Mosse's (2005) ethnography of the Indo-British Rain-Fed Farming Project (IBRFP), funded by the United Kingdom's Overseas Development Administration (ODA) and Department for International Development (DFID), illustrates how the process of induced participation works in a large, scaled-up, donor-driven project. Mosse studied the project over several years and was involved in it in various capacities—as a planner, social expert, soil and water conservation consultant, and adviser—as it evolved through different planning and implementation phases. He studied all of its phases, from inception, in 1992, as a participatory project geared toward bringing agricultural technologies and innovations to the tribal Bhil population in central India; to its assessment by the development community, in 1995, as an "exemplary success"; to its culmination, in 1998–99, by which time it was declared a failure. ODA–DFID's Indian partner organization was a fertilizer company, which Mosse found to be unusually committed to the participatory ethic. The company hired a large field staff of community organizers and trained a large number of village-level volunteers, called *jankars* ("knowledgeable people"), who gradually emerged as crucial local mediators and brokers.

The project began with a "village entry" participatory rural appraisal. The very nature of a participatory rural appraisal—which is typically held in the courtyard of a village headman or other notable—subjects it to a high degree of bias and reflects the effects of local power. The type of knowledge that was communicated, the tone of the discourse, and the words used all reflected the biases of the more active, articulate members of the village, who defined the community's needs and then became crucial links for the community organizations in the initial trust-building phase of the project. The poorer members of the community were usually unwilling, inarticulate participants in such processes. In response, the community organizations gradually changed their tactics. They approached women and nonelites for more discreet, informal rural appraisal–type exercises, which had repercussions for their position in relation to village elites.

Matters were hardly as simple as ensuring that all points of view were represented, however: villagers quickly learned to anticipate the outsider's point of view, sense project staff's capacities for providing assistance, and structure their demands accordingly. The project soon came to be seen as a patron of particular activities and constituencies. The participatory rural appraisal and planning stage became, in effect, a process of mutual collusion in which "local knowledge" and desires were effectively domesticated by the project's vocabulary, as community perspectives seamlessly melded with the project's interests. Although planners continued to use the language of participation and empowerment, villagers viewed the project as just another kind of patronage. Better-off villagers hoped for various forms of assistance in terms of capital investment (seeds, inputs, loans for pump sets); worse-off villagers came to view the project as a source of wage labor and credit.

Was there anything wrong with the way this participatory project progressed? The answer depends on what hopes one harbors for "participation." Rather than evaluating the project from an abstract ideal, Mosse studied various dynamics. The community organizations and other field staff had to undergo a tricky process of earning the trust of community members. Doing so required them to become familiar with local notables, institutional figures, and bureaucrats. As they did so, they gradually became implicated in various village hierarchies and factions and in local networks of exchange, favors, and mutual assistance. The village-level *jankars* became more or less "empowered" over time (although their fortunes could wax and wane with the fortunes of the project), although this empowerment arose mainly through relations with outsiders. This process, Mosse argues, is one of the generic dilemmas of participatory approaches: such projects often demand not less but more intensive agency presence, they may be less cost-efficient, and they may foster dependency and patronage (Mosse 2005).

So when did things begin to go "wrong" with this project? Two interpretations must be separated: Mosse's evaluation of the implementation stage of the project and the organizational judgments that first declared the project a success and then a failure.

In Mosse's view, the implementation stage brought with it entirely new organizational dynamics: prioritizing quantifiable targets, setting numerical goals, moving away from learning and experimentation. This transition created a "regime of implementation" (2005, 109). Staff members faced growing pressure to meet implementation targets, set from above and demanded from below. The *jankars,* working closely with but junior to the community organization project staff, began to "regard themselves primarily as project employees (if not private contractors), with the power to assess work and sanction payment" (Mosse 2005, 114). As one senior project employee reported, "we rather skewed the potential of *jankars* as real agents of a more indigenous type of development. They became the delivery mechanisms, which [was a departure] from the original thinking" (114). As for the villagers, "although they were now familiar with the official rhetoric of 'people's participation' (*janasabhagita*), in common parlance 'participation' (*bhagidari*) implied simply that a contribution (of money or labor) had to be made . . . the extent and nature of villager's *bhagidari* (contribution) was a matter for negotiation and agreement with outsider patrons" (114). By this phase, participatory rural appraisal "became largely symbolic. Staff now knew how to write them [participatory appraisals] up; how to move swiftly to expenditure. . . . As the logic of implementation pushed practice toward standardization, it was virtually impossible to ensure that 'participatory planning' involved local problem solving or even choosing between alternatives. In fact, the 'quality' of the "participatory process' mattered less and less" (116).

Mosse's analysis describes the phase shift typically experienced by most participatory projects, from a somewhat open-ended planning phase to a more structured implementation phase. It is possible to conceive of it as a kind of rhythm of participatory projects, which could, therefore, have been anticipated.

More damaging, according to Mosse, was the effect of this shift on the service delivery aspect of the project and the kind of demands that should have been but were not factored in. "Villagers themselves had little control over project processes and budgets. Rather than implementing their own 'village development plan,' they found that components of the plan (individual schemes and subsidies) would be delivered on an item-by-item basis—instead of in logically related bundles—by an administrative system that was unknown and unpredictable. One example of a logical bundle was a request by a group of women in a village for support for a project consisting of an interlinked package of activities—ducks, goats, *rabi* seeds, and a pump set" (Mosse 2005, 263). Mosse argues that one of the key problems in the shift from the planning to the implementation phase is that once a set of practices is in place, the system generates its own priorities, activities, and goals, which may be quite different from the formal goals regarding community participation and empowerment expressed in policy papers or even project design documents. The relationship between policy and practice in participatory interventions therefore needs careful consideration.

Another problem is that there are stratified, relatively autonomous levels of project actors with narrow points of overlap (Mosse describes this relationship as an "hourglass"), as illustrated in Mosse's multisited ethnography of head offices, consultants, budget specialists, project staff, village-level community organizations, volunteers, and villagers. This hourglass relationship is crucial to the question of how to scale up projects. Mosse describes a wrong turn, a transition point in the project, as "DFID–imposed disorder" caused by a "grossly simplified view of 'up-scaling,' 'mainstreaming,' 'fast-tracking,' and 'replication.'" As a result, "a huge burden was placed on a complex and shaky system: the project had to create a new organizational structure, to quadruple the size of its operations . . . fast-track its process (reduce village entry time) . . . create further linkages [to both the local government and the rural commercial sectors], while retaining its intense focus on participation . . ." (Mosse 2005, 185).

Most strikingly, throughout the period in which the project was first declared a success and then a failure, field activities, levels of work, and modes of engagement remained more or less the same, and project actors maintained relative autonomy. This meant, according to Mosse, that the project's "fall from grace" was not a result of a shift in design or implementation but a result of changing policy fashions. The late 1990s saw an increased emphasis on partnerships with state structures; parastatal projects lost favor, as they were not seen to be "replicable models" (Mosse 2005, 199). What Mosse finds worrisome is that with policy fashion cycles becoming shorter, the ability to gain the trust of local populations may be increasingly compromised, as projects abruptly dispense with groups that no longer serve their policy objectives.

Several lessons emerge from Mosse's account:

- The expectation of abrupt shifts in policy has adverse effects at every level of the project—and crucially contributes to the shallowness of the intervention. If the project is seen as ending within a very proximate period rather than contributing to sustainable change, higher-level project officials will spend their time trying to frame the intervention as a success rather than working to lay the foundation for lasting change.
- The expectation of abrupt shifts in policy influences the quality and character of mobilization. Because the intervention is seen as time bound, people participate largely in order to reap material gain. They take what they can from the resources the

project brings and say what they have to say to gain access to those material benefits. Although such behavior may create some short-term improvements in material well-being, it does not result in a lasting shift in power relationships and stronger mechanisms for voice and mobility.

- Even if the intervention is long lasting, participatory change takes time. A short project cycle that initiates but then terminates a trajectory of change can leave communities hanging off a cliff.

- Participatory projects work well when they are given the freedom to learn by doing, to constantly experiment and innovate based on feedback from the ground. As the project expands, however, experimentation becomes more difficult, and efforts are directed more toward meeting the letter rather than the spirit of project goals.

- Facilitators play a crucial role in participatory projects.

Implementation Challenges: The Role of Facilitators

Facilitators are at the frontline
of induced participation . . .

Facilitators are at the frontline of induced participation. They identify the failures of local civil society, markets, and government; design interventions to repair them; and look for ways to repair the associated civic failures, seek political opportunities, and mobilize the community to exploit them. Facilitators are paid to play the role that the social activist would play in an organic participatory movement. Their incentives are rarely aligned in a manner that results in truly empowered change, however. For example, although their job requires flexibility, time, and constant engagement with experimentation, facilitators are given targets (mobilize X communities in Y days). Because they are poorly compensated and know the project will end in two or three years, they are constantly looking for other work. They are often poorly monitored, allowing them to submit false reports on the achievement of project targets.

Perhaps of greatest concern, facilitators working under these conditions may take shortcuts to persuade or force people to participate, using messages for recruitment that are quite different from stated project goals. For example, they may try to meet their participation targets by using messages with a strong emotional impact or by luring people with the implicit promise of monetary benefit. Instead of being seen as agents of change, facilitators may be perceived as part of the existing nexus of accommodation. The question, then, is whether they can legitimately affect radical change when they are perceived as part of the state apparatus? When change requires radical advocacy, do these facilitators, who report upward to people who may not permit them to advocate radical change, face the right incentives? More fundamentally, what can facilitators accomplish? Within which spaces can they work for change? Can induced participatory development really generate political and social empowerment? Many factors affect the answers to these questions, but it is clear that interventions will not succeed without higher levels of government being actively committed to the development of active civic engagement at the local level.

> . . . but their incentives are often not set up to truly empower communities.

Implementation Challenges: Trajectories of Change

A major problem with donor-induced participation is that it works within an "infrastructure template." Donors' institutional structures and incentives are optimally suited to projects with short timelines and linear trajectories of change with clear, unambiguous projected outcomes. When a bridge is built, for instance, the outcome is easily verified, the trajectory of change is predictable, and the impact is almost immediate. Participatory interventions, which engage in the much more complex task of shifting political and social equilibriums, have very different trajectories.

> Donors' institutional structures and incentives are optimally suited to projects with short timelines and linear trajectories of change with clear, unambiguous projected outcomes . . .

Unfortunately, most participatory projects that emerge from donor agencies are designed within the same assumed trajectory and three- to five-year cycles as infrastructure projects. At the end of the project cycle, these projects are expected to have met various civic objectives (better social capital, community empowerment, improved accountability). Almost all community-driven projects go farther, projecting gains in outcomes such as a poverty reduction, school enrollment, sanitation and health, and so forth. The assumption is that within the period of the project cycle, the intervention will activate civic capacity to the extent that it will repair political and market failures enough to have an observable impact on "hard" outcomes.

> . . . but civic change is a highly unpredictable process.

Three assumptions are inherent in this thinking:

- Civic engagement will be activated in the initial period of the project.

- Civic capacity will be deepened enough to repair government and market failures.
- This improvement in the quality of governments and markets will result in a measurable change in outcomes.

Figure 3.1 illustrates the problems with these assumptions. The project-based assumption (illustrated by the dotted lines) shows a path in which civil society and governance outcomes improve in a predictable linear manner that is congruent with changes in measurable outcomes. The problem with this reasoning is that civic change is a highly unpredictable process; many things have to take place to make it happen. Individuals have to believe that collective mobilization is worth the effort and be willing to participate; civic groups have to solve the collective action problem and exploit political opportunities to effect change; the nexus of accommodation in government has to be disrupted by the rising cost of ignoring citizens' interests, so that politicians and bureaucrats change their actions; and their new actions have to result in changes in outcomes. A change in outcomes has to be preceded by an improvement in civic capacity, which possibly unleashes a series of changes that will change outcomes (Woolcock 2009). The reality is depicted by the solid lines in figure 3.1.

Predicting when meaningful change will occur in each node is extremely difficult because a number of factors come into play,

Figure 3.1   Possible trajectories of local participation

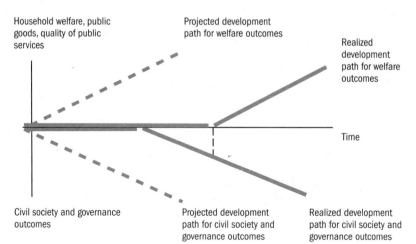

including the nature of the cooperative infrastructure; the history of civic engagement and politics; the level of development; the extent to which the state has committed to the process of change and is therefore effectively incentivizing, enforcing, and monitoring the actions of its agents; the level of literacy; information flows—in other words, all of the factors that affect civic failure. Social equilibrium is hard to change because it has evolved after years of repeated interactions within particular economic, political, and social environments.

Therefore, whether at the micro or the macro level, civic engagement often tends to be absorbed, in its early stages, within the nexus of accommodation, with the leaders co-opted by elites. Furthermore, as discussed earlier in this chapter, until citizens are convinced that the high cost of fighting for their interests and resisting elite domination is worth the effort, they are unlikely to engage in an effective manner. Widespread participation occurs when a tipping point is reached— when enough people are convinced of the value of participation, when they sense a fundamental change in the nature of politics and power, and when enough people convince enough others to engage, resulting in a participatory cascade. Borrowing from evolutionary biologists, sociologists describe this process as one of "punctuated equilibrium" (Koopmans 2007)—a process in which long periods of stability are punctuated by brief periods of extremely rapid change. At the local level, the wide diversity in the nature of communities reinforces this unpredictability in the timing of change. Each community is likely to have a different change trajectory.

Thus, particularly when it is packaged within a project, induced participation is almost set up for failure because of unrealistic predictions that emerge from bureaucratic imperatives. The challenge of policy interventions is to figure out where each community is within this complex trajectory of change and to create an enabling environment in which that change can occur in a manner that improves development objectives. For induced participatory projects to have a chance of meeting their objectives, they have to attempt to adopt the spirit of experimentation, learning, and persistent engagement that characterizes organic participatory change. Unfortunately, donors are bound by strict timelines; imperatives to disperse money quickly and effectively; and internal incentives that make honest and effective monitoring and evaluation a low priority at the project level, despite the rhetoric in support of it.

Particularly when it is packaged within a project, induced participation is almost set up for failure because of unrealistic predictions that emerge from bureaucratic imperatives.

Deriving Hypotheses

Public spending to improve living conditions for the most disadvantaged is widely accepted as the cornerstone of any credible development strategy. There is also a sense that any serious policy shift in this direction needs to include a larger role for civil society. In line with this, many developing countries have devolved the management of key public services, have decentralized the implementation of targeted poverty reduction programs, and are increasingly providing local public goods through mechanisms that induce some type of community participation. At the core of these efforts is the idea that greater civic engagement can make resource allocation both more responsive and more accountable, with the greatest benefits realized by people with the least influence and the least capacity to opt for private alternatives.

The traditional economic justification for local provision of public goods and services is that it allows subjurisdictions to tailor the level, quality, and cost of services to the preferences of local residents. Governments are assumed to be largely benign and citizens mobile, able to "vote with their feet" by moving to areas where regulations, taxes, and services best match their preferences and needs.

Most public goods and services (schools, drinking water, sanitation, roads) are inherently local; they serve a reasonably well-defined group from which nonresidents can be effectively excluded. In such cases, devolution should increase both efficiency and equity, because it frees up a distant center from having to acquire costly information on local preferences and the supply of local public goods. Local agents may also have access to emerging information, such as recent adverse shocks, that may be only poorly reflected in the types of data available to distant central administrators. To the extent that some of the salient characteristics of poverty are also location specific, decentralizing the identification of beneficiaries may also increase the efficiency of resource allocation. Citizen mobility also creates external performance pressure on subjurisdictions to compete for the best talent and the most productive and profitable businesses, which curbs excessive rent-seeking by public officials and increases service quality. Menes (2003) argues that this process accounts for the decline in municipal corruption in the United States at the turn of the 20th century. As railroads were developed and the frontier became accessible, the capacity of local government officials to extract rents declined (see also Rondinelli, Mccullough, and Johnson 1989; Khan 2002).

If citizens are mobile and governments benign, there seem to be few efficiency arguments for centralized resource allocation, except when significant intercommunity coordination problems arise from spillovers, externalities, or economies of scale that require centralized management. (Rules and regulations regarding environmental pollution, vaccination programs, and defense are good examples.)

The situation is quite different in most developing countries, where the main arguments for decentralization center on accountability. In this view, the fundamental problem with the central provision of public goods and services is bureaucratic inefficiency and rampant rent-seeking. Localizing resource allocation decisions brings ordinary citizens, who have the greatest stake in the quality of services provided as well as the greatest incentive to restrict rent-seeking, into closer proximity with relevant decision makers. Decentralization allows citizens to observe the actions of officials and providers, to use this information to induce higher levels of transparency, and to generate social pressure for policy reform.

Concerns about corruption have amplified the accountability argument for decentralization.[2] Over the past decade, the view that corruption poses a major threat to development has acquired considerable currency. Corruption is seen as adding substantially to the cost of providing basic public goods and services; dampening the redistributive objectives of poverty reduction programs; and, perhaps worst of all, changing the incentives facing both citizens and public officials.[3] As reform efforts directed at legal and financial institutions at the center have produced little success, the push for more local solutions has grown, with the greatest emphasis on civil society oversight and monitoring of public officials and providers.[4]

This emphasis on local accountability has effectively created a new justification for the decentralization of resource allocation decisions that remains relevant even when there is no significant variation in preferences for public goods. Arguments for state and donor support to local participatory institutions are couched in terms of giving voice to the most disadvantaged members of society in order to create demand for better governance.

Influential voices on the other side of the debate over participation point out that shifting the locus of decision making downward need not have salutary effects if social structures reflect long histories and deeply entrenched power hierarchies. In such contexts, they argue, local inequalities of wealth and power can acquire much greater significance,

> The main argument for decentralization in most developing countries is that it increases accountability, thereby reducing corruption.

113

as important resource allocation decisions shift downward; in the extreme, they can exacerbate local inequality and perpetuate or even reinvigorate local power relations.

Where localities are also heterogeneous in other respects, such as in their ethnic, racial, or tribal composition, there may be additional coordination challenges and greater potential for redistributive projects to generate or exacerbate local conflicts. Some researchers, such as Henkel and Stirrat (2001), even argue that although the language used by participatory programs is designed precisely to manage such underlying dissent, the search for "consensus" often simply results in the subordination of minority voices or the proliferation of formal governance rules that make participation costly, particularly for the people with the least capacity. In the presence of significant group heterogeneity, electoral incentives can also induce political agents to allocate resources to satisfy more parochial interests, at the cost of broader investments in public goods and services.

Whether or not local governments or participatory programs can be responsive to local needs may depend to a significant degree on the resources they can access relative to their mandate and the discretion they have over the allocation of resources across diverse needs. For many reasons, including the political context in which central governments undertake decentralization, in most developing countries, devolution of responsibility for taxation has been far more contentious than the devolution of responsibilities for expenditure, particularly when local governments are elected. With few exceptions, however, and regardless of the type of decentralization undertaken, local governments obtain the bulk of their resources as transfers, whether formula based or discretionary and ad hoc, from central or intermediate-level governments; taxation authority is rarely devolved to any substantial degree. As a result, there is an unavoidable tension between central and lower levels of governments regarding accountability and fiscal discipline at the local level. Local officials blame the center for their failures in service provision by claiming that the center has assigned unfunded mandates to them, limiting their ability to meet their responsibilities. Discretionary transfers from the center are considered particularly detrimental for local provision of public goods and services, because they not only limit the local government's ability to plan investments and expenditures, they also leave local governments vulnerable to various types of manipulation from the center. For their part, central governments bemoan

> Whether local governments or participatory programs can be responsive to local needs may depend to a significant degree on the resources they can access relative to their mandate . . .

> . . . and the discretion they have over the allocation of resources across diverse needs.

local governments' "soft budget constraints," a situation in which local governments that are unconstrained by their revenue-raising capacity are tempted to overspend and then ask the center for a bailout in the form of supplemental transfers from tax revenues generated elsewhere. Of course, such overspending may itself be a response to an unfunded expenditure mandate.

In principle, local governments could raise some or all of their resources directly from their constituents, through taxes and fees, and there are important arguments in favor of devolving revenue-raising responsibilities. Some researchers have even gone as far as to argue that central transfers should be contingent on such revenue-raising efforts, as such a move would force local governments to accept responsibility for poor service provision and incentivize citizens to monitor local officials' performance more closely. In practice, however, devolving revenue raising to the local level is difficult.

Central governments also have a mandate to mitigate interregional disparities through appropriately targeted fiscal transfers, which can include considerations of need intensity and demographic size. As Cai and Treisman (2004) argue, when regional differences in the productivity of specific factors are significant (because of location, agglomeration externalities, or the endowment of resource), local taxation authority can unleash a race to the bottom. As local governments compete to attract the wealthy, less well-endowed localities become weaker and more dependent on central transfers. This situation can exacerbate regional disparities in government services and increase horizontal wealth inequality. The worst-off areas may also have the least incentive to give up rent-seeking activities.

Some observers suggest that the timelines and objectives of donor-funded projects can exacerbate these challenges. Donor-funded projects, they argue, value the rapid disbursement of inputs, the creation of community organizations, the achievement of predetermined rates of return on investments, and improvements in the income and assets of beneficiaries. These evaluation criteria create an incentive to select areas that are easily reached and organized and to target project benefits to households that are able to quickly absorb project funds in productive activities.[5]

A key concern is the possibility of civil society failure (defined in chapter 2). A group might be unable to act collectively, or collective action could occur in a well-coordinated but dysfunctional manner that

> In practice, devolving revenue raising to the local level is difficult.

> Donors' evaluation criteria create incentives to select areas that are easily reached and organized . . .

> . . . . and to target project benefits to households that are able to quickly absorb project funds in productive activities.

When civic participation is likely to be the best solution to government and market failures, and when it is not, is highly contextual. . . .

. . . and thus best determined by turning to the evidence.

reduces the welfare of the average citizen (as in the case, for example, of an organized fringe group that uses terror and violence to further its extremist ends at high social cost).

When is civic participation likely to be the best answer to government and market failures, and when is it not? The answers are deeply contextual, fundamentally conditioned by social structures and historical trajectories, and different for every community. A policy that works in one village may fail miserably in another. Moreover, as effective collective action depends on the cooperative infrastructure provided by a strong state, it is not at all clear that strong civil society creates strong governments; the reality is more complex and nuanced. Similarly, although empowering civic groups may often lead to good outcomes, doing so is not always superior to a pure market-based strategy for raising incomes or to a strategy that strengthens the role of central bureaucrats to, say, improve social services. Keeping this in mind, the decision about whether, when, and how to promote local participation should be made with an understanding of the tradeoffs involved in moving decisions to local communities—in a particular country, within a particular region in a country, and at a particular time.

Theorizing and thinking through the conceptual foundations of these questions can yield important insights, but several open questions are best answered by examining the evidence. When does participation work, and when does it fail to achieve specific objectives? How important is capture? Does handing over large sums of money to community groups empower the poor, or do elites use it to enrich themselves? What mechanisms are most effective in improving the capacity for collective action and building social capital? What methods reduce civic inequality and elite capture and truly empower the poor? Do participatory projects result in choices that are better aligned with people's preferences? Does fostering participation enhance social cohesion? Does it strengthen civil society? Does it produce more resilient and inclusive local institutions? To what extent does group heterogeneity and illiteracy affect the quality of participation? Does participation improve development outcomes at the local level? Does it help the sustainable management of local resources? Chapters 4–6 provide a broad and comprehensive review of the evidence on these and many related questions.

For the reasons outlined in chapter 1, the focus of the review of the evidence is on large-scale participatory projects that have been evaluated based on representative samples of target populations with good counterfactuals—studies that have a valid control group for the communities targeted (or "treated") by the intervention. Generally speaking, this means that the findings come from econometric analysis, although some well-designed qualitative research is examined to inform the results.

Notes

1. Needs can be unlimited, however. Normative theories of fiscal federalism and decentralization consequently pay equal attention to the budget constraints associated with financing expenditure and the tax assignments of federal and local jurisdictions. Although these fundamental issues on the supply side of decentralization are not the focus of this report, they are important to keep in mind.
2. The World Bank and the U.S. Agency for International Development (USAID) have been leading champions of this new emphasis on fighting corruption. See the *World Development Report 2004* (World Bank 2004) on the effect of corruption on service delivery
3. Tanzi and Davoodi (1997) show that corruption can reduce public revenue and increase income inequality by allowing well-positioned individuals to benefit unduly from government programs intended for the poor.
4. Myerson (1993) and Persson, Roland, and Tabellini (1997) provide theretical arguments for the relationship between political institutions and corruption. Bardhan and Mookherjee (2006) provide a good overview of the conceptual literature on the relationship between decentralization and corruption and review much of the empirical evidence.
5. Bernard and others (2008) find evidence on the proliferation of community organizations in Burkina Faso and Senegal that appears to be consistent with this hypothesis. They report a dramatic growth in both market- and community-oriented village organizations over the two-decade period between the early 1980s, when participatory approaches first became popular popularity, to about 2002. In Burkina Faso, where 22 percent of sample villages had village organizations in 1982, 91 percent had at least one village organization by 2002; in Senegal, where 10 percent of sample villages had at least one village organization in 1982, the figure rose to 65 percent. Household participation in village organizations also rose dramatically, with 57 percent of households in Burkina Faso and 69 percent in Senegal participating in at least one village organization. However, one-fifth of all registered organizations had not undertaken any activity by the time of the survey, and among those that had, most members reported that the projects undertaken were either incomplete or had not yielded any significant benefits.

References

Acemoglu, D., and J. A. Robinson. 2006. *Economic Origins of Dictatorship and Democracy.* New York: Cambridge University Press.

Appadurai, A. 2004. "The Capacity to Aspire: Culture and the Terms of Recognition." In *Culture and Public Action,* ed. V. Rao and M. Walton, 59–84. Stanford, CA: Stanford University Press.

Bardhan, P., and D. Mookherjee. 2006. *Decentralization and Governance in Developing Countries.* Cambridge, MA: MIT Press.

Basu, K. 2011. *Beyond the Invisible Hand: Groundwork for a New Economics.* Princeton, NJ: Princeton University Press.

Bernard, T., M.-H. Collion, A. De Janvry, P. Rondot, and E. Sadoulet. 2008. "Do Village Organizations Make a Difference in African Rural Development? A Study for Senegal and Burkina Faso." *World Development* 36(11): 2188–204.

Cai, H., and D. Treisman. 2004. "State Corroding Federalism." *Journal of Public Economics* 88(3–4): 819–43.

Comaroff, J., and J. Comaroff. 1999. *Civil Society and Political Imagination in Africa.* Chicago: University of Chicago Press.

Cooke, B., and U. Kothari. 2001. *Participation: The New Tyranny?* London: Zed Books.

Elster, J. 1989. *Nuts and Bolts for the Social Sciences.* Cambridge, U.K.: Cambridge University Press.

Evans, P. 2004. "Development as Institutional Change: The Pitfalls of Monocropping and the Potentials of Deliberation." *Studies in Comparative International Development* 38(4): 30–52.

Fung, A., and E. O. Wright. 2003. "Thinking about Empowered Participatory Governance." In *Deepening Democracy: Institutional Innovations in Empowered Participatory Governance,* ed. A. Fung and E. O. Wright, 3–42. New York: Verso.

Gibson, C., and M. Woolcock. 2008. "Empowerment, Deliberative Development and Local Level Politics in Indonesia: Participatory Projects as a Source of Countervailing Power." *Studies in Comparative International Development* 2(43): 151–80.

Harriss, J. 2001. *Depoliticizing Development: The World Bank and Social Capital.* New Delhi: LeftWord.

Henkel, H., and R. Stirrat. 2001. "Participation as Spiritual Duty; Empowerment as Secular Subjection." In *Participation: The New Tyranny?* ed. B. Cooke and U. Kothari, 168–84. London: Zed Books.

Hirschman, A. O. 1970. *Exit Voice and Loyalty: Responses to Decline in Firms, Organizations and States.* Cambridge, MA: Harvard University Press.

Hoff, K., and J. E. Stiglitz. 2001. "Modern Economic Theory and Development." In *Frontiers of Development Economics,* ed. G. Meier and J. Stiglitz, 389–459. Oxford, U.K.: Oxford University Press.

Khan, M. H. 2002. "Corruption and Governance in Early Capitalism: World Bank Strategies and Their Limitations." In *Reinventing the World Bank,* ed. J. Pincus and J. Winters, 164–84. Ithaca, NY: Cornell University Press.

Koopmans, R. 2007. "Protest in Time and Space: The Evolution of Waves of Contention." In *The Blackwell Companion to Social Movements*, ed. D. A. Snow, S. A. Soule, and H. Kriesi, 19–46. New York: Blackwell.

Kriesi, H. 2007. "Political Context and Opportunity." In *The Blackwell Companion to Social Movements*, ed. D. A. Snow, S. A. Soule, and H. Kriesi, 67–90. New York: Blackwell.

Levy, B., and F. Fukuyama. 2010. *Development Strategies: Integrating Governance and Growth*. Washington, DC: World Bank.

Menes, R. 2003. "Corruption in Cities: Graft and Politics in American Cities at the Turn of the Twentieth Century." NBER Working Paper 9990, National Bureau of Economic Research, Cambridge, MA.

Migdal, J. S. 1988. *Strong Societies and Weak States: State-Society Relations and State Capabilities in the Third World*. Princeton, NJ: Princeton University Press.

Mosse, D. 2005. *Cultivating Development: An Ethnography of Aid Policy and Practice*. London: Pluto Press.

Myerson, R. B. 1993. "Effectiveness of Electoral Systems for Reducing Government Corruption: A Game-Theoretic Analysis." *Games and Economic Behavior* 5(1): 118–32.

Oates, W. 1972. *Fiscal Federalism*. New York: Harcourt Brace Jovanovich.

Persson, T., G. Roland, and G. Tabellini. 1997. "Separation of Powers and Political Accountability." *Quarterly Journal of Economics* 112(4): 1163–202.

Rao, V., and P. Sanyal. 2010. "Dignity through Discourse: Poverty and the Culture of Deliberation in Indian Village Democracies." *Annals of the American Academy of Political and Social Science* 629(May): 146–72.

Rondinelli, D. A., J. S. Mccullough, and R. W. Johnson. 1989. "Analyzing Decentralization Policies in Developing-Countries: A Political-Economy Framework." *Development and Change* 20(1): 57–87.

Rose-Ackerman, S. 2008. "Corruption and Government." *International Peacekeeping* 15(3): 328–43.

Scott, J. 1990. *Domination and the Art of Resistance: Hidden Transcripts*. New Haven, CT: Yale University Press.

Tanzi, V., and H. Davoodi. 1997. "Corruption, Public Investment, and Growth." IMF Working Paper 97/139, International Monetary Fund, Washington, DC.

Warren, M. E. 1995. "The Self in Discursive Democracy." In *The Cambridge Companion to Habermas*, ed. S. K. White, 167–200. Cambridge, U.K.: Cambridge University Press.

Woolcock, M. 2009. "Towards a Plurality of Methods in Project Evaluation: A Contextualized Approach to Understanding Impact Trajectories and Efficacy." *Journal of Development Effectiveness* 1(1): 1–14.

World Bank. 2004. *World Development Report 2004: Making Services Work for Poor People*. Washington, DC: World Bank.

CHAPTER FOUR

How Important Is Capture?

A KEY ASSUMPTION UNDERLYING SUPPORT FOR PARTICIPATORY programs and local decentralization is that they increase the involvement of the poor and the marginalized in local decision making, thereby enhancing "voice" and reducing capture and corruption. How empirically grounded are these assumptions?

This chapter attempts to answer this question. It first examines whether the real worry should be corruption narrowly defined or more routine and legal forms of rent-seeking, including clientelism. It then reviews the evidence for elite capture in participatory programs and discusses potential implications for the inclusion and empowerment objectives of such programs. The next two sections look at the impact of democratic decentralization on the behavior of local political agents. The last section summarizes the broad lessons that emerge from the evidence.

Theorists have written a good deal on local accountability in the context of political decentralization; the body of empirical literature is also large. This chapter does not attempt to do justice to either body of research. Instead, it uses the literature somewhat selectively to frame the questions that are most relevant to understanding the "demand side" of local governance and to highlight the empirical studies that have informed this debate. Attention is confined, for the most part, to empirical studies of developing countries.

Corruption and Local Accountability

Corruption adds substantially to the cost of providing basic public goods and services . . .

. . . it can also change the incentives citizens and public officials face.

Civic engagement is often seen as key to reducing corruption.

Corruption—defined narrowly as theft, graft, and bribes—has come to be viewed as a major threat to development.[1] It adds substantially to the cost of providing basic public goods and services; dampens the redistributive objectives of poverty-reduction programs; and, perhaps worst of all, changes the incentives both citizens and public officials face. Reducing corruption through legal and financial reforms is rarely an option. Instead, most international donor organizations, notably the World Bank and the U.S. Agency for International Development (USAID), have come to see decentralization and civic engagement as an alternative route to increasing accountability in both the public and private sphere.

The view that decentralization is needed to combat corruption is not unchallenged. Some observers argue that decentralization could increase opportunities for theft, bribes, and graft.[2] There is also a concern that devolution could simply shift the form of rent-seeking from outright theft and graft to other, more pernicious and ostensibly legal, avenues of resource capture. In the extreme, both equity and efficiency could decline as a result, even as measured levels of corruption fall. Too sharp a focus on corruption defined narrowly can divert attention from the true welfare cost of rent-seeking under decentralized resource allocation, particularly where there are significant opportunities for capture by local elites. Bardhan (2002) and Bardhan and Mookherjee (2006a) advocate a broader view that includes all types of political corruption, in addition to theft, bribes, and graft.[3] The literature on corruption is reviewed here with these concerns in mind.

Only a few studies examine the relationship between decentralized resource allocation and the level of corruption. This literature includes a series of papers using cross-country data that by and large argue that corruption tends to be lower in countries that are more decentralized, but only when local governments face "hard budget constraints" (that is, rely less on fiscal transfers from the center and more on their own revenues).[4] For example, Estache and Sinha (1995) report a positive association between expenditure decentralization and levels of infrastructure provided by local governments, but only when both revenue generation and expenditure responsibilities are decentralized.

Fisman and Gatti (2002a, 2002b) find similar results. Using data from the United States for 1976–87, they report a positive correlation between a state's dependence on fiscal transfers from the center and convictions for abuse of state public office (Fisman and Gatti 2002a). In a second study, based on cross-country data for 1980–95, they find a negative association between expenditure decentralization and perceived corruption (Fisman and Gatti 2002b). However, both studies are plagued with problems of potential reverse causality and unobserved heterogeneity across the units of analysis, making the results difficult to interpret.

Using roughly the same sample of countries over the same time period as Fisman and Gatti (2002b), Treisman (2007) shows that the key result in their study is sensitive to the set of controls used. The negative association between expenditure decentralization and corruption (using a range of measures of both) disappears once an additional control, the proportion of Protestants in the population, is added. Apparently, countries with more Protestants tend to be both less corrupt and more decentralized.[5]

The metric of corruption used in these studies is also problematic. For the most part, country-level corruption measures are either aggregated from corruption perception surveys or derived from country-risk analyses. Most studies that compare perception data with data on the actual incidence of corruption find that perception data correlate poorly with the actual incidence of corruption, however defined.[6] They also find that perceptions may be sensitive to the absolute level of corruption, as measured by the number of occurrences, rather than just relative corruption levels. Thus, perceptions of corruption tend to be greater in larger countries. The relationship between perceptions of corruption and absolute and relative corruption levels weakens as levels of corruption rise. The use of perception data may therefore be more warranted in low-corruption than high-corruption settings.

More recent cross-country studies attempt to overcome some of these problems by using a more objective metric of corruption. Fan, Lin, and Treisman (2009) examine how political decentralization affects the odds of bribe extraction by corrupt officials. They attempt to rectify the problems with perception data by combining a cross-country data set on decentralization with a firm-level survey conducted in 80 countries that provides information on the experiences of firms with graft and bribes. Their results suggest that decentralization can increase opportunities for corruption when the number of tiers of public employees increases, particularly when governments are also strapped for funds and public sector

> The use of perception data to measure corruption may be more warranted in low-corruption than high-corruption settings.

> Decentralization can increase opportunities for corruption.

123

employees are poorly paid and have few resources. Overall, their results suggest that as the complexity of governance structures and the number of tiers increases, as it does under decentralization, there is a danger of more uncoordinated rent-seeking and higher net levels of corruption.[7]

By and large, however, attention has moved to within-country analyses that use more carefully constructed data and objective measures of corruption. This newer body of literature also attempts to identify causal effects by focusing on specific policy shifts, such as audits, increased monitoring, a change in access to information, or variation in the political incentives of incumbents, which allow for a clearer analysis of the relationship between decentralized resource allocation and corruption.[8]

This literature has produced some important insights. Studies confirm substantial levels of graft and theft in decentralized programs (although few compare levels of corruption with and without decentralization). They also highlight the potential risks of incomplete and differential access to information. In particular, they find that opportunities for corruption are greater when some individuals or communities are less well placed to benefit from information. This literature also underscores the manifold constraints that communities—particularly those which are poorer, more remote, and more unequal—face in monitoring and sanctioning corrupt officials or service providers.

Overall, the evidence suggests that corruption tends to be higher in remote communities that have low education levels and low exposure to media—qualities that tend to be positively correlated with poverty and inequality—and that within such communities, the costs of corruption are higher for the poor. Perhaps more surprisingly, interventions from the center appear to constrain corrupt local practices—particularly when they augment citizen "voice" at the local level by increasing information on resource flows through well-publicized audits or media campaigns. On balance, therefore, there appears to be little reason to be sanguine about community-based monitoring or information provision in the absence of a strong reform-minded center, an active and independent media, and highly able communities.

Reinikka and Svensson (2004, 2005, 2007) examine the extent of corruption in the allocation of public resources for education in Uganda during the 1990s. They study a large government program that provided grants to primary schools to cover their nonwage expenditures. The program was managed by the central government but used district

> Corruption tends to be higher in remote communities that have low education levels and low exposure to media . . .

> . . . and within such communities, the costs of corruption are higher for the poor.

> The center can constrain corrupt local practices by augmenting citizen "voice" through advertised audits and media campaigns.

offices as distribution channels. Their measure of corruption is the difference between disbursed flows from the central government to lower tiers of government and the resources actually received by final beneficiaries. The data come from a public expenditure tracking survey.

Reinikka and Svensson (2004) show that primary schools in Uganda received only 13 percent of the grants allocated to them for nonwage expenditures; local officials and politicians captured the rest. The allocation of the amounts that did reach schools was also quite regressive. Schools in the poorest communities fared worst, obtaining significantly smaller shares of their entitlements.[9] A benefit incidence analysis of the program, conducted in 1996 by the World Bank, found that the poorest quintile received about as much as the richest quintile. This finding highlights the difficulty of using benefit incidence analysis to understand the distributional impact of public spending when allocated expenditure rather than actual spending is used. It also highlights the potential for local capture to completely undo and even reverse the redistributive goals of poverty reduction programs.

Reinikka and Svensson (2007) examine the extent to which information on the flow of funds can restrain corruption. In response to the enormous leakage of funds found in the first public expenditure tracking survey, the central government initiated a campaign in which national newspapers, including their local language editions, began publishing the monthly transfer of capitation grants to districts. Reinikka and Svensson show that schools that were closer to newspaper outlets managed to claim a significantly larger part of their entitlement after the newspaper campaign was initiated and that head teachers in such schools were also more knowledgeable of the rules governing the grant program as well as the timing of fund release by the central government. They also find significant increases in enrollment and student learning outcomes following the information campaign (Reinikka and Svensson 2005), with much larger effects for schools located near newspaper outlets.

Bjorkman (2006) confirms these results. Using district-level data, she finds that districts that were more exposed to the newspaper campaign obtained a larger share of their allocated budget and had substantially greater increases in student test scores.

Francken, Minten, and Swinnen (2009) use a measure of corruption similar to the one Reinikka and Svensson (2005) use to examine the impact of media on the local capture of public education funds in

> Local officials and politicians captured 87 percent of the grants allocated to primary schools in Uganda for nonwage expenditures.

Madagascar. They find very little evidence of capture in resource flows from the center, where the education bureaucracy was closely monitored, to the district. In contrast, they observe significant levels of capture at the district level, with capture increasing with distance from the center. These results point to the importance of central monitoring for accountability at the local level. The study also finds a strong negative effect of media access on corruption, with substantially larger negative effects in more educated communities, which were presumably better able to use information on budgets to monitor providers. In line with earlier findings on capture, the authors note that the misappropriation of funds was greater in districts in which the program director was a member of the local elite or had a lower level of education.

Relative to the better-off, the poor had less and worse-quality information on India's National Rural Employment Guarantee Scheme and were less likely to participate in it.

Shankar, Gaiha, and Jha (2010) highlight the risk of differential information access in their study of India's National Rural Employment Guarantee Scheme (NREGS). This targeted workfare program was launched with a nationwide effort to disseminate information through the media and through village-level meetings organized by the local government. The program has been plagued with problems of resource misappropriation, including the fudging of muster rolls, the manipulation of wages, and outright bribe-taking by local officials. Survey data reveal that the nonpoor had more and better-quality information on the program and were also more likely to participate. Better-informed participants were also more likely to obtain the full benefits of the program in terms of wages, the timing of payment, and hours worked. Poorer participants were more likely to report having paid bribes. This finding is particularly important given concerns about the level of corruption in this program.[10]

An intensive top-down audit reduced corruption as measured by missing expenditures . . .

. . . but it appears to have increased nepotism.

Few studies assess the relative effectiveness of bottom-up and top-down anticorruption interventions. The best study is by Olken (2007), who reports the results of a field experiment conducted in villages supported by the Kecamatan Development Program (KDP) in Indonesia, which builds local infrastructure using a community-driven development approach. The experiment assessed the relative effectiveness of community-based versus external monitoring of KDP road construction projects by inducing random variation in the mechanism by which corruption could be detected. A subset of study villages was assigned to the bottom-up intervention, in which citizens were encouraged to participate in village-level meetings at which project officials documented their expenses in relation to the use of public funds for the construction of local roads; a second subset was assigned to the top-down intervention, in which villages were informed that road construction expenses would be closely monitored by local officials. The odds of an audit in this group were 100 percent. In the control villages, the usual process of government audit was expected; the odds of an audit were about 4 percent. The study finds that intensive top-down audits reduced missing expenditures on materials and wages by about 8 percentage points. In contrast, grassroots monitoring reduced only missing wage expenditures. Given the larger budget share of nonwage expenditures, the overall impact of community monitoring was negligible.

These results suggest that community monitoring may be constrained, for several reasons. There may be freeriding, in the sense that community members may be unwilling to monitor providers when benefits are largely nonexcludable (as they are for roads), or they may be unable to detect corruption when the activity entails technical inputs. Although the study cannot separate out these channels, the fact that villagers were able to detect missing wage payments but appear to have had a harder time knowing how much of any construction input was actually used in the road suggests that capacity constraints are likely to be at least part of the story.

Although the intensive top-down audit reduced corruption as measured by missing expenditures, it appears to have increased nepotism. Relatives of members of the implementation committee, including the village leader, were significantly more likely to be hired, suggesting the need for a broader view inclusive of all types of political corruption, in line with Bardhan and Mookherjee (2006a).

The level of resource capture that should be considered problematic is somewhat fuzzy. The pursuit of a policy designed primarily to minimize corruption may make little sense if there are other, possibly conflicting, policy goals (see Mookherjee 1997; Waller, Verdier, and Gardner 2002). The key issue, therefore, may not be whether decentralization eliminates capture but rather how large the implied efficiency and equity losses are and the extent to which they attenuate the poverty reduction agendas of development projects.

Olken's (2006) study of losses in Indonesia's subsidized rice program (Operasi Pasar Khusus [OPK]) is instructive in this regard. The program allowed eligible households to purchase up to 20 kilograms of rice a month. Roughly half of rural households were eligible to participate, and the implied subsidy was significant.[11] About 18 percent of the rice went missing, and ineligible households purchased a large amount of OPK rice. Much of the corruption was concentrated in a small fraction of villages, most of which were located in the most corrupt districts.[12] One-half to two-thirds of total program benefits were lost to corruption and mistargeting, making the project welfare reducing in net terms. What is perhaps most interesting is that losses from mistargeting far outweighed losses from outright corruption.

These results highlight the point that a focus on corruption defined narrowly as outright theft, bribes, or graft may miss the larger problems of resource capture through other, often legal, forms of rent-seeking or resource losses caused by the poor implementation and monitoring capacity of project staff or community members. This issue is examined in the sections that follow.

> A narrow focus on corruption may miss the larger problems of resource capture through rent-seeking and resource losses caused by poor implementation and monitoring capacity.

Participation and Resource Allocation in Induced Community-Driven Development Programs

A small number of studies have looked carefully at who participates in organizations formed by community-driven development projects. Overall, the evidence suggests that participants tend to be disproportionately from wealthier, more educated, and more politically connected households. They also tend to belong to ethnic or tribal groups that enjoy higher status. In Bolivia and Burkina Faso, wealthier households were not only more likely to be active in local associations; they also had more memberships per household. In Indonesia, poorer and less educated households tended to participate less; the wealthiest also spent less time and money on community organizations, suggesting an inverted U-shape in participation (Grootaert, Oh, and Swamy 2002).[13]

> Participants in community organizations tend to be disproportionately from wealthier, more educated, and more politically connected households.

Burkina Faso and Senegal reveal a similar pattern of exclusion (Arcand and Fafchamps 2012). Arcand and Fafchamps find little evidence that community organizations created by donor-sponsored projects are more inclusive than other community groups. On the contrary, they find that members of externally funded community organizations were more likely to be older and to have more land wealth.

Elite dominance is also evident in Indonesia's Second Urban Poverty Project (UPP2), which provided one-time allocations to support implementation of community development plans through access to credit, mobilization of community members, and financing of small infrastructure. Pradhan, Rao, and Rosenberg (2009) find that groups managing fund allocation decisions were more likely to have members who were educated, affluent, politically connected, and male; while members of groups implementing funded projects, were more likely to be less affluent, less educated, and female.

In rural Pakistan, villagers who belong to community organizations supported by the Pakistan Poverty Alleviation Fund (PPAF) are far more likely to own land than villagers who do not belong (Mansuri 2012b). They are also significantly more likely to have some schooling and to belong to households that are connected to traditional village leaders and local politicians. On average, community organization members have twice as much land as nonmembers and almost one additional year of schooling. However, village characteristics matter. In villages with a larger fraction of household heads with some schooling, landlessness is less of a barrier to community organization membership. Conversely, in more unequal villages, lower-caste households are less likely to belong to a community organization, although this discouragement effect is dampened as the proportion of low-caste households in the village rises.[14]

One explanation for elite dominance in participatory bodies may be that members of a society who are well endowed, whether in wealth or ability, may be the only ones who possess the requisite resources, capabilities, and leisure to represent their community's interests. Educated community members may also be best placed to articulate community demands with external actors and facilitate the application procedures projects require. Better-educated people may also be more altruistic as leaders and thus less likely to engage in resource misappropriation of all types. On the other hand, the most disadvantaged may be least able to spare the time or resources needed for participatory decision making. They may also be least equipped to deal with its technical demands. In sum, the mere fact that participants at the community level are from the elite may not be sufficient evidence of capture: by virtue of their education, exposure, networks, and greater leisure time, members of the elite may have both the ability and the willingness to effectively represent the community.

These findings raise several important questions. Does the identity of participants in community-based organizations affect the allocation of resources for intended beneficiaries? Can participatory programs serve their empowerment and inclusion objectives if participation itself

Participation by poor and low-caste residents is lower in more unequal communities . . .

. . . and higher in communities with above-average levels of education.

The mere fact that participants at the community level are from the elite may not be sufficient evidence of capture.

129

is not democratized? These questions are particularly important if not all spending on public goods and services benefits the poor equally. Investments in primary schooling, basic health facilities, and safe drinking water are likely to yield larger benefits for poorer households than investments in higher education and hospitals. Investments in public irrigation systems may be even more exclusionary, because only people who own land may be well placed to benefit from higher productivity and higher land values.

The first set of studies examined looks at the extent to which community level projects funded by social funds or community-driven development programs are well aligned with the stated priorities of the poor or other disadvantaged groups, including women. Rao and Ibanez (2005) look at this issue using retrospective data from survey respondents in communities funded by the Jamaica Social Investment Fund. They find that the match between the projects funded and the preferences of community members was poor overall. In only two of the five communities studied did the project match the preferences of a majority in the community. Overall, better-educated and better-networked people were more likely to obtain projects that matched their preferences. Some 80 percent of respondents nevertheless reported satisfaction with the project. The authors argue that this high level of satisfaction may reflect "benevolent" capture, in which the elite are best informed about true community needs, feasible projects, or both and act altruistically to obtain benefits for their communities.

> In Jamaica, better-educated and better-networked people were more likely to obtain projects that matched their preferences.

Dasgupta and Beard (2007) find similar results in their study of the performance of community development boards in Indonesia's Urban Poverty Project (UPP). Communities were selected for this case study in part because they had high levels of social cohesion, as measured by the authors. The authors find that community development boards that were dominated by elite groups delivered more benefits to the poor, who fared much worse under apparently more egalitarian community development boards. Based on their findings, they argue that elite control over local decision making must be distinguished from elite capture.

Other researchers argue that even when it induces no change in selected projects, the deliberative process creates a sense of satisfaction and legitimacy, because people like to be consulted, even when the consultative process does not yield a change in resource allocation.[15] Olken (2007) examines whether observed project choice in Indonesia reflects, in part, the underlying participatory mechanism adopted by the KDP program. To test this hypothesis, he randomized the final project selection method across villages. In one group, projects were selected publicly, at a village meeting; in the other, they were chosen by secret ballot. The list of proposed projects was subject to an earlier process of selection about which little is known, except that village elites were in attendance during their selection. The study finds no impact of the political mechanism on project choice, despite high turnout in the election and sparse attendance at the village meeting, which attracted mainly the village and supra-village elite.

However, the election mechanism increased satisfaction with the proposed project, even though there was no change in the project selected. Olken argues that this finding may indicate a preference for greater participation; specifically more equitable participation may have a normative aspect, creating greater satisfaction as well as greater "buy-in" for the policies and choices adopted regardless of the impact on substantive outcomes. A potential problem with this interpretation is that given the balloting process, village residents would also have needed more information ex ante on the set of projects proposed in order to vote on them. The study cannot separately identify the potential impact of information and voting on satisfaction. What it does indicate is that a considerable level of exclusion is possible in the type of deliberative process that community-driven development projects typically employ. In this case, village and supra-village elites dominated the initial process of selecting the menu of projects on which the rest of the community could vote.

These limitations notwithstanding, this set of studies suggests that evidence of elite influence need not indicate malevolent intent. For one thing, the preferences of nonelite groups could change as a result of community deliberation over the use of funds, particularly if they are initially less informed about the feasibility or potential benefits of specific projects. If this is the case, what appears to be capture could well reflect a more altruistic or benevolent process, with local elites taking the lead in advocating for public goods that the community most needs and acting as intermediaries between the implementing agency and the beneficiary community. Some observers argue that this is indeed what often happens. The projects finally selected are often the projects that best serve the needs of the most disadvantaged in the community, even though they were not initially proposed by them. White (2002) notes, for example, that the disproportionate number of schools and health facilities funded by social funds reflects the preferences of the "prime

> The deliberative process may create a sense of satisfaction and legitimacy, even when it does not yield a change in resource allocation.

Community facilitators' preferences may heavily influence the deliberation process.

movers" behind these projects, who are often school teachers or health workers.

Platteau and Gaspart (2003), among others, take a very different position. They argue that any assessment that elicits community preferences ex post may not reveal much about the extent of elite capture or corruption in the use of funds, because poor villagers may be unable or unwilling to express reservations about the funded project, or the role of the elite, for fear of repercussions or loss of resources. They suggest that community facilitators often play an influential role in the process of project selection, that facilitator preferences are likely to heavily influence the deliberation process, and that it is these preferences, as much as the preferences of prime movers within the community, that are reflected in project proposals (see also Murphy 1990; Mohan and Stokke 2000).

Separating these issues is difficult in practice. Doing so requires data on the projects specific groups or individuals prefer before and after any deliberative process; the facilitation and deliberation process within communities; the preferences of facilitators; the location of projects, proposed and selected; and the identity of beneficiaries. In practice, the data collected on preferences, process, project location, and beneficiaries tend to be fairly coarse. Most studies ask questions about the top three needs of the community or its main problems, without reference to a budget; the expected cost share for beneficiaries; or, most critically, project location. Survey respondents may thus state that upgrading roads or drinking water sources in the community is a priority, but it is unclear which road or drinking water source they wish to upgrade. It is rarely the case, however, that a "community" inhabits an area small and cohesive enough to allow everyone to benefit equally from all infrastructure investments. In most cases, roads, drinking water schemes, and irrigation channels are provided to specific neighborhoods or habitations, and location determines who benefits. Data on the nature of the facilitation process or its role in modifying or shaping preferences are even rarer.

In line with the concerns of critics like Platteau and Gaspart (2003), recent experimental work by Humphreys, Masters, and Sandbu (2006) finds that facilitator preferences significantly predict the choices of participants in consultative meetings. They use data from a national forum held in São Tomé and Príncipe to discuss policy issues related to the use of newly discovered oil reserves. About 5 percent of the adult population attended small group meetings, whose leaders were randomly assigned.

Groups led by women were more likely than groups led by men to prioritize investments in local health clinics over hospitals. Unlike groups led by men, they also preferred investments in improving transportation services rather than investments in improving roads and expanding road networks. They were also more likely to accept higher taxation of windfall earnings and to opt for saving rather than spending windfalls. Furthermore, groups led by older adults were more likely than groups led by younger people to emphasize health as a national priority and to favor commercial transport over passenger transport and better roads over public transportation services. Meetings led by women and older people also reached much higher levels of consensus than meetings led by men and younger people.

The only published study that has collected ex ante preference data for public good projects is Labonne and Chase (2009). They find substantial evidence of capture by local leaders at the project proposal stage but only in more unequal villages with a less politically active population. Local leaders in such villages, they find, exercise greater influence over resource allocation at meetings at the supra-village level, where proposed projects are approved.

Gugerty and Kremer (2008) take a different approach. They look at the impact of a participatory agricultural project in rural Kenya on group membership and agricultural productivity. The project provided leadership training and agricultural inputs to small self-help organizations, most of whose members were poor women with little education. The project spent $674 per group, or an average of $34 per member, half of which was allocated to agricultural inputs, which were provided to the group as a whole. As the typical comparison group had $243 in assets before the project started, this spending represented a large increase in the group's capital stock.[16] The study finds that the groups selected for the intervention were far more likely to attract new members and that new members were also likely to be more educated, to have formal sector income, and to take over group leadership positions.[17] Moreover, although exit rates were similar in program and comparison groups, more members left the program groups because of intragroup conflicts. Older female members, who were among the most vulnerable, were also disproportionately more likely to leave.

In sum, the program appears to have unleashed a process in which group membership and leadership moved into the hands of younger and better-educated women. It also induced the entry of more men and

One study finds substantial evidence of capture by local leaders at the project proposal stage . . .

. . . but only in more unequal villages with a less politically active population.

A rapid increase in resources may serve only to increase exclusion.

more efforts on the part of government officials to build links to the groups. However, despite the large injection of funds, the project yielded unimpressive gains in agricultural productivity. The authors conjecture that a rapid increase in resources may serve only to increase exclusion.

In a somewhat similar vein, Mansuri (2012a) compares the distribution of beneficiaries of village level infrastructure projects built by a participatory program and projects built by government line departments in the same villages and at comparable size and cost (see chapter 5 for a fuller discussion of this study). She finds that benefits from the participatory project were no better distributed than benefits from the relevant government project and that the share of the landless, the poor, and people from low castes was far below their population share in both cases. Moreover, investment in the most excludable schemes—irrigation channels—tended to be the least pro-poor. Beneficiaries were also far more likely to be members of a community organization, and as discussed above, members of community organizations were far more likely to be drawn from people with land wealth, education, or political networks.

Local inequality may reduce the odds that a community selects a pro-poor project.

Another way to assess whether capture is benevolent is to determine whether community characteristics affect the allocation of resources. Araujo and others (2008) assess the relationship between community inequality and the odds of selecting a more pro-poor excludable project in Ecuador's social fund. They find that local inequality significantly reduced the odds that a community selected a pro-poor project. They also find that the impact of inequality on project choice was amplified in communities that had a larger share of indigenous households, suggesting that ethno-linguistic heterogeneity can exacerbate capture by local elites.[18]

Community inequality can reduce access to private transfers.

Community inequality can also reduce access to private transfers. Galasso and Ravallion (2005) find that greater land inequality significantly worsened targeting in the program in Bangladesh that they studied. They also find that targeting was less effective in remote and isolated villages. Bardhan, Mookherjee and Torrado (2010) find that villages with greater land inequality allocate a significantly smaller share of private benefits to scheduled castes and tribes. Shankar, Gaiha, and Jha (2010) find that poor and low-caste households are considerably less likely to participate in the National Rural Employment Guarantee Scheme (NREGS) program in Indian villages with greater wealth inequality.

Conning and Kevane (2002) identify some of these patterns in a review of community-based targeting that focuses on the tradeoff between better information and local capture. They conclude that communities are more effective than outside agencies in targeting programs to the poor only when they are relatively egalitarian, have open and transparent systems of decision making, and establish clear rules for determining who is poor. Communities with a low capacity to mobilize information and monitor disbursements are more vulnerable to corruption and capture by elites, as are more heterogeneous communities, where multiple and conflicting identities can create competing incentives.

In sum, context matters a great deal in the degree to which participatory programs achieve their inclusion objectives, as do the specifics of program design and implementation. Overall, however, poorer, less educated, and more marginalized groups tend to participate less, as do women of all socioeconomic backgrounds. Higher average literacy levels are almost uniformly beneficial for pro-poor participation, and wealth inequality and remoteness of location tend to reduce participation by the poor.

Participation also affects the allocation of resources. A reasonable amount of evidence shows that elite domination of the participatory process is not without consequence and should not be routinely viewed as benign. What does appear to be the case, however, is that a well-articulated deliberative process may build legitimacy for the resource allocation decisions made by the elite even when they are not apparently well aligned with the initial preferences of the poor. The evidence here is thin, however; much more is needed in order to draw any sensible conclusion.

There is also some evidence that an increase in external funding can displace the most vulnerable people by inducing greater participation by the more educated, wealthy, and young. This finding is consistent with the case several critics make that short-duration donor-funded projects can create conditions under which program implementers have strong incentives to rapidly mobilize communities in order to disburse project funds. As doing so is easier in relatively developed and accessible localities, programs tend to focus on them and on the relatively well placed and influential within them. This finding resonates with the worry that co-financing requirements and competition for access to project funds—common features in many participatory projects—can

> Elite domination of the participatory process is not without consequence and should not be routinely viewed as benign.

encourage disproportionate participation by people in a position to contribute or with a greater capacity to propose viable projects (see the discussion in chapter 5). Program design may therefore matter a good deal.

Participation and Resource Allocation under Decentralization

Democratic decentralization may limit outright capture . . .

A significant body of theoretical literature suggests that political elites may be just as likely as traditional elite groups to engage in rent-seeking behavior, including the use of public resources to woo particular constituencies in order to gain electoral advantage (see, for example, Cox and McCubbins 1986; Persson and Tabellini 2000). It is important in this context to understand the distinction between outright corruption and clientelism. Democratic decentralization may limit outright capture, but insofar as it increases opportunities for clientelism, the consequences for development can be equally negative, as discussed in chapter 3. Clientelism can lead to the unequal treatment of the equally deserving, exacerbating inequality and causing resources to be used inefficiently as a result of the prioritization of short-term political gains.

. . . but insofar as it increases opportunities for clientelism, the consequences for development can be equally negative.

How important clientelism and capture are is, of course, an empirical question. One way to assess their importance is to check whether electoral results predict future resource allocations or past allocations predict future electoral results. Several studies confirm such patterns. Following the 1994 elections in Brazil, federal deputies allocated more resources for local public goods to municipalities in which they had received the greatest number of votes. Looking at the allocation of public works from 1996 to 1999, Finan (2004) finds that a 10 percent increase in vote shares for a candidate in the previous election, implied an expected increase of R$75,174 in public works for a municipality during the electoral cycle. Miguel and Zaidi (2003) find that administrative districts in Ghana in which the ruling party won all parliamentary seats in the 1996 election received 27 percent more school funding in 1998–99. Bratton and van de Walle (1997) cite several cases in Africa where state resources were used to reward faithful supporters. They note that by "electively distributing favors and material benefits to loyal followers who are not citizens of the polity so much as the ruler's clients," rulers often ensure the political stability of their regime and personal political survival.

De Janvry, Nakagawa, and Sadoulet (2009) test this hypothesis using electoral data from Zambia. They match local election results in 1998, 2001, and 2006 with ward-level data on resource allocation under three social fund programs (CRP I, CRP II, and ZAMSIF). They examine whether the percentage of votes received by the majority party's candidate for the district council influenced the allocation of project resources in the ward and whether past allocations to a ward affected the political fortunes of incumbents. On the first question, they find that in highly decentralized districts, a 10 percent increase in the majority party's share of the vote was associated with a 32 percent increase in per capita resources in the ward. Interestingly, the increase occurred only in wards with high literacy rates. They also find that incumbents were rewarded for higher per capita budgets: a doubling of the allocated per capita budget in the three years preceding an election increased an incumbent's odds of reelection by 4–5 percent. This effect is large, given that only 24 percent of the wards in subject districts received a project and that 39 percent elected a councilor from the incumbent district majority. The authors find no evidence of a trade-off between pro-poor program targeting and the political use of public resources, however, as the poorest wards were both more likely to be funded and more likely to vote for the district majority party.

Schady (2000) finds that expenditures on projects funded by the Peruvian social fund FONCODES increased significantly before national elections over the period 1991–95. Projects were also more likely to be directed at poorer provinces, which returned smaller shares of votes for the incumbent president in the previous election. He suggests that funding decisions were made on the basis of both political and poverty criteria.

In Mexico, municipal-level expenditures by PROGRESA–Oportunidades, a national conditional cash transfer program, increased the incumbent party's share of the vote by about 4.3 percent (Rodriguez-Chamussy 2009). This effect was particularly strong when the Partido de la Revolución Democrática (PRD) was the incumbent party. Incumbent opposition party mayors also benefitted, however, presumably by successfully claiming some credit for benefits delivered to their constituents.

Manacorda, Miguel, and Vigorito (2011) study a large government-initiated poverty reduction program in Uruguay. They find that program beneficiaries were 21–28 percent more likely to support the current government than nonbeneficiaries.

Expenditures on projects funded by the Peruvian social fund increased significantly before national elections.

Camacho and Conover (2011) examine the targeting performance of a poverty score card issued by the Colombian government to determine eligibility for a wide range of programs, including unemployment benefits, housing improvement grants, food aid for the elderly, educational subsidies, and a publicly provided health insurance program. The central government designed the scoring system but allowed municipalities discretion over the administration and timing of the door-to-door interviews. The authors find sharp discontinuities in the score, precisely at the eligibility threshold of 47. They find that in municipalities in which a relatively high proportion of families had identical interview answers, an overwhelming number with identical answers obtained scores below 47. Scores calculated using the disaggregated data largely agree with the assigned scores, suggesting that the manipulation occurred mainly through the recording of fake answers at the local level rather than an overwriting of the score at a later point. This evidence of local manipulation is strengthened by their finding that the sharp discontinuity in the score density emerged only after the score algorithm was released to municipal officials and households became aware that eligibility was based on the score. In fact, 91 percent of families with suspicious scores were interviewed after 1997, when the score algorithm became well known to municipal officials. The authors also find a larger discontinuity at the poverty threshold in more competitive elections, where additional votes were more valuable.

Several studies from India find a similar pattern. Using data from four Indian states, Markussen (2006) finds that villagers who belong to the political party of the leader (*pradhan*) of the *gram panchayat* (village council) were 32 percent more likely to receive Below Poverty Line (BPL) cards intended for the poor, regardless of their economic and social status. A more nuanced finding concerns the interplay between land inequality and electoral accountability. Membership in the *pradhan*'s party increased the likelihood of receiving benefits only in *gram panchayats* in which land inequality was above a certain threshold.

Besley, Pande, and Rao (2005, 2007) show that the households of *pradhans* and other *gram panchayat* leaders are significantly more likely to be assigned BPL cards. In their study, this tendency was substantially muted in villages with higher historical literacy rates. In these villages, the landless and illiterate were also more likely to attend *gram sabha* (village assembly) meetings. *Gram sabhas* are expected to be held at least once a year; several public programs rely on these meetings to generate

In India, villagers who belonged to the political party of the leader of the *gram panchayat* were more likely to receive Below Poverty Line (BPL) cards, regardless of their economic and social status.

beneficiary lists. The benefits of higher village literacy did not extend to women, however.

Bardhan and Mookherjee (2006b) find that poverty, land inequality, and the fraction of low-caste households substantially increases capture in the allocation of resources by local governments for public goods. Local governments in West Bengal, India, selected projects that generated less employment for the poor in villages in which a larger fraction of the population was poor or low caste and land was more unequally distributed. They find much less evidence of capture in the allocation of private transfers—mainly credit and the supply of agricultural inputs—distributed by the government, although here, too, the share of the poor was smaller in more unequal villages and villages with larger shares of low-caste households.

Research also points to the significance of legislative malapportionment on the allocation of resources at the local level and the performance of local governments under decentralization. Malapportionment occurs when there is a discrepancy between the share of legislative seats held by a geographical unit and its population share, so that some votes count more than others in legislative decision making at the center. Samuels and Snyder (2001) argue that some malapportionment may be necessary in the transition to democracy at the local level in order to appease antidemocratic elites, who demand that their privileges be protected. Malapportionment may therefore be more important in rural areas with entrenched local elites and significant wealth inequality or in areas with a history of ethnic or linguistic conflict. The authors find that the overrepresentation of rural districts and counties seems to be typical in emerging democracies. In Latin America, for example, malapportionment tends to favor conservative rural districts at the expense of more urban or politically progressive districts.

Ansolabehere, Gerber, and Snyder (2002) show that counties in the United States that were overrepresented relative to their populations received relatively more per capita transfers from the state before the court order mandating redistricting in the 1960s. Following redistricting, these inequities were largely eliminated, as almost $7 billion a year moved from formerly overrepresented to formerly underrepresented counties.

One implication of malapportionment is that central governments that rely on overrepresented, nondemocratic localities to secure national legislative majorities may also tend to tolerate subnational authoritarian

Poverty, land inequality, and the fraction of low-caste households substantially increased capture in the allocation of resources by local governments for public goods in West Bengal.

Central governments that rely on nondemocratic localities to secure national legislative majorities may also tolerate subnational authoritarian enclaves and be unresponsive to efforts to reform local politics.

Bolivia's decentralization process doubled the share of national tax revenues devolved to municipalities . . .

. . . and required that resources be allocated strictly on a per capita basis.

enclaves and be unresponsive to efforts to reform local politics.[19] Emerging democracies will then tend to undergo a period in which democracy is simultaneously strengthened at the center and undermined at the local level.

Several political theorists have noted a relationship between political and economic liberalization at the national level and the maintenance of authoritarian regimes at the subnational level (see, for example, O'Donnell 1993; Fox 1994; Snyder 1999). There is very little empirical evidence from developing countries on whether legislative malapportionment protects authoritarian enclaves at the local level.

Faguet (2004) provides some evidence on how an effort to reduce malapportionment in the resource allocation process can help improve local accountability in a developing country. In Bolivia, the decentralization process not only doubled the share of national tax revenues devolved to municipalities, it also required that resources be allocated strictly on a per capita basis—which limited ad hoc and clientelistic resource assignment. At the same time, a redistricting effort created 198 new municipalities (64 percent of the total) and expanded existing municipalities to include suburbs and surrounding rural areas. Together, these changes led to a massive shift of resources in favor of smaller and poorer districts in which the largest beneficiaries were districts with the worst demographic indicators and the poorest infrastructure endowment. Before decentralization, Bolivia's three largest cities received 86 percent of all devolved funds; the remaining 14 percent was divided among 308 municipalities. After decentralization, these shares were reversed, with the three largest cities receiving just 27 percent of devolved funds.

Using data on political, institutional, administrative, and governance indicators for all 311 Bolivian municipalities over the period 1987–96, Faguet shows that decentralization shifted public investment toward significantly higher investments in human capital and social services and that the reallocation was well aligned with local needs. Education investments were higher in areas with lower literacy; water and sanitation investments were higher in areas with lower water and sewerage connection rates; and investments in water management and agriculture were higher in areas at greater risk of malnutrition. This alignment of investments with local needs was driven in large part by the 250 smallest and poorest municipalities. Popular participation in local governments was formalized through local oversight committees (*comités de vigilancia*), which were empowered to exercise oversight over municipal allocations of "popular participation funds" and to freeze disbursements to local governments that misused funds.

De Janvry, Nakagawa, and Sadoulet (2009) also find a shift in resource allocation with decentralization. They look at the allocation of the Zambia social fund (ZAMSIF) across districts that vary in the discretion they can exercise in the allocation of these resources. They find greater diversity in funded projects in more decentralized districts, as well as a shift toward income-generating projects as opposed to broad public goods, such as education, health, and water supply/sanitation. However, the increased investments appeared to benefit the poor, and there was an overall shift of resources in favor of the poorest wards.

Can Electoral Incentives Reduce Rent-Seeking?

Ultimately, of course, the question of interest is whether a shift toward democracy at the local level reduces capture on balance. There is very little good evidence on this issue. What there is suggests that local democracy has the potential to mitigate capture, albeit not always most efficiently, and that electoral rules such as term limits, the political context in which decentralization occurs, and the ability of the center to oversee resource allocation at the local level matter a great deal.

There is little good evidence on whether a shift toward democracy at the local level reduces capture.

Foster and Rosenzweig (2004) develop a model of two-party democracy in which local governments need to allocate the public budget across three types of goods: a public good (roads) that disproportionately benefits the poor, by raising wages; a club good (irrigation facilities) that disproportionately benefits landowners; and a neutral public good (schools). The model establishes that an increase in the share of landless households should lead to larger investments in road construction under a democratic regime relative to a regime that specifically favors the local elite. Using data from 250 villages in rural India, Foster and Rosenzweig show that an increase in the population weight of the poor induces resource allocations that favor the poor. Their evidence suggests that public irrigation investment crowds out private irrigation investment, so that the shift toward more pro-poor public goods also implies a net gain in total output.

Political economy agency models, such as those by Barro (1973) and Ferejohn (1986), predict that incumbent politicians will refrain from maximizing rent extraction in their first term in order to get reelected and enjoy future rents. Persuasive empirical evidence that this is indeed the case has emerged based on term limits of U.S. state governors. Besley and Case (1995) show that governors eligible for reelection were significantly more likely to reduce taxes and expenditures than governors not facing reelection.

List and Sturm (2006) show that electoral rules affect even secondary policies, such as environmental protection. They find that environmental spending is higher when governors are eligible for reelection and that the spending gap between eligible and final-term governors increases in states with a large pro-environmental population.

Evidence on the relationship between term limits and political incentives has also started to emerge for developing countries. Ferraz and Finan (2011) look at mayoral elections in Brazilian municipalities. Using data from the 2003 audits conducted by the Brazilian central government, they examine the allocation of federal resources by local governments. Municipalities were selected by lottery for an audit each month; audit reports were made available on the Internet and sent to all levels of government about two months after completion. Ferraz and Finan find that the share of total audited resources that was misappropriated was 27 percent larger in municipalities with second-term mayors, who did not have reelection incentives because of term limits, and that the effects were more pronounced in municipalities with less access to information and in municipalities in which the likelihood of judicial punishment was lower. Overall, their findings suggest that electoral rules that enhance political accountability play a crucial role in constraining corrupt behavior. Assuming that in the absence of reelection incentives, first-term mayors would behave like second-term mayors, they estimate that reelection incentives reduced the misappropriation of resources by about $160 million.

De Janvry, Finan, and Sadoulet (forthcoming) provide additional evidence of the impact of term limits on the performance of mayors in Brazilian municipal elections. They focus on the impact of term limits on the effectiveness of the Bolsa Escola program on student dropout rates.[20] The authors find that municipalities governed by a first-term mayor eligible for reelection had an additional 2 percentage point reduction in the dropout rate, which represented a 36 percent improvement in program performance compared with municipalities governed by a second-term mayor not eligible for reelection. Once the potential

Results from Brazil suggest that electoral rules that enhance political accountability play a crucial role in constraining corrupt behavior.

selection of children into the program is accounted for, the reduction in dropout rates is about 8 percentage points, representing a decline of 52 percent relative to the preprogram dropout rate of 15 percent.[21] Various robustness checks validate these results. The authors also find some evidence for heterogeneity in program impact. Wealthier municipalities generally do better, but so do municipalities that have more open and competitive electoral practices, which display less evidence of nepotism and administrative politicization.

De Janvry, Finan, and Sadoulet attempt to understand the channel through which mayoral effort translates into lower dropout rates by looking at differences in program implementation.[22] Their findings indicate that first-term mayors were somewhat more likely to rely on the registration of children through schools and to involve social councils in various ways in implementing the program. In contrast, second-term mayors were somewhat more likely to register children in the mayor's office and to send program coordinators to the homes of children who did not comply with the program's attendance requirements. The authors argue that in-school registration of children is more transparent and indicates higher levels of effort. One could argue the opposite—that in-school registration could favor the inclusion of lower-risk (and potentially better-off) children, whereas registration through the mayor's office, along with follow-up through program coordinators, may induce more noncompliers to openly drop out. If this is the case, dropout rates could be higher for second-term mayors precisely because they select poorer and riskier children and enforce the conditionality stipulated by the program, whereas reelection incentives may make first-term mayors more likely to engage in clientelistic behavior, as Khemani and Wane (2008) argue, than to deliver higher-quality public services. Disentangling these effects requires data on the child's household characteristics and compliance with the program.

The reelection incentives of local politicians, including the need to reward supporters, can also influence resource allocation in participatory development projects. Arcand and Bassole (2008), for example, show that, on average, the village of the *Conseil Rural* (rural council) president was 18.5 percent more likely to receive funding for a subproject under the Programme National d'Infrastructures Rurales, a large community-driven development program in Senegal. Baird, McIntosh, and Özler (2009) find that wards and districts in which elected representatives were not from the ruling party generated fewer applications for projects funded by Tanzania's Social Action Fund (TASAF), suggesting the use of decentralized project resources to build support for the incumbent party.[23] Case (2001) finds that block grants provided by the Albanian social assistance program were distributed across communities in a manner consistent with the core-supporter model.

Several recent studies examine the restraining effect of election incentives on corruption in local governments. Ferraz and Finan (2008) examine whether access to information on the corrupt practices of local politicians affects voter behavior by comparing municipalities in Brazil that were randomly audited before the elections with municipalities that were audited after the elections. They find that the disclosure of audit reports had a significant impact on the reelection rates of corrupt mayors and that exposure to media was important, with larger effects in municipalities with radio stations.

Henderson and Kuncoro (2011) find that Indonesia's move toward decentralized local governance in 2001 decreased the level of corruption as measured by the reported bribes paid by firms to government line departments for activities under local control. The extent of the reduction was greater in districts where Islamic (rather than secular) parties, whose local platforms emphasized anticorruption policies, were elected in 2001. The authors see this evidence as pointing to the importance of corruption as a political issue in the selection of local leaders and indicative of the potential for democracy at the local level to constrain corruption.

Brollo (2009) focuses on the political opportunity that the audits of local government can provide to the central government. This study reveals that much of the observed impact on the reelection odds of incumbent mayors in Brazil occurs because the central government uses audit reports to strategically reward and punish allies and competitors. Brollo finds that municipalities in which two or more instances of corruption were found received smaller transfers from the center, but corrupt mayors who were affiliated with the president's political party were actually compensated with larger transfers in order to avoid future political losses caused by any reputational effects. In contrast, pure reputation effects dominated only when information was released close to the election. This finding suggests that when localities are largely dependent on fiscal transfers from the center, as Brazilian municipalities are, the central government can use devices such as audits to control local political selection. It also suggests that voters may care far more

> When localities are largely dependent on fiscal transfers from the center, the central government can use devices such as audits to control local political selection.

about the delivery of public goods and transfers than about the extent to which politicians, who are able to deliver these services, are corrupt.

Bobonis, Camara-Fuertes, and Schwabe (2011) examine whether the public disclosure of information about political corruption affects the re-election odds and future behavior of politicians. They find that audits do little to reduce corruption but can be instrumental in improving the odds of re-election. Using data on publicly released audits of municipal governments in Puerto Rico, they find that audited levels of corruption in municipalities that were audited before the previous election and municipalities that were not are similar. However, mayors were able to translate the reputational gain provided by a good audit into higher odds of reelection and higher levels of rent-seeking in future periods.

Litschig and Zamboni (2007) and Di Tella and Schargrodsky (2003) focus on the impact of judicial institutions and "corruption crack-downs" on resource misappropriation and fiscal mismanagement. These studies point to the importance of mechanisms other than electoral and social accountability for improving governance.

Litschig and Zamboni (2007) exploit exogenous variation in the location of state judiciary branches to assess the impact of judicial institutions on corruption by civil servants in local governments in Brazil.[24] Using audit data to construct an estimate of offenses per civil servant in counties, with and without state judiciary branches, they find that offenses per civil servant were about 35 percent lower in counties with a branch of the judiciary.[25]

Di Tella and Schargrodsky (2003) study the price paid for basic inputs during a crackdown on corruption in public hospitals in Buenos Aires in 1996–97. The crackdown was conducted by a newly elected city government, which collected and compared prices paid by all public hospitals for a set of homogenous basic inputs for which quality differences should not have been a concern. The authors find that the prices paid by hospitals for basic inputs fell about 18 percent during the first six months of the crackdown. Although there was some increase afterward, prices remained significantly below the pre-crackdown phase nine months later. The longer-term effects were larger when procurement officers were better paid.

These studies suggest that institutions at the local level cannot substitute for weak and corrupt formal institutions of accountability. Instead, local oversight over the use and management of public resources is likely

> Mechanisms other than electoral and social accountability, such as judicial reforms, are important for improving governance.

> In Buenos Aires, the prices public hospitals paid for basic inputs fell about 18 percent during the first six months of a crackdown on corruption.

to be effective only when other institutions of accountability, including institutions at the center, function well and communities have the relevant information and the capacity to sanction lax or corrupt providers and others in charge of public resources.[26] In addition, broader reforms that enhance judicial oversight, allow for independent audit agencies, and protect and promote the right to information and a free media appear to be necessary for effective local oversight.

Conclusions

The literature on decentralization identifies a central trade-off between the advantages of local information and the hazards of local capture. The evidence reviewed in this chapter indicates that in many cases, the hazards of local capture can outweigh the benefits of local information.

In the majority of cases, participants in community-driven development projects belong to the elite, whose preferences are often reflected in the resource allocation process. The extent to which their dominance distorts the poverty reduction intent of decentralized public programs depends on the extent to which elite dominance can be construed as capture. Community characteristics—including inequalities of wealth and political power, geographic isolation, and ethnic heterogeneity—appear to play a decisive role in this regard. Malevolent forms of capture are more likely in communities with greater wealth inequality, communities that are isolated or poor and communities in which caste, race, and gender disparities are important and are embedded in a hierarchical structure which valorizes particular groups.

Participatory programs attempt to deal with these concerns by using local facilitators to build community capacity. However, little is known about the facilitation process, the training received by facilitators, or the incentive structures they face. There is also little evidence of any self-correcting mechanism through which community engagement counteracts the potential capture of public resources. Instead, the bulk of the evidence suggests that the more unequal the initial distribution of assets, the better positioned the nonpoor are to capture the benefits of external efforts to help the poor. Local actors may have an informational and locational advantage, but they appear to use it to the benefit of the disadvantaged only where institutions and mechanisms to ensure local accountability are robust.

Local actors may have an informational and locational advantage . . .

. . . but they appear to use it to the benefit of the disadvantaged only where institutions and mechanisms to ensure local accountability are robust.

146

Other dimensions of community capacity also matter a great deal. Participatory programs face far greater challenges in remote or isolated localities and in areas with lower literacy levels and higher levels of poverty. Such localities also tend to be less well served by mass media and other sources of information and are less likely to have adequate central oversight.

Local democracy can have both favorable and unfavorable effects on the level and distribution of public resources. The outcome is context dependent. It varies with the nature of political institutions, at both the national and the local level; the level of voter awareness; and the accountability mechanisms in place. The potential for resource capture by political elites appears to be considerable.

The literature also indicates that democratic decentralization can lead to a greater use of public budgets to reward particular constituents for their loyalty and to improve the fortunes of political allies.

The important question is whether democratic decentralization narrows the overall scope for capture. The answer appears to warrant cautious optimism, provided political institutions and rules are designed to address perverse incentives. On balance the ballot box, though far from perfect, provides a clearer mechanism than less formal deliberation for sanctioning unpopular policy choices or excessive rent-seeking by traditional or political elites. It is less clear how citizens can collectively sanction negligent or corrupt officials or local leaders where such venues for the exercise of citizen voice are not available. This suggests that community-driven development projects may be able to induce greater accountability by mandating inclusion and using electoral processes to select community representatives.

In sum, far from being a substitute for weak and corrupt formal institutions of accountability, local oversight over the use and management of public resources is effective only when institutions of accountability at the center function well and communities have the capacity to effectively monitor service providers and others in charge or public resources. This finding appears to increase, rather than diminish, the need for a functional and strong center and vigilant and able implementing agencies. There is little evidence that donors can substitute for a nonfunctional central government as a higher-level accountability agent. Effective local oversight appears to require reforms that enhance judicial oversight, allow for independent audit agencies, and protect and promote the right to information and a free media.

> Participatory programs face far greater challenges in remote or isolated localities and in areas with lower literacy levels and higher levels of poverty.

> Local democracy can have both favorable and unfavorable effects on the level and distribution of public resources. The outcome is context dependent.

> On balance, the ballot box provides a clearer mechanism for sanctioning unpopular policy choices or excessive rent-seeking by traditional or political elites than less formal deliberation.

> Institutions at the local level cannot substitute for weak and corrupt formal institutions of accountability.

> Effective local oversight requires well-functioning institutions at the center . . . and reforms that enhance judicial oversight, allow for independent audit agencies, and protect and promote the right to information and a free media.

Notes

1. See in particular Mauro (1995). The causal relationship between corruption and economic development has been argued both ways. Glaeser and others (2004) argue that corruption tends to decline as economic progress occurs.
2. See, for example, Shleifer and Vishny (1993); Manor (1999); and Bardhan and Mookherjee (2006b). Recent theoretical work on incentives in principal-agent models also shows that decentralization can raise the propensity of individuals to accept bribes (see, for example, Carbonara 2000).
3. Several writers argue that it may not always be sensible to pursue a policy designed to minimize corruption, narrowly defined as bribes, graft, and theft, particularly when there are other, possibly conflicting policy goals (see, for example, Waller, Verdier, and Gardner 2002). The implications of corruption for efficiency have been a somewhat contested issue. Some writers, like Huntington (1968) argue that bribes, graft, and theft are necessary for greasing the "squeaking wheels" of a rigid bureaucracy or that they are an unpleasant but unavoidable side effect of needed government intervention to prevent market failure (Acemoglu and Verdier 2000). Others point out that corruption can skew the incentives of the most economically efficient people away from socially productive activities toward rent-seeking activities and that the people who "grease the wheels" may simply be the most successful at rent-seeking rather than production (Treisman 2000). Rose-Ackerman (2008) argues that the use of public office to influence resource allocation or move legislation in favor of particular groups or causes should not be viewed as corruption, as constituency-based politics can motivate voters to monitor the actions of their representatives, thereby reducing incentives for outright corruption.
4. An important strand in the cross-country literature on corruption focuses on the relationship between corruption and a country's level of economic development, its political institutions, and aspects of its culture. Much of this literature tests hypotheses that have emerged from theoretical studies that seek to explain the relative prevalence of corruption across countries (see, for example, Olson 1993; Shleifer and Vishny 1993; and Campante, Chor, and Do 2009). Studies that look at the relationship between economic development and corruption find evidence for a strong negative relationship. Higher levels of economic development are associated with lower levels of corruption, although the direction of causality is not clear. Some writers argue that development reduces corruption (see Treisman 2000); others argue that countries with lower corruption levels experience more economic development (see Kaufmann and Kraay 2002). Studies also find that other features of the economy, including the level of economic inequality, natural resource endowments, and exposure to foreign competition, influence the extent of corruption. You and Khagram (2005) argue that in more unequal societies, the wealthy have greater incentives and opportunities to skew resources and power in their favor through corruption, while the poor are more vulnerable to extortion and less able to

hold the rich and powerful to account. Ades and Di Tella (1999) find that corruption tends to be higher in countries with greater income inequality. Leite and Weidmann (1999) find that larger natural resource endowments are associated with more corruption. Myerson (1993) and Persson, Roland, and Tabellini (1997) provide theoretical arguments for the relationship between political institutions and corruption.

5. Corruption also appears to be higher in countries that have fewer political rights, in ex-communist regimes (Triesman 2000), and in countries that have less press freedom (Brunetti and Weder 2003). Corruption levels are lower in countries that have a history of common law and procedural fairness, such as former British colonies; in countries that pay higher wages to their civil bureaucrats; and countries with larger numbers of ethno-linguistic groups (Treisman 2000; on wages see Evans and Rauch 2000). Some researchers argue that corruption levels are also lower where women play a greater role in the government and the economy (see, for example, Dollar, Fisman, and Gatti 2001; Swamy and others 2000).

6. Donchev and Ujhelyi (2009) show that factors commonly found to "cause" corruption—religion, the level of development, democratic institutions—are better at explaining perceptions of corruption than actual levels of it. Controlling for such variables, they find at best a very weak relationship between corruption and indexes of corruption perception, for all the measures of corruption experience the use. Olken (2007) and Donchev and Ujhelyi (2009) show that corruption perceptions vary systematically by individual and household characteristics such as education, age, gender, and income. A number of studies find a positive correlation between perceptions of corruption and a range of societal characteristics. Several studies find that reported perceptions of corruption are positively correlated with levels of local inequality and ethnic heterogeneity (see, for example, Mauro 1995; La Porta and others 1999; and Olken 2007). Others find a negative relationship between social capital, measured by levels of trust and civic activism, and corruption (on the relationship between social capital and corruption, see Putnam 1993; Paldam and Svendsen 2002; Bjornskov 2003). These studies cannot rule out reverse causality (high levels of corruption reducing trust and civic activism).

7. This finding is consistent with the theoretical model developed by Shleifer and Vishny (1993).

8. Moving from perception data to data on actual corruption experience is not always straightforward. In general, different measures of corruption do not produce the same conclusions. Moreover, the impact of a policy shift can vary across measures of corruption and possibly with the level of social tolerance for corruption in a society, as Mendez and Sepulveda (2010) show. Ades and Di Tella (1999) argue that hard data on corruption, such as the number of reported fraud cases, are likely to reflect the classification system used in each country as well as both the incidence of corruption and the corruption deterrence system in place.

9. Public expenditure tracking data collected in other African countries yields a similar pattern of missing expenditures.

10. A number of other studies show that governments tend to be more responsive when the electorate is better informed. The mass media have an important role to play in this regard. Drèze and Sen (1990) make this argument forcefully in noting the relative success that India, which has a free media, has had avoiding famines compared with China. Besley and Burgess (2002) show that Indian states with higher newspaper circulation (which also had higher literacy rates and greater election turnout) were more likely to be responsive to food shortages. Stromberg (2004a, 2004b) shows how access to media can affect the allocation of resources to specific groups and thus influence the incidence of redistributive programs. A number of cross-country studies find a negative correlation between press freedom and corruption (Stapenhurst 2000; Brunetti and Weder 2003; Ahrend 2002). Djankov and others (2003) find a negative relationship between state ownership of the media and measures of good governance, including political rights, service delivery, and social outcomes. However, the independence of the media (and the degree of state ownership) may itself depend on the size of political rents and thus the scale of opportunities for resource misappropriation. Besley and Prat (2006) argue that the press is more likely to be free where political rents are small and there is scope for a multiplicity of media outlets and sources for advertising revenue. Mullainathan and Shleifer (2002) point out that greater media concentration need not imply less media autonomy if competition generates a struggle for market share that leads to the publication of more stories that tend to confirm the prior beliefs of readers.

11. OPK rice was available at 60 percent below market price, implying a subsidy of about 9 percent of preprogram monthly household expenditures for a median household purchasing its full allotment of subsidized rice.

12. The measure of corruption is obtained by comparing administrative data on the amount of rice distributed with survey data on the amount households actually received. A potential issue is that the survey data provide information only on whether a household obtained any subsidized rice, without naming the program or the number of times it did so. Olken (2006) therefore assumes that each household that received rice received its full monthly allotment and that the rice was obtained from the OPK.

13. The study incorporates data from various sources, including focus group interviews with households and community leaders on service quality and on local institutions, data on service coverage and administration, and a household survey that included information on participation in local associations and the use of specific services.

14. The study uses census data from 155 villages. The villages are a random subset of all the villages in which an NGO, the National Rural Support Program, was active. The National Rural Support Program is funded through the Pakistan Poverty Alleviation Fund, a World Bank–supported community-driven development program.

15. See chapter 6 for more on deliberative councils and their role in resource allocation.

16. The inputs provided were sufficient to cultivate at least 3.5 acres of land.

17. The control group was generated by randomizing the order in which groups entered the program.

18. To obtain representative measures of community poverty and inequality, Araujo and others (2008) use poverty mapping techniques to combine household and census data. They then combine these with administrative data on project type and cost at the community level.

19. Redistricting could also create new constituencies of swing voters, allowing politicians to better target communities whose electoral choices could be influenced by the provision of public goods (Lindbeck and Weibull 1987; Dixit and Londregan 1996; Persson and Tabellini 2001). The swing voter is theorized to be closest to the center of the political spectrum. There is empirical support for the swing voter model in both developed and developing countries. Levitt and Snyder (1997) show that in the United States, government spending increases the incumbent's vote share in congressional elections. Sorribas-Navarro and Sole-Olle (2008) confirm this result in national elections in Spain. Dahlberg and Johansson (2002) find that incumbent governments in Sweden distributed temporary grants for ecologically sustainable development programs to regions with more swing voters.

20. Bolsa Escola gives conditional cash transfers to poor mothers of school-age children if the children attend school on a regular basis. Municipalities were allocated a fixed number of stipends and were responsible for identifying beneficiary children. By design, households with a monthly per capita income of less than R$90 (about $40) were eligible. They were offered a transfer of R$15 per child, up to a maximum of R$45 per household.

21. Selection is likely to be important, as almost half of eligible children were left out of the program because of limits on stipends at the municipality level. Beneficiary children had an initial dropout rate that was less than a third the dropout rate of nonbeneficiaries. The authors deal with this problem by estimating the treatment effect after controlling for child fixed-effects and by allowing children with a different pretreatment drop-out status to have different year effects. Identification is then based on a comparison of the change in dropout levels between treated children and their comparable untreated counterparts.

22. Program implementation varied greatly across municipalities, despite clear eligibility rules at the federal level. Implementation processes varied, for example, in the location at which children were registered, the manner in which the school attendance conditionality was monitored, and the extent to which program coordinators were involved in verifying compliance. Much of this variation appears to be tied to whether the municipality was led by a first-term or second-term mayor.

23. In his study of Indonesia's Urban Poverty Project, Fritzen (2007) finds that electoral incentives induced more pro-poor actions by elected members of community development boards, which are responsible for selecting and managing all activities funded by the project. A concern with this study is that the key variables used to determine elite capture are perceptions of the board members whose behavior was being assessed, making any

inference difficult. The data on perceptions are also aggregated into scores in a somewhat obscure manner.

24. State judiciary branches are assigned only to the most populous county among contiguous counties forming a judiciary district. Counties with nearly similar populations but without a local judicial presence serve as the counterfactual case.

25. Ferraz and Finan (2011) also find that the presence of a judge reduces corruption among second-term mayors. Litschig and Zamboni (2007) are unable to find evidence of any impact of mayoral incumbency on corruption levels. However, their strategy makes their results not directly comparable to the studies by Ferraz and Finan (2008, 2011).

26. A comprehensive review of the case study evidence on civil society engagement in reducing corruption (Grimes 2008) finds that community efforts at monitoring and sanctioning corrupt practices have bite only when there is a strong and engaged advocate at the center. In the absence of such conditions, civil society efforts are able to succeed in only a limited way, largely by inducing resignations through naming and shaming and through protests to raise awareness.

References

Acemoglu, D., and T. Verdier. 2000. "The Choice between Market Failures and Corruption." *American Economic Review* 90(1): 194–211.

Ades, A., and R. Di Tella. 1999. "Rents, Competition, and Corruption." *American Economic Review* 89(4): 982–93.

Ahrend, R. 2002. "Press Freedom, Human Capital, and Corruption." DELTA Working Paper Series 36, Ecole Normale Supérieure, Paris.

Ansolabehere, S., A. Gerber, and J. M. Snyder Jr. 2002. "Equal Votes, Equal Money: Court-Ordered Redistricting and Public Expenditures in the American States." *American Political Science Review* 96(4): 767–77.

Araujo, M. C., F. H. G. Ferreira, P. Lanjouw, and B. Özler. 2008. "Local Inequality and Project Choice: Theory and Evidence from Ecuador." *Journal of Public Economics* 92(5–6): 1022–46.

Arcand, J.-L., and L. Bassole. 2008. "Does Community Driven Development Work? Evidence from Senegal." CERDI-CNRS, Université d'Auvergne, France.

Arcand, J.-L., and M. Fafchamps. 2012. "Matching in Community-Based Organizations." *Journal of Development Economics* 98(2): 203–19.

Baird, S., C. McIntosh, and B. Özler. 2009. *The Squeaky Wheels Get the Grease: Applications and Targeting in Tanzania's Social Action Fund.* World Bank, Washington, DC.

Bardhan, P. 2002. "Decentralization of Governance and Development." *Journal of Economic Perspectives* 16(4): 185–205.

Bardhan, P., and D. Mookherjee. 2006a. "Decentralization, Corruption, and Government Accountability." In *International Handbook on the Economics of Corruption,* ed. S. Rose-Ackerman. Cheltenham, United Kingdom: Edward Elgar.

―――. 2006b. "Pro-poor Targeting and Accountability of Local Governments in West Bengal." *Journal of Development Economics* 79(2): 303–327

―――. Forthcoming. "Land Reform and Farm Productivity in West Bengal." *American Economic Journal, Applied Economics.*

Bardhan, P., D. Mookherjee, and M. P. Torrado. 2010. "Impact of Political Reservations in West Bengal Local Governments on Anti-Poverty Targeting." *Journal of Globalization and Development* 1(1): 1–34.

Barro, R. 1973. "The Control of Politicians: An Economic Model." *Public Choice* 14: 19–42.

Besley, T., and R. Burgess. 2002. "The Political Economy of Government Responsiveness: Theory and Evidence from India." *Quarterly Journal of Economics* 117(4): 1415–51.

Besley, T., and A. Case. 1995. "Does Electoral Accountability Affect Economic Policy Choices? Evidence from Gubernatorial Term Limits." *Quarterly Journal of Economics* 110(3): 769–98.

Besley, T., R. Pande, and V. Rao. 2005. "Participatory Democracy in Action: Survey Evidence from South Rural India." *Journal of the European Economic Association* 3(2–3): 648–57.

―――. 2007. "Just Rewards? Local Politics and Public Resource Allocation in South India." LSE, STICERD Research Paper DEDPS49, Suntory and Toyota International Centres for Economics and Related Disciplines, Lond School of Economies, London.

Besley, T., and A. Prat. 2006. "Handcuffs for the Grabbing Hand? Media Capture and Government Accountability." *American Economic Review* 96(3): 720–36.

Bjorkman, M. 2006, "Does Money Matter for Student Performance? Evidence from a Grant Program in Uganda." Working Paper 326, Innocenzo Gasparini Institute for Economic Research (IGIER), Universitá Bocconi, Milan.

Bjornskov, C. 2003. "Corruption and Social Capital." Working Paper 03-13, Aarhus School of Business, Aarhus, Germany.

Bobonis, G. J., L. Camara-Fuertes, and R. Schwabe. 2011. "The Dynamic Effects of Information on Political Corruption: Theory and Evidence from Puerto Rico." Working Paper 428, Department of Economics, University of Toronto, Toronto, ON.

Bratton, M., and N. Van de Walle. 1997. *Democratic Experiments in Africa.* Cambridge, U.K.: Cambridge University Press.

Brollo, F. 2009. "Who Is Punishing Corrupt Politicians—Voters or the Central Government? Evidence from the Brazilian Anti-Corruption Program." Institute for Economic Development Working Paper dp-168, Department of Economics, Boston University, Boston.

Brunetti, A., and B. Weder. 2003. "A Free Press Is Bad News for Corruption." *Journal of Public Economics* 87(7–8): 1801–24.

Camacho, A., and E. Conover. 2011. "Manipulation of Social Program Eligibility." *American Economic Journal-Economic Policy* 3(2): 41–65.

Campante, F. R., D. Chor, and Q. Do. 2009. "Instability and the Incentives for Corruption." *Economics and Politics* 21(1): 42–92.

Carbonara, E. 2000. "Corruption and Decentralisation." Dipartimento di Scienze Economiche, Working Paper 342/83, University of Bologna, Italy.

Case, A. 2001. "Election Goals and Income Redistribution: Recent Evidence from Albania." *European Economic Review* 45(3): 405–23.

Conning, J., and M. Kevane. 2002. "Community-Based Targeting Mechanisms for Social Safety Nets: A Critical Review." *World Development* 30(3): 375–94.

Cox, G. W., and M. D. McCubbins. 1986. "Electoral-Politics as a Redistributive Game." *Journal of Politics* 48(2): 370–89.

Dahlberg, M., and E. Johansson. 2002. "On the Vote-Purchasing Behavior of Incumbent Governments." *American Political Science Review* 96(1): 27–40.

Dasgupta, A., and V. A. Beard. 2007. "Community Driven Development, Collective Action and Elite Capture in Indonesia." *Development and Change* 38(2): 229–49.

De Janvry, A., F. Finan, and E. Sadoulet. Forthcoming. "Local Electoral Incentives and Decentralized Program Performance." *Review of Economics and Statistics.*

De Janvry, A., H. Nakagawa, and E. Sadoulet. 2009. "Pro-Poor Targeting and Electoral Rewards in Decentralizing to Communities the Provision of Local Public Goods in Rural Zambia." University of California, Berkeley.

Di Tella, R., and E. Schargrodsky. 2003. "The Role of Wages and Auditing During a Crackdown on Corruption in the City of Buenos Aires." *Journal of Law and Economics* 46(1): 269–92.

Dixit, A., and J. Londregan. 1996. "The Determinants of Success of Special Interests in Redistributive Politics." *Journal of Politics* 58(4): 1132–55.

Djankov, S., C. McLeish, T. Nenova, and A. Shleifer. 2003. "Who Owns the Media?" *Journal of Law and Economics* 46(2): 341–81.

Dollar, D., R. Fisman, and R. Gatti. 2001. "Are Women Really the 'Fairer' Sex? Corruption and Women in Government." *Journal of Economic Behavior and Organization* 46(4): 423–29.

Donchev, D., and G. Ujhelyi. 2009. "What Do Corruption Indices Measure?" Department of Economics, University of Houston, Houston, TX.

Drèze, J., and A. Sen, eds. 1990. *The Political Economy of Hunger: Entitlement and Well-Being, World Institute for Development Economics Research Studies in Development Economics vol. 1.* Oxford: Oxford University Press.

Estache, A., and S. Sinha. 1995. "Does Decentralization Increase Spending on Public Infrastructure?" Policy Research Working Paper 1457, World Bank, Washington, DC.

Evans, P. B., and J. E. Rauch. 2000. "Bureaucratic Structure and Bureaucratic Performance in Less Developed Countries." *Journal of Public Economics* 75(1): 49–71.

Faguet, J. P. 2004. "Does Decentralization Increase Government Responsiveness to Local Needs? Evidence from Bolivia." *Journal of Public Economics* 88(3–4): 867–93.

Fan, C. S., C. Lin, and D. Treisman. 2009. "Political Decentralization and Corruption: Evidence from around the World." *Journal of Public Economics* 93(1–2): 14–34.

Ferejohn, J. 1986. "Incumbent Performance and Electoral Control." *Public Choice* 50: 5–25.

Ferraz C. and F. Finan. 2008. "Exposing Corrupt Politicians: The Effects of Brazil's Publicly Released Audits on Electoral Outcomes." *Quarterly Journal of Economics* 123(2): 703–45.

———. 2011. "Electoral Accountability and Corruption: Evidence from the Audits of Local Governments." *American Economic Review* 101(4): 1274–311.

Finan, F. 2004. "Political Patronage and Local Development: A Brazilian Case Study." Working Paper, Department of Agricultural and Resource Economics, University of California, Berkeley.

Fisman, R., and R. Gatti. 2002a. "Decentralization and Corruption: Evidence across Countries." *Journal of Public Economics* 83(3): 325–45.

———. 2002b. "Decentralization and Corruption: Evidence from U.S. Federal Transfer Programs." *Public Choice* 113(1–2): 25–35.

Foster, A., and M. Rosenzweig. 2004. "Democratization and the Distribution of Local Public Goods in a Poor Rural Economy." Working Paper 01-056, Penn Institute for Economic Research, University of Pennsylvania, Philadelphia.

Fox, J. 1994. "The Difficult Transition from Clientelism to Citizenship: Lessons from Mexico." *World Politics* 46(2): 151–84.

Francken, N., B. Minten, and J. F. M. Swinnen. 2009. "Media, Monitoring, and Capture of Public Funds: Evidence from Madagascar." *World Development* 37(1): 242–55.

Fritzen, S. A. 2007. "Can the Design of Community-Driven Development Reduce the Risk of Elite Capture? Evidence from Indonesia." *World Development* 35(8): 1359–75.

Galasso, E., and M. Ravallion. 2005. "Decentralized Targeting of an Antipoverty Program." *Journal of Public Economics* 89(4): 705–27

Glaeser, E. L., R. La Porta, F. Lopez-de-Silanes, and A. Schleifer. 2004. "Do Institutions Cause Growth?" *Journal of Economic Growth* 9(3): 271–303.

Grimes, M. 2008. "The Conditions of Successful Civil Society Involvement in Combating Corruption: A Survey of Case Study Evidence." QoG Working Paper 22: 21, Department of Political Science, University of Gothenburg, Sweden.

Grootaert, C., G. T. Oh, and A. Swamy. 2002. "Social Capital, Household Welfare and Poverty in Burkina Faso." *Journal of African Economies* 11(1): 4–38.

Gugerty, M. K., and M. Kremer. 2008. "Outside Funding and the Dynamics of Participation in Community Associations." *American Journal of Political Science* 52(3): 585–602

Henderson, V. J., and A. Kuncoro. 2011. "Corruption and Local Democratization in Indonesia: The Role of Islamic Parties." *Journal of Development Economics* 24(2): 164–80.

Humphreys, M., W. A. Masters, and M. E. Sandbu. 2006. "The Role of Leaders in Democratic Deliberations: Results from a Field Experiment in São Tomé and Principe." *World Politics* 58(4): 583–622.

Huntington, S. P. 1968. *Political Order in Changing Societies.* New Haven, CT: Yale University Press.

Kaufmann, D., and A. Kraay. 2002. "Growth without Governance." *Economia: Journal of the Latin American and Caribbean Economic Association* 3(1): 169–215.

Khemani, S., and W. Wane. 2008. "Populist Fiscal Policy." Policy Research Working Paper 4762, World Bank, Washington, DC.

La Porta, R., F. Lopez-de-Silanes, A. Shleifer, and R. Vishny. 1999. "The Quality of Government." *Journal of Law Economics & Organization* 15(1): 222–79.

Labonne, J., and R. S. Chase. 2009. "Who Is at the Wheel When Communities Drive Development? Evidence from the Philippines." *World Development* 37(1): 219–31.

Leite, C., and J. Weidmann. 1999. "Does Mother Nature Corrupt? Natural Resources, Corruption, and Economic Growth." IMF Working Paper 99/85, International Monetary Fund, Washington, DC.

Levitt, S. D., and J. M. Snyder. 1997. "The Impact of Federal Spending on House Election Outcomes." *Journal of Political Economy* 105(1): 30–53.

Lindbeck, A., and J. Weibull. 1987. "Balanced Budget Redistribution as the Outcome of Political Competition." *Public Choice* 52: 273–97.

List, J. A., and D. M. Sturm. 2006. "How Elections Matter: Theory and Evidence from Environmental Policy." *Quarterly Journal of Economics* 121(4): 1249–81.

Litschig, S., and Y. Zamboni. 2007. "The Effect of Judicial Institutions on Local Governance and Corruption." Discussion Paper 0607-15, Department of Economics, Columbia University, New York.

Manacorda, M., E. Miguel, and A. Vigorito. 2011. "Government Transfers and Political Support." *American Economic Journal: Applied Economics* 3(3): 1–28.

Manor, J. 1999. *The Political Economy of Democratic Decentralization.* Washington, DC: World Bank.

Mansuri, G. 2012a. "Bottom Up or Top Down; Participation and the Provision of Local Public Goods." World Bank, Poverty Reduction and Economic Management, Washington, DC.

———. 2012b. "Harnessing Community: Assortative Matching in Participatory Community Organizations." World Bank, Poverty Reduction and Economic Management, Washington, DC.

Markussen, T. 2006. "Inequality and Party Capture: Theory and Evidence from South India." Discussion Paper 10-26, Department of Economics, University of Copenhagen, Copenhagen, Denmark.

Mauro, P. 1995. "Corruption and Growth." *Quarterly Journal of Economics* 110(3): 681–712.

Mendez, F., and F. Sepulveda. 2010. "What Do We Talk about When We Talk about Corruption?" *Journal of Law, Economics & Organization* 26(3): 493–514.

Miguel, E., and F. Zaidi. 2003. "Do Politicians Reward Their Supporters? Public Spending and Incumbency Advantage in Ghana." University of California, Berkeley.

Mohan, G., and K. Stokke. 2000. "Participatory Development and Empowerment: The Dangers of Localism." *Third World Quarterly* 21(2): 247–68.

Mookherjee, D. 1997. "Incentive Reforms in Developing Country Bureaucracies Lessons from Tax Administration." Paper prepared for the Annual Bank Conference on Development Economics, World Bank, Washington, DC.

Mullainathan, S., and A. Shleifer. 2002. "Media Bias." NBER Working Paper 9295, National Bureau of Economic Research, Cambridge, MA.

Murphy, W. 1990. "Creating the Appearance of Consensus in Mende Political Discourse." *American Anthropologist* 92(1): 24–41.

Myerson, R. B. 1993. "Effectiveness of Electoral Systems for Reducing Government Corruption: A Game-Theoretic Analysis." *Games and Economic Behavior* 5(1): 118–32.

O'Donnell, G. 1993. "On the State, Democratization and Some Conceptual Problems (A Latin American View with Glances at Some Post-Communist Countries)." *World Development* 21(8): 1355–69.

Olken, B. 2006. "Corruption and the Costs of Redistribution: Micro Evidence from Indonesia." *Journal of Public Economics* 90(4–5): 853–70.

———. 2007. "Monitoring Corruption: Evidence from a Field Experiment in Indonesia." *Journal of Political Economy* 115(2): 200–49.

Olson, M. 1993. "Dictatorship, Democracy, and Development." *American Political Science Review* 87(3):567–76.

Paldam, M., and T. Svendsen. 2002. "Missing Social Capital and the Transition in Eastern Europe." *Journal for Institutional Innovation, Development and Transition* 5: 21–34.

Persson, T., G. Roland, and G. Tabellini. 1997. "Separation of Powers and Political Accountability." *Quarterly Journal of Economics* 112(4): 1163–202.

Persson, T., and G. Tabellini. 2000. *Political Economics: Explaining Economic Policy.* Cambridge, MA: MIT Press.

———. 2001. "Political Institutions and Policy Outcomes: What Are the Stylized Facts?" CESifo Working Paper 459, CESifo Group, Munich.

Platteau, J.-P., and F. Gaspart. 2003. "The Risk of Resource Misappropriation in Community-Driven Development." *World Development* 31(10): 1687–703.

Pradhan, M., V. Rao, and C. Rosenberg. 2009. *The Impact of the Community Level Activities of the Second Urban Poverty Project.* World Bank, Washington, DC.

Putnam, R. 1993. *Making Democracy Work: Civic Traditions in Modern Italy.* Princeton, NJ: Princeton University Press.

Rao, V., and A. M. Ibanez. 2005. "The Social Impact of Social Funds in Jamaica: A 'Participatory Econometric' Analysis of Targeting, Collective Action, and Participation in Community-Driven Development." *Journal of Development Studies* 41(5): 788–838.

Reinikka, R., and J. Svensson. 2004. "Local Capture: Evidence from a Central Government Transfer Program in Uganda." *Quarterly Journal of Economics* 119(2): 679–705.

———. 2005. "Fighting Corruption to Improve Schooling: Evidence from a Newspaper Campaign in Uganda." *Journal of the European Economic Association* 3(2–3): 259–67.

———. 2007. "The Returns from Reducing Corruption: Evidence from Education in Uganda." CEPR Discussion Paper 6363, Center for Economic Policy and Research, London.

Rodriguez-Chamussy, L. 2009. "Local Electoral Rewards from Centralized Social Programs: Are Mayors Getting the Credit?" Department of Agricultural and Resources Economics, University of California, Berkeley.

Rose-Ackerman, S. 2008. "Corruption and Government." *International Peacekeeping* 15(3): 328–43.

Samuels, D., and R. Snyder. 2001. "The Value of a Vote: Malapportionment in Comparative Perspective." *British Journal of Political Science* 31(4): 651–71.

Schady, N. R. 2000. "The Political Economy of Expenditures by the Peruvian Social Fund (FONCODES), 1991–95." *American Political Science Review* 94(2): 289–304.

Shankar, S., R. Gaiha, and R. Jha. 2010. "Information and Corruption: The National Rural Employment Guarantee Scheme in India." ASARC Working Paper 32-32, Australia South Asia Research Centre, Australian National University, Canberra.

Shleifer, A., and R. W. Vishny. 1993. "Corruption." *Quarterly Journal of Economics* 108(3): 599–617.

Snyder, R. 1999. "After Neoliberalism: The Politics of Reregulation in Mexico." *World Politics* 51(2): 173–204.

Sorribas-Navarro, P., and A. Sole-Olle. 2008. "The Effects of Partisan Alignment on the Allocation of Intergovernmental Transfers. Differences-in-Differences Estimates for Spain." *Journal of Public Economics* 92(12): 2302–19.

Stapenhurst, R. 2000. *The Media's Role in Curbing Corruption*. Washington, DC: World Bank Institute.

Stromberg, D. 2004a. "Mass Media Competition, Political Competition, and Public Policy." *Review of Economic Studies* 71(1): 265–84.

———. 2004b. "Radio's Impact on Public Spending." *Quarterly Journal of Economics* 119(1): 189–221.

Swamy, A., S. Knack, Y. Lee, and O. Azfar, 2000. "Gender and Corruption." CDE Working Paper Series, Center for Development Economics, Williams College, Williamstown, MA.

Treisman, D. 2000. "The Causes of Corruption: A Cross-National Study." *Journal of Public Economics* 76(3): 399–457.

———. 2007. "What Have We Learned about the Causes of Corruption from Ten Years of Cross-National Empirical Research?" *Annual Review of Political Science* 10(June): 211–44.

Waller, C. J., T. Verdier, and R. Gardner. 2002. "Corruption: Top Down or Bottom Up?" *Economic Inquiry* 40(4): 688–703.

White, H. 2002. "Social Funds: A Review of the Issues." *Journal of International Development* 14(5): 605–10.

World Bank. 2004. *World Development Report 2004: Making Services Work for Poor People*. Washington, DC: World Bank.

You, J. S., and S. Khagram. 2005. "A Comparative Study of Inequality and Corruption." *American Sociological Review* 70(1): 136–57.

CHAPTER FIVE

Does Participation Improve
Development Outcomes?

MUCH OF THE IMPETUS FOR INVESTMENT IN PARTICIPATORY poverty reduction projects and decentralization efforts has come from the hope that greater civic engagement will lead to faster and more equitable development. In line with this notion, many countries have shifted the provision of basic public services to the local level, and there has been much greater emphasis on citizen engagement in service delivery through community health groups, school management committees, and similar groups. Common-pool resources are also increasingly managed more locally, and small-scale infrastructure is often provided through decentralized poverty reduction programs, social funds, and community-driven development projects. Community-based livelihood programs, which focus more directly on increasing income and employment, have also become an important component of large-scale poverty reduction programs.

This chapter assesses the extent to which this shift toward the local has enhanced the pace of development, increased equity in access to public programs, and improved the sustainability of development efforts. The first section reviews efforts to decentralize the identification of beneficiary households and communities for poverty reduction and social insurance programs. The second section reviews efforts to devolve the management of common-pool resources and summarizes the evidence for greater resource sustainability and equity. The third section examines local infrastructure delivered through participatory mechanisms. The fourth section reviews efforts to induce greater community oversight in the delivery of health and education services. The fifth section assesses the evidence on the poverty impacts of participatory projects. The last section sums up the broad lessons learned.

161

Identification of Beneficiaries

A common approach to evaluating the relative efficiency of alternative targeting mechanisms has been to compare leakage and undercoverage rates. Much of the literature focuses almost exclusively on leakage and the extent to which it reflects resource capture by elites.[1] Although this aspect of targeting is important, an exclusive focus on the identity of beneficiaries can draw attention away from what is ultimately of greatest interest: whether the poverty reduction objectives of targeted programs are achievable given the size and distribution of the budget (see Ravallion 2009b).

Participatory poverty reduction programs typically use a combination of targeting methods to identify beneficiary households and communities. When the government manages and implements programs, the center may allocate resources to subnational jurisdictions, using administrative criteria to satisfy broad political economy concerns, such as support to the poorest areas or the need to ensure horizontal equity. Local governments may then be required to identify the poor, or the most poorly served by public services, within their jurisdiction. Geographic and poverty targeting at higher levels is often combined with a demand-driven process at the community level to generate beneficiary lists for infrastructure projects. Community-driven development and social fund programs often do this by working with local nongovernmental organizations (NGOs) and community activists. Elected or selected local leaders are usually responsible for identifying beneficiaries when programs are implemented through local governments.

The process of beneficiary identification at the local level also varies substantially, both within and across projects, and is often left fuzzy. Critics worry that this leaves the process open to rent-seeking. One response to the problem has been to use poverty monitoring tools to select beneficiaries at the very local level.[2] The use of such tools is not without costs, however, as it devalues the relevance of information at the local level—precisely the level at which such information is likely to be most valuable. The evidence reviewed below sheds some light on this issue.

Participatory programs that invest in local public goods also rely on community and household self-selection. All social funds, for example, require community co-financing, with or without competition for funds. Communities as a whole, or specific community groups, must decide whether or not to submit a proposal for a project based on the

> The process of beneficiary identification at the local level varies substantially, both within and across projects, possibly leaving the process open to rent-seeking.

implied level of benefits and the cost of participation. The assumption for targeted social funds is that the level of benefits is too low to make participation advantageous for the better-off.

Co-financing has long been seen as a cornerstone of participatory development. It can be in the form of free or low-wage labor, cash, or materials. It is believed that community co-financing ensures community engagement in all aspects of the project, at construction and after, thereby ensuring that investments are sustainable. As the community, along with the government or donor agency, decides on the level of provision of the good or service, co-financing is sometimes seen as a lump-sum tax on public good provision.

However, many observers view co-financing as an egregious aspect of participatory projects, one that forces people with the least to either pay more for their development needs than the better-off do or to opt out and be excluded altogether from project benefits. Free labor provision by community members has even been compared with forced or *corvée* labor (see chapter 1).[3]

When communities compete for funds, with or without co-financing requirements, the overall targeting performance of projects also depends on the capacity of eligible communities to submit adequate proposals. Communities that have low capacity or cannot meet co-financing requirements are often unable to submit projects for consideration. Even the best-intentioned implementing agencies cannot prevent this type of initial exclusion: although the use of administrative criteria, such as the number of poor households served, can improve targeting among applicants, it cannot reverse exclusion in the pool of submitted projects.

Program conditions such as the resources allocated to building community capacity or the information available to potential beneficiaries can therefore determine who applies for benefits as well as who gets approved. Many community-based projects have remedial mechanisms that are intended to ensure that all eligible communities can submit feasible projects. Nonetheless, there is a pervasive concern in the literature about the extent to which better-off communities—communities with greater capacity, political networks, or wealth—are more likely to propose and win subprojects. This issue is addressed in the review that follows, as far as is possible, by examining the targeting strategy and its outcomes at different stages of the targeting process—that is, by looking at factors such as program reliance on administrative targeting, a

Many observers view co-financing—a cornerstone of participatory development projects—as an egregious tax on the poor.

There is a pervasive concern in the literature about the extent to which better-off communities are more likely to propose and win subprojects.

competitive fund allocation process, self-selection to determine eligibility, and the extent to which program participation entails costs such as co-financing or a challenging application process.

Central versus Local Targeting of Private Transfers

Some studies suggest that local co-financing requirements can exacerbate horizontal inequities, particularly when eligibility thresholds are also decentralized.

Most studies that have examined the relative targeting performance of the center versus local areas in assigning private benefits find support for more pro-poor targeting at the local level. However, the increase in targeting performance is small, with programs only mildly pro-poor on balance. Moreover, some evidence suggests that the local targeting of poor areas or households is substantially improved when the center provides stronger incentives for pro-poor targeting by local governments or implementing agencies, often by retaining control over key design features of the program, such as eligibility thresholds. Some studies suggest that local co-financing requirements can exacerbate horizontal inequities, particularly when eligibility thresholds are also decentralized.

Evidence from an Albanian economic support program (the Ndihme Ekonomika) indicates that local officials were able to target recipients better than the center could have done using proxy entitlement indicators (Alderman 2002). The program provided social assistance to some 20 percent of the population through a block grant to communes. Local officials determined eligibility and the amount of the transfer to beneficiary households.

Galasso and Ravallion (2005) find similar evidence for a decentralized poverty program in Bangladesh. The Food-for-Education program distributed fixed food rations to selected poor households conditional on their school-age children attending at least 85 percent of classes. The center was responsible for identifying eligible *union parishads*, the lowest level of local government. Villages in eligible *union parishads* were then made responsible for identifying program beneficiaries. The program was mildly pro-poor (slightly more poor than nonpoor households received rations). Although the targeting differential was small—the program achieved about one-fifth the maximum targeting differential—almost all of it occurred because beneficiaries were well targeted within villages.[4]

The center is often better at targeting poor communities than identifying poor households within such communities.

A series of other studies broadly supports these findings. Coady (2001) examines a large Mexican cash transfer program (Progresa), which selected poor households on the basis of census data without any community involvement. He finds some support for the center's ability to target eligible communities but, in line with other studies, finds that the center is far less able to identify poor households within targeted poor communities.

In their study of the Trabajar 2 program in Argentina, Ravallion (2000) and Jalan and Ravallion (2003) demonstrate the center's role in providing incentives for more pro-poor targeting by local governments. This World Bank–supported program, introduced in 1997, expanded an earlier workfare program, Trabajar 1, in order to provide an additional period of short-term work to poor households and to locate socially useful projects in poor areas. Under Trabajar 2, the central government allocated funds to the provinces, making an effort to provide more program funding to poorer provinces. Provincial governments then allocated funds to projects within the provinces. Local governments and NGOs proposed subprojects and bore their nonwage costs. The results show that self-targeting in the program worked well, with participants overwhelmingly drawn from among the poorest households. The studies also find some improvement in reaching poorer areas within provinces. About a third of the overall improvement came from better targeting of provinces; the rest came from better targeting of poor areas within provinces.[5]

However, a more recent assessment of the targeting performance of this program (Ronconi 2009) finds greater leakage and smaller income effects. It also finds some evidence that nontargeted beneficiaries were more politically connected.

A number of studies use data from rural India to examine whether participation in mandatory village assemblies (*gram sabhas*) called by elected village councils (*gram panchayats*) to discuss resource allocation decisions in the village improved the allocation of central transfer programs. These programs provide an array of government schemes, ranging from subsidized food through the public distribution system to housing schemes and free hospitalization to poor households. In collaboration with state government officials, through a census, the *gram panchayat* identifies households eligible to receive Below Poverty Line (BPL) cards. The list of BPL households, as well as the subsequent selection of beneficiaries for specific schemes, needs to be ratified at public *gram sabha* meetings. The Indian Planning Commission reports that there is a perception of significant mistargeting in the allocation of BPL cards.

Some evidence suggests that villages in India that hold a *gram sabha* do a better job of targeting the most disadvantaged.

Besley, Pande, and Rao (2005, 2007) find that villages that hold a *gram sabha* do a better job of targeting BPL cards to the most disadvantaged villagers. People without any formal schooling, for example, fare substantially better in villages that hold *gram sabhas*. However, not all villages hold such meetings, and among those that do, only about a fifth discuss beneficiary selection for public programs. Consequently, most local politicians in their sample (87 percent of the 540 surveyed) believed that they, rather than the *gram sabha*, were responsible for benefit allocation decisions.

Bardhan and others (2008) also find that villages that had greater *gram sabha* participation rates were more pro-poor in their allocation of benefits. Although they are careful to point out that this finding does not provide evidence of a causal impact of *gram sabha* meetings on targeting, they argue that it is consistent with the hypothesis that village meetings "formed a channel of accountability of *gram panchayats* to poor and low caste groups" (p. 7). Besley, Pande, and Rao (2007) also find support for the disciplinary effect of the *gram sabha* on capture. They show that the odds of a politician's household receiving a BPL card were lower in villages in which a *gram sabha* was held.

These results are only suggestive, as the design of these studies does not allow the authors to determine why some villages hold meetings and others do not. Several studies using data from India have tried to identify village characteristics that predict the holding of *gram sabhas* as well as household characteristics associated with participation. Bardhan and others (2008) find that participation rates were higher in villages in which the proportion of landless and scheduled caste households was lower. Besley, Pande, and Rao (2007) find higher participation rates for the landless and low caste in villages with higher average levels of education.

Kumar (2007) looks at the effect of community participation on the targeting of BPL cards in India. Her data come from the state of Madhya Pradesh, where a participatory development project, the District Poverty Initiatives Project (DPIP), was initiated in 2001. She assesses the extent to which DPIP, which aims to build political awareness and confidence among the disadvantaged, affects the allocation of BPL cards to eligible households. Her results indicate that the targeting of BPL cards is indeed more pro-poor in DPIP villages, where a greater fraction of BPL cardholders are landless and belong to lower castes. (See also the discussion in chapter 6.)

Ravallion (2009a) examines the relationship between central and local targeting, using data from the implementation of Di Bao, a decentralized urban poverty reduction program in China. The program aims to provide all urban households with a transfer payment sufficient to bring their incomes up to a predetermined poverty line. The center set the guidelines and provided about 60 percent of the program's costs on average, making some effort to bear a larger share of the cost in poorer provinces.[6] Municipalities were allowed to set the eligibility threshold for benefits and identify beneficiaries.

The question of interest is whether poorer municipalities had incentives under these conditions to understate their poverty problems by setting lower thresholds. The analysis shows that poorer cities did indeed set lower poverty lines and thus had lower participation rates. As a result, equally poor families ended up with very different levels of access to the program, with the poor in the poorest cities typically faring worst. This problem greatly diminished the program's ability to reach the poor.

An important dimension of inducing greater civic engagement in the identification of beneficiaries is that local perceptions of need may not coincide with the ways the center determines program eligibility. This divergence in perceptions may account for some of the perceived leakage in transfer programs when such programs are assessed using means tests or other information that external agents can observe. The literature in this area is sparse, but the evidence suggests that local determination of need may take into account variables not observed by the center, possibly creating a divergence in notions of eligibility between the center and localities.

> Local determination of need may take into account variables not observed by the center.

In a case study of famine relief efforts in Southern Sudan, Harragin (2004) finds that local ideas of how food should be distributed differed from the ideas of aid workers, resulting in a poorly designed project. Ethnographic and case study evidence supports the view that the mechanisms used to identify beneficiaries are crucial in determining how pro-poor decentralized targeting will be, especially when community members have unequal access to project implementers.

> The mechanisms used to identify beneficiaries are crucial in determining how pro-poor decentralized targeting will be, especially when community members have unequal access to project implementers.

Alatas and others (2012) report on a field experiment designed to understand how community methods fare relative to a proxy means test in targeting resources to the poor.[7] They collected proxy means test information for all households in all sample villages, randomly varying its use in assigning eligibility. In a third of sample villages, only the proxy means test was used to assign eligibility; in another third, beneficiaries were selected through a community ranking exercise; in another third, the proxy means test was used to determine eligibility of people identified by the community. The authors find very little support for the benefits of community targeting over the proxy means test when poverty status is measured based on per capita expenditures. This finding is somewhat surprising given the substantial leakage and exclusion that can occur under even the best-designed proxy means test. One would expect that in very small communities like the ones the authors worked with, access to relevant information on recent shocks might at least improve coverage of the eligible based on per capita consumption.

The authors also find no evidence that meetings confined to the village elite produced worse targeting outcomes than meetings that included a more representative group. Furthermore, households more closely connected to elites were not more likely to benefit when meetings were confined to elites. Despite poorer targeting outcomes, community targeting resulted in higher satisfaction levels.

Alatas and others (2012) use data on poverty perceptions to make sense of these results. They check the correlation of a household's subjective ranking of itself and other households against rankings from the community targeting exercise and the proxy means test. They find a higher correlation of self-perception with the rankings obtained under community targeting. Taken together, they argue, their results suggest that communities employ a concept of poverty that is different from per capita expenditure and that this difference explains the ostensibly worse performance of community targeting. As communities use different criteria to ascribe poverty status, they contend, it is understandable that a strategy that valorizes their preferences yields greater satisfaction levels.

Gugerty and Kremer (2006) also find that the women's groups they study in Kenya reported more satisfaction with group leadership. There was little improvement in objective measures of group activity, however, and the women did not have better attendance rates than the comparison groups.

Although these results are interesting, it is difficult to know how to assess their validity. In the study by Alatas and others (2012), for example, the treatment provided a one-time transfer that was a little less than a third of the monthly transfer received by eligible households under the Indonesian government's main transfer program, the Bantuan Langsung Tunai (BLT), potentially limiting the gains from capture. Equally important, aware that this was a small study and distinct from

> Meetings confined to the village elite may not produce worse targeting outcomes than meetings that include a more representative group.

the BLT, village elites and government administrators may have found it opportune to demonstrate transparency. The careful design of the community-based targeting meeting, along with the very small and relatively homogeneous subvillages or neighborhoods that were selected for the study, may also have affected the results. Much of the evidence from studies of large-scale transfer programs, including programs in Indonesia, points to substantial heterogeneity in the manner in which community input is solicited and to significant capture of funds (see chapter 4).

Much of the evidence from studies of large-scale transfer programs points to substantial heterogeneity in the manner in which community input is solicited and to significant capture of funds.

Central versus Local Targeting of Public Goods

Several studies of social funds find pro-poor geographic targeting by the center in allocating local public goods. Some, however, find weaker central capacity to target the poor within eligible areas. Chase and Sherburne-Benz (2001) and Pradhan and Rawlings (2002), for example, find that investments made under the Zambia social fund (ZAMSIF) and the Nicaragua social fund were generally well targeted to both poor communities and poor households. In Zambia, however, targeting was effective only in rural communities; in urban areas, better-off communities and households were selected. A review of social fund projects by the World Bank's Independent Evaluation Group (2002) also finds this bias. Araujo and others (2008) find that geographic targeting at the level of the community appears to have worked well in Ecuador's social fund, with poorer communities more likely to be selected for subproject funding.

Paxson and Schady (2002) assess the poverty targeting of the Peruvian social fund using district-level data on expenditures and poverty. They find that the fund, which emphasized geographic targeting, reached the poorest districts but not the poorest households in those districts: better-off households were slightly more likely than poor households to benefit. Using propensity score matching techniques, Chase (2002) finds similar results in Armenia. Although the social fund was successful in targeting communities with the poorest infrastructure, these communities were not always among the poorest, and the fund was slightly regressive in targeting households in rural areas.

Several studies of social funds find pro-poor geographic targeting by the center . . .

De Janvry, Nakagawa, and Sadoulet (2009) explore the relationship between decentralization and pro-poor targeting within districts under the third phase of ZAMSIF. Districts were grouped into three categories

. . . but some find weaker central capacity to target the poor within eligible areas.

based on administrative capacity. In districts with the lowest capacity, targeting remained fully centralized. Districts with greater capacity were given progressively more control over resources, culminating in full decentralization of decision making for some.

Decentralization did not affect the allocation of funds across districts, but it did affect a district's capacity to allocate resources across its wards. Using two measures of welfare (school enrollment and an index of housing conditions), the authors find that the center's targeting of districts was not progressive—and was even somewhat regressive in some phases. In contrast, the within-district targeting of wards became more progressive over time in all districts, especially districts given greater discretion. A caveat regarding these results is that the districts that had greater discretion over resource allocation decisions also had greater managerial capacity. It is unclear, therefore, whether more progressive targeting in these districts reflected greater decentralization or greater capacity. Interestingly, within-district effects in the higher-capacity districts were driven almost entirely by wards with high literacy levels.

Baird, McIntosh, and Özler (2009) focus on the process by which Tanzania's Social Action Fund (TASAF) allocated subprojects within districts. Using administrative data on project submission and approval, they find that the demand-driven application process was strongly regressive, with many more applications originating from wealthier and more literate districts. The political affiliation of ward and district representatives also influenced the allocation of TASAF money. Wards that were aligned with the party in power were significantly more likely to apply; wards in which both the ward and the district representatives were from the opposition party were significantly less likely to apply. Ironically, a strongly pro-poor allocation of district-level budgets from the center managed to undo much of this regressivity in applications, leaving a mildly pro-poor program overall, although the poverty reduction objectives of the center were considerably attenuated.

Labonne and Chase's (2009) work on the KALAHI-CIDSS project in the Philippines also provides a good example of the tension between pro-poor targeting and a competitive demand-driven process of subproject elicitation. As in other community-driven development and social fund projects, facilitators in KALAHI-CIDSS help communities identify priorities and prepare and submit proposals. After review at a municipal-level meeting, a subset of proposed projects is funded.

A study in Tanzania finds that demand-driven application processes were strongly regressive.

In the study, respondents were asked to name the three most pressing issues in the village before any project activities got under way. Combining these data with administrative data on projects proposed and accepted, the authors assessed whether the preferences of specific groups mattered at the project proposal and acceptance stage. Consistent with other studies, they find that the competitive subproject proposal and approval process led to fewer applications from poorer and less politically connected villages. In addition, while the village leader's preferences on both project type and location appeared to be influential in determining which projects were put forward, these preferences were much less likely to sway the outcome at the municipal level. In fact, as in Tanzania, municipal allocation rules undid some of the regressivity in proposed projects. Given the initial bias in proposed projects, however, municipal allocation rules had limited success, and funded proposals remained well aligned with the village leader's preferences. The influence of the village leader was much greater in villages with greater wealth inequality. Controlling for poverty, more unequal villages were also more likely to have their projects approved, indicating that local leaders in more unequal villages may also exercise greater influence over the inter-village approval process.

As discussed above, China's Di Bao program (Ravallion 2009a) suggests that the poorest communities may underparticipate or self-select out of programs that require them to foot part of the bill for private benefits or local public goods. This tendency may partly account for the lack of applications from poorer districts and wards in the TASAF program. A key similarity between the two programs is that eligibility criteria are decentralized and a portion of the funds come from the center, which progressively targets poorer localities (districts in TASAF and municipalities in Di Bao). Under TASAF, participation by poorer districts is depressed at the application stage, whereas under Di Bao, municipalities have an incentive to depress their participation rates in the program in the face of budget constraints. In both cases, the net effect is that despite progressive targeting from the center, the overall poverty impact of the program is attenuated. Chase (2002) also argues that mandatory community contributions in the Armenia Social Fund may have led to a selection bias against the poorest communities, which are often unwilling or unable to contribute.

In the TASAF and ZAMSIF studies, weak community capacity also appears to be a deterrent to participation. Unlike the Di Bao program,

> The poorest communities may underparticipate or self-select out of programs that require them to foot part of the bill for private benefits or local public goods.

wealthier districts in TASAF or KALAHI-CIDSS were also not able to target their own poor better than poorer districts, suggesting greater capture of program benefits by the relatively well off.

Sustainable Management of Common-Pool Resources

Institutions for local resource governance have increased substantially over the past two decades . . .

Local institutions for resource governance have increased substantially over the past two decades, at least in numbers, as national governments have created new institutional arrangements to engage local populations in the governance of natural resources (Stern, Dietz, and Ostrom 2003). Estimates place the share of the world's natural forests officially managed with some form of popular participation at about 12 percent (Sunderlin, Hatcher, and Liddle 2008)—and this figure probably significantly underestimates the actual figure, as it excludes forests that are officially managed by the state but actually managed by local communities and private individuals.

. . . accompanied by a more enfranchising view of decentralized natural resource management, which represents a major shift from the past.

This expansion has been accompanied by a more enfranchising view of decentralized natural resource management, which represents a major shift from the past. Historically, popular participation in the management of natural resources was closely associated with colonial efforts to extend control over local resources. In the case of forests, an expansion in local participation under colonial rule was precipitated by industrialization and higher prices for timber and other forest products. In the case of water for irrigation, local participation increased when colonial governments made large investments in irrigation infrastructure, which also created greater management needs.[8] Many newly independent nations chose to reverse this process, initially, by recentralizing and consolidating power at the center.

Decentralization efforts around natural resource management gained momentum in development policy circles only in the 1970s, largely under outside pressure from international aid organizations and donors, motivated by both concerns about the accountability of central governments and recognition of resource depletion and climate change.[9] By the 1980s, decentralized natural resource management had come to be associated with the broader project of poverty reduction[10] and the building of democratic local institutions (Ribot, Lund, and Treue 2010).[11]

The push for localizing natural resource management has thus paralleled the broader move toward participatory development over the past two decades. A large body of literature, based largely on case studies, has been extremely influential in this process. It has established the pervasive presence of local institutions in the management of natural resources, with or without state support, and demonstrated the viability of community management as an alternative to either privatization or management by a centralized state bureaucracy.[12]

In practice, the local management of common-pool resources takes many institutional forms, and there is often substantial divergence between formal and de facto community control as well as the types of decision making transferred to local governments or user communities. The extent and type of central government involvement also varies a great deal with the value placed on the resource. The scale of national and international interest in a common-pool resource also depends on the size of the externality it creates. With forests, the interests of the global community can also be relevant; they can determine the form of management as well as the allocation of benefits. In contrast, in the case of irrigation water or pastures, the main concerns are likely to be capture by insiders and local incentives and capacity to maintain the resource base.

It is important to distinguish community-based natural resource management (CBNRM) and decentralization. Like community-driven development, CBNRM refers to the direct or indirect involvement of local communities at a relatively small scale to shape the use, distribution, and management of resources. Democratic decentralization—under which local representative authorities receive powers in the name of local citizens—can be considered a manifestation of CBNRM, but the devolution of powers to user groups, chiefs, NGOs, private corporations, or private individuals is not decentralization. Likewise, transfers to local line ministries (that is, deconcentration) is not a form of CBNRM.[13]

These distinctions are borne in mind in the literature review presented in this chapter. The review is selective, with a focus on the following questions: When does community engagement in resource management enhance resource sustainability (regenerated forests, increased forest cover, more sustainable fish and livestock harvesting, better water storage and use systems)? Is local management more inclusive and more equitable than central management or an unmanaged commons? In each case, to what extent is success shaped or constrained by preexisting community characteristics? Can local management systems be designed

Community management of common-pool resources has come to be seen as a viable alternative to privatization or management by a centralized state bureaucracy.

to overcome adverse local characteristics—that is, can design induce the right type and level of participation? How dependent is success on the role played by the central state?

The literature on community involvement in the management of natural resources is large and multidisciplinary, but most of it is based on case studies. Well-done case studies can add greatly to the understanding of processes; they are often less helpful, however, in establishing causal relationships between the structural features of communities, the institutions of governance established within them, and their impact on measures of system performance. The few research studies that use large datasets and attempt to deal with problems of selection into community management, are therefore highlighted in the discussion below.

Local Management and Resource Sustainability

Much of the literature on CBNRM and decentralized resource management focuses on the conditions under which the commons can be better governed—that is, the conditions under which community participation leads to greater resource sustainability (see, for example, Wade 1985; Ostrom 1990; Baland and Platteau 1997). This focus is in large part driven by Hardin's concerns about the fate of an unregulated commons. Many case studies suggest the viability of community management of natural resources with or without state assistance (see Agrawal and Benson 2010 for a review). The verdict on government-initiated institutions for community resource management has been bleaker.[14]

Several studies based on large data sets suggest that it may be possible for governments to successfully induce natural resource management on a large scale.

However, several studies that use large data sets to examine the impact of government-initiated institutions of community forest management show that it may be possible for governments to successfully induce natural resource management on a large scale. A key point made by all of these studies is that there is considerable selection in community management of natural resources, because community takeover is usually voluntary. Case studies cannot deal with such selection or with spillover effects, which can also bias results considerably.

Edmonds (2002) uses data from Nepal to determine the impact on the level of extraction of wood for fuel of a government-initiated program that transferred management of forests to local user groups. The evidence suggests that there was a significant reduction in wood extraction in areas with forest user groups.[15]

Somanathan, Prabhakar, and Singh (2005) assess the impact of local forest councils (*van panchayats* [VPs]) on forest degradation in the Indian state of Uttaranchal. Unlike Edmonds, they use satellite-based measures of forest quality (principally predictors of canopy cover) over a large geographical region that included VP and non VP forests in Uttaranchal. This methodology circumvents the problem of using community reported measures of local forest quality. The authors assess the long-run impact of decentralized management by village councils on forest stocks. Their study is also the only one that compares the cost of state and community management.[16]

The results indicate that broadleaved forests, which are of much greater relevance for local use, improved significantly under VP management but that there was no improvement in pine forests (VP–managed pine forests did no worse than comparable state-managed forests). At the same time, community management was far more cost effective than state management. The authors' calculations suggest that transferring state forests to community management would generate annual savings equal to the value of the total annual production of firewood from state forests.

Baland and others (2010) also assess the impact of VPs on forest degradation in Uttaranchal, using a wider set of measures of forest quality. They find that VP management improved the extraction of wood for fuel and fodder but did not lead to broader improvements in forest quality, such as canopy cover or forest regeneration. Their results indicate that VPs had little impact on tree-cutting or timber extraction, which may be a much greater source of forest degradation than the extraction of wood for fuel and fodder. However, the improvement that did occur was not at the cost of neighboring non VP forest parcels.[17] Their findings suggest that community management is often a response to the degradation of local forests. If this is the case, then any simple comparison of community-managed forests with forests managed by the state, or not managed at all, will tend to show no or even negative impact, as Agrawal and Chhatre find in their study of the Indian Himalayas (2006).

The impact of inequality on collective action has been at the center of a number of theoretical and empirical studies of management by communities or users, particularly in the fisheries sector and in the management of irrigation. It has also been an important focus in the case study literature on common-pool resource management. Ostrom, Lam, and Lee (1994) and Ostrom (1990) show that farmer-managed irrigation schemes have more equitable water distribution, for example,

A study of India suggests that community management of state forests would generate annual savings equal to the value of total annual production of firewood from state forests.

Maintenance of irrigation
systems tends to be
worse in more unequal
and heterogeneous
communities . . .

. . . but adequate local
discretion may be able
to overcome problems
created by inequality among
resource users.

A great deal of forest
conservation and regeneration
has been achieved under
community management in
Nepal and some Indian states.

but they do not compare the functioning of farmer-managed systems in more and less equal communities.

Studies that look explicitly at the impact of local inequality on the maintenance of irrigation systems find by and large that maintenance is worse in more unequal communities. Dayton-Johnson (2000) develops a model of cooperation in small irrigation systems, which he tests with data from a survey of Mexican irrigation societies. He finds that social heterogeneity and landholding inequality are consistently and significantly associated with lower levels of maintenance. Bardhan (2000) finds similar results in South India.

Dayton-Johnson and Bardhan (2002) attempt to reconcile views from the field study literature with Olson's (1965) view that inequality should be good for collective action. Their study pulls together data from a number of irrigation systems, including three large-scale studies from Nepal, southern India, and central Mexico. Overall, the findings suggest that however it is defined, heterogeneity weakens a group's ability to use social norms to enforce collective agreements and generally has a negative impact on cooperation. Moreover, even after controlling for social heterogeneity, inequality in the distribution of wealth continues to exercise a significant and largely negative effect. The authors conclude that although "Olson effects" are theoretically plausible under certain conditions, they do not seem to be operative in the irrigation systems they examine. They do find some evidence for a *U*-shaped relationship between inequality and collective action, with conservation possible only when inequality is very low or very high, not in between. In a similar vein, Bardhan, Ghatak, and Karaivanov (2007) show that when private inputs, such as land, are complementary in production with collective inputs, such as irrigation water, inequality in the ownership of private inputs tends to worsen maintenance.

A number of studies note, however, that adequate local discretion can overcome problems created by inequalities among resource users. Adhikari and Lovett (2006) use data from forest user groups in Nepal to argue that successful collective action can be achieved even when inequalities among resource users exist, provided that communities can exercise discretion in creating institutions for resource management.

A number of other case studies of forestry management highlight the same point. Hobley (1996) finds that in some states in India, as well as in Nepal, a great deal of forest conservation and regeneration has been achieved under community management. Adhikari and Lovett (2006) and Hobley (1996) report on cases in which user communities were able to exercise substantial discretion and had clear incentives to manage and preserve the resource.

In Africa, accounts of failure far outnumber accounts of success, except in Cameroon, Malawi, and Tanzania. Ribot, Lund, and Treue (2010), who review a large number of case studies, blame this failure on weak local governments and poorly thought-out donor programs. They note that donor-supported projects often fail to empower representative and downwardly accountable local bodies, relying instead on disenfranchising colonial practices oriented toward extraction and control (see also Ribot 2007; Ribot, Chhatre, and Lankina 2008).

These results suggest that successful collective action requires the establishment of clear and credible systems of accountability and that such rules may not be forthcoming in unequal communities, creating a space for central effort in setting the rules of the game. Dayton-Johnson and Bardhan's (2002) analysis provides an important insight. They note that heterogeneity affects not just the extent of cooperation, given a set of rules, but the type of rules chosen. Furthermore, not all rules are equally conducive to good performance or equity, and unequal communities are less likely to pick effective and equitable rules.

Ribot (2004) notes that when externalities are significant, it is particularly important that standards and rules be set at a higher level. If, for example, conversion is forbidden as a precondition for local control of the forests, incentives may need to be put in place that link conservation with livelihoods. In the absence of such incentives, there is no inherent reason to believe that local people will not sell off or convert forests if doing so is the most lucrative option.

Is Local Management More Equitable?

Community management is expected to satisfy the twin goals of attaining resource sustainability and increasing equity in the distribution of benefits. But these objectives are not necessarily complementary. Ribot, Lund, and Treue (2010) argue that in much of Africa, the devolution of responsibilities to communities has been mainly about maintaining opportunities for rent-seeking or ensuring resource sustainability for the benefit of higher-level national groups or international interests, with the costs borne mainly by local inhabitants.

Donor-supported projects often fail to empower local bodies, relying instead on disenfranchising colonial practices oriented toward extraction and control.

Successful collective action requires the establishment of clear and credible systems of accountability, which may not be forthcoming in unequal communities.

When externalities are significant, it is particularly important that standards and rules be set at a higher level.

In much of Africa, the devolution of responsibilities to communities has been mainly about maintaining opportunities for rent-seeking or ensuring resource sustainability for the benefit of higher-level groups or international interests . . .

. . . with the costs borne mainly by local inhabitants.

When local structures are not accountable to communities, decentralization can create perverse outcomes for the poorest and most vulnerable groups.

Several other studies also suggest that decentralization can create perverse outcomes for the poorest and most vulnerable groups when local structures are not accountable to communities. In India, Kumar (2002) reports that the joint management of Sal *(Shorea robusta)* forests has, if anything, deepened poverty because, despite community participation in the management of these forests, the emphasis has remained on high forests and timber production, which originated under colonial rule as an aspect of "scientific forestry." As the forest canopy closes, however, nonwood forest products, which are of particular importance for the poor, decline, deepening poverty.

In Tanzania, Lund and Treue (2008) find that the taxation and licensing system for the production of timber and charcoal that was introduced under decentralized forest management has created new entry barriers for the poorest producers, making them more dependent on town-based traders and village leaders. Wood (1999) argues that larger farmers in the more backward state of Bihar in India routinely negotiate preferential access to irrigation systems by paying bribes to local officials.

The poor may have greater motivation to maintain resources such as forests or pastures, because they depend on them for a larger share of their income.

The poor are often more dependent than the nonpoor on access to natural resources. Jodha (1986, 2001) estimates that 15–25 percent of the incomes of the rural poor in India comes from natural resources. In their survey of a large number of studies of India and West Africa, Beck and Nesmith (2001) also find higher levels of reliance on common-pool resources among the landless poor. Gregerson and Contreras (1989) estimate that more than a third of the world's population relies on local forests to meet basic household needs. Studies also indicate that the relatively better-off tend to benefit more from common-pool resources, although the poor are far more dependent on such resources (that is, the share of forest income in their total income is higher), perhaps indicating some scope for redistribution (Cavendish 2000; Campbell 2003; Fisher 2004; Narain, Gupta, and Van't Veld 2005; Lund and Treue 2008). The products the poor derive from the forest—fuel, water, fodder, and food—also have few affordable market alternatives and thus also constitute an important safety net (Pattanayak and Sills 2001; McSweeney 2005). As a result, some researchers argue that poorer members of a community may have a greater motivation to maintain resources such as forests or pastures, given the right set of incentives, as the risk-adjusted return to doing so may be higher for them.

In practice, however, rules regarding access and fees are rarely changed when management becomes more local. One reason is that the poor, who rely the most on the forest, are often also a minority group whose interests do not coincide with those of village leaders or the village majority. The choice of local institutions and the rules regulating such institutions are set by higher-level institutions that reflect a multitude of values and interests, ranging from concerns with resource sustainability, biodiversity, and carbon storage to the desire for a strategic political advantage or enhanced opportunities for rent-seeking. The choices these institutions make are influenced by national elites as well as a host of international interests, including bilateral and multilateral donors (Ferguson 1996; Blaikie 2006; Ribot, Lund, and Treue 2010). As a result, policies originally designed to favor elites under colonial structures are often maintained, even when countries officially promote popular participation in natural resource management. Mustalahti and Lund (2010), for example, find that despite official policies supporting community participation in forestry in the Lao People's Democratic Republic, Mozambique, and Tanzania, local communities were systematically prevented from sharing in the returns from commercially valuable forest resources. A number of other studies raise similar concerns regarding the disproportionate advantages obtained by the rich, powerful, and well connected (see, for example, Ribot 1995; Larson and Ribot 2007; Lund and Treue 2008).

> In practice, however, local management seems to disproportionately benefit the rich, powerful, and well connected.

Beck and Nesmith's (2001) review suggests that a process of progressive exclusion of the poor from natural resource–based livelihood sources may be underway even where conservation has been successful, as in India and Tanzania. They caution that unless management regimes are specifically designed to include poor people, CBNRM may end up as little more than donor-supported control by elites. Dasgupta and Mäler (1995) illustrates how this cycle can lead to an environmental poverty trap. Nerlove (1991) shows that increasing rates of deforestation may lead to greater population growth and even faster rates of deforestation.

> Unless management regimes are specifically designed to include poor people, community-based natural resource management may end up as little more than donor-supported control by elites.

Several studies caution against assuming that the introduction of simple participatory mechanisms can ensure downward accountability in the absence of clear mechanisms for ensuring compliance. Two case studies from Tanzania and Senegal are illustrative. Lund (2007) reports that a new requirement in Tanzania that elected forest committee members provide oral accounts of all forest-related incomes and expenditures at quarterly village assemblies led to greater equity in the distribution of forest-related incomes. However, as Ribot, Lund, and Treue (2010) note, such simple changes in rules, though powerful, may work only

Without credible sanctions, community members have no ability or capacity to monitor corrupt officials, who know that allegations of misappropriation can be denied or ignored with impunity.

when there is clear support from higher tiers of government and commensurate mechanisms to sanction local leaders are in place. They note that in the Tanzanian case, a watchful donor and an involved district council and forest office provided this support. In contrast, they note that in Senegal, which lacked such support, community members had no ability or capacity to monitor corrupt officials, who knew that allegations of misappropriation could be denied or ignored with impunity.

Common-pool resources also vary widely in their potential impact on livelihoods and in the number of actors at various levels who have a stake in their use, conservation, and regeneration. Forests, for example, can generate tremendous value at the local and national level, but forest preservation and regeneration often yield large positive externalities at the global level. In contrast, the returns to small irrigation schemes are plausibly confined to a limited number of local actors. Communities that live in or near specific natural resources can therefore face very different incentives to engage, individually or collectively, in efforts to preserve or restore the resource base.

Local governments or community user groups are often given management rights over forests that have few livelihood improvement opportunities . . .

. . . leaving them with the largely unfunded costs of management and with little by way of returns.

The question of who benefits from forest land is an important case in point. A common issue highlighted in the literature is that local governments or community user groups are often given management rights over forests that have few livelihood improvement opportunities. In contrast, private interests or the central state control productive forests. Even in countries like Tanzania, where there is significant decentralized forest management, most joint forest management agreements have been made in relation to the *montane* rainforests, where laws prohibit use in order to maintain national and international biodiversity. Where productive forests are under joint management, by village councils or community-based groups, they either yield low-value nontimber forest products for subsistence use (Topp-Jorgensen and others 2005; Meshack and others 2006) or are degraded or of low value with little by way of immediate livelihood opportunities, at least in the short run (Lund 2007; Mustalahti and Lund 2010). The result is that local communities are often required to bear the largely unfunded costs of management and with little by way of returns.

There are also issues about what constitutes the "community," as the case of people who live on the borders of forests demonstrates. On the one hand, living near a forest can leave them more vulnerable to crop damage and livestock losses from protected forest wildlife. On the other hand, they can be restricted in expanding their farmland if the forest border becomes "hard" (Lund and Treue 2008). Similar issues arise for pastoralist and agro-pastoralist groups, who are often not represented in community user groups or local councils.

Several studies question the assumption underlying the move toward CBNRM—namely, that viable and well-functioning local institutions exist to which decision-making power simply needs to be transferred. They argue that CBNRM is in the main a process of creating the necessary institutional structures at the local level, to which specific responsibilities can then be devolved. Although these new institutions may be based on historical forms, the creation of accountable institutions at the local level implies a much greater involvement of the state in resource governance arrangements. Thus, even where communities and local groups have long-standing rights to manage local resources, such rights require at least the implicit if not explicit sanction of the state. For resources that are deemed valuable—such as timber and fish—local rights typically exist as a result of explicit actions by government and state agencies (Ribot, Lund, and Treue 2010; Agrawal 2010). Agrawal (2010) notes that of the 400 million hectares of tropical forests currently under formal community control, more than half was transferred to community management in the past quarter century. Fujiie, Hayami, and Kikuchi (2005) look at the creation of irrigation association groups in the Philippines, which were formed as part of the broader decentralization process. They find that only 20 percent of the irrigation association groups included in their study had communal irrigation systems in existence before the National Irrigation Authority got involved (see also Mosse 2005 on India and Wilder and Lankao 2006 on Mexico).

State intervention thus seems to determine the impact of participation on natural resource management, equity, and local livelihoods, much as it does for other programs or reform processes that induce greater local participation. The distribution of responsibilities and resources between the center and the locality as well as the mandate local citizens have to protect, improve, monitor, and benefit from the natural resource are critical.

Baird (2006) highlights another significant issue: the impact of donor and government reporting requirements and incentive structures on the quality of local management. The central government in Lao PDR provided incentives to provinces to expand aquaculture ponds but not fish sanctuaries. In response, provinces met the central government's quota by reporting fish sanctuaries as aquaculture ponds. Similarly, irrigation

> The existence of viable local institutions cannot be assumed. Such institutions need to be created through deliberate effort.

> State intervention seems to determine the impact of participation on natural resource management, equity, and local livelihoods.

Communities and local governments can obtain significant benefits if more effective management of the common-pool resource increases public revenues for local investment.

reports in India provided by local officials to higher levels often inflate the areas covered by irrigation in order to "meet" targets (Wood 1999).

Communities and local governments can obtain significant indirect benefits if more effective management of the common-pool resource increases public revenues for local investment. Ribot, Lund, and Treue (2010) argue that such benefits can provide the right incentives for conservation when management of the forest itself is unlikely to be a lucrative venture. They argue that revenue raising is one of the most prominent outcomes of decentralized forest management in Africa. In Uganda, for example, local governments are entitled to keep 40 percent of the revenues from the management of national forest reserves (Muhereza 2006; Turyahabwe and others 2007), even though they are effectively sidelined as far as management of these reserves goes. Revenues have also increased substantially for rural communities in Cameroon and Tanzania in community forestry areas (Oyono and Efoua 2006; Oyono and Nzuzi 2006; Lund 2007). These funds are used to cover the direct costs of forest management as well as to fund public infrastructure and services such as roads, schools, and health clinics (Ribot, Lund, and Treue 2010), or to provide micro loans, as in Nepal (Pokharel 2009).

Participation and the Quality of Local Infrastructure

Participatory development programs usually invest a good deal in building community infrastructure. The argument for doing so is twofold. First, lack of adequate infrastructure—connector roads, wholesale markets, irrigation channels, electricity, school buildings, sanitation, and the like—significantly constrains prospects for development, and this lack is far more acute in the poorest communities. Second, it is expected that devolving responsibility to the local level will produce projects that are not only better aligned with the preferences and needs of final users, but are also of higher quality, and more likely to be well maintained.

Ideally, participatory programs are expected to work with communities to ensure need, feasibility, and adequacy of scale; to monitor the project over the construction cycle; and to create systems for project maintenance. Most programs require some form of community cofinancing as a mechanism for inducing greater community engagement and "ownership" of the project. Some also require upfront community commitment of resources for project maintenance. Many participatory projects also restrict the menu of feasible subprojects, either overtly or de facto, to a small set of public goods (typically roads, culverts, and drainage systems; drinking water and sanitation facilities; and schools, and clinics). Although this appears to be contradictory to a demand-driven process of project selection, in practice, it may serve to restrict choice to a small set of public goods that communities are better able to maintain or where the opportunities for capture are limited.[18] Competition in the project selection process is also intended to weed out bad projects and to encourage communities to put in the requisite effort to align the proposed project with program objectives.

How successful are these efforts? Does local provision create infrastructure that is better designed, better constructed, and better maintained? Does this imply less capture? Are projects of better quality than similar types of infrastructure created by central line departments? How important are community characteristics such as wealth inequality, ethnic heterogeneity, remoteness, and low levels of education or poverty? Can the right incentives (such as interjurisdictional competition for funds) or the right investments (such as community capacity building) mitigate the impact of potentially negative community characteristics? Specifically, can local provision create "good" projects in "bad" communities, and do the poor gain as a result? The following subsections present the evidence on these questions.

Bottom-up versus Top-down

Given the resources allocated to social funds of various types, surprisingly few studies compare the relative performance of subprojects built by local governments or community groups and subprojects built by central line departments. Even fewer simultaneously address the question of infrastructure quality and the distribution of benefits. Yet it is far from clear that benefits, even from well-designed and constructed projects, are more equitably distributed.

The first study to carefully assess this question used data from 132 infrastructure projects in 99 randomly selected rural communities across northern Pakistan, where the Agha Khan Rural Support Program (AKRSP) has promoted participatory rural development for more than 30 years. Khwaja (2004, 2009) compares infrastructure projects provided by the community, with AKRSP support, with similar projects provided by government line departments. His research yields three interesting findings. First, community engagement, with AKRSP

Competition in the project selection process is intended to weed out bad projects and encourage communities to align projects with program objectives.

Community engagement in Pakistan substantially improved project maintenance . . .

. . . but only when participation was confined to the nontechnical aspects of the project. Community involvement in technical decisions was detrimental.

facilitation, substantially improved project maintenance (the main outcome of interest) but only when participation was confined to the nontechnical aspects of the project. When communities got involved in technical project decisions, participation was detrimental. The intuition behind this claim is that decisions requiring local information are more likely to be sensitive to the community's investment, whereas decisions that require technical information should be more responsive to the external agency's investment. Second, communities were less able to maintain projects that were technically complex or new.[19] They did better when preexisting projects were refurbished or the project selected was one in which they had previous experience. Third, inequality in the incidence of project benefits (across both participatory and government provided projects) has a *U*-shaped effect on maintenance. As inequlity in the distribution of project benefits increases, maintenance levels first fall then rise.[20] As Khwaja notes, under perfect inequality in the distribution of benefits, the project is effectively privatized, and maintenance no longer requires any coordination.[21] This *U*-shaped relationship between inequality and project maintenance is similar to the tradeoff between resource sustainability and wealth inequality in the literature on common pool resources.

Mansuri (2012a) uses data from the three largest provinces of Pakistan to provide further insights on the relationship between participation and project quality. Her study combines administrative, census, and survey data from 230 infrastructure projects in 80 villages.[22] About half of the projects were constructed by government line departments; while the rest were built by the community with support from the National Rural Support Program (NRSP).[23] The study assesses two aspects of project quality: design and construction, and current condition and maintenance. The first aspect, provides evidence of capture, in the narrow sense of theft and corruption, in construction, while the second reflects a communities' capacity for coordination and is therefore more comparable with Khwaja's (2004, 2009) work.

Compared with the northern areas, the rest of Pakistan has far greater levels of local inequality and ethnic heterogeneity. Land ownership, which is almost entirely hereditary, is extremely skewed, with the top 5 percent of landowners owning more than 40 percent of all land while more than half of rural households are landless. The caste (*zaat*) structure is also extremely hierarchical. Given these features, Mansuri's findings are encouraging.

Mansuri finds that participatory projects in the study villages appear to be better designed and constructed than comparable projects delivered by government line departments and the effects are economically large. This finding suggests that the scope for outright rent-seeking through the diversion of project funds can be considerably muted when infrastructure is provided with community engagement. NRSP-supported projects are also better maintained, in line with the evidence provided by Khwaja (2009). This may be due, at least in part, to NRSP's (and AKRSP's) approach to project maintenance. Maintenance costs are built into project costs at the proposal stage and although the community is entirely responsible for project maintenance postconstruction, NRSP (and AKRSP) continue to provide technical assistance as needed. This is very much in line with the following discussion on the importance of building community capacity to undertake resource management.

That said, project quality alone can reveal only so much about capture. If project benefits are effectively privatized at the local level, there may be little incentive to engage in the type of rent-seeking that could reduce the quality of project construction. The results here are far less encouraging. As discussed in chapter 4, Mansuri (2012b) finds that benefits from the participatory project are no better distributed than benefits from the relevant government project. In both types of projects, the share of the landless, the poor, and people from low castes was far below their share in the population.

> The scope for outright rent-seeking through the diversion of project funds was considerably muted when infrastructure in Pakistan was provided with community engagement. . . .
>
> . . . but benefits were no better distributed than in projects directed from the center.

Can "Good" Programs Compensate for "Bad" Communities?

An important premise in the literature on participatory programs is that well designed and implemented projects can overcome adverse community characteristics. Specifically, that the challenge to collective action posed by local inequality, ethnic divides, and exclusionary practices of various types, can be overcome by inducing participation through a well-implemented program. Khwaja's (2009) analysis provides an encouraging assessment. Project characteristics, which include the participatory delivery mechanism facilitated by AKRSP, significantly outweigh community characteristics, suggesting that well-designed participatory efforts can, to a large degree, overcome the negative effects of wealth inequality and community heterogeneity. The study also finds that the quality of local leadership matters: projects in communities

> Well-designed participatory efforts can overcome the negative effects of wealth inequality and community heterogeneity to a large degree.

in the northern areas of Pakistan that had more educated leaders, and leaders who were actively engaged in community affairs, were better maintained.[24]

Mansuri (2012a) finds that after controlling for participation (that is, facilitation by the NRSP), inequality does not affect project maintenance much. However, projects were far better maintained in communities with above average levels of schooling. The impact of inequality on construction quality is different, however. The quality of construction of NRSP-supported projects worsens significantly in villages that are more unequal, and this effect is amplified when projects are also more technically complex or are built on older preexisting (usually government-provided) projects. The study thus shows that although participation appears to dampen opportunities for rent-seeking, greater effort is required to ensure the quality of projects in more unequal communities.

A number of large participatory development programs use some form of interjurisdictional competition to improve community incentives to allocate funds in a more transparent and equitable manner. Grant funds from the central government can also induce competition across localities if they are tied to the achievement of specific outcomes, reform processes, and so forth.

In more competitive subdistricts in Indonesia, the set of projects submitted and funded had larger community contributions, a more pro-poor allocation of project benefits, and lower unit costs.

Chavis (2009) is perhaps the only study that has looked at the impact of competition on the quality of infrastructure subprojects. The study used administrative data from the Indonesian Kecamatan Development Program (KDP), funded by the World Bank. Like other community-driven development programs, KDP involves communities in the allocation of funds for the construction of local public goods. In the KDP, each funded *kecamatan* (subdistrict) receives a block grant, based on population. The grants are allocated at the village level by a competitive process of project selection that is managed by an intervillage council with representation from each village. As a result, subdistricts with more villages face a greater competition for funds. Chavis proposes that this competitive pressure is plausibly exogenous and that it changes the process by which the block grant is allocated, inducing greater compliance with KDP rules and thus higher-quality projects in more competitive subdistricts.[25] He tests this hypothesis using administrative data on more than 3,000 road project proposals received in a single year (road projects typically account for almost half of all KDP subproject funds). The results indicate that in more competitive subdistricts, the set of projects submitted and funded had larger community contributions, a more pro-poor allocation of project benefits, and lower unit costs.

A potential limitation of using reported unit costs and distribution of beneficiaries at the time of proposal submission and approval is that there are no independent data against which these claims can be checked. Chavis attempts to overcome this problem by using corroborative evidence from an earlier study by Olken (2007), which shows a considerable amount of overinvoicing of labor and materials in the stated costs of KDP road projects (see discussion in chapter 3). Using data from this study, Chavis confirms that there is also less theft in road projects in more competitive subdistricts, bolstering the finding on lower reported unit road costs in project proposals.

Recall, however, that demand-driven application processes can be strongly regressive (see the first section of this chapter). Taken together, these results suggest that high project construction quality and maintenance do not imply an equitable distribution of resources. There can be a significant trade-off between equity and sustainability.

Community Capacity and Project Quality

Several of the studies reviewed in the previous sections point to the relevance of building community capacity for project quality and maintenance. This section reviews studies that suggest that lack of community capacity is often the key constraint on project quality.

> Lack of community capacity is often the key constraint on project quality.

Katz and Sara (1997) cite inadequate technical support from project implementers as one of the key reasons for the failure of water projects in their global review. They note that in the absence of community supervision or management, projects were often left in the hands of private contractors, whose incentives can be suspect. Community members were unable to make informed choices about the type of project to build, monitor the work of contractors, or maintain projects after they were constructed without adequate training.

Isham and Kahkonen (2002) make similar points in their analysis of water projects in India, Indonesia, and Sri Lanka. They find that communities often require considerable support in understanding the technical aspects of projects.

> Communities often require considerable support in understanding the technical aspects of projects.

Newman and others (2002) raise similar concerns in their evaluation of the Bolivian social fund. They find that water projects improved water quality only when community-level training was also provided.

Water projects in Bolivia improved water quality and access to water only when community-level training was also provided.

Results of an experiment in Kenya suggest that water projects are better maintained when water management committees are given funds to carry out regular maintenance.

Large donors often support communities in the construction of projects . . .

. . . but provide little support for postconstruction activities.

They attribute the significant reduction in under-five mortality associated with the provision of health clinics to the fact that investments in health went beyond providing infrastructure to providing other necessary technical inputs as well. In contrast, education projects led to little change in education outcomes, because no resources were provided beyond the building of schools.

In a more recent study, Leino (2007) provides further support for this hypothesis from a field experiment in Kenya. The study, which allocated funds for maintenance to a random subset of water management committees, finds that water projects were better maintained when water management committees were given funds to carry out regular maintenance activities.

Very few studies attempt to assess the long-term sustainability of participatory infrastructure projects. Kleemeier (2000) is an exception. She looks at a rural piped water program in Malawi. Only half of the schemes, which were 3–26 years old, were performing well; the rest were performing poorly or had failed entirely. Moreover, the schemes that were in good working condition were either small or new. Kleemeier notes that her findings are an indictment not of the participatory process itself but of the lack of attention implementers paid to the weak link between communities and external agencies with the requisite technical capacity. Community groups were capable of making small repairs necessary to keep water flowing, but they were unable to undertake more substantive preventative maintenance and repairs. In the end, the water department had to send in government-employed monitoring assistants and supervisors to ensure that preventive maintenance was performed.

Kleemeier notes that CARE, a large international NGO, was confronted with much the same situation in Indonesia (see also Hodgkin and Kusumahadi 1993). Although it supported communities in the construction of projects, it provided little support for postconstruction activities. Although small and simple schemes can survive this neglect, larger schemes that require external technical inputs cannot. In a related study, Uphoff (1986) notes that local organizations can be effective only if they have adequate links with political and administrative centers.

Community Engagement in Public Service Delivery

Much of the effort to improve accountability in the allocation of resources for public services focuses on expanding citizen oversight and engagement. These efforts have taken a number of forms, ranging from the decentralization of service delivery to local governments and the signing of contracts with private providers and NGOs to programs that induce greater community participation in service provision and quality by transferring resources directly to community organizations.

The review of the evidence focuses on outcomes related to improvements in service quality, as measured by learning, school retention, infant and maternal mortality, and access to services. As Bardhan and Mookherjee (2005) caution, the distributional and welfare consequences of decentralized delivery are likely to be as important as the impact on service quality. In essence, if local governments or participatory programs are beholden to local elites, they may overprovide some services and undercharge for the services they do provide, leaving the poor to bear a disproportionate cost of service provision.

If local governments or participatory programs are beholden to elites, they may underprovide some services and overcharge for the services they do provide . . .

. . . leaving the poor to bear a disproportionate cost of service provision.

School-Based Management and the Decentralization of Education

The decentralization of education takes many forms. The review here divides the literature broadly into decentralization efforts directed at schools (generally referred to as "school-based management") and the decentralization of education services to local governments.

School-based management is a form of decentralization in which decision making is devolved, either from a central line ministry or a lower-tier government, whether provincial or municipal, to the school or community. As with the devolution of authority in other domains, increased school and community discretion is expected to improve school quality (as measured by student performance and use of the school budget) and enhance satisfaction with the quality of service provision.

School-based management typically involves setting up a school management committee or council that includes the school principal, teachers, and members of the school community, in particular parents but also local leaders and other community members. School committees are usually tasked with monitoring school performance and providing oversight on the use of resources. Less frequently, such committees are granted authority over teacher hiring and firing and decisions about the curriculum and the allocation of school budgets.

Many developing countries have adopted school-based management programs over the past two decades, often as part of a larger effort to decentralize resource allocation and service delivery. The extent to which resources and decision-making authority are transferred, as well as the agents to whom authority is transferred, varies widely. There is also a great deal of variation in the extent to which community and parent engagement is mandated, the form it takes, and the type of oversight local and higher-level governments provide.

Barrera-Osorio and Linden (2009) categorize school-based management approaches along two dimensions: who has the power to make decisions and the degree of decision making devolved to the school level. They note that "with so many possible combinations of these two dimensions, almost every school-based management reform is unique" (p. 4).

Bruns, Filmer, and Patrinos (2011) divide school-based management programs into three broad groups: strong versions, in which school councils have significant authority over both staffing and school budgets; intermediate versions, in which school councils have some say in curriculum but very limited authority over resources or staffing decisions; and weak versions, in which school councils are largely advisory in nature. They also provide a useful framework for understanding the channels through which school-based management can enhance accountability, highlighting four facets: increasing choice and participation, giving citizens a stronger voice, making information about school performance widely available, and strengthening school level incentives for effective service delivery for the poor (see Bruns, Filmer, and Patrinos 2011 for a comprehensive review of school-based management). The review here focuses on evidence for the second channel, insofar as studies can unpack multifaceted interventions to identify the impact of a specific component.

In all cases, the decentralization of education is expected to induce greater efficiency in the use of education budgets and create better performance incentives for local officials and school staff. The expectation is that decentralization can deliver improvements in a range of schooling outcomes, from enrollment and retention to better student performance on standardized tests, and that it can do so cost-effectively.

As with all decentralization efforts, there is the usual set of risks. Programs can be captured, with resources flowing to better-off locations or schools or siphoned off for private use. Local government agents may also lack the capacity to manage funds or make effective decisions regarding resource allocation, staffing, or curriculum. Theory would predict that both types of problems would tend to be worse in communities that are poorer, more unequal, or in which citizens are more alienated from the political process.

Caldwell (2005) notes that as with broader decentralization efforts, governments have supported school-based management for a variety of reasons. Governments on the left have initiated school management reforms as part of larger efforts to increase community empowerment. Governments on the right have often justified school-based management on the basis of greater freedom or more choice, which has also been interpreted as an effort to create a market among schools in public education systems.

These divergent motives have made school-based management politically contentious, with little agreement on what the expected outcomes should be. In recent years, however, a consensus has been forged that the primary purpose of school-based management is the improvement of educational outcomes. With this, evidence on the effects of school-based management on educational outcomes has also started to emerge. According to Caldwell (2005), early studies were marred by the lack of a clear objective for school-based management as well as by the lack of data. In contrast, what he calls third-generation studies, starting in the late 1990s, look at programs in which improvement in learning outcomes is a central objective and adequate data are available to assess impact.

Before examining the evidence, it is useful to point out that few, if any, studies are able to measure the extent or quality of community engagement or identify its influence on school management. Studies that do attempt to separate out community participation from other aspects of decentralization, such as school autonomy, tend to assume that the level of community or parent participation, usually self-reported, is independent of unobserved community or student characteristics that could influence outcomes. Similar assumptions are made about reported levels of school autonomy. Gunnarsson and others (2009) make an important point in this regard. They find that levels of reported school autonomy and parental participation are not only poorly correlated with each other but that both vary more within countries than between them.[26]

A smaller body of literature looks at the impact of decentralizing education to local governments. A general concern with studies that look at the impact of decentralization is that the scope, timing, and extent of decentralization usually depend on a number of political economy considerations that are neither evident ex post nor malleable ex ante. As such, strong assumptions about the plausible exogeneity of the timing or extent of decentralization are often required. The extent to which

A consensus has been forged that the primary purpose of school-based management is the improvement of educational outcomes.

The scope, timing, and extent of decentralization usually depend on a number of political economy considerations that are neither evident ex post nor malleable ex ante.

191

the results of such studies are credible depends in part on the extent to which panel data, along with some feature of the decentralization, can be used to construct a credible counterfactual against which outcomes under decentralization can be compared.

Overall, the evidence suggests that decentralization in any form improves school access. There is also some evidence that student retention rates and attendance improve and grade repetition is reduced. There is little evidence, however, of any improvement in learning outcomes.

Most evaluations do not cover the time periods typically associated with improvements in learning outcomes. As Bruns, Filmer, and Patrinos (2011) point out, much of the evidence from developed countries indicates that it can take up to eight years to see an impact on student learning. This lack of impact on student learning is consistent with a basic concern highlighted in chapter 2. Reform processes that attempt to change structures of authority and power may require longer time spans to realize gains than the timeline of impact studies allows. It may also be easier to observe gains in some dimensions than others. Outcomes may also worsen before they improve. Some studies, for example, show a decline in student quality at school entry, as children from less privileged backgrounds enter school for the first time. Their entry may partly account for the negligible improvement in learning despite improvement in attendance and school retention. Even in studies with longer time frames, however, results for learning outcomes are mixed, as shown below.

Social fund–supported school infrastructure investments. Although social funds have invested substantial resources in upgrading school infrastructure, only a few studies look at the impacts of such investments on schooling outcomes. The few that have find an improvement in school access. No study looks at learning outcomes.

Paxson and Schady (2002) find that the Peruvian social fund increased school attendance, particularly among younger children. Other researchers find similar results for social funds in Armenia (Chase 2002) and Zambia (Chase and Sherburne-Benz 2001); Chase and Sherburne-Benz also find that children were in more appropriate grades. Household expenditure on schooling in Zambia was also higher in communities that used social funds to rehabilitate schools, probably because of the higher fees charged by parent-teacher associations in such

Decentralization in any form seems to improve school access . . .

. . . but there is little evidence of any improvement in learning outcomes over the periods studied.

Reform processes that attempt to change structures of authority and power may require longer time spans to realize gains than the timeline of impact studies allows . . .

. . . and outcomes may actually worsen before they improve.

Several studies find that social funds increased school attendance, particularly among younger children.

schools. Although increased spending need not be welfare enhancing for poor households, the authors argue that taken together with improved attendance rates and grade-appropriate placement of children, it is indicative of unmet demand for schooling in these communities.

School-based management.   Several countries have implemented strong versions of school-based management. An early program is the Educación con Participación de la Comunidad (Education with Community Participation [EDUCO]) program in El Salvador. Under this program, the state bore all schooling costs (tuition, uniforms, textbooks). Parents were expected to contribute time and labor to the school. Each school had an Association for Community Education (ACE), with elected parent members. The ACEs managed the school budget; they could hire and fire teachers and monitor teacher performance (Sawada and Ragatz 2005). Half of all rural students in grades 1–9 were enrolled in an EDUCO school by 2001 (Di Gropello 2006).

Jimenez and Sawada (1999, 2003) find that students in EDUCO schools had higher attendance and lower dropout rates than students in traditional schools. Attending an EDUCO school raised the odds of school retention by about 64 percent. As the decision to enroll in an EDUCO school is endogenous, the authors use the availability of EDUCO at the municipality level as an instrument for a school being in the EDUCO program. They attempt to isolate the channel through which the EDUCO effect is realized by adding a community participation variable to the estimation. This estimation yields a positive and significant effect, leading the authors to conclude that EDUCO worked mainly through community participation.

These results are interesting, but the empirical strategy is not convincing. In practice, any number of municipal characteristics could influence a municipalities' eligibility for the EDUCO program and thus the odds of a school entering the program. Similarly, any number of community characteristics could affect the odds of a school selecting into the program as well as the observed dropout effects.

Jimenez and Sawada (1999) and Sawada (1999) also find positive changes in teacher attitudes and behavior, particularly teacher absenteeism. Sawada and Ragatz (2005) uses propensity score matching to identify the impact of EDUCO on a range of outcomes. Their results also indicate lower teacher absenteeism. Community associations and parents also report much greater influence over administrative processes, including teacher hiring and firing. There is also some, albeit limited, evidence of an improvement in student test scores. The authors note that EDUCO schools tend to be located in poorer, more remote, and more rural communities which could explain the lower comparative test scores.

A school autonomy reform in Nicaragua that gave school councils decision-making authority had no impact on average student learning.

A similar school autonomy reform in Nicaragua allowed school councils to hire and fire the school principal and make decisions about school maintenance and student learning. King and Özler (1998) look at the impact of the program on student test scores. They use matching methods to find comparable nonautonomous public and private schools. The study finds no impact of the reform on student learning on average. However, students performed better in schools that reported exercising greater de facto autonomy. The results, though interesting, are difficult to interpret, because the study cannot identify why some schools exercised greater autonomy. A subsequent study (King, Özler, and Rawlings 1999) that tried to determine which aspects of community decision making were responsible for the improved learning finds that the school council's autonomy over staffing decisions had the greatest impact.

In contrast Eskeland and Filmer (2002), who assess the decentralization of education in Argentina, find positive impacts of school autonomy but not of parental participation. They theorize that while greater school autonomy increases the ability of school officials to extract rents, greater participation by parents in schools can channel this discretionary power toward improved learning. The expectation is that community and parental engagement in schools can constrain rent-seeking by local officials or school administrators. The question is whether communities have the capacity, ability, or incentive to play this monitoring role, particularly in poorer and less developed areas, which may be most in need of education reform. Interestingly, they find that, consistent with their model, school autonomy has a larger impact on learning in communities that have higher levels of participation.

In contrast, giving oversight power to community members in Kenya improved both teacher attendance and student performance.

These results are broadly corroborated by a randomized experiment in Kenya that, among other things, increased community monitoring of teachers through local school committees. Duflo, Dupas, and Kremer (2008) find that giving oversight power to community members—in this case through local school committees—improved teacher attendance and student performance.[27]

Gunnarsson and others (2009) cast light on why the learning impacts of school autonomy and community participation are so mixed. They use data from eight Latin American countries to argue that local managerial effort, at the level of the school as well as the community, is likely to be endogenous. Their results demonstrate that correcting for the endogeneity of school autonomy and parental participation can completely reverse the positive and significant effects of school autonomy. Encouragingly, in their sample countries, the positive effect of community participation remains positive and is strengthened when the endogeneity of participation is addressed.

Chaudhury and Parajuli (2010) study a school-based management program in Nepal that transferred school management to the community. School management committees, composed of parents as well as "influential local citizens," were given the authority to repost government teachers, hire and fire community-recruited teachers, and index teacher salaries to school performance. The committees were also given untied block grants to invest in school improvement. Exogenous variation in program participation, which was voluntary, was randomly induced in some communities through an advocacy group that persuaded treatment communities to participate in the program. Two years into the program, results show an increase in school access but no effect on learning.

In some school-based management programs, community groups play a more consultative role, with very limited discretion over budgets or teacher hiring and firing decisions. One such program is the Programa Escuelas de Calidad (Quality Schools Program [PEC]) in Mexico, which provides five-year grants of up to $15,000 to schools that commit to invest in education quality. In exchange for PEC grants, schools need to prepare an education improvement plan in collaboration with parent associations. During the first years of the grant period, all investments must be made in upgrading school facilities and providing learning materials. The last installment of the grant can be used in part for teacher training and development. Participation in PEC is voluntary, but the program targets disadvantaged urban schools.

Using two years of nationally representative panel data, Skoufias and Shapiro (2006) find significant declines in dropout, grade repetition, and failure rates. Dropout rates decreased by 0.24 points, failure rates by 0.24 points, and repetition rates by 0.31 points.

A school-based management program in Nepal was associated with an increase in school access but not learning.

A school-based program in the Philippines appears to have had a positive but modest effect on learning.

Grade failure and grade repetition in Mexico declined following introduction of a school-based management program.

Murnane, Willet, and Cardenas (2006) use longitudinal data from all seven years of PEC, which allows them to control for pre-PEC trends in relevant outcomes in both PEC and non-PEC schools. Using only schools that entered PEC in the program's second year of operation and had similar historical trends as non-PEC schools, they find that PEC decreased dropout rates by about 6 percent over three years of participation. The largest effects occurred in states that were more developed.

A similar school-based program in the Philippines funded infrastructure along with teacher training, curriculum development, and the provision of textbooks. This program required schools to develop a five-year school improvement plan in partnership with the community. Khattri, Ling, and Jha (2010) evaluate the program using retrospective administrative data along with propensity score matching to identify counterfactual schools. They find positive but modest effects on learning.

The Apoyo a la Gestión Escolar (School Management Support [AGE]) program in Mexico provided parent associations with resources that could be used to rehabilitate and upgrade school infrastructure. The funds were subject to being audited annually on a random basis. Gertler, Patrinos, and Rubio-Codina (2007) find substantial positive effects of giving parent associations more management responsibilities.[28] Their results indicate a reduction in both grade failure and grade repetition of about 0.4 percentage points in AGE beneficiary schools. Given a mean failure rate of 10 percent and a mean repetition rate of 9.6 percent at baseline, these values imply about a 4 percent decrease in the proportion of students failing and the proportion of students repeating a grade. The effects are larger for schools that received benefits for more than one year.[29]

A couple of recent studies have examined interventions in India designed to induce greater community monitoring of school-based committees. Banerjee and others (2010) report on a randomized evaluation that had three intervention arms. The first arm provided information to villagers about the role of an existing institution, the village education committee. Baseline data indicated very little awareness of its existence, even among its own members. The second arm added to the first by also providing information on student test scores and how to evaluate a child's learning level. The third arm supplemented the first two arms by teaching volunteers in the village a simple technique for teaching children how to read in an after-school reading program. Each intervention arm was implemented in 65 villages; a fourth group of 85 villages formed the control group.

The authors find virtually no impact of the first and second arms of this intervention. Even village education committee members themselves were not significantly more likely to be aware that they were on the village education committee following the intervention. What effects the authors do observe appear to reflect a decline in awareness in the control group. The first two interventions also had no effect on children's learning. In villages that received the third intervention arm, however, children were 1.7 percent more likely to read letters and 1.8 percent more likely to read words or paragraphs. The authors note that this small increase should be viewed with some optimism, given the small number of children who attended the after-school reading program.

Pandey, Goyal, and Sundararaman (2011) present findings from another study that provided information to communities about their roles and responsibilities in school management in the Indian states of Karnataka, Madhya Pradesh, and Uttar Pradesh. At baseline, there were significant differences across states in test scores, teacher absence, and parental awareness of the village education committees. In line with Banerjee and others (2010), they find that only 8 percent of parents in Uttar Pradesh knew about the village education committee and only 2 percent could name its chair. In contrast, in Karnataka, 63 percent of parents were aware of the village education committee and 44 percent knew the name of its chair. The information campaign was also more intense and prolonged than the one studied by Banerjee and others (2010).[30] The findings also differ in important ways. Pandey, Goyal, and Sundararaman find significant gains in teacher attendance, teaching time, and the functioning of school committees. They also find higher levels of parental and community engagement and higher student math scores, with much larger impacts in the two lagging states, Uttar Pradesh and Madhya Pradesh. The emergence of some learning gains is encouraging. The percentage of children receiving benefits from government entitlement programs (cash stipends, uniforms, midday meals) also rose, although in the more backward states of Madhya Pradesh and Uttar Pradesh, these benefits were provided mainly to high-caste students.

Decentralization of schooling to local governments. Decentralization of schooling to municipal governments appears to have had little impact on average student learning, although there is some evidence of improvement in learning outcomes in wealthier and administratively

In India, inducing better monitoring of schools by providing more information and training to communities about school management has had mixed effects.

Decentralization of schooling to municipal governments appears to have little impact on average student learning.

Average test scores in Argentina rose following decentralization . . .

. . . but all of the increase was concentrated in wealthier schools located in municipalities and provinces that had greater administrative capacity.

more capable localities. Madeira (2007) finds that school decentralization in the Brazilian state of São Paolo increased dropout and failure rates across all primary school grades, widening the gap between "good" and "bad" schools ranked by their initial dropout rates. These negative effects occurred despite an increase in school resources and a reduction in class size and student teacher ratios. Worse yet, the negative effects were significantly larger for schools in poorer, more rural, and more unequal communities, and the effects intensified with the number of years the school was decentralized.[31]

Similar results emerge from a study by Galiani, Gertler, and Schargrodsky (2008), who find an increase in average test scores in Argentina in schools that were decentralized. However, all of the increase was concentrated in wealthier schools located in municipalities and provinces that had greater administrative capacity. Decentralization actually decreased scores for schools in poorer areas and in municipalities that were in provinces that had run fiscal deficits before decentralization.

Kosec (2011) shows how preferences over public spending can differ systematically across localities that vary in initial wealth. The study focuses on investment in public preprimary education across municipalities in Brazil following legal changes that increased resources for education.[32] Kosec shows that poorer municipalities used significantly more resources to enhance the availability of public preprimary education, which then had a substantial payoff in student learning. In contrast, wealthier municipalities used the funds largely to enhance the quality of primary education. Investments in public preprimary education were lower in municipalities that were more unequal, suggesting that polarization can undermine the influence of the poor on public policy.

Madeira (2007) attributes some of the perverse learning effects in Brazil to the democratization of schooling, which expanded school access for less well-prepared students, especially in grades 1 and 2. Rodriguez (2006) assesses the impact of school decentralization in Colombia, using a strategy that compares the performance of students in public and private schools on standardized tests. She finds that once the change in the composition of children in public schools as a result of decentralization is accounted for, the average standardized test scores of public school students improved significantly more than the scores of students in private schools.[33]

Pradhan and others (2011) study an intervention aimed at strengthening school committees in Indonesia. They find that measures that increased linkages between schools and local government officials were the most effective in improving schooling outcomes and the legitimacy of the participatory process, particularly when combined with better accountability of the school committees themselves through open elections. In contrast, interventions that provided funds and training to incumbent school committee members had no effect. Moreover, even the most effective intervention (election with linkage) did not alter parental willingness to invest time or resources in the school committee though it did increase the amount of time parents devoted to homework, by about 80 minutes a week.[34]

A number of intermediate outcomes also improved. Specifically, the election intervention improved perceptions of school committee effectiveness by teachers, suggesting that elections may improve legitimacy. Elections also improved teacher motivation and effort. Elections alone increased teaching time by 0.63 hours a day, mostly in lesson preparation time. Elections plus linkage increased daily teaching time by 1.1 hours, mostly in time spent grading. The proportion of teachers observed in the classroom at the time of the survey decreased with the election intervention, however, which is puzzling. The authors also find no impact on student dropout or repetition rates in any arm, although they find some improvement in student learning in the linkage and election plus linkage arms.

The results from a companion qualitative study suggest an interesting tension. On the one hand, school committees appreciated receiving grants that were directly under their control and reported this control as the impetus for more face-to-face dialogue with the community. On the other hand, the grants seem to have resulted in greater conflict between the school committee and the principal (as might be expected). There were also some challenges in implementing elections, with school committees resisting changes in membership. When elections were conducted as designed, however, they enhanced community awareness and participation in school committee activities and legitimized the committee. Simply providing training to incumbent committee members had little effect, either qualitatively or quantitatively. The key finding in this study is that the linkage process created a partnership between the school committee and the village

In Indonesia, partnership between school committees and village councils resulted in concrete actions by the village council and significant impacts that school committees could not have achieved alone.

council that resulted in concrete actions by the village council and led to significant schooling impacts that school committees alone could not have achieved.

Community Engagement in Delivering Primary Health Care Services

Many developing countries have experimented with community-based health care models. Often cited examples of success include Costa Rica and Jamaica, where community-level health education programs and community-based service provision are believed to have led to major reductions in mortality, despite fairly stagnant economic conditions (Riley 2005).

Community-based health service provision encompasses a wide range of programs. Most programs supply trained health care providers, who work at the community level and are often charged with activating communities in some fashion, usually through women's groups. The main focus of community-based health provision is on maternal and child care and household health behaviors. Most programs also rely on community volunteers or facilitators to build trust, mobilize local resources, coordinate group activities, or complement services provided by trained staff.

A number of randomized control trials yield evidence on the health impacts of such interventions. Most are small-scale interventions but some work directly with existing government health delivery systems or test mechanisms that can be scaled up through existing health delivery systems.

A small but growing body of literature by and large confirms the potentially beneficial impact of community-based health programs, particularly for maternal and child health.

This small but growing body of literature by and large confirms the potentially beneficial impact of community-based health programs, particularly for maternal and child health. A potential caveat is that the role of community engagement per se is often difficult to isolate, because most programs undertake a bundle of activities.

Only a few evaluations separate the role of community engagement from other bundled interventions. These studies find that community volunteers and health groups can positively affect both health behaviors and health outcomes—but only when they complement other inputs, such as trained health professionals and improved health services. There is also some evidence on the efficacy of transferring the management of community-based health programs to local governments and the role of public-private partnerships in the delivery of health services. The findings suggest positive, significant, and economically large effects of decentralizing health service delivery to local governments. In contrast, the findings on public-private partnerships in the delivery of health services are more mixed.

The literature on community-based health delivery can be grouped into four categories: community engagement in the allocation of resources for health-related investments, community engagement in providing health-related services and information, community monitoring of health care providers, and decentralization of basic health services to local governments or NGOs. The literature on each category is reviewed below.

Community engagement in resource allocation.

Communities often choose to allocate resources from social funds or community-driven development projects to upgrading or building primary health care facilities. Few evaluations have anything to say about the impact of such investments on health behaviors or outcomes. Among the few that do is an early study of social funds by Chase and Sherburne-Benz (2001), which finds an increase in the use of primary care services in communities that invested in a health facility constructed by ZAMSIF, the Zambia social fund. Under ZAMSIF, communities received social investment funds for investment in small infrastructure projects such as the rehabilitation of community health posts. Chase and Sherburne-Benz find that social fund beneficiaries were more likely to go first to a health post rather than a hospital when they sought treatment. They were also significantly more likely to report an illness, although they were no more likely than controls to seek treatment. The study also finds more limited evidence that the vaccination prevalence rate rose in areas with rehabilitated health posts.[35]

Arcand and Bassole (2008) find an increase in the use of basic health services and access to clean drinking water in communities that participated in the Programme National d'Infrastructures Rurales in Senegal. Access to basic health services rose 24 percentage points and access to clean drinking water 22 percentage points. The program was also associated with positive nutritional impacts (as measured by height for age, weight for age, and weight for height) for children, which were substantially larger for children from poorer households. The channel through which improvements occurred is not clear, however, as discussed next.

Decentralizing health service delivery to local governments appears to produce positive, significant, and economically large effects.

Community engagement in the provision of health care services.
A number of randomized control trials have attempted to assess the effectiveness of demand-side interventions in primary health care. A randomized pilot study of Ghana's Community Health and Family Planning Project (Navrongo) casts some light on the added benefits of engaging community volunteers in the provision of health services (Binka and others 2007). One arm of the intervention tested the impact of adding community-based, volunteer-provided health services to the basic set of clinical services, along with revolving funds and user fees to ensure organizational sustainability. Trained supervisors from the community recruited community health volunteers, organized community supervision of their work, and managed essential health resources. User fees and revolving accounts sustained this work. A second arm deployed trained nurses to villages as "community health officers." A third arm engaged the community in ensuring that the trained nurses would be available. A fourth arm was held as the control. In the third arm, community members helped construct housing for nurses using volunteer labor, ensuring that nurses could reside in the village. They also provided other types of community assistance and supported services provided by resident nurses.

The findings suggest that over an eight-year period, posting nurses to community locations reduced childhood mortality rates substantially relative to control areas. In contrast, volunteer services had no impact on child survival. However, where volunteers worked alongside trained nurses, outcomes were superior to the first two interventions. Working in concert with chiefs, village elders, and community volunteers, community-based nurses helped develop various types of social insurance mechanisms, such as deferred payment. These mechanisms allowed formal care to substitute for traditional care, reducing the delay in health seeking that tends to precipitate childhood mortality (see Nyonator and others 2005 for a detailed discussion). The authors interpret these results as reflecting the limited ability of volunteers alone to change entrenched behaviors like seeking traditional healers.

Linnemayr and Alderman (2011) evaluate an intervention in Senegal that focused on the provision of nutrition-related information to mothers of young children through a community-based mechanism. The nutrition intervention was undertaken as a pilot program within the Programme de Renforcement de la Nutrition, which included cooking workshops and a monthly community-level meeting on nutritional

> Working with chiefs, village elders, and community volunteers, community-based nurses in Ghana helped develop social insurance mechanisms that allowed formal care to substitute for traditional care.

practices, targeted at mothers. The program also provided vitamin and iron supplements, bednets, and deworming.

The pilot was randomized across 212 villages in three poor rural regions.[36] The results indicate significant improvements in health care practices in program villages but no effect on child growth measures, at least in the full sample of children. The one exception is children who were born or of breastfeeding age during the intervention. The nutritional status of these children rose significantly. Because of the bundled nature of the intervention, however, the role of each of its components remains unclear.

A number of studies assess the role of community facilitators in motivating better health practices. Manandhar and others (2004) report on one such study, in a district in Nepal. The sample consisted of 12 pairs of village development committees, one of which was randomly assigned to treatment.[37] The study collected baseline data on almost 29,000 eligible women from some 28,000 households. Follow-up data were collected two years after the intervention. In each intervention cluster, a local facilitator was recruited (nominated by the local community or identified by word of mouth or through an advertisement). The facilitator conducted a monthly women's group meeting in every ward (the level below the village development committee). Each facilitator held 10 group meetings. A number of issues were discussed in the meetings, including the identification and prioritization of health issues related to pregnancy and childbirth and potential solutions, including community-generated funds, stretcher schemes, and home visits by group members. The role of the facilitator was to activate and support the women's groups, not to provide health support. Health services were strengthened in both the control and intervention clusters, through the provision of supplies at local health facilities, the provision of newborn care kits, and the training of community health workers.

Over the two-year trial period, the neonatal mortality rate in intervention clusters fell 30 percent, though there was no difference in stillbirth rates. Maternal mortality also declined 80 percent (2 maternal deaths versus 11 in control clusters). There were significant improvements in health behaviors, such as antenatal care, the use of supplements, the share of births in health facilities with trained attendants, and use of clean kits. Birth attendants were more likely to wash their hands, and maternal and child illness was more likely to be treated at a health facility. Moreover, 95 percent of the groups remained active after the trial period. These results were achieved with only 37 percent of newly pregnant women (8 percent of married women) ever attending the women's meetings.

Tripathy and others (2010) conducted a similar trial in Jharkhand and Orissa, two of India's poorest states, where neonatal and maternal mortality rates are higher than the national average. In treatment villages, local facilitators were trained to support women's groups, which met about 20 times in all over three years. Health committees were formed in both intervention and control clusters to discuss health entitlements from service providers, particularly for mothers and newborns.[38]

This intervention witnessed a 45 percent reduction in early neonatal deaths (0–6 days). By the third year of the trial, there was also a 57 percent reduction in moderate depression among mothers. There were no significant differences in health care–seeking behavior, but there were significant improvements in home care practices (use of safe kits, hand washing by birth attendants, boiling of threads used to tie the cord, and so forth). More infants were also exclusively breastfed at six weeks. The cost per life-year saved was about $33 ($48 with health-service strengthening activities). Although the availability of delivery kits increased in both control and intervention clusters, women's groups generated more uptake of the kits in intervention areas.

Olken, Onishi, and Wong (2011) evaluate a pilot program in Indonesia (PNPM Generasi) that provided block grants to villages to encourage investments intended to improve specific health and education indicators.[39] In some communities, the grant was incentivized, in that the amount of the grant the following year was based partially on the village's performance on each of the 12 targeted health and education indicators. The performance bonus was competitively allocated among villages within the same subdistrict. For the evaluation, program villages were randomly assigned to receive either the incentivized or the nonincentivized grant. The data come from three survey waves, conducted between 2007 and 2010.

The study finds that the program reached beneficiaries and had very significant effects on a range of intermediate behaviors, at both midline and endline. For health, the strongest intermediate impacts were on growth monitoring and the distribution of iron sachets to pregnant women. The intervention was also associated with a 9.6 percent reduction in malnutrition and a significant increase in prenatal visits and immunizations. Health impacts were also larger in incentivized areas.

A program in Indonesia that gave block grants to villages to encourage them to improve specific health and education indicators achieved positive midline results . . .

Incentives did not affect education indicators, however, and some health impacts also disappeared by endline. For example, the project had large impacts on reducing neonatal and infant mortality at midline, but these impacts disappeared by the endline. The endline results also show no impact on learning.

Importantly, nontargeted indicators also improved across the board, with an average improvement of 0.0362 standard deviation, with statistically significant improvements in indicators such as facility-based deliveries. The grant also appears to have been most effective in more disadvantaged areas.

In looking at the mechanisms through which the project worked, the authors suggest that Generasi appears to have had the greatest impact on community effort. It mobilized cadres working at village health posts and ratcheted up participation in meetings about health education and related topics. Households in Generasi areas also felt that both health and education services had improved.

In terms of overall service provision, however, there were no statistically significant impacts. If anything, there was a slight decrease in health provider inputs and effort and some increase in the prices charged by providers. There is also some evidence of deterioration in the quality of care. Combined with the fact that the main effects come from greater community effort in direct service provision, these results are disturbing from the point of view of sustainability, as is the finding that there was no impact of the program on any indicator of community outreach or monitoring and no spillover to other community activities.

Community monitoring of health care providers.   Perhaps the best-known assessment of the efficacy of community monitoring in improving health service delivery is of a randomized citizen's report card project in Uganda (Bjorkman and Svensson 2007). The main objective of the project was to improve the quality of basic health services by improving community capacity to monitor service providers. The report card intervention was randomly assigned to half of 50 rural communities across 9 districts. Meetings of users and providers were held at which the information collected in the report cards was disseminated together with practical information on how best to use this information.[40]

The authors find large and significant improvements in a number of treatment practices, from staff absenteeism to waiting time and the quality of preventive care. They find a 16 percent increase in the use of health facilities, along with greater community satisfaction with

... but many results were not sustained.

Following the introduction of citizen report cards in Uganda, the under-five mortality rate fell 33 percent and vaccination rates and infant weight rose.

205

service providers. Some health outcomes also improved substantially. In particular, the under-five mortality rate fell 33 percent and vaccination prevalence rates and infant weight increased. During this period, there was no increase in government funding or investment in health facilities or services.

Given the size of the effect on under-five mortality, understanding the precise channel through which change occurred, as well as the role of community monitoring, is clearly of great value. The intervention suggests three competing channels through which service quality changes could have come about: greater community monitoring (a demand-side channel), provision of information to providers regarding their performance relative to expectations (a supply-side channel), and the bringing together of the community and providers (which could increase both the efficacy of information and community willingness to monitor). The authors test for the relevance of the demand- versus supply-side channels by replacing treatment indicators with measures of staff and community engagement as explanatory variables. They find that the coefficients on community engagement are positive, statistically significant, and larger than the coefficients on treatment indicators. In contrast, the coefficients on staff engagement are not significant or have the wrong sign. The authors posit that these results are more supportive of the demand-driven explanation. Although this finding is encouraging, the results are at best suggestive, as it is unclear precisely what the community or staff engagement variables are capturing.

An interesting descriptive study by Uzochukwu, Akpala, and Onwujekwe (2004) casts valuable light on potential hurdles in scaling up community engagement in service delivery. The authors report on the Bamako Initiative program in Nigeria, which aimed to strengthen primary health care by increasing community engagement. The program created village- and district-level health committees and gave them substantial authority. The committees' mandate was to supervise the activities of traditional birth attendants; select, supervise, and pay village health workers; manage revenues and profits from drug sales; set the remuneration of health workers; and make decisions about the level of user fees and rules for exemption. Despite very broad-based participation and awareness of its functions, the committee focused largely on ancillary functions, such as the provision of health education and a waste disposal system. It remained entirely outside all important decision-making processes, such as hiring and payment of staff, setting user fees, or providing oversight over budgets. There was also some disconnect between reports from health facility heads and community members about the extent of community involvement, with health facility heads claiming far greater community engagement in planning and management decisions than community members did.

Few if any empirical studies collect this type of qualitative data that could help elucidate the channels through which participation works to improve outcomes and the potential constraints that could limit effective community engagement. Moreover, no careful empirical study has been conducted of the Bamako program that could bring these participation results together with results on service quality and health outcomes.

Decentralization of basic health services to local governments or NGOs.

Decentralization of basic health care services to local governments appears to have been successful overall. The evidence suggests substantial gains on a number of child health outcomes as well as on a wider range of health behaviors. Some studies also find improvements in labor market outcomes and decreased fertility.

The devolution of health service provision to NGOs appears to have been less successful, although there is evidence of some positive outcomes. In particular, when programs are devolved to NGOs, improvements in health tend to be confined to outcomes specifically targeted by the program. There are also some perverse effects of the imposition of user fees.

Much of the evidence on the benefits of decentralized delivery of basic health services comes from a set of studies on Brazil's family health program, the Programa Saude da Família (PSF). The PSF was first rolled out in 1994, as a small pilot initiative covering a few areas. By 2006, it had expanded into a nationwide program; by 2009, the program covered more than 90 percent of Brazilian municipalities.

Municipal governments manage the PSF, under the supervision of the Brazilian Ministry of Health. PSF teams—which usually consist of a doctor, a nurse, an assistant nurse, and six community health workers, as well as a dental and a social work professional in some cases—are responsible for monitoring the health status of about 3,000–4,500 people (about 1,000 households). Teams make home visits and perform community-based health promotion activities. All services are delivered free of charge to ensure access by the most disadvantaged. Assessments

Decentralization of basic health care services to local governments appears to have been successful overall.

Devolution of health service provision to NGOs appears to have been less successful, although there is evidence of some positive outcomes.

Assessments of Brazil's decentralized family health program find positive and economically large effects on health outcomes and behaviors.

of the program find positive and economically large effects on health outcomes, particularly for neonates, and health behaviors. They also find substantial gains in child school attendance, adult labor supply, and employment and a decline in fertility.

Macinko and others (2007) uses the differential adoption and expansion rates of the PSF as a quasi-experiment to assess the relationship between changes in PSF coverage over time and changes in health outcomes that are most likely to be sensitive to primary care. Their data cover six years (1999–2004) and include 557 Brazilian micro-regions in 27 states. Each micro-region includes several municipalities.

This study finds a significant reduction in postneonatal mortality (deaths of children from 30 days to 1 year) and mortality from diarrheal diseases. In exploring the mechanisms through which PSF might work, the authors note that areas with greater PSF coverage also have higher prevalence rates of behaviors stressed by community health workers, such as breastfeeding, use of oral rehydration therapy, and child immunizations. The authors provide a back of the envelope estimation of program costs of about $30 per capita.[41]

A related study (Macinko, Guanais, and DeSouza 2006) finds high levels of satisfaction with PSF among users, with more than 75 percent reporting that child health services were of good quality. The presence of the program in a given municipality was also associated with better perceived health.

A potential limitation of the study by Macinko, Guanais, and DeSouza (2006) is that variation in the timing or rate of PSF adoption could be endogenous. Well-governed municipalities could decentralize health services early, for example, or municipalities with the worst outcomes could decentralize first. In either case, estimated impacts would be biased, with the direction of the bias not clear.[42]

Rocha and Soares (2009) also use the differential adoption and expansion rates of the PSF as a quasi-experiment. They use municipal panel data from 1995 to 2003. These data include information on a range of demographic and socioeconomic characteristics in addition to program coverage and mortality. Difference-in-difference estimates suggest a substantial decline in mortality, especially during the first year of life.[43] Municipalities that had been in the program for three years, for example, reduced infant mortality by 1.5 more infants per 1,000 live births than comparable municipalities that did not adopt PSF. Based on the 1993 average infant mortality rate in Brazil of 27 per 1,000 live births, this difference corresponds to a 5.6 percent reduction in the infant mortality rate. For a municipality eight years into the program, infant mortality declined by 5.4 deaths per 1,000 live births, a 20 percent decline relative to the 1993 national average.[44] Gains were largest in the two poorest regions (the North and the Northeast), which also provided fewer public goods.[45] Gains were also larger in less urbanized municipalities and municipalities with less access to treated water and poorer sanitation systems. The largest impacts of the program on infant mortality were associated with complications during pregnancy; infectious diseases (diarrhea and other intestinal diseases, influenza); and respiratory diseases (asthma, bronchitis)—precisely the sorts of conditions for which the presence of a community-based health program would be most effective.

The authors also look at the effects of PSF on household behavior, using several rounds of census data. They find no effects on child labor supply. In contrast, they find that school enrollment was 4.5 percent higher eight years after PSF exposure. In addition, adult labor supply was 6.8 percentage points higher and employment 11 percentage points higher.

The other case on which there is robust evidence of improvements in infant mortality is Pakistan's Lady Health Worker Program (formally known as the National Program for Family Planning and Primary Health Care), introduced by the government in 1994. Lady health workers are typically young women who have at least eight years of schooling and live in the community they serve. They are given 15 months of training to deliver care in community settings.

Lady health workers make home visits and are expected to be available at their own home, which is known as a "health home." They provide antenatal care, contraceptive advice, growth monitoring, and immunization services, with each worker responsible for about 1,000–1,500 people (about 175 households). Although the program is a federal program, lady health workers report to basic health units and rural health centers, which are managed by provincial and district governments.

Bhutta and others (2011) present the results of a randomized cluster trial in which lady health workers in treatment villages were given additional training in group counseling; the promotion of specific

The program was also associated with increases in school enrollment, adult labor supply, and employment and a decline in fertility.

health behaviors; the establishment of linkages with traditional birth attendants; and the recognition of urgent care cases and the need to refer them to basic health units, rural health centers, or hospitals. In addition, the trial created volunteer community health committees in treatment villages, with the aim of promoting maternal and newborn care in the village. Community health committees were expected to conduct advocacy work with community elders and local political leaders, organize an emergency fund for transporting the sick to an appropriate facility, and help lady health workers conduct group education sessions.[46]

The study finds a 15–20 percent reduction in perinatal and newborn mortality in the intervention area. It also finds improvement in 16 household behaviors related to maternal and early newborn care, with gains rising over time. The largest improvements were in antenatal care and facility (instead of at-home) births.

The authors point out that these gains occurred despite implementation through the government health system rather than by workers employed directly by the research team, in a difficult to reach and underdeveloped area. Although lady health workers were unable to complete the full set of activities they were expected to engage in, they still managed to successfully deliver a package of preventive and promotive health care services. However, the authors stress, in order to be effective, community health workers and programs need close oversight.

This study points to the importance of carefully assessing the additional gain from organizing volunteer-based community health committees. Given that the largest gains were in facility births, the role of the community health committees in organizing transport may have been key, but the importance of transport is not clear from the study. The study also cannot separate the effect of the additional training provided to lady health workers from the effect of setting up community health committees.

Jokhio, Winter, and Cheng (2005) report on an earlier cluster-randomized trial in rural Pakistan that trained traditional birth attendants in antenatal and newborn care. Traditional birth attendants were also provided with clean delivery kits from primary health care centers and linked to lady health workers. Concurrently, outreach clinics were established in intervention clusters (two clinics in each of three clusters), where obstetricians conducted eight outreach sessions during the six-month trial.

Lady health workers in Pakistan successfully delivered a package of preventive and promotive health care services . . .

. . . but to be effective, they need close oversight.

The study finds a reduction in neonatal mortality of 30 percent, identical to the outcome in Nepal's experiment with women's groups and larger than the results from the lady health worker trial. However, the sample consists of only seven clusters, including both treatment and control areas. It also fails to distinguish the impact of training birth attendants, and hence using existing structures, from the impact of outreach clinics. In practice, however, 91 percent of the women in the intervention group received care from traditional birth attendants, with only 16 percent visiting outreach clinics.

The Projahnmo project in Bangladesh tested a model similar to the lady health worker program, with one difference (Baqui and others 2008). Two treatment arms were established, in order to test the efficacy of a home-based care model against a community-based care model. In both intervention arms, male and female community mobilizers held group meetings on birth and newborn care preparedness. Community resource people were enlisted to encourage women to attend these meetings and seek antenatal care.

In the home care intervention, one community health worker was recruited (by an NGO) per four villages with a total population of about 4,000 people. The community health worker was trained for six weeks in behavior change communication and the clinical assessment and management of illnesses in neonates. He or she was responsible for tracking pregnancies during routine surveillance activities, making scheduled antenatal and postnatal home visits, diagnosing illnesses for referral, and administering penicillin to neonates who could not be taken to health facilities for treatment. In the community care arm of the intervention, only group meetings with mobilizers and resource people were held; no home visits were made. However, female volunteers (including traditional birth attendants) were recruited to identify pregnant women, encourage them to attend meetings held by mobilizers, and receive routine antenatal and early postnatal care. These volunteers were responsible for about 18,000 people.

This study finds very significant improvements in neonatal mortality but only in the home care arm, which saw a 30 percent decline in neonatal mortality during the last 6 months of the 30-month trial (relative to the control arm). In the home care clusters, there was also a sizable and statistically significant improvement in the use of supplements during pregnancy, the use of clean equipment, and newborn care practices. In contrast, there was no significant improvement in health behaviors in

An intervention in Bangladesh that created community health groups had no impact on any outcomes.

In contrast, a home care intervention was associated with a 30 percent decline in neonatal mortality as well as improvements in other health outcomes.

211

the community care arm. Furthermore, each community health worker in this trial was responsible for 4,000 people, a ratio similar to the primary health care worker-to-population ratio in Bangladesh's health care system, suggesting an easy route for scaling up existing health infrastructure.

Two studies look at the impact of devolving primary health care provision to NGOs. Kremer and others (2006) evaluate the effects of a pilot program under which the Cambodian Ministry of Health contracted with NGOs to run public health facilities in 12 districts. The project, which ran from 1999 to 2003, covered 1.26 million people, about 11 percent of Cambodia's population. In some districts ("contracting in" districts), contracted NGOs were expected to work within the existing government system to procure drugs, equipment, and supplies and to use Ministry of Health personnel. They could request transfers of personnel but not hire or fire staff; their operating expenses were financed through the government budget. In others districts ("contracting out" districts), NGOs had full management authority. They could hire and fire staff; bring in health workers from other parts of the country; and procure drugs, supplies, and equipment from any source. [47] Staff members from the Ministry of Health were allowed to join the NGO by taking a leave of absence from the civil service. If fired by the NGO, they were allowed to return to government service in another district.[48]

The study finds that both contracting out and contracting in had significant positive effects on most measures of health center management, including the health center's hours of service, staff presence during unannounced visits, and availability of equipment, supplies, and vaccines.[49] The authors also look at the impact on the specific health outcomes targeted by the program. They find that both contracting in and contracting out had positive and significant effects on the use of public health facilities for curative care consultations, as well as on antenatal care, vitamin A distribution to children, and child immunization. In contrast, there was less systematic improvement in nontargeted outcomes, such as the treatment of diarrhea and knowledge about HIV risk factors.

Yoong (2007) studies the Rogi Kalyan Samiti (Patient Welfare Committee [RKS]) program, in the Indian state of Madhya Pradesh, which transferred control over some aspects of hospital management to a local NGO.[50] The study used the phased implementation of this transfer of authority to identify its impact on child immunization rates.

Using difference-in-difference estimates, the study finds that children ages 0–3 received significantly fewer appropriate vaccines per year of exposure after a hospital was transferred to the NGO. Interestingly, the reduction in immunization rates was confined to the relatively better-off, with no negative effect on the poor, who were exempt from the user fees charged by the NGO. It is useful to note that vaccination is not generally a candidate for decentralization, because of significant interpersonal and interjurisdictional externalities.[51]

The Poverty Impact of Participatory Projects

Evidence on the poverty impacts of participatory development projects and decentralization reforms is scarce. This section draws some lessons from the little evidence there is, with some important qualifiers: the number of studies is small; the studies examine fairly disparate interventions; and, with a few exceptions, outcomes are typically assessed within a relatively short time span, even though, as discussed in chapter 3, some outcomes, such as changes in income or assets, are likely to be realized only over much longer time periods. It is also unclear whether most projects operate at a scale that could plausibly affect average poverty levels in program communities or even effect a permanent change in the income or assets of participating households.

Participatory projects provide a bundle of interventions, of which the encouragement or facilitation of participation is but one. Most provide resources for local public goods, productivity-enhancing investments, or private transfers, and many provide all three, often bundled with some form of microcredit. All of these interventions inject resources into communities and could thus have an independent effect on income.

Many community-driven development programs are also moving decisively toward greater support for livelihood activities. Such projects tend to encompass a broad array of productive activities, including crop production and nontraditional agricultural activities, such as aquaculture and medicinal plants, livestock, agro-forestry, fishing, and fish farming. Most programs also support postproduction activities, which can include agro-processing enterprises as well as rural marketing services. Projects usually provide some type of grant to eligible members or groups for productive investments, which can be either individual or collective and often include a training component, which may cover

Evidence on the poverty impacts of participatory development projects and decentralization reforms is scarce.

Participatory projects provide a bundle of interventions.

project formulation, skill enhancement, or the basics of business management and marketing. Many projects include innovative multisectoral programs, including linkages with government line ministries at many levels. Careful evaluations of these efforts would add much to the knowledge base on the effectiveness of participatory poverty reduction programs.

The literature reviewed below provides a mixed picture. Some studies find improvements in assets or income, other do not. Studies that present longer-term results tend to find that income gains either disappear or survive only for specific subgroups, not always the poorest or most disadvantaged. There are also concerns about evaluation strategies. The review excludes studies that use extremely poor data or an evaluation strategy that is flawed in a fundamental way.

An evaluation of the long-running KALAHI-CIDSS program in the Philippines finds a 5 percent increase in consumption, concentrated among poor households (Labonne 2011).[52] The program was also associated with higher labor force participation rates for both men and women and greater income diversification, as evident in reported participation rates at midline (2006), particularly for women. Interestingly, during the financial downturn, the participation rate for both men and women fell significantly, but mainly in control areas. The program thus appears to have had a protective effect on employment and participation rates, particularly for women.

Reported impacts are likely to be significantly biased, however— and the bias is likely to be in the direction of finding positive income impacts, since the results do not correct appropriately for sample size or initial differences between program and control groups.[53]

A careful evaluation of the KDP program in Indonesia (Voss 2008) finds no impact on average household consumption. However, there are significant gains among households in the bottom quintile of the consumption distribution and similar losses for households in the top quintile.[54] In the matched household sample, per capita consumption by the bottom quintile rose about 5 percent. The author carefully demonstrates that the estimated impact is likely to be robust to problems in the data.

A potential problem with this study is that the 2002 survey (SUSENAS) appears to have mismeasured household consumption. As a result, households whose consumption was erroneously understated in 2002 registered an increase in consumption in 2007, and households

The evidence on the impact of participatory projects on poverty is mixed . . .

. . . and most studies find that income gains disappear over time or survive only for subgroups, which are not always the poorest or most disadvantaged.

A careful evaluation of the KDP program in Indonesia concludes that it led to significant consumption gains by the bottom quintile.

whose consumption was erroneously overstated in 2002 registered consumption losses. This concern is not significant when looking at average changes, because program placement and mismeasurement are not likely to be correlated. It is a concern when disaggregating the data into quintiles using 2002 poverty status or per capita consumption, because the quintile level estimates may be biased. The authors use two alternative strategies to demonstrate that this bias is unlikely to be large.[55] Interestingly, the study finds no impact on the consumption of other disadvantaged groups, such as households with low levels of education or households headed by women, which suffer from more severe poverty, suggesting that consumption growth in the bottom quintile was concentrated among poor households near the poverty line.

A randomized evaluation of GoBifo, another World Bank–funded project, in Sierra Leone also finds no impact on household income four years after project inception (Casey, Glennerster, and Miguel 2011).[56] The evaluation sample included 238 villages, half of which were randomly held as controls. The baseline evaluation was conducted in 2005 and the follow-up in 2009.

GoBifo provided block grants of $4,667 (roughly $100 per household) to rural communities for construction of local public goods and for skills training and small business start-up capital. The project required village development committees to submit development plans for grant use to district councils through ward development committees for review and approval. The government implemented the project. Community facilitators supported GoBifo communities by encouraging inclusive decision making; greater participation of marginalized groups, such as women and youth; and transparent budgeting practices.

The results indicate some gains in household assets, such as housing quality and durables, as well as impacts on intermediate outcomes, such as the number of petty traders in the village and the range of goods available for sale. However, the authors do not discuss whether these gains accrued to poor or otherwise disadvantaged households. It is not clear whether this study collected detailed consumption data.

The Programme National d'Infrastructures Rurales (PNIR) was implemented in 90 of the poorest *communautés rurales* in Senegal.[57] Its main objective was to support the decentralization and fiscal reform process by providing resources for rural infrastructure investments which were allocated using a participatory mechanism. At the village level, the program set up a community development committee (*Comité de*

Concertation et de Gestion), with mandated inclusion of women and other marginalized groups.

Evaluation of the program used a quasi-experimental approach (Arcand and Bassole 2008). Eligibility for PNIR was based on an index of access to basic services at the *communauté rurale* level, allowing the authors to choose control communities using the same set of indicators and regional controls.[58]

The evaluation finds no reduction in household poverty, as measured by consumption expenditures, when villages that received the program are compared with controls, regardless of whether the program village received any PNIR funding. This comparison comes closest perhaps to a test of the impact of participation per se on income, as PNIR villages should differ from controls only in the community mobilization effort of PNIR rather than because of project funds. This comparison does find significant improvements in the nutritional status of children (as measured by weight for age, height for age, and weight for height), however, with larger gains for poorer households. It also finds improvements in access to clean drinking water, which rose 22 percentage points, and basic health services, which rose 24 percentage points. It is unclear what drove these improvements, however.

When the study confines attention to program villages and compares outcomes for households in villages with completed projects with outcomes in villages without completed projects, it finds large and significant impacts on consumption, particularly for the poor, but no impact on child nutrition. This finding suggests that nutritional gains do not vary because of investments in local public goods, whereas income and consumption do. These results are less robust than results that compare PNIR communities to control communities since it is unclear what determines the odds of a PNIR village actually getting a project.[59] The study also finds that poverty is reduced only in villages that invested in income-generating agricultural projects and, curiously, in schools rather than in drinking water or public health facilities.

An evaluation of the District Poverty Initiative Program (DPIP) in Andhra Pradesh (Deininger and Liu 2009) also yields mixed results. The authors use two rounds of data, from 2004 and 2006, collected from three districts in the state (Anantapur, Adilabad, and Srikakulam) to evaluate program impacts. As all the municipalities (*mandals*) in their sample benefitted from DPIP, they construct a counterfactual using years in the program. Specifically, control *mandals* are *mandals* that

Analysis of India's District Poverty Initiative Program finds no change in consumption or nutrition.

entered the program two and half years after treatment *mandals* and so have fewer years of exposure to the program. The sample includes 41 programs and 10 controls *mandals*, selected through propensity score matching to eliminate bias because of initial selection.[60] The authors assess program impact on household consumption, nutritional intake, and nonfinancial assets. Using the full sample of matched households, they find no change in consumption or nutrition, though there was a significant (16 percent) improvement in nonfinancial assets.

DPIP began in 2001, with the objective of using women's self-help groups, which had been organized in Andhra Pradesh under earlier development projects, to promote economic and social empowerment.[61] The bulk of DPIP support was directed at building the capacity of self-help groups and providing them with a one-time grant to promote microcredit and savings through a "community investment fund."[62] The presence of women's self-help groups was an important factor in the selection of the first DPIP districts.

Confining attention to self-help group participants, the authors find an 11 percentage point increase in consumption, a 10–12 percentage point increase in nutrition, and a 23 percentage point increase in non-financial assets. This comparison is valid only insofar as self-help group membership was driven by the same factors in the old and new DPIP districts. The widespread prevalence of self-help groups in the old DPIP districts much before the program was initiated, casts some doubt on this. That said, the results suggest that benefits were confined largely to members, which seems sensible given that benefits were mainly in the form of transfers to organized self-help groups (the project created no public goods). Disaggregating by poverty status, the authors find that benefits were entirely concentrated among the poor, with the greatest benefits going to the poorest.

Four other studies find little or no impact on poverty. Park and Wang (2009) evaluate China's Poor Village Investment Program—a community-based poverty alleviation program initiated in 2001 that financed investments in infrastructure projects in "poor" villages.[63] Projects were to be selected through a participatory mechanism. The study finds no impact of the project on mean income or consumption growth—although income and consumption among the better-off rose significantly.[64] For the nonpoor, per capita household income rose 6.6 percent and per capita consumption expenditure rose 8.8 percent.[65] The program also reduced the odds of migration by nonpoor households

China's flagship community-based poverty alleviation program had no impact on mean income or consumption growth . . .

. . . although there were substantial positive effects on income and consumption among the better-off.

by 5.2 percent. In contrast, there was no effect on the migration odds of the poor.

The study uses panel data on some 666 eligible villages and 5,500 households surveyed in 2001 and 2004. The identification strategy relies on the gradual phasing in of planned investments within designated poor villages. Hence, the main concern for identification is not the potential bias because of village selection but the bias induced by the timing of program investments. The authors use propensity score matching with time-invariant variables, or variables measured before the start of the program, to deal with this problem.[66]

The implied transfer of wealth to the relatively better off is considerable, given the authors' estimates that in 2004 the central government allocated some Y 32.7 billion (about $4 billion)—more than 5 percent of the central government budget—to poverty investment programs.

An evaluation of the Southwest China Poverty Reduction Project (SWP) provides a rare longer-run perspective on program impact (Chen, Mu, and Ravallion 2009). The SWP was introduced in 1995 in the counties of Guangxi, Guizhou, and Yunnan with the explicit goal of achieving a large and sustainable reduction in poverty in the poorest villages in these counties.[67] Like other participatory programs, the SWP included a bundle of interventions along with community-based participation in the selection of beneficiaries and activities. Within selected villages, it was expected that virtually all households would benefit from infrastructure investments such as improved rural roads, power lines, and piped water supply. Broad-based benefits were also expected from improved social services, including upgrading village schools and health clinics and training teachers and village health care workers. People with school-age children also received tuition subsidies, as a conditional cash transfer. Individual loans were available for investments in a wide range of productive activities, ranging from investments in yield improvement and animal husbandry to nonfarm enterprises. Microloans accounted for more than 60 percent of all disbursements.

The project yielded sizable and statistically significant improvements in mean household income in participating villages during the project cycle. But four years after the project had ended, these gains had largely disappeared.[68] The only group that was able to sustain income gains were initially poor but relatively well-educated households, which may have been genuinely credit constrained because of poverty. Given the numerous interventions bundled in this program, the authors do not

The Southwest China Poverty Reduction Project yielded sizable improvements in mean household income in participating villages during the project cycle . . .

attempt to isolate the effects of community participation. Given the observed heterogeneity in long-term gains, they do attempt to infer the potential impact of using participatory practices to identify beneficiaries for loans. They conclude that the weak overall performance of the project may have been caused by a participatory beneficiary selection process that apparently favored the better-educated overall but, perhaps because of program capture, failed to provide enough opportunities for the educated poor.

The authors also point to a broader concern with the assessment of the longer-term impacts of programs that are geographically placed, even when program assignment is random. Additional funding from participatory programs could simply displace local government spending in project areas, or governments could increase funding in non-project areas. There is some evidence for such displacement in their study areas. Comparison villages appear to catch up with project villages. Early gains in project villages disappeared as enrollment in control villages rose, for example. The authors note that this process may account, in part, for the smaller long-term impacts they observe, but the size of the bias introduced does not indicate that it could fully account for the absence of an average income impact over the longer term.

Fearon, Humphreys, and Weinstein (2009) study a community-driven reconstruction project implemented by the International Rescue Committee in post conflict northern Liberia. This careful study finds no impact of the project on livelihoods or access to public goods or services. The authors also find no evidence that the community-driven reconstruction program reduced the need for households in treatment communities to walk to key services. However, they do find that school-age children and young adults in treatment communities had higher school attendance rates, and there was a significant increase in female employment (see also the discussion of this study in chapter 6).

Two recent studies use randomized designs to study World Bank–funded community-driven development programs that provide support to individuals to obtain skills and business training and to establish or expand microenterprises. Blattman, Fiala, and Martinez (2011) assess the Youth Opportunities Program, implemented under the Northern Uganda Social Action Fund (NUSAF). This program provided substantial grants (worth almost 1.5 years of salary) to young adults chosen by lottery. About 60 percent of the grant was invested in vocational training or productive assets, with a substantial portion of the rest used

. . . but four years after the project had ended, these gains had largely disappeared.

Additional funding from participatory programs could simply displace local government spending in project areas, or governments could increase funding in nonproject areas.

A participatory project in postconflict northern Liberia had no apparent impact on livelihoods or access to public goods or services.

for working capital, savings, and consumption. The results at midline suggest a significant increase in the number of hours worked as well as a 50 percent increase in net income. Given the interest rates facing young adults, these investments would likely not have been made in the absence of grant funding, underscoring the need to expand access to capital markets for the poor and for young people, who lack assets as well as employment experience.

Gine and Mansuri (2012) assess a program to provide business training and microloans to members of rural community organizations established by the National Rural Support Program (NRSP) and funded by the Pakistan Poverty Alleviation Fund (PPAF). Many community organization members already had some experience with microcredit loans from NRSP.

Community organizations were randomized into two groups, one of which was offered the opportunity to obtain eight days of business training at no cost. About two-thirds of people offered training took it. Both groups were also offered the opportunity to apply for a loan that was about five times the size of the standard loan (the base loan was about Rs. 20,000, about six to seven months of daily wage labor earnings for one household member). Access to the loan was randomized through a lottery in which about half of applicants were chosen.

Gine and Mansuri find that business training reduced business failure and that the best businesses survived. Training also raised consumption, increased income (by about 12 percent), and improved business practices. However, the gains were confined largely to men.[69] Uptake of the loan was modest, with less than a third of eligible members applying, and the authors find no additional income gain for lottery winners.

Alwang, Gacitua-Mario, and Centurion (2008) report on PRODECO, a project that supports group-based income-generating activities in the southern departments of Itapua, Misiones, and Neembucu in Paraguay. Its main objectives are to empower marginalized groups and to strengthen local government capacity to identify, design, implement, and monitor community development projects. PRODECO provides grants to eligible groups for productive investments. Groups are formed in targeted communities by "development agents," which can be NGOs or public sector employees. Once the income-generating activity is identified, groups are trained in project formulation, technical skills related to the project, and business management and marketing basics. Approved projects can receive up to $30,000.[70]

Business training in Pakistan reduced business failure, raised consumption and income, and improved business practices . . .

. . . but the gains were confined largely to men.

The evaluation finds significant poverty impacts, but the design of the evaluation is unclear. Survey data were collected on participant and nonparticipant households. However, the authors do not specify how this sample was created. The authors then use a matching technique as well as an instrumental variables strategy to deal with selection. They do not discuss the matching variables or indicate when they were measured. The district-level instrument is a measure of political participation through voting; it is unclear how it can deal with selection at the household level. The second instrument is ownership of a refrigerator. Use of this measure ostensibly exploits the targeting criteria of the project, but as the data come years after the project is implemented, it is unclear why household assets years after the program was implemented should satisfy the exclusion restriction. Moreover, the data suggest that program participants are more likely than nonparticipants to own a refrigerator. Finally, the evaluation says nothing about the participatory process through which projects were identified, approved, and ultimately run.

A qualitative study by Marcus (2002) underscores the lack of longer-term sustainability of participatory efforts. Marcus's study includes a desk review of three social funds and an analysis of qualitative data from beneficiary communities. The projects reviewed were implemented by Save the Children in Mali, Mongolia, and Tajikistan. The review finds that, on balance, project investments were not sustainable, particularly for the poorest, once targeted assistance in the form of school fees and food subsidies was phased out.

Participatory project investments in Mali, Mongolia, and Tajikistan were not sustainable, particularly for the poorest.

Conclusions

The literature on decentralized targeting identifies a trade-off between the advantages of local information and the hazards of local capture. On balance, the evidence appears to indicate that local capture can overwhelm the benefits of local information.

Project design and implementation rules also play a critical role in determining whether participatory programs are captured. Demand-driven, competitive application processes can exclude the weakest communities and exacerbate horizontal inequities. Under some conditions, co-financing requirements—which have become the sine qua non of participatory projects—can exacerbate the exclusion of the poorest

On balance, the evidence appears to indicate that local capture can overwhelm the benefits of local information.

Demand-driven, competitive application processes can exclude the weakest communities and exacerbate horizontal inequities.

households and communities and attenuate the impacts of poverty reduction programs.

Community contributions and a demand-driven competitive project approval process are expected to generate higher-quality projects that are better aligned with community needs. They are also expected to enhance the sustainability of community infrastructure by giving beneficiaries a real stake in maintaining local public goods. At the same time, if the most disadvantaged among the eligible have the least capacity to propose viable projects and are thus more likely to opt out of the process altogether, the intended poverty reduction impacts of the program are attenuated and cross-community inequities in capacity and resources can increase.

The political relationship between the center and localities also matters, as do the incentives of local politicians under democratic decentralization. The objectives of the center and localities can diverge widely.

Involving Communities

On balance, the evidence suggests that greater community involvement tends to improve resource sustainability and the quality of infrastructure. However, four concerns permeate the literature:

- Inequality tends to reduce both efficiency and equity, and there can be important tradeoffs between resource sustainability and equity.
- Transferring management responsibilities for a resource or an infrastructure scheme does not usually involve handing over control to a cohesive organic entity with the requisite capacity; often it requires creating local management capacity. In the absence of deliberate efforts to create such capacity and provide resources for ongoing maintenance and management, investments in infrastructure are largely wasted and natural resources poorly managed.
- Clear mechanisms for downward accountability are critical. The literature is rife with cases in which decentralization is used to tighten central control and increase incentives for upward accountability rather than to increase local discretion. The absence of robust mechanisms for downward accountability tends to go hand in hand with complex reporting and planning

Co-financing requirements—which have become the sine qua non of participatory projects—can exacerbate the exclusion of the poorest households and communities and attenuate the impacts of poverty reduction programs.

On balance, the evidence suggests that greater community involvement tends to improve resource sustainability and the quality of infrastructure.

requirements, which are usually beyond the capacity of local actors and become a tool for retaining control and assigning patronage. Most of these requirements are holdovers from past rules designed to extract resources from local rather than benefit communities.

- Communities need to benefit from the resources they manage. For natural resources that create substantial externalities, the benefit should be commensurate with the size of the externality created by the resource and should at least compensate communities for the alternative uses to which they could put the resource for immediate gain. These concerns imply considerable engagement of higher-tier governments or implementing agencies in building local capacity, monitoring outcomes, and setting the broad parameters under which management is devolved—with a view to enhancing downward rather than upward accountability while leaving sufficient discretion at the local level.

Decentralizing Delivery of Education and Health

The evidence on the extent to which decentralizing the delivery of education and health has improved service access for the poor and other disadvantaged groups and led to improvements in service quality is mixed. Because efforts to engage communities in improving basic health services or primary schools usually also involve a substantial injection of funds for other activities (trained health personnel, upgraded facilities, stipends, uniforms, school meals), unpacking the impact of community engagement is d ifficult. The few studies that try to do so suggest that encouraging community participation can be beneficial when projects also provide technical support, such as community-based trained health personnel, or make investments in upgrading health and school facilities.

The evidence also suggests that the most successful programs are implemented by local governments that have some discretion and are downwardly accountable. Devolving programs to NGOs works less well, on average. Interventions that provide information to households and communities about the quality of services in their community as well as government standards of service tend to improve outcomes even when no additional resources are expended.

The most successful programs are implemented by local governments that have some discretion and are downwardly accountable.

223

Improving Livelihoods

A few studies find that projects with large livelihood components perform better than other participatory projects, but more evaluations are needed.

Few studies of participatory poverty reduction programs find clear poverty impacts. Some positive income effects emerge for subgroups, although in most cases the methodology used to generate these results is questionable. There is some evidence, however, that projects with larger livelihood components (credit, skills) perform better than other participatory projects, at least in the short run. Given this potential, such projects should be carefully evaluated.

Notes

1. Leakage occurs when benefits accrue to people other than the intended beneficiaries. Undercoverage occurs when some intended beneficiaries cannot be covered, because of budget constraints.
2. A poverty monitoring tool allows eligibility to be enforced though an administrative process, using indicators of household or community welfare that are intended to proxy for income, which is costly and often difficult to observe. The process usually involves some type of means test based on easily observed and verified aspects of a household's or community's poverty status, such as demographic and socioeconomic characteristics that are expected to be strongly correlated with relative deprivation.
3. Although private transfers can also include some stipulations to contribute labor (as in the case of workfare programs) or undertake specific behaviors (such as vaccinating one's children or enrolling them in school), the benefits are largely internalized by the household in the form of income or gains from improved health and schooling. This is not the case for the provision of free labor for a nonexcludable local public good, as the labor-providing household can internalize only a fraction of the benefits.
4. As Galasso and Ravallion (2005) note, the requirement that all *thanas* (municipalities or county subdivisions) participate in the program is likely to have constrained the scope for pro-poor geographic targeting at the center. Such political economy constraints tend to be a common feature of social programs.
5. Despite their higher allocations, the provinces were initially less able to target their poor areas, possibly because wealthier areas were better able to propose and co-finance feasible projects. In response, a project monitoring tool was developed to continuously update targeting performance at the district level. Ravallion (2000) shows that this simple but powerful tool—which can be adapted for regular project monitoring and evaluation—was able to substantially improve the intraprovincial targeting of the poor.
6. Because data on the shares obtained by provinces are not available, it is unclear how successful this effort was.

7. Proxy means tests are increasingly being used to target beneficiaries precisely because of concerns about program capture. They tend to impose uniform eligibility requirements, with some regional variation, leaving little room for discretion in the identification of beneficiaries at the local level.

8. Mustafa (2007), for example, views British colonial water development projects in India and Pakistan as an effort to increase the power of the state and ensure security. British authorities sought to "increase government control of the local populations by encouraging them to take up settled agriculture and thereby minimize the security threat they might pose to the power of the state." Mosse (2001) emphasizes that political control has always been a component of decentralized task management in India; it was part of a political process that allowed chiefs to maintain and extend their control

9. These developments were reflected in the title of the Eighth World Forestry Congress—"Forests for People"—held in 1978. The same year, both the Food and Agriculture Organization and the World Bank presented policy papers indicating the change in focus (Hobley 1996; Arnold 1998; Wardell and Lund 2006; see also Dasgupta 2009).

10. In 1992, the Rio Declaration and Agenda 21 called for participatory natural resource management strategies as means of increasing efficiency and equity in natural resource use and management. The emphasis on poverty reduction was strengthened even more in the United Nations Millennium Declaration (United Nations 2000).

11. Forestry, for example, historically focused on establishing plantations and woodlots. The handing over of rights to existing natural forests to rural communities emerged only in the 1980s (Arnold 1998).

12. Scholarship on common property regimes spans many disciplines. Anthropologists, resource economists, environmentalists, historians, political scientists, rural sociologists, and others have contributed to the growing body of literature, which also comprises political ecological, ethnographic, and historical approaches. Although Ostrom's work has clearly been the most influential in this regard, Dasgupta, Agarwal, Ribot, Bardhan, and others have also made important contributions. Recent empirical work on the commons draws significantly on theories of property rights and institutions. For a review of some of this literature, see; Bates (1989); Libecap (1989); Eggertsson (1990); North (1990); and the introduction in Ensminger (1992), which discusses the early foundations of this literature in the work of Coase (1960), Cheung (1970), Commons (1970), and Alchian and Demsetz (1972).

13. As Ribot, Lund, and Treue (2010) note, democratic decentralization is specifically about including whole populations—all citizens—in decision making based on representative authority, whereas CBNRM defines a community for each intervention (the user group, "stakeholders," fishers). Under CBNRM, the mode of representation of the "community" is variously defined through appointed committees, elected committees, stakeholder forums, participatory processes, customary chiefs, project

personnel, and so forth. In contrast, democratic decentralization involves transfers to elected local government authorities, and the community is defined simply as the citizens who live in the jurisdiction.

14. See also Morrow and Hull's (1996) study of the Yanesha Forestry Cooperative in Peru.

15. As the paper relies on a single cross-section and forest user groups were not placed randomly, the author uses a number of creative econometric strategies, including the use of administrative data to control for heterogeneity in the placement of forest groups. The results remain robust. The main outcome measure is self-reported collections of firewood and fodder.

16. Their empirical strategy involves comparing adjacent VP and non–VP forest parcels in order to control for unobservable community characteristics. They also control for a number of geographical attributes (such as slope, aspect, altitude, and distance from the village) that affect forest quality.

17. The study uses a large sample of randomly selected forest parcels and objective measures of forest quality, including canopy cover, height, girth, species of trees, and lopping and regeneration rates. The authors deal with unobserved heterogeneity in the existence of a VP by comparing conditions in VP and non–VP forest patches that are adjacent to a particular village. This methodology allows them to control for time-invariant characteristics of local geography, climate, and communities. They address the potential for negative externalities to neighboring non–VP forests by including controls for distance to the nearest VP forest.

18. Khwaja (2009), for example, notes that communities often report choosing a particular type of project simply because they believed that it was one the external agency could or would approve; asking for a different type of project, they believed, would lead to not getting any project at all.

19. Project complexity was measured by whether the project required cash or skilled labor and the community's experience in maintaining such a project.

20. Controlling for inequality in wealth (land ownership), an increase in the heterogeneity index from the first to the third quartile (0.25–0.43) is associated with a 7 percent drop in maintenance.

21. The argument is that as a member's share of project returns increases, her share of maintenance costs may not increase commensurately if free riding is possible and maintenance costs are increasing. However, as inequality in returns increases further, people with substantial shares may become willing to bear the necessary maintenance costs, perhaps by contracting out the work.

22. Survey data included engineers' assessments of the quality of project construction, the physical condition of the project on the survey date, and beneficiary assessments of project performance. Information on household landholdings, assets, caste, education, and other characteristics for all households in study villages came from the census.

23. The NRSP operates much like the Agha Khan Rural Support Program. Both are now substantially funded by an apex institution, the Pakistan Poverty Alleviation Fund, which is financed by the World Bank.

24. An increase in the quality of the leader from the first to the third quartile increased the quality of maintenance by almost 8 percentage points.

25. The exogeneity argument relies on the fact that both the subdistrict and the village are administrative units based on population and geography and are thus not likely to be influenced by the presence of the KDP. However, it is not clear that the number of villages per subdistrict is uncorrelated with other unobserved subdistrict characteristics, such as ethnic heterogeneity or geography, which could exert an independent effect on project quality. For example, location and geography could influence local labor market conditions, the cost of materials and transportation, construction methods, and pre–KDP stocks of village infrastructure. Similarly, if ethnic/religious identity is part of the calculation in setting administrative boundaries, subdistricts with greater ethnic diversity could have a larger number of more homogeneous villages. If such villages are also more cohesive, with higher levels of village monitoring, average project quality could be higher in subdistricts that comprise more villages. Given the limitations this study faces in relying exclusively on administrative data from the KDP, it deals with these issues well.

26. Gunnarsson and others (2009) use data from eight Latin American countries. They find that differences across countries explain just 9 percent of the variation in school autonomy and 6 percent of the variation in community participation, although cross-country differences in mandated levels of autonomy and participation are substantial. Educational systems are highly nationalized in Bolivia and the Dominican Republic; more locally managed in Brazil, Chile, and Colombia; and somewhere in between in Argentina and Peru. Interestingly, the two countries with the greatest parental participation, Colombia and the Dominican Republic, are at opposite ends of the range of legal centralization. Cuba has both extremely low levels of autonomy and participation and extremely high educational achievement.

27. The program they evaluate sought to address the challenges created by the introduction of free primary education in Kenya and the associated influx of new students with varying levels of academic preparation.

28. A second component of this program was a training program for parent associations, which provided training in the management of school funds and in the participatory management process. The authors do not evaluate this component, which was introduced at a later stage.

29. The authors use the gradual phasing in of the intervention to identify average treatment effects using a pipeline approach. An index of school quality (which included student density; teacher student ratio; and failure, repetition, and dropout rates) was used to target schools for AGE. The authors use this index to check whether schools that received AGE during the study period were similar at baseline to schools that received AGE later. They also use school fixed effects and a school-specific linear time trend. Although this strategy cannot deal with unobserved time-variant school characteristics that are correlated with both the timing of AGE treatment and the quality outcomes of interest, the authors argue correctly that such

unobserved time-variant school characteristics are unlikely to be driving the results. The authors also find little evidence that changes in unobserved student ability drove the results. Not only did they find no effect on the dropout rate in treatment schools but, compared with preintervention trends, enrollment levels actually improved.

30. The film, poster, and calendar conveyed information on the detailed roles and responsibilities of the three state-specific school oversight committees. The intervention was conducted in three rounds in each *gram panchayat* (village council), separated by a period of two to three weeks. Each round consisted of two to three meetings in different neighborhoods of the *gram panchayat*. The campaign also included the distribution of posters and take-home calendars and the convening of neighborhood meetings to ensure participation by members of disadvantaged castes. The tools were the same in all three states (the information communicated was state specific, pertaining to the School Development and Monitoring Committee (SDMC) in Karnataka, the parent-teacher association in Madhya Pradesh, and the village education committee in Uttar Pradesh). In addition to the information campaign treatment in each of the three states, a second treatment was tested only in Karnataka. The only dimension in which the second treatment was different from the first was that the film had an additional one- to two-minute component at the end. To increase awareness about the economic benefits of schooling, this component showed average wages in the state for different levels of schooling and encouraged the audience to become involved in monitoring outcomes at the school.

31. The school reform in the state of São Paolo allowed municipalities to take over any primary or secondary school. During the period of the study, municipal governments took over more than half of all state-run schools. The author uses this gradual takeover to identify the impact of school decentralization on intermediate outcomes. As municipal governments could decide which schools to decentralize, the impact of school decentralization cannot be assessed without accounting for this selection effect. The direction of the bias is unclear, as municipalities could choose to decentralize either the best- or the worst-performing schools in order to show the greatest impact from decentralization. The author deals with this problem by using an eight-year school panel. The data include a large number of time-variant characteristics for each school and its community and span the period before and after decentralization, allowing the author to conduct robustness checks, including a check for parallel trends, to deal with the potential bias caused by initial selection.

32. Municipal governments in Brazil are required to provide primary education; preprimary education is offered on an optional basis, with substantial variation in provision levels. Kosec uses changes in the law that occurred in 1998 (FUNDEF) and 2007 (FUNDEB) and panel data on municipal education policy over a 13-year period (1995–2008).

33. Both Galiani, Gertler, and Schargrodsky (2008) and Rodriguez (2006) rely on variation in the timing of decentralization across provinces to identify the impact of decentralization.

34. School committees were randomly assigned to receive or not receive a grant. All funded school committees then received one of three interventions: training, democratic election of school committee members, or a facilitated collaboration between the school committee and the village council (linkage), yielding eight study arms in all. The sample included 520 schools in 9 districts and 44 subdistricts in the provinces of Java and Yogyakarta; 100 schools were left as controls. The data come from three surveys: a baseline (administered in 2007), a midterm (administered in early 2008), and an endline (administered in late 2008).

35. The study uses a combination of pipeline and matching methods to estimate the impact of social fund investments.

36. There was considerable deviation from assigned status. To deal with this problem, the authors report estimates of impact using assigned treatment status (that is, "intent to treat") as well as actual treatment status, using assigned status as an instrument as well as an input into the propensity score in a matching approach.

37. A village development committee has a population of about 7,000. Forty-two village development committees were matched into 21 pairs on the basis of ethnic composition and population density; 12 random pairs were selected for the study (1 intervention and 1 control cluster in each pair).

38. The sample comes from 36 rural clusters in 3 districts (12 per district), with a total population of 228,000. Eighteen clusters were randomly allocated to the treatment group, the other 18 were held as controls. All women 15–49 who had given birth during the study period (July 2005–July 2008) could participate; women could enter anytime if they gave birth. Baseline mortality rates were established over a nine-month period.

39. The grants—whose average size ranged from $8,500 in 2007 to $18,200 in 2009—could be used for a range of health-related activities, including hiring extra midwives or teachers for the village, subsidizing the costs of prenatal and postnatal care to women, providing supplementary meals to children, offering scholarships, improving health or school facilities, and rehabilitating roads to improve access to health and education facilities during the rainy season. Activities had to be used to support one of the 12 indicators of health and education service delivery identified by the program, which included antenatal and postnatal care, childbirth assisted by trained birth attendant, immunization, school enrollment, and school attendance, among others.

40. Facilitators from local NGOs led three meetings: a meeting with community members, a meeting with the staff of the relevant health facility, and a meeting that brought the community and health facility staff together. At the community meeting, facilitators provided community members with an assessment of the performance of the relevant primary health care facility, both in absolute terms and relative to other local providers and the government standard for health service delivery at the dispensary level. Communities were then encouraged to identify the key problems and the best way to monitor the provider. The health facility staff meeting was held at the health facility. At this meeting, the facilitators contrasted

information on the quality of service provision they had obtained from the baseline survey with the information provided by the facility. At the third meeting, community representatives and health facility staff developed a shared action plan, or a contract, outlining what needed to be done and how and when it would be done, as well as who would be responsible. After the initial meetings, the community was expected to monitor the provider. However, facilitators supported this process through follow-up meetings. These meetings took place during the facilitator's day-to-day interaction with the community-based organizations in the village.

41. In 2005, federal government transfers to municipalities totaled R\$5.7 billion (about \$2.6 billion), which represents about \$14 per person covered. This figure does not include the municipal contributions, which varied from zero to almost 100 percent.

42. The authors add micro-region fixed effects as well as a number of other time-variant regional variables to reduce potential selection problems; they do not test for parallel trends before the study period, however, without which the conditional exogeneity of program expansion rates cannot be assumed.

43. The authors do a careful job of dealing with selection issues. To deal with time-invariant differences across municipalities, such as differences in initial mortality rates or health service quality, they add municipal fixed effects to the difference-in-difference specification. Time-variant differences, such as the occurrence of health shocks, are more problematic. The authors include state-specific time dummies to deal with this issue. Because the number of municipalities was large, they could not use municipality-specific time trends. Instead, they add a wide range of municipality variables, including immunization coverage, health and education infrastructure, and municipality population. They cluster standard errors at the municipality level.

44. For mortality of children ages 1–4, the coefficients correspond to reductions of 6.4 percent (0.07 in absolute terms) for municipalities three years into the program and 25 percent (0.28 in absolute terms) for municipalities eight years into the program.

45. In the North, a municipality eight years into the program is estimated to experience a reduction of 15.0 infant deaths per 1,000 live births. The reduction in the Northeast is 13.8 per 1,000 live births.

46. Sessions were to be held quarterly, in a local household, with adolescent girls, women of reproductive age, and older women. Lady health workers and traditional birth attendants were expected to facilitate these sessions using materials specifically developed for this purpose, including a docu-drama on pregnancy and newborn care.

47. The 12 districts selected for the study were randomly assigned to three groups: four were eligible to receive "contracting-in" bids, four were eligible to receive "contracting-out" bids, and four served as a comparison group. The authors collected data on individual health care outcomes and care-seeking behavior from a random sample of 30 villages in each of the 12 districts involved in the contracting project. About 20,000 people in 3,700

households were included in the samples. A baseline survey was conducted in 1997; a full follow-up was conducted in 2003. Although the same villages were sampled in both survey years, within villages a new random sample of households was taken each time. The data are thus a panel at the village level and a repeated cross-section at the household level. In treated districts, the management of government health care services was put out to competitive bid by qualified organizations, such as NGOs and private firms. For each district, the organization with the highest combined score on the technical quality of the proposal and price was awarded a contract to manage the district's government health care service. In the end, only international NGOs, firms, and universities submitted bids. All the winners were international NGOs. The comparison districts continued to be managed by local employees.

48. In the end, only a few staff members were fired. Salaries in the "contracting in" districts were based on the civil service pay structure, plus additional amounts decided by the contractors that could be raised from user fees. In "contracting-out" districts, NGOs were free to implement the pay structure of their choosing.

49. Not all districts in the initial treatment groups were actually treated. The authors report "treatment on treated" effects using assignment to treatment as an instrument.

50. Each hospital continued to receive the same line-item grants from the state government to ensure preform levels of funding. The RKS also raised its own money through user fees, the leasing of hospital property, loans, and donations. It had full autonomy over the use of hospital assets but no authority over government-appointed doctors.

51. It identified transfer of control as the date at which the RKS became active, as reflected in the date at which it started to collect revenue. It aggregated RKS activity at the district level and grouped districts into high- and low-exposure, within which it measured exposure as the number of years in a high-exposure district. The estimation includes district and cohort fixed effects as well as controls for maternal demographics and child characteristics.
The poor are identified as holders of Below Poverty Line (BPL) cards, issued by the government for a range of poverty-related benefits.

52. Participating municipalities receive an annual grant, equivalent to ₱300,000 for each *barangay* (the smallest administrative unit, often a village). The grant is then allocated competitively among *barangays* in the municipality. The annual per capita allocation is about ₱300. The project was implemented in the poorest quartile of municipalities. The study uses propensity score matching to create comparison municipalities. As the program was provided at the municipal level, matching was done at the municipal level. The final sample included 16 municipalities, half of which received the program and half of which served as controls. Comparison municipalities were clearly better off at baseline, but a check for parallel trends finds no significant differences between treatment and control municipalities once standard errors are corrected for intramunicipality

correlation. Data were collected at three points in time: baseline (2003), midline (2006), and endline (2010).

53. Since treatment assignment was at the municipal level while analysis was at the household level, a correction needs to be done to account for the intracluster correlation of standard errors at the municipal level. Given the small number of municipalities included in the study, this correction is likely to substantially increase standard errors. Although this correction is made for the parallel trends estimation—wiping out all differences between treatment and control municipalities, as one might expect—no standard error correction is reported for the impact results.

54. The author uses propensity score matching methods to create a matched sample of 300 treatment and control subdistricts. The treated subdistricts were drawn from treated subdistricts in the 2002 SUSENAS survey, which also serves as the baseline, in conjunction with the 2003 PODES village census. Control subdistricts were drawn from non–KDP subdistricts in the same survey that did not benefit from similar government programs. A matched sample of about 6,000 households was also created using available household characteristics. The follow-up data were collected in 2007.

55. The baseline and midline surveys were also conducted at different times, with the follow-up overlapping Ramadan, the Muslim month of fasting, followed by the Eid festival, when consumption is higher, particularly among the poor.

56. Chapter 6 discusses the study's findings on social cohesion and collective action.

57. A *communauté rurale* is an administrative unit with 42 villages on average and a population of about 13,000,

58. The study uses data from 36 *communautés rurales,* half of which were controls. The sample includes 71 villages, 750 households, and 1,000 children. Analysis is done at the village, household, and child level, using baseline and follow-up data. Village, household, and child fixed effects are included, depending on the level of analysis. The authors check for parallel trends across treatment and control communities in the key outcome variables before PNIR and cannot reject the null hypothesis of similar trends. However, this check for parallel trends is run at the level of the *communauté rurale*, whereas the analysis is conducted at the child, household, and village level.

59. Political influence variables at the village level are used as instruments to deal with potential selection in project awards. A concern with this strategy is that it is not clear whether political influence affects village outcomes only through its effects on accessing PNIR funds. If political influence can also be used to attract other public or private resources to the village, the exclusion conditions necessary for the use of political influence variables as instruments would be violated.

60. The authors do not check for parallel trends in outcome variables before program inception. It is therefore unclear whether the propensity score matching exercise and difference-in-difference technique can take care of selection bias from time-invariant or time-variant sources.

61. A typical program self-help group consists of 10–15 members who meet regularly to discuss social issues and activities, make a small deposit into a joint account, and make decisions on loans.

62. In later years, the program also tried to increase the availability of rice to low-income households through bulk purchases from the public distribution system and resale to poor village households at a discounted price. Rice was provided as an in-kind loan for self-help group members. The provision of grain as in-kind credit when needed was also expected to boost meeting attendance, saving, and repayment.

63. The program covered 148,000 villages officially designated as poor, which represent about 21 percent of all villages in rural China. Some 140 million people (about 15 percent of China's rural population) live in these villages.

64. The authors find a substantial increase in overall spending on public infrastructure in program villages with completed projects. This increased spending occurred because of larger investments by both the government and the village community, suggesting that community financing was used to leverage government funds, as is the practice in community-driven development projects. Interestingly, however, the program had no effect on what the authors describe as village *corvée* labor. It is not clear whether the supply of such labor failed to increase because villages were not required to contribute labor to the projects or because villagers responded by reducing labor on other communal activities. There is also some heterogeneity in the financing of infrastructure investments in western versus nonwestern regions. The increase in investment was twice as large in nonwestern villages, entirely because of larger contributions from the community, including village labor. In contrast, communal labor inputs were reduced in western villages that began investments under the project.

65. Of the 588 villages in the matched sample, 552 had at least one poor household, 484 had at least one nonpoor household, and 448 villages had both nonpoor and poor households. The restricted sample included the 448 villages with both types of households. A comparison of results for nonpoor and poor households using the restricted sample is analogous to controlling for village fixed effects, as the authors compare the average change in income for the village poor (nonpoor) with the average change for the village poor (nonpoor) in the matched village. As villages with both nonpoor and poor households are more heterogeneous with respect to poverty, a comparison of estimates for the restricted and full samples also suggests how program impacts may vary along this dimension.

66. By the end of 2004, 55 percent of poor villages (366 sample villages) had completed plans and 37 percent (244 sample villages) had begun investments based on the plans. According to the authors, a main reason why most villages had yet to begin planned investments three years after the program began was that county governments generally concentrated annual program allocations in a subset of villages. The decision to fund village plans sequentially rather than simultaneously reflected practical concerns, such as economies of scale in investments and the fixed costs associated with supervising the design and implementation of plans in

each village. The village data confirm that the increase in treated villages over time reflected the gradual expansion of investments in new villages within rather than across counties.

67. Some 1,800 of a total of 7,600 villages were selected in the three counties, using specific and objective criteria.

68. As program placement was targeted based on geography and poverty, the authors obtain a counterfactual set of villages by selecting randomly from non–SWP villages in the same counties and then using propensity score matching methods to arrive at a plausible counterfactual.

69. Neither study includes data on the longer-term sustainability of impact from the grant or skills and business training.

70. Targeting of the poorest was ensured through a two-step process. In the first stage, the poorest districts in the three departments were identified using a poverty map. In the second stage, households were screened based on eligibility criteria (in rural areas, households could not own more than two cows or farm more than 10 hectares; in all areas, households could not own an air conditioner, a refrigerator, or a four-wheel vehicle). Participatory targeting was not used to identify beneficiaries, despite the participatory intent of the program.

References

Adhikari, B., and J. C. Lovett. 2006. "Institutions and Collective Action: Does Heterogeneity Matter in Community-Based Resource Management?" *Journal of Development Studies* 42(3): 426–45.

Agrawal, A. 2010. "Environment, Community, Government." In *In the Name of Humanity*, ed. I. Feldman and M. Ticktin, 190–217. Durham, NC: Duke University Press.

Agrawal, A., and C. Benson. 2010. "Local Resource Governance Institutions: Outcomes and Explanations." Background paper for Policy Research Report, World Bank, Washington, DC.

Agrawal, A., and A. Chhatre. 2006. "Explaining Success on the Commons: Community Forest Governance in the Indian Himalaya." *World Development* 35: 149–66.

Agrawal, A., A. Chhatre, and R. Hardin. 2008. "Changing Governance of the World's Forests." *Science* 320: 1460–62.

Alatas, V., A. Banerjee, R. Hanna, B. A. Olken, and J. Tobias. 2012. "How to Target the Poor: Evidence from a Field Experiment in Indonesia." *American Economic Review* 102(4): 1206–40.

Alchian, A., and H. Demsetz. 1972. "Production, Information Costs, and Economic Organization." *American Economic Review* 62: 777–95.

Alderman, H. 2002. "Do Local Officials Know Something We Don't? Decentralization of Targeted Transfers in Albania." *Journal of Public Economics* 83(3): 375–404.

Alwang, J., E. Gacitua-Mario, and V. Centurion. 2008. "Economic and Social Impacts on Participating Households of a Community-Driven Development Project in Southern Paraguay." World Bank, Washington, DC.

Araujo, M. C., F. H. G. Ferreira, P. Lanjouw, and B. Özler. 2008. "Local Inequality and Project Choice: Theory and Evidence from Ecuador." *Journal of Public Economics* 92(5–6): 1022–46.

Arcand, J.-L., and L. Bassole. 2008. "Does Community Driven Development Work? Evidence from Senegal." CERDI–CNRS, Université d'Auvergne, France.

Arnold, M. 1998. "Managing Forests as a Common Property." Working Paper 136, Food and Agricultural Organization, Rome.

Baird, I. G. 2006. "Strength in Diversity: Fish Sanctuaries and Deep-Water Pools in Laos." *Fisheries Management and Ecology* 13(1): 1–8.

Baird, S., C. McIntosh, and B. Özler. 2009. *The Squeaky Wheels Get the Grease: Applications and Targeting in Tanzania's Social Action Fund.* Development Economics Research Group, World Bank, Washington, DC.

Baland, J. M., P. Bardhan, S. Das, and D. Mookherjee. 2010. "Forests to the People: Decentralization and Forest Degradation in the Indian Himalayas." *World Development* 38(11): 1642–56.

Baland, J. M., and J. P. Platteau. 1997. "Coordination Problems in Local-Level Resource Management." *Journal of Development Economics* 53 (1): 197–210.

Banerjee, A. V., R. Banerji, E. Duflo, R. Glennerster, and S. Khemani. 2010. "Pitfalls of Participatory Programs: Evidence from Randomized Experiments in Education in India." *American Economic Journal: Economic Policy* 2(1): 1–30.

Baqui, A. H., S. El-Arifeen, G. L. Darmstadt, S. Ahmed, E. K. Williams, H. R. Seraji, and I. Mannan. 2008. "Effect of Community-Based Newborn-Care Intervention Package Implemented Through Two Service-Delivery Strategies in Sylhet District, Bangladesh: A Cluster-Randomised Controlled Trial." *Lancet* 371: 1936–44.

Bardhan, P. 2000. "Irrigation and Cooperation: An Empirical Analysis of 48 Irrigation Communities in South India." *Economic Development and Cultural Change* 48(4): 847–65.

Bardhan, P., M. Ghatak, and A. Karaivanov. 2007. "Wealth Inequality and Collective Action." *Journal of Public Economics* 91(9): 1843–74.

Bardhan, P, S. Mitra, D. Mookherjee, and A. Sarkar. 2008. "Political Participation, Clientelism, and Targeting of Local Government Programs." Discussion Paper, Economic Research Unit/2008-03, Indian Statistical Institute, Calcutta.

Bardhan, P., and D. Mookherjee. 2005. "Decentralization, Corruption, and Government Accountability: An Overview." In *International Handbook of Economic Corruption*, ed. S. Rose-Ackerman. Northhampton, MA: Edward Elgar Publishing.

Barrera-Osorio, F., and L. L. Linden. 2009. "The Use and Misuse of Computers in Education: Evidence from a Randomized Experiment in Colombia." Policy Research Working Paper 4836, World Bank, Washington, DC.

Bates, R. 1989. *Toward a Political Economy of Agrarian Development in Kenya.* Cambridge, U.K.: Cambridge University Press.

Beck, T., and C. Nesmith. 2001. "Building on Poor People's Capacities: The Case of Common Property Resources in India and West Africa." *World Development* 29(1): 119–33.

Besley, T., and R. Kanbur. 1993. "The Principles of Targeting." In *Including the Poor,* ed. M. Lipton and J. Van der Gaag, 67–90. Washington, DC: World Bank.

Besley, T., R. Pande, and V. Rao. 2005. "Participatory Democracy in Action: Survey Evidence from Rural India." *Journal of the European Economic Association* 3(2–3): 648–57.

———. 2007. "Just Rewards? Local Politics and Public Resource Allocation in South India." Development Economics Paper, London School of Economics and the Suntory and Toyota International Centres for Economics and Related Disciplines, London.

Bhutta, Z. Q. A., S. Soofi, S. Cousens, S. Mohammad, Z. A. Memon, I. Ali, and A. Feroze. 2011. "Improvement of Perinatal and Newborn Care in Rural Pakistan Through Community-Based Strategies: A Cluster-Randomised Effectiveness Trial." *Lancet* 377: 403–12.

Binka, F. N., A. A. Bawah, J. F. Phillips, A. Hodgson, M. Adjuik, and B. Macleod. 2007. "Rapid Achievement of the Child Survival Millennium Development Goal: Evidence from the Navrongo Experiment in Northern Ghana." *Tropical Medicine and International Health* 12: 578–83.

Bjorkman, M., and J. Svensson. 2007. "Power to the People: Evidence from a Randomized Field Experiment of a Community-Based Monitoring Project in Uganda." Policy Research Working Paper 4268, World Bank, Washington, DC.

Blaikie, P. 2006. "Is Small Really Beautiful? Community-Based Natural Resource Management in Malawi and Botswana." *World Development* 34(11): 1942–57.

Blattman, C., N. Fiala, and S. Martinez. 2011. "Can Employment Programs Reduce Poverty and Social Instability? Experimental Evidence from a Ugandan Aid Program (Mid-Term Results)." Yale University, New Haven, CT.

Bruns, B., D. Filmer, and H. A. Patrinos. 2011. *Making Schools Work New Evidence on Accountability Reforms.* Washington, DC: World Bank.

Caldwell, B. J. 2005. *School-Based Management.* Education Policy Series. Paris: International Institute for Educational Planning (IIEP) and International Academy of Education (IAE).

Campbell, T. 2003. *Quiet Revolution: Decentralization and the Rise of Political Participation in Latin American Cities.* Pittsburg, PA: University of Pittsburg Press.

Casey, K., R. Glennerster, and E. Miguel. 2011. "Reshaping Institutions: Evidence on External Aid and Local Collective Action." NBER Working Paper 17012, National Bureau of Economic Research, Cambridge, MA.

Cavendish, W. 2000. "Empirical Regularities in the Poverty-Environment Relationship of Rural Households: Evidence from Zimbabwe." *World Development* 28(11): 1979–2003.

Chase, R. S. 2002. "Supporting Communities in Transition: The Impact of the Armenian Social Investment Fund." *World Bank Economic Review* 16(2): 219–40.

Chase, R. S., and L. Sherburne-Benz. 2001. "Household Effects of Community Education and Health Initiatives: Evaluating the Impact of the Zambia Social Fund." World Bank, Social Development Unit, Washington, DC.

Chaudhury, N., and D. Parajuli. 2010. "Giving It Back: Evaluating the Impact of Devolution of School Management to Communities in Nepal." World Bank, Washington, DC.

Chavis, L. 2009. "Decentralizing Development: Allocating Public Goods via Competition." Kenan-Flagler Business School, University of North Carolina, Chapel Hill.

Chen, S., R. Mu, and M. Ravallion. 2009. "Are There Lasting Impacts of Aid to Poor Areas?" *Journal of Public Economics* 93(3–4): 512–28.

Cheung, S. 1970. "The Structure of a Contract and the Theory of Non-Exclusive Resources." *Journal of Law and Economics* 13(1): 49–70.

Coady, D. 2001. "An Evaluation of the Distributional Power of Progresa's Cash Transfers in Mexico." FCND Discussion Paper, International Food Policy Research Institute, Washington, DC.

Coase, R. H. 1960. "The Problem of Social Cost." *Journal of Law and Economics* 3(1): 1–44.

Commons, J. R. 1970. *The Economics of Collective Action*. Madison, WI: University of Wisconsin Press.

Dasgupta, P. 2009. "Trust and Cooperation among Economic Agents." *Philosophical Transactions of the Royal Society* 364: 3301–09.

Dasgupta, P. and K. G. Mäler. 1995. "Poverty, Institutions, and the Environmental Resource-Base." In *Handbook of Development Economics*, vol. III(A), ed. J. Behrman and T. N. Srinivasan, 2371–63. Amsterdam: North-Holland.

Dayton-Johnson, J. 2000. "Choosing Rules to Govern the Commons: A Model with Evidence from Mexico." *Journal of Economic Behavior & Organization* 42(1): 19–41.

Dayton-Johnson, J., and P. Bardhan. 2002. "Inequality and Conservation on the Local Commons: A Theoretical Exercise." *Economic Journal* 112(481): 577–602.

Deininger, K., and Y. Liu. 2009. "Longer-Term Economic Impacts of Self-Help Groups in India." Policy Research Working Paper 4886, World Bank, Washington, DC.

De Janvry, A., H. Nakagawa, and E. Sadoulet. 2009. "Pro-Poor Targeting and Electoral Rewards in Decentralizing to Communities the Provision of Local Public Goods in Rural Zambia." University of California, Berkeley.

Di Gropello, E. 2006. "A Comparative Analysis of School-Based Management in Central America." Working Paper 72, World Bank, Washington, DC.

Duflo, E., P. Dupas, and M. Kremer. 2008. "Peer Effects, Pupil-Teacher Ratios, and Teacher Incentives: Evidence from a Randomized Evaluation in Kenya." Online Working Paper CCPR 055-08, California Center for Population Research, University of California, Los Angeles.

Edmonds, E. V. 2002. "Government-Initiated Community Resource Management and Local Resource Extraction from Nepal's Forests." *Journal of Development Economics* 68(1): 89–115.

Eggertsson, T. 1990. *Economic Behavior and Institutions.* Cambridge, U.K.: Cambridge University Press.

Ensminger, J. 1992. *Making a Market: The Institutional Transformation of an African Society.* New York: Cambridge University Press.

Eskeland, G. S., and D. Filmer. 2002. "Autonomy, Participation, and Learning in Argentine Schools: Findings and Their Implications for Decentralization." Policy Research Working Paper 276, World Bank, Washington, DC.

Fearon, J. D., M. Humphreys, and J. M. Weinstein. 2009. "Can Development Aid Contribute to Social Cohesion after Civil War? Evidence from a Field Experiment in Post-Conflict Liberia." *American Economic Review* 99(2): 287–91.

Ferguson, J. 1996. *The Anti-Politics Machine. Development, Depolitization, and Bureaucratic Power in Lesotho.* Cambridge, U.K.: Cambridge University Press.

Fisher, M. 2004. "Household Welfare and Forest Dependence in Southern Malawi." *Environment and Development Economics* 9(2): 135–54.

Fujiie, M., Y. Hayami, and M. Kikuchi. 2005. "The Conditions of Collective Action for Local Commons Management: The Case of Irrigation in the Philippines." *Agricultural Economics* 33(2): 179–89.

Galasso, E., and M. Ravallion. 2005. "Decentralized Targeting of an Antipoverty Program." *Journal of Public Economics* 89(4): 705–27.

Galiani, S., P. Gertler, and E. Schargrodsky. 2008. "School Decentralization: Helping the Good Get Better, but Leaving the Poor Behind." *Journal of Public Economics* 92: 2106–20.

Gertler, P., H. Patrinos, and M. Rubio-Codina. 2007. "Empowering Parents to Improve Education: Evidence from Rural Mexico." Policy Research Working Paper 3935, World Bank, Washington, DC.

Gine, X., and G. Mansuri. 2012. "Money or Ideas? A Field Experiment on Constraints to Entrepreneurship in Rural Pakistan." World Bank, Washington, DC.

Gregerson, H. M., and A. H. Contreras. 1989. *Economic Analysis of Forestry Projects.* Rome: Food and Agriculture Organization.

Gugerty, M. K., and M. Kremer. 2006. *Outside Funding and the Dynamics of Participation in Community Associations.* Cambridge, MA: Harvard University Press.

Gunnarsson, V., P. F. Orazem, M. A. Sanchez, and A. Verdisco. 2009. "Does Local School Control Raise Student Outcomes? Evidence on the Roles of School Autonomy and Parental Participation." *Economic Development and Cultural Change* 58: 25–52.

Harragin, S. 2004. "Relief and an Understanding of Local Knowledge: The Case of Southern Sudan." In *Culture and Public Action,* ed. V. Rao and M. Walton, 307–27. Stanford, CA: Stanford University Press.

Hobley, M. 1996. "Institutional Change within the Forestry Sector: Centralized Decentralization." Working Paper 92, Overseas Development Institute, London.

Hodgkin, J., and M. Kusumahadi. 1993. "A Study of the Sustainability of Care-Assisted Water Supply and Sanitation Projects, 1979–1991." Associates in Rural Development, Burlington, VT.

Isham, J., and S. Kahkonen. 2002. "Institutional Determinants of the Impact of Community-Based Water Services: Evidence from Sri Lanka and India." *Economic Development and Cultural Change* 50(3): 667–91.

Jalan, J., and M. Ravallion. 2003. "Estimating the Benefit Incidence of an Antipoverty Program by Propensity-Score Matching." *Journal of Business and Economic Statistics* 21(1): 19–30.

Jimenez, E., and Y. Sawada. 1999. "Do Community-Managed Schools Work? An Evaluation of El Salvador's Educo Program." *World Bank Economic Review* 13(3): 415–41.

———. 2003. "Does Community Management Help Kids in Schools? Evidence Using Panel Data from El Salvador's Educo Program." Faculty of Economics, University of Tokyo.

Jodha, N. S. 1986. "Common Property Resources and Rural Poor in Dry Regions of India." *Economic and Political Weekly* 21(27): 1169–81.

———. 2001. *Common Property Resources in Crisis.* New Delhi: Oxford University Press.

Jokhio, A. H., H. R. Winter, and K. K. Cheng. 2005. "An Intervention Involving Traditional Birth Attendants and Perinatal and Maternal Mortality in Pakistan." *New England Journal of Medicine* 325: 2091–99.

Katz, T., and J. Sara. 1997. "Making Rural Water Supply Sustainable: Recommendations from a Global Study." World Bank, Washington, DC.

Khattri, N., C. Ling, and S. Jha. 2010. "The Effects of School-Based Management in the Philippines: An Initial Assessment Using Administrative Data." Policy Research Working Paper 5248, World Bank, Washington, DC.

Khwaja, A. I. 2004. "Is Increasing Community Participation Always a Good Thing?" *Journal of the European Economic Association* 2(2–3): 427–36.

———. 2009. "Can Good Projects Succeed in Bad Communities?" *Journal of Public Economics* 93(7–8): 899–916.

King, E. M., and B. Özler. 1998. "What's Decentralization Got to Do with Learning? The Case of Nicaragua's School Autonomy Reform." World Bank, Development Economics Research Group, Washington, DC.

King, E. M., B. Özler, and L. B. Rawlings. 1999. "Nicaragua's School Autonomy Reform: Fact or Fiction?" Working Paper 19, Impact Evaluation of Education Reforms Series, World Bank, Washington, DC.

Kleemeier, E. 2000. "The Impact of Participation on Sustainability: An Analysis of the Malawi Rural Piped Scheme Program." *World Development* 28(5): 929–44.

Kosec, K. 2011. "Politics and Preschool: The Political Economy of Investment in Pre-Primary Education." Policy Research Working Paper Series 5647, World Bank, Washington, DC.

Kremer, M., E. Bloom, E. King, I. Bhushan, D. Clingingsmith, B. Loevinsohn, R. Hong, and J. B. Schwartz. 2006. *Contracting for Health: Evidence from Cambodia.* Cambridge, MA: Harvard University Press.

Kumar, N. R. 2007. "Pro-Poor Targeting and Participatory Governance: Evidence from Central India." Working Paper dp-176, Institute for Economic Development, Department of Economics, Boston University, Boston, MA.

Kumar, S. 2002. "Does 'Participation' in Common Pool Resource Management Help the Poor? A Social Cost-Benefit Analysis of Joint Forest Management in Jharkhand, India." *World Development* 30: 763–82.

Labonne, J. 2011. "The KALAHI–CIDSS Impact Evaluation: A Synthesis Report." World Bank, Washington, DC.

Larson, A., and J. C. Ribot. 2007. "The Poverty of Forestry Policy: Double Standards on and Uneven Playing Field." *Journal of Sustainability Science* 2(2): 189–204.

Leino, J. 2007. "Ladies First? Gender and the Community Management of Water Infrastructure in Kenya." Graduate Student and Research Fellow Working Paper 30, Harvard University, Center for International Development, Cambridge, MA.

Libecap, G. 1989. *Contracting for Property Rights.* New York: Cambridge University Press.

Linnemayr, S., and H. Alderman. 2011. "Almost Random: Evaluating a Large-Scale Randomized Nutrition Program in the Presence of Crossover." *Journal of Development Economics* 96: 106–14.

Lund, J. F. 2007. "Is Small Beautiful? Village Level Taxation of Natural Resources in Tanzania." *Public Administration and Development* 27(4): 307–18.

Lund, J. F., and T. Treue. 2008. "Are We Getting There? Evidence of Decentralized Forest Management from the Tanzanian Miombo Woodlands." *World Development* 36(12): 2780–800.

Macinko, J., M. F. M. De Souza, F. C. Guanais, and C. C. D. S. Simoes. 2007. "Going to Scale with Community-Based Primary Care: An Analysis of the Family Health Program and Infant Mortality in Brazil, 1999–2004." *Social Science & Medicine* 65: 2070–80.

Macinko, J., F. C. Guanais, and M. D. M. De Souza. 2006. "Evaluation of the Impact of the Family Health Program on Infant Mortality in Brazil, 1990–2002." *Journal of Epidemiology and Community Health* 60: 13–19.

Madeira, R. 2007. "The Effects of Decentralization on Schooling: Evidence from the São Paulo State Education Reform." Department of Economics, Boston University, Boston, MA.

Manandhar, D. S., D. Osrin, B. P. Shrestha, N. Mesko, J. Morrison, K. M. Tumbahangphe, and S. Tamang. 2004. "Effect of a Participatory Intervention with Women's Groups on Birth Outcomes in Nepal: Cluster-Randomised Controlled Trial." *Lancet* 364: 970–79.

Mansuri, G. 2012a. "Bottom up or Top Down: Participation and the Provision of Local Public Goods." World Bank, Poverty Reduction and Equity Unit, Washington, DC.

————. 2012b. "Harnessing Community: Assortative Matching in Participatory Community Organizations." World Bank, Poverty Reduction and Equity Unit, Washington DC.

Marcus, R. 2002. "Social Funds as Instruments for Reducing Childhood Poverty: Lessons from Save the Children's Experience." *Journal of International Development* 14(8): 653–66.

McSweeney, K. 2005. "Natural Insurance, Forest Access, and Compounded Misfortune: Forest Resources in Smallholder Coping Strategies before and after Hurricane Mitch, Northeastern Honduras." *World Development* 33(9): 1453–71.

Meshack, C. K., B. Ahdikari, N. Doggart, and J. C. Lovett. 2006. "Transaction Costs of Community-Based Forest Management: Empirical Evidence from Tanzania." *African Journal of Ecology* 44(4): 468–77.

Morrow, C. E., and R. W. Hull. 1996. "Donor-Initiated Common Pool Resource Institutions: The Case of the Yanesha Forestry Cooperative." *World Development* 24(10): 1641–57.

Mosse, D. 2001. "People's Knowledge, Participation, and Patronage: Operations and Representations in Rural Development." In *Participation: The New Tyranny*, ed. B. Cooke and U. Kothari. London: Zed Books.

————. 2005. *Cultivating Development: An Ethnography of Aid Policy and Practice*. London: Pluto Press.

Muhereza, F. 2006. "Decentralizing Natural Resource Management and the Politics of Institutional Resource Management in Uganda's Forest Sub-Sector." *Africa Development* 31: 67–101.

Murnane, R. J., J. B. Willet, and S. Cardenas. 2006. "Did the Participation of Schools in Programa Escuelas De Calidad (PEC) Influence Student Outcomes?" Working Paper, Harvard University Graduate School of Education, Cambridge, MA.

Mustafa, D. 2007. "Social Construction of Hydro-Politics: The Geographical Scales of Water and Security in the Indus Basin." *Geographical Review* 97(4): 484–501.

Mustalahti, I., and J. F. Lund. 2010. "Where and How Can Participatory Forest Management Succeed? Learning from Tanzania, Mozambique, and Laos." *Society & Natural Resources* 23(1): 31–44.

Narain, U., S. Gupta, and K. Van't Veld. 2005. "Poverty and Environment: Exploring the Relationship Between Household Incomes, Private Assets, and Natural Assets." Discussion Paper 05-18, Resources for the Future, Washington, DC.

————. 2008. "Poverty and Resource Dependence in Rural India." *Ecological Economics* 66(1): 161–76.

Nerlove, M. 1991. "Population and the Environment: A Parable of Firewood and Other Tales." *American Journal of Agricultural Economics* 73(4): 1334–47.

Newman, J., M. Pradhan, L. B. Rawlings, G. Ridder, R. C. And, and J. L. Evia. 2002. "An Impact Evaluation of Education, Health, and Water Supply Investments by the Bolivian Social Investment Fund." *World Bank Economic Review* 16(2): 241–74.

Nkonya, E., D. Phillip, T. Mogues, J. Pender, M. K. Yahaya, G. Adebowale, T. Arokoyo, and E. Kato. 2008. "From the Ground Up Impacts of a Pro-Poor Community-Driven Development Project in Nigeria." Discussion Paper 00756, International Food Policy Research Institute, Washington, DC.

North, D. C. 1990. *Institutions, Institutional Change, and Economic Performance.* Cambridge, U.K.: Cambridge University Press.

Nyonator, F. K., J. K. Awoonor-Williams, J. F. Phillips, T. C. Jones, and R. A. Miller. 2005. "The Ghana Community-Based Health Planning and Services Initiative for Scaling Up Service Delivery Innovation." *Health Policy and Planning* 20(1): 25–34.

Olken, B. 2007. "Monitoring Corruption: Evidence from a Field Experiment in Indonesia." *Journal of Political Economy* 115(2): 200–49.

Olken, B. A., J. Onishi, and S. Wong. 2011. "Indonesia's PNPM Generasi Program: Final Impact Evaluation Report." World Bank, Social Development Department, Washington, DC.

Olson, M. 1965. *The Logic of Collective Action: Public Goods and the Theory of Groups.* Cambridge, MA: Harvard University Press.

Ostrom, E. 1990. *Governing the Commons: The Evolution of Institutions for Collective Action.* New York: Cambridge University Press.

Ostrom, E., W. F. Lam, and M. Lee. 1994. "The Performance of Self-Governing Irrigation Systems in Nepal." *Human Systems Management* 13(3): 197–207.

Oyono, P. R., and S. Efoua. 2006. "Qui représente qui? Choix organisation-nels, identités sociales et formation d'une élite forestière au Cameron." *Africa Development* 31(2): 147–82.

Oyono, P., and F. Nzuzi. 2006. "Au sortir d'une longue 'nuit' institutionnelle, nouvelles transactions entre les politiques forestières et les sociétés rurales en RD Congo post-conflit." *Afrique et Développement* 31(2): 183–214.

Pandey, P., S. Goyal, and V. Sundararaman. 2011. "Does Information Improve School Accountability? Results of a Large Randomized Trial." Discussion Paper 49, World Bank, Washington, DC.

Pandey, S. K., and E. C. Stazyk. 2008. "Antecedents and Correlates of Public Service Motivation." In *Motivation in Public Management: The Call of Public Service,* ed. J. L. Perry and A. Hondeghem, 101–17. Oxford, U.K.: Oxford University Press.

Pandey, S., B. Wright, and D. Moynihan. 2008. "Public Service Motivation and Interpersonal Citizenship Behavior in Public Organizations: Testing a Preliminary Model." *International Public Management Journal* 11(1): 89–108.

Park, A., and S. Wang. 2009. "Community-Based Development and Poverty Alleviation: An Evaluation of China's Poor Village Investment Program." Draft background paper for the 2006 China Poverty Assessment, World Bank, Washington, DC.

Pattanayak, S. K., and E. O. Sills. 2001. "Do Tropical Forests Provide Natural Insurance? The Microeconomics of Non-Timber Forest Product Collection in the Brazilian Amazon." *Land Economics* 77(4): 595–613.

Paxson, C., and N. R. Schady. 2002. "The Allocation and Impact of Social Funds: Spending on School Infrastructure in Peru." *World Bank Economic Review* 16(2): 297–319.

Pokharel, R. P. 2009. "Pro-Poor Programs Financed through Nepal's Community Forestry Funds: Does Income Matter?" *Mountain Research and Development* 29: 67–74.

Pradhan, D. S. M., A. Beatty, M. Wong, A. Alishjabana, A. Gaduh, and R. P. Artha. 2011. "Improving Educational Quality through Enhancing Community Participation: Results from a Randomized Field Experiment in Indonesia." Faculty of Economics and Business Administration, University of Amsterdam.

Pradhan, M., and L. B. Rawlings. 2002. "The Impact and Targeting of Social Infrastructure Investments: Lessons from the Nicaraguan Social Fund." *World Bank Economic Review* 16(2): 275–95.

Ravallion, M. 2000. "Monitoring Targeting Performance When Decentralized Allocations to the Poor Are Unobserved." *World Bank Economic Review* 14(2): 331–45.

———. 2009a. "Decentralizing Eligibility for a Federal Antipoverty Program: A Case Study for China." *World Bank Economic Review* 23(1): 1–30.

———. 2009b. "How Relevant Is Targeting to the Success of an Antipoverty Program?" *World Bank Research Observer* 24(1): 205–31.

Ribot, J. C. 1995. "From Exclusion to Participation: Turning Senegal's Forestry Policy Around?" *World Development* 23(9): 1587–99.

———. 2004. *Waiting for Democracy: The Politics of Choice in Natural Resource Decentralizations.* Washington, DC: World Resources Institute.

———. 2007. "Institutional Choice and Recognition in the Consolidation of Local Democracy." *Democracy* 50: 43–49.

Ribot, J. C., A. Chhatre, and T. Lankina. 2008. "Institutional Choice and Recognition in the Formation and Consolidation of Local Democracy." *Conservation and Society* 6(1): 1–11.

Ribot, J. C., J. Lund, and T. Treue. 2010. "Forestry and Democratic Decentralization in Sub-Saharan Africa: A Review." Background paper prepared for Policy Research Report, World Bank, Washington, DC.

Riley, J. C. 2005. *Poverty and Life Expectancy: The Jamaica Paradox.* Bloomington, IN: Indiana University Press.

Rocha, R., and R. R. Soares. 2009. "Evaluating the Impact of Community-Based Health Interventions: Evidence from Brazil's Family Health Program." Global Development Network, New Delhi.

Rodriguez, C. 2006. "Households' Schooling Behavior and Political Economy Trade-Offs After Decentralization." Working Paper, Universidad de los Andes, Colombia.

Ronconi, L. 2009. "Estimates of the Benefit Incidence of Workfare." *Journal of LACEA Economia (Latin American and Caribbean Economic Association)* 8587.

Sawada, Y. 1999. "Community Participation, Teacher Effort, and Educational Outcome: The Case of El Salvador's Educo Program." Working Paper 307, William Davidson Institute, University of Michigan, Ann Arbor, MI.

243

Sawada, Y., and A. Ragatz. 2005. "Decentralization of Education, Teacher Behavior, and Outcomes." In *Incentives to Improve Teaching*, ed. E. Vegas. Washington, DC: World Bank.

Skoufias, E., and J. Shapiro. 2006. "The Pitfalls of Evaluating a School Grants Program Using Non-Experimental Data." Policy Research Working Paper 4036, World Bank, Washington, DC.

Somanathan, E., R. Prabhakar, and B. Singh. 2005. "Does Decentralization Work? Forest Conservation in the Himalayas." Indian Statistical Institute, New Delhi.

Stern, P. C., T. Dietz, and E. Ostrom. 2003. "The Struggle to Govern the Commons." *Science* 302: 1907–12.

Sunderlin, W. D., J. Hatcher, and M. Liddle. 2008. "From Exclusion to Ownership? Challenges and Opportunities in Advancing Forest Tenure Reform." Rights and Resources Initiatives, Washington DC.

Topp-Jorgensen, E., M. K. Poulsen, J. F. Lund, and J. F. Massao. 2005. "Community-Based Monitoring of Natural Resource Use and Forest Quality in Montane Forests and Miombo Woodlands of Tanzania." *Biodiversity and Conservation* 14(11): 2653–77.

Tripathy, P., N. Nair, S. Barnett, R. Mahapatra, J. Borghi, S. Rath, and S. Rath. 2010. "Effect of a Participatory Intervention with Women's Groups on Birth Outcomes and Maternal Depression in Jharkhand and Orissa, India: A Cluster-Randomised Controlled Trial." *Lancet* 375: 1182–92.

Turyahabwe, N., C. J. Geldenhuys, S.Watts, and J.Obua. 2007. "Local Organizations and Decentralised Forest Management in Uganda: Roles, Challenges, and Policy Implications. *International Forestry Review*. 9(2):581–96.

United Nations. 2000. "Millennium Declaration." United Nations, New York.

Uphoff, N. 1986. *Local Institutional Development: An Analytical Sourcebook with Cases*. Sterling, VA: Kumarian Press.

Uzochukwu, B. S. C., C. O. Akpala, and O. E. Onwujekwe. 2004. "How Do Health Workers and Community Members Perceive and Practice Community Participation in the Bamako Initiative Programme in Nigeria? A Case Study of Oji River Local Government Area." *Social Science and Medicine* 59: 157–62.

Voss, J. 2008. "Impact Evaluation of the Second Phase of the Kecamatan Development Program in Indonesia." World Bank, Jakarta.

Wade, R. 1985. "The Market for Public Office: Why the Indian State Is Not Better at Development." In *The Economics of Corruption and Illegal Markets*, ed. G. Fiorentini and S. Zamagni. Cheltenham, U.K.: Edward Elgar Publishing.

Wardell, D. A., and C. Lund. 2006. "Governing Access to Forests in Northern Ghana: Micro-Politics and the Rents of Non-Enforcement." *World Development* 34(11): 1887–906.

Wilder, M., and P. R. Lankao. 2006. "Paradoxes of Decentralization: Water Reform and Social Implications in Mexico." *World Development* 34: 1977–95.

Wood, G. 1999. "Private Provision after Public Neglect: Bending Irrigation Markets in North Bihar." *Development and Change* 30(4): 775–94.

World Bank. 2002. "Social Funds: Assessing Effectiveness." Operations Evaluations Department, World Bank, Washington, DC.

Yoong, J. 2007. "Does Decentralization Hurt Childhood Immunization?" Department of Economics, Stanford University, Stanford, CA.

CHAPTER SIX

Does Participation Strengthen Civil Society?

PARTICIPATORY DEVELOPMENT PROJECTS OFTEN INCLUDE BUILD-
ing "social capital" and hearing the "voices of the poor" as key objectives. This chapter reviews the literature on how effective participatory
development projects have been in achieving these goals. It presents
evidence on several important questions. How do deliberative processes
actually work in developing countries? Is deliberation equitable? Is it
sustainable? Under what conditions does it build the capacity to engage?
Can local inequalities in power and social structure be remedied by
mandating the inclusion of women and discriminated minorities in
leadership positions? Does participation build "social capital"? Can
inducing participation improve a community's capacity to address disputes and improve cohesion in postconflict settings? Is there evidence
that induced participation enhances social cohesion and the "voice" of
marginalized groups in local decision-making bodies?

Participatory Decision Making and Social Cohesion in Induced Development Projects

Participatory development projects expend considerable resources and
effort building community-level organizations with the expectation that
doing so not only allows disadvantaged groups to participate directly
in decision-making processes but that it can also encourage dialogue
between groups otherwise separated by wealth, gender, or social status,
thereby creating the basis for greater social cohesion. If this is the case,
induced participation may help build social cohesion and strengthen
democratic values and practices even in communities where there are

important social cleavages caused by inequality, ethnic heterogeneity, or conflict.

> The hypothesis that induced participation may help build social cohesion turns out to be a particularly difficult one to evaluate.

The hypothesis that induced participation may help build social cohesion turns out to be a particularly difficult one to evaluate. The measurement of social outcomes is itself challenging, because projects usually provide resources for local public goods, private transfers, microcredit, and skills training, in addition to community mobilization. The provision of resources makes it difficult to isolate the impact of participation on social outcomes. Exposure to participatory messaging may also make members of program communities more likely to indicate more willingness to cooperate or to report higher levels of trust and support for democracy regardless of any substantive change in attitudes or practices. Local facilitators spend considerable time with community members elucidating the benefits of program participation, community collective action, self-help groups, contributions to development projects, and so forth. Isolating the impact of participation on preferences, trust, networks, or cooperation is therefore likely to be difficult even in the best-designed evaluation. Self-reported retrospective accounts of change are perhaps the least reliable source of information.

To make matters worse, very few evaluations of community-driven development or social fund projects have been able to deal effectively with the problem of identifying comparison communities for assessing project impact. In the majority of cases, comparison groups are created by identifying communities that did not get the program but look otherwise similar to program communities. Because matching communities on the relevant social variables (trust, cooperation, density of social networks, political participation, and so forth) is rarely an option, most studies match on the usual set of sociodemographic variables available in national income statistics and expenditure surveys. Matching in this way is particularly problematic if, as is often the case, participatory programs rely on community "willingness" or "readiness" to participate rather than on clear eligibility criteria. Although matching in this way may be sensible from a programmatic perspective, it makes causal inference challenging, because outcomes of interest (such as greater political awareness) may be precisely why a community was selected in the first place, rather than an outcome of the program.

These challenges affect both the quantity and quality of the literature on participation and social cohesion. Three recent studies, all of which focus on community-driven reconstruction projects, are exceptions.

The first evaluates a community reconstruction project implemented by the International Rescue Committee in northern Liberia (Fearon, Humphreys, and Weinstein 2009).[1] Survey results indicate a reduction in social tension and an increase in trust in local leadership, as well as an increase in participation by marginalized groups in community decision-making activities. The authors use a behavioral public goods game to augment and validate these survey-based findings on the impact of participation on social cohesion and cooperation.[2] They find that a larger percentage of households in the program communities (71 percent versus 62 percent in the comparison communities) contributed the maximum amount. However, the difference was driven mainly by contributions from internally displaced persons who had returned to their villages after the war and benefited from this project as well as other programs directed at resettling them. Moreover, the evidence does not support any increase in broader collective action or in democratic values or practices in program villages. There was also no change in the attitudes of traditional leaders toward community decision making.

The second study is an ongoing evaluation of a community-driven reconstruction program in Afghanistan. It also finds some positive, albeit preliminary, evidence on the impact of a national community-driven reconstruction project (the National Support Program) on political attitudes and social cohesion (Beath, Christia, and Enikolopev 2011).[3] The results from an initial follow-up suggest significant shifts in political attitudes (regarding trust in government and local leaders, in women's role in the community, and in women as leaders, for example) and in social cohesion. A caveat is that self-reports of political attitudes such as trust in government or greater community cooperation can be difficult to interpret in the absence of corroborating evidence on outcomes. There is little evidence that village elites in program villages were less likely to exercise influence in village development councils or that there was any change in the types of households that benefited from government programs. As discussed in earlier chapters, communities that have community-driven development projects routinely report greater social cohesion and levels of satisfaction, and self-reports are generally more positive when questions are posed in language that more closely evokes the language used by facilitators.[4]

The third study, by Casey, Glennerster, and Miguel (2011), finds less positive results. The GoBifo (Move Forward) project in Sierra Leone, funded primarily by the World Bank, provided block grants

A project in Liberia shows an increase in trust and participation by marginalized groups and a reduction in social tension. But there is no evidence of an increase in broader collective action capacity.

An ongoing evaluation of a community-driven reconstruction project in Afghanistan finds preliminary positive evidence on political attitudes and social cohesion.

A study from Sierra Leone finds no evidence that a community-driven program had any impact on social cohesion or collective action.

worth about $5,000 per community (roughly $100 per household) for local public goods, skills training, and microentrepreneurship. The project staff also provided training in democratic decision making and encouraged the participation of socially marginalized groups (mainly women and youth) in local decision-making bodies.[5] Like the first two studies, this study randomly assigned eligible communities to program and comparison status and combined survey methods with what they refer to as "structured community activities." These activities assessed how communities responded to a matching grant opportunity to invest in a small public good (building materials), made communal decisions between two alternatives, and allocated a small endowment among community members. Despite the careful design and the long evaluation period (four years between baseline in 2005 and endline in 2009), the study finds no evidence that the program had an impact on any measure of social cohesion or collective action used (local fundraising capacity, decision-making processes, and so forth). There was also no evidence of a shift in social attitudes or norms with respect to women's participation in public activities.

Another approach to measuring social cohesion is to assess the extent to which community-level organizations bring together diverse groups of people who may otherwise not have an opportunity to interact with one another, thereby creating a new deliberative space. A growing body of literature on participatory councils is starting to generate interesting evidence on this issue in the context of local decentralization, but only three studies look at the extent to which community organizations are cohesive in their membership patterns. Doing so is important, because community-driven projects often work through self-help groups, which are endogenously formed. A community or village may therefore have several such groups, which may or may not be brought together into higher-level organizations.

Arcand and Fafchamps (2012) look at community organizations in Burkina Faso and Senegal. They find that community organizations tend to sort sharply by wealth and status. Survey research in São Paulo and Mexico City also finds that citizens who participate in associations are likely to be highly stratified by education, gender, labor market status, and other factors (Houtzager, Acharya, and Lavalle 2007). Mansuri (2012) finds that community organizations supported by the National Rural Support Program in Pakistan were highly segregated along wealth, ethnicity, education, and political power within villages, in addition to almost complete sorting by gender. However, she finds that some communities do much better than others. Sorting on status (education, land, and caste) is significantly dampened in villages with above-average levels of schooling but similar levels of land inequality and caste composition. In contrast, sorting by land intensifies in villages that are more unequal in land wealth, and sorting by caste status intensifies in villages that have more low-caste households.

Four other studies provide some interesting insights, though their evaluation designs are flawed. Chase, Christensen, and Thongyou (2006) use data from an evaluation of the Thailand Social Fund to assess whether the fund selected villages with specific characteristics and whether implementation of the program had an impact on the level of social capital in the selected villages. Using a combination of household survey and qualitative data, they find that the social fund provided funding to villages with particular preexisting social capital characteristics (greater norms of self-sacrifice, higher levels of trust among neighbors, and a history of collective action). They also find some evidence that exposure to the program enhanced social cohesion.[6] These results are suggestive at best, as the social capital variables were generated after program implementation, making any causal inference difficult. Moreover, program effects were weak, with social fund villages performing significantly better than control villages on only 19 percent of the social capital measures listed in the study.

Labonne and Chase (2008) study KALAHI–CIDSS, a large community-driven development program in the Philippines. Using data from 135 villages in 16 municipalities, the authors assess the program's impact on social capital indicators such as participation in local governance activities, village group membership, and relationships between local officials and citizens. They find that trust in local officials increased in villages that received funding—even though the proportion of households that requested services decreased.

Two studies use data from the District Poverty Initiatives Project (DPIP) in India to measure changes in social capital and political empowerment. The DPIP supported the formation of women's self-help groups to promote economic and social empowerment.

Deininger and Liu (2008) use recall data to measure changes in social capital and political participation in treatment and control groups in Andhra Pradesh between 2000 and 2004.[7] They find a significant increase in the level of social capital and political participation in DPIP areas, with identical effects across participants and nonparticipants.[8] They interpret this finding as evidence that the program had large positive social externalities. However, the design of the evaluation does not allow for a clean test of this effect, because it is unclear whether control communities are comparable on the relevant measures of social cohesion or social capital at baseline. The measures of social cohesion used are also closely linked to the rhetoric of participatory projects.

Kumar (2007) examines whether participation in DPIP, which runs parallel to and outside the local government structure, helped poor and lower-caste households engage effectively with the participatory processes organized by local governments in Madhya Pradesh. She finds a significant impact on political participation by poor rural women in program areas. Households in program villages not only had greater political awareness and better knowledge of other government programs, but they were also more likely to participate in village affairs, to know about *gram sabha* (village assembly) meetings, and to participate in them. They also reported being more active participants, and speaking, voting, or objecting to decisions more often than other participants. As in the study by Deininger and Liu, however, this paper's evaluation strategy is problematic, because it cannot identify why some villages were selected into DPIP and others were not.[9]

There is also fair bit of suggestive evidence that localities in which civic institutions are more vibrant have better outcomes. Few, if any, of these studies are able to identify a causal link from decentralization or participation in a community-drive development program to the quality of civic institutions, however. Olken (2006) finds that villages with more social organizations (community self-help groups, religious study groups, women's organizations) were less likely to experience both outright corruption in the form of missing rice and less leakage to village elites. Camacho and Conover (2011) find that municipalities in Colombia that had better monitoring by community organizations experienced less leakage from targeted programs. Galasso and Ravallion (2005) find that Bangladeshi villages in which the Grameen Bank was present received more program resources from the center and that these resources were better targeted to the poor. Arcand, Bassole, and Tranchant (2008) examine the extent to which participatory governance bodies, such as the *Conseil de Concertation et de Gestion* (CCG) in Senegal, are able to compete with local elected leaders from the *Conseil Rural* in attracting project funds to their communities. The community-driven development project designed the CCG as a parallel participatory institution to ensure the representation of vulnerable and marginalized groups that were less likely to be represented in the *Conseil Rural* through the electoral process. The authors find that villages with more CCG members who were not in the *Conseil Rural* were more likely to receive a project, suggesting that although political elites may direct projects to their own villages, villagers who engage in participatory governance structures can enhance resource flows to their communities.

Representation Quotas and Inclusion Mandates

This section focuses on how reservations and quotas in local councils and inclusion mandates have been used to address specific types of social exclusion and make democratic institutions (and political incentives) more responsive to people who would otherwise have little voice. Many of the results come from the literature on mandated representation in Indian village councils (*gram panchayats*). These studies look at whether leaders from disadvantaged groups have incentives to align their actions with the interests of their particular group or the general public.

Effects on Women

Women are systematically excluded from collective bodies, and from positions of power, in many parts of the world. Looking at what she calls "participatory exclusions" in community forestry groups in India and Nepal, Agarwal (2001) finds that fewer than 10 percent of the members of groups with decision-making authority are women, even though women are required to do much of the work involved in forest management. Women's underrepresentation affects the decisions made by these groups and thus has distributional consequences. It also reduces the effectiveness of the organizations, by failing to make use of the information and skills women may have. Such exclusion can have a reinforcing impact on discrimination against women.

On the basis of fieldwork conducted over two years, Agarwal finds that participatory exclusions occur for a variety of reasons. Social norms exclude women from participating in public spaces, and gendered norms of "acceptable" behaviors restrict women's attendance

Some evidence suggests that localities in which civic institutions are more vibrant have better outcomes . . .

. . . but whether decentralization, or participation in a community-driven development program, improved the quality of civic institutions remains unclear.

at public gatherings. Women find men's behavior "aggressive." Restrictions on women's visibility and mobility affect their ability to participate, they face negative stereotypes about their ability to contribute effectively to proceedings that have public implications, and they face norms that relegate them to work on women-specific tasks. Many groups also have exclusionary rules, such as allowing only one person per household to belong to a forestry group, which effectively excludes women.

To get around social restrictions of this kind, in 1992 India adopted a constitutional amendment mandating that one-third of all seats on village councils and a third of all presidencies of these councils be reserved for women. Many states randomly rotate the council seats and presidencies reserved for women. A series of studies has exploited this random allocation to study the impact of mandating seats for women on a variety of outcomes.

Chattopadhyay and Duflo (2004b) analyze survey data from 265 village councils in the states of West Bengal and Rajasthan. In the Birbhum district of West Bengal, the share of women among participants in the village council was significantly higher when the president was a woman (rising from 6.9 percent to 9.8 percent), and female presidents in reserved villages were twice as likely as male presidents to have addressed a request or complaint to the *gram panchayat* in the previous six months. In contrast, in Rajasthan the fact that the president was a woman had no effect on women's participation in the village council or on the incidence of women's complaints.

The authors also look at the effect of the policy of reserving seats for women on the provision of public goods. They find that the gender of the president affected the provision of public goods in both West Bengal and Rajasthan, with significantly more investments in drinking water in *gram panchayats* in which the president was a woman. In West Bengal, *gram panchayats* were less likely to have set up informal schools when the presidency was reserved for a woman. The evidence on roads was mixed, with roads receiving significantly more funding in *gram panchayats* reserved for women in West Bengal and less in *gram panchayats* reserved for women in Rajasthan. In both states, the provision of public goods in reserved constituencies was more closely aligned with the preferences of women than with the preferences of men. Women invested less in public goods that were more closely linked to men's concerns (education in West Bengal and roads in Rajasthan).

Duflo and Topalova (2004) look at the effects of political reservation for women with data from a larger geographical area (11 states in India). They present evidence on three aspects of women's performance in office (as measured by the quality and quantity of various public goods provided and the likelihood of taking bribes) as well as evidence on perceptions of their performance by voters in India's village councils. Consistent with the results in Chattopadhyay and Duflo (2004b), they find that reservation for women led to more investment in drinking water infrastructure, with significantly more public drinking water taps and hand pumps when the leadership of the *gram panchayat* was reserved for a woman and weak evidence that the drinking water facilities were in better repair. Overall, the average effect of reservation on the availability of public goods in a village was positive and statistically significant. The average effect of the reservation on the quality of public goods was positive as well but not significant. The authors conclude that women leaders did a better job than men at delivering drinking water infrastructure and at least as good a job delivering other public goods.

Duflo and Topalova also find that both men and women reported being less likely to pay a bribe to obtain a service when the *gram panchayat* presidency was held by a woman. However, respondents in villages with female presidents were also 2 percent less likely to declare that they were satisfied with the public goods they received. Interestingly, respondents also reported being significantly less satisfied with the quality of the public health services in villages with women presidents, despite the fact that health services were centrally administered and not under the jurisdiction of *panchayat*s in any of the 11 states during the study period.

Beaman and others (2009) compare villagers' attitudes toward hypothetical and actual women leaders in councils that have been reserved for women once, twice, or never in West Bengal. Random allocation of reservation implies that a difference in voter attitudes in reserved and unreserved villages captures the causal effect of mandated reservations. An important innovation of this study is the collection and use of detailed survey and experimental data on voters' taste for female leaders, their perceptions of gender roles, and of the effectiveness of female leaders. The authors examine explicit and implicit measures of voters' tastes. Explicit tastes are captured through voters' stated feelings toward the general idea of male and female leaders; implicit tastes are captured through Implicit Association Tests (IATs).[10]

Reservation of *gram panchayat* seats for women led to more investment in drinking water infrastructure . . .

. . . and to less spending on public goods preferred by men.

Both men and women in India perceive women as less effective leaders than men.

To examine voter perceptions of leader effectiveness, the authors asked villagers to evaluate the effectiveness of hypothetical female and male leaders described through vignettes and recorded speeches in which the leader's gender is experimentally manipulated. The results show that in villages that never experienced political reservation, villagers, particularly men, disliked the idea of female leaders. On a scale of 1–10, the average man rated his feeling toward female leaders one point below his feelings toward male leaders. Men perceived female leaders as less effective than male leaders. The average male villager rated the same speech and vignette describing a leader's decision 0.05 standard deviations lower when the leader's gender was experimentally manipulated to be female. Female villagers' evaluation of hypothetical female leaders, although less negative, was not statistically different from that of male villagers'.

Mandated exposure to a female leader did not affect villagers' stated taste for male leaders. Neither the "feeling" rating of leaders nor the taste IAT showed increased approval of female leaders in villages reserved for a female leader. However, among male villagers, it weakened the stereotype (as measured by the occupation IAT) that men are associated with leadership activities and women with domestic activities. It also radically altered perceptions of the effectiveness of female leaders among male villagers. In the speech and vignette experiments, male villagers who were required to have a female leader considered hypothetical female and male leaders equally effective. This reduction in bias was absent among female villagers. The authors provide evidence suggesting that a likely reason for this difference is the lower levels of political knowledge and exposure to local politics among women. Consistent with the experimental data, they find that prior exposure improved villagers' evaluation of their actual leader along multiple dimensions.

Reserving *gram panchayat* seats for women may elevate the aspirations parents have for their daughters and the aspirations of girls themselves . . .

. . . but reserving seats for women has not always led to positive effects.

Analyzing data from the same sample, Beaman and others (2012) find that the reservation of seats for women has effects outside the political sphere. According to their study, reservations positively affected both the aspirations parents had for their daughters and the aspirations of girls themselves. They examine the impact of women's reservations on parents' preferences for their children not to become housewives, to hold a job requiring a good education, not to marry before 18, to receive higher education, and to be the president of a village. The gap between mothers and fathers in *gram panchayats* in which positions for women were never reserved was large, ranging from 24 percent for their child not marrying before 18, to 75 percent for their daughter not becoming a housewife. This gap was, on average, 20 percentage points smaller in *gram panchayats* with a randomly assigned woman president. The authors also surveyed adolescents ages 11–15. They find that the gender gap in their career and education aspirations was 32 percentage points smaller in villages that reserved seats for women.

Bhavnani (2009) assesses the long term impact of the reservation of seats for women on municipal councils in Mumbai by examining the relative change in political power in councils that had previously been reserved for women. He tests for the continuing effects of the 1997 reservations on various aspects of the 2002 elections. His main finding is that women won 21.6 percent of wards that had been reserved for women in 1997 but were open to both genders in 2002 (treatment wards) and only 3.7 percent of wards that were open to both men and women in 1997 and 2002 (control wards). Women's chances of winning ward elections in 2002 were thus more than quintupled by the reservation of seats five years earlier. Bhavnani also examines the mechanisms through which the electoral chances for women may have increased in the previously reserved constituencies. He finds that the increase is explained by both an incumbency effect and an increase in the number of woman candidates running in the previously reserved constituency.

Some studies show that reserving seats for women has not always led to positive effects. Bardhan, Mookherjee, and Torrado (2010) examine all 16 rural districts in West Bengal (89 villages in 57 *gram panchayats*), drawing on the results of a household survey conducted between 2003 and 2004. Using a stratified random sample of 20 households per village, they examine the determinants of access to a variety of local government programs, including provision of toilets, participation in public works, receipt of Below Poverty Line (BPL) cards, and access to agricultural minikits. They find that the reservation of seats for women led to no improvement in intravillage household targeting to female-headed households and a worsening of targeting to households from schedule castes and tribes. These effects were mitigated in villages that had high land inequality. The authors interpret these findings to suggest that female leaders are inexperienced and weak and that their leadership exacerbates clientelistic allocations. In high inequality areas, female leaders are also from elite families, which makes them more effective.

Ban and Rao (2009) draw on community-level and household survey data and surveys of village presidents in four southern Indian states.

They find no significant effect of women's leadership on participation in public village meetings or the existence of women's organizations in the community. They also find that women presidents in reserved *gram panchayats* were significantly less likely than male presidents to meet with higher-level officials. Relative to unreserved *gram panchayats*, *panchayat*s reserved for women invested significantly more in education-related activities. But on the vast majority of activities, female presidents behaved no differently from male presidents. In contrast to Chattopadhyay and Duflo (2004a), Ban and Rao find no evidence that female presidents acted in accordance with women's preferences.

Ban and Rao find considerable heterogeneity in their results. In particular, female presidents in reserved *gram panchayats* were unambiguously more effective when they were more experienced. Women in reserved *gram panchayats* performed worse when most of the land in the village was owned by upper castes, suggesting that caste structures may be correlated with structures of patriarchy in ways that make conditions particularly difficult for women. The authors also find that female presidents in reserved *gram panchayats* performed best in states where reservations had been in place longest, indicating the importance of the maturity of the reservation system. This effect, in conjunction with the positive effect of the president's political experience, points toward a hopeful future, as it suggests that as women acquire more experience and the system continues to mature, women will become more effective leaders.

> More experienced female presidents in reserved *gram panchayats* were unambiguously more effective than less experienced ones.

Leino (2007) examines whether incentives for female participation improved the maintenance of infrastructure in Kenya. The intervention aimed to increase women's participation in the maintenance of water sources by encouraging them to attend community meetings at which water management committees were elected. Once elected, the water management committees were trained by a facilitating NGO to manage maintenance tasks for water schemes. The meetings were held at times convenient for women, and NGO facilitators emphasized the importance of women's participation at each meeting.

The intervention was successful in increasing the number of women on water management committees. It also increased the number of women holding leadership positions in the committee, more than doubling the odds that a woman was a committee chair. This effect appears to have persisted through the three-year period of the study. The increase in female leadership on the water management committees had no impact on the quality of infrastructure maintenance, however. There is thus little evidence of any efficiency gain because of greater female participation—although, as the author notes, the more interesting result may be that increased inclusion can be achieved with no apparent efficiency cost.

Effect on Disadvantaged Castes

Chattopadhyay and Duflo (2004a) examine how the type and location of public goods differs in unreserved *gram panchayat*s and *gram panchayats* in which presidencies were reserved for historically disadvantaged Scheduled Castes (SC) in West Bengal.[11] Identification of the caste reservation effect was based on the random assignment of *gram panchayats* reserved for scheduled castes. The authors studied investments in drinking water facilities, irrigation facilities, roads, and education centers, measured using a participatory survey in which a representative group of villagers was shown a village map that depicted the location of all infrastructure schemes and then was asked which investments had been built or repaired since the last election.

The authors find that SC presidents did not significantly change the types of investments in public goods relative to presidents from unreserved *gram panchayats*. SC hamlets in SC–reserved *gram panchayats* received 14 percent more investment in public goods than SC hamlets in unreserved *gram panchayats*.

Chin and Prakash (2010) assess the extent to which reservation for disadvantaged castes and tribes improves living conditions for the poorest. Using panel data from 16 Indian states over the period 1960–92, they examine the effect of state-level reservations for SCs and Scheduled Tribes (STs) on state-level measures of overall poverty. The main question of interest is whether on balance, minority political representation is welfare enhancing for all of the poor. The authors find that reservations for SCs reduced overall poverty—that is, benefits to minority groups did not appear to have come at a cost to poor or near-poor nonminorities. Reservation policies for STs were more effective in reducing poverty in rural than in urban areas, suggesting some caution in generalizing findings in the absence of more empirical work.

Using data from four southern Indian states, Besley and others (2004) examine the effect of reservations for SCs and STs on the distribution of low-spillover and high-spillover goods within and

In Kenya, incentives for inclusion increased female leadership on water management committees, but the increase had no impact on the quality of infrastructure maintenance.

between villages at the *gram panchayat* level. They measure access to low-spillover (household-level) public goods through a household survey that defines access as having had a house or toilet built under a government scheme or having received a private water or electricity connection through a government scheme since the last *gram panchayat* election. They measure access to high-spillover public goods (public goods that are easily accessed across groups and neighborhoods) using data on *gram panchayat* activity from an independent audit of village facilities. An index constructed from these data measures whether the *gram panchayat* undertook any construction or improvement activity on village roads, drains, streetlights, or water sources since the last *gram panchayat* election.

Using a household-level regression with village fixed effects, the authors find that low-spillover public goods (access to which is more easily restricted to particular groups and neighborhoods) were targeted more toward SC/ST households. On average, a household from an SC/ST was 6 percent more likely to receive such a public good than a non–SC/ST household. The extent of such targeting was enhanced by living in a reserved *gram panchayat*. Relative to living in a nonreserved *gram panchayat*, living in a reserved *gram panchayat* increased a SC/ST household's likelihood of getting such a low-spillover public good by 7 percent.

Besley and others (2004) consider the village-level incidence of high-spillover public goods, as measured by the *gram panchayat* activity index. They find that on average, this index was 0.04 points higher in the president's village. Thus, for high-spillover public goods, proximity to the elected representative matters. In contrast, for low-spillover public goods, sharing the politician's group identity matters most.

Besley, Pande, and Rao (2005) show that reservation makes it more likely that SC/ST households will receive a Below Poverty Line card, which provides access to targeted benefits. This finding suggests that SC/ST leaders favor members of their own group.

Bardhan, Mookherjee, and Torrado (2010) find that SC/ST reservation has a positive effect on per capita benefits allocated to the village as a whole. It also improves intrahousehold targeting to both female-headed and SC/ST households—a sharp contrast to their results on women's reservations. In a related paper combining theory with an analysis of the same data set, Bardhan and Mookherjee (2012) find that the effects of SC/ST reservation are entirely consistent with a model of clientelism. This result is also consistent with the results of Besley and others (2004).

This literature details the largely positive impacts of inclusion mandates. Other studies find that reservation mandates have had a mixed impact in terms of giving groups more voice or aligning the interests of caste leaders with the preferences of their groups.

Palaniswamy and Krishnan (2008) identify the effects of SC/ST political reservation in the Indian state of Karnataka by exploiting the random allocation of reservations, conditional on village population size and the proportion of the SC/ST population in the village. In looking at the distribution of grants within village councils, they find that villages represented in the village council by SC/ST members attract fewer resources. They also find that reservations for other backward classes (OBCs) allow some politically dominant castes (Vokkaligas and Lingayats) to run in these reserved constituencies. Such villages are likely to receive more resources, suggesting that elite capture may persist despite the presence of reservations.

Dunning and Nilekani (2010) use a regression discontinuity design to compare the impact of caste reservations on otherwise similar village councils in Karnataka. They find very weak policy and redistributive effects.

Munshi and Rosenzweig (2009) analyze survey data on Indian local governments at the ward level over multiple terms. They show that reservations for disadvantaged castes can have adverse village-level outcomes, by increasing the odds of electing lower-quality politicians who are able to attract fewer public resources. The caste system, the authors contend, serves as a commitment-enforcing device. Fearing social sanctions, a leader elected with the support of his or her caste is more likely to make decisions that reflect the preferences of the caste. When a caste group is large, it is able to elect its most able leader and to ensure that the leader implements a policy that does not deviate from the policy preferred by the median member of the caste. However, political reservations for disadvantaged castes make it less likely that a leader will be elected from a numerically dominant caste. Setting the main explanatory variable as the existence of a numerically dominant caste, the authors run a ward-level regression (the dependent variables are the characteristics of the elected ward leader and the ward-level provision of public goods). As they observe the same ward over multiple electoral terms, they are able to isolate within-ward variations in the identity

The majority of studies find that India's constitutionally mandated rules on inclusion have given disadvantaged groups more benefits. . . .

. . . but some studies find that reservation mandates have had adverse effects.

of leaders from a numerically dominant caste. The results show that, without a caste reservation, the existence of a dominant caste results in the election of a wealthier leader, as well as a leader who is more likely to be in an occupation involving independent decision making (farm operator, business person, or professional), and this appears to increase the overall level of local public resources the ward receives by about 16 percent.

In sum, while mandates thus seem to increase the representation of women and excluded groups in leadership positions and can be an effective mechanism for promoting greater inclusion in local councils. Their effects on resource allocation and the effectiveness of local governments seem to depend on the context. In particular, while women leaders are more effective in more mature reservation systems, their political effectiveness continues to be hampered by land inequality, the strength of existing structures of patriarchy, and the power of dominant caste groups.

In contrast, caste reservation seems to affect the local political economy by changing the incentives for clientelistic allocations. For the most part, clientelism seems to narrowly benefit SC/ST households with potentially detrimental effects for the majority of village residents.

The evidence also hints at the possibility that reservation rules are sometimes not properly enforced but instead captured by male-dominated structures of power. The vast majority of the evidence derives from Indian village democracies, however. The effects in non-democratic settings may be different.

Community-Driven Reconstruction

The active involvement of citizens in public life has come to be viewed as an important mechanism for managing or mitigating conflict at all levels; participatory development projects are seen as an important mechanism for reengaging citizens in public life. In the aftermath of widespread conflict, participation usually takes the form of reconstruction projects. The basic argument is that broad-based involvement in reconstruction planning can play an important role in rebuilding citizenship and trust in government institutions in a context in which state-society relations are frayed (Cliffe, Guggenheim, and Kostner 2003; World Bank 2011).

The conflict-reducing role of participatory development goes beyond postconflict conditions, however. Community-driven development projects are usually implemented in contexts where formal governance institutions are weak and access to judicial institutions, courts, or the local police is limited largely to people with wealth or political power. In such settings, ordinary conflicts over property rights, the use of natural resources, and violence (domestic or communal) must often be arbitrated within the community itself, often through informal justice institutions. The impartiality of such informal mechanisms may be limited for marginalized groups within a community.

In such environments, participatory projects could change the conditions under which disputes emerge and are resolved. On the one hand, the new informal institutional structures created by such projects could empower marginalized groups to demand more even and effective judicial services, from both formal and informal providers. On the other, they could create new struggles over the allocation of project resources and the distribution of power within localities, which could exacerbate local conflicts.

There is as yet little reliable evidence on the relative effectiveness of community-driven reconstruction projects as a means of delivering development aid or (re)building civil society under conditions of conflict. What evidence there is, is not altogether encouraging, though there are some positive findings.

Strand and others (2003) review 14 World Bank–funded community-driven reconstruction projects. They find that although community-driven reconstruction projects may provide a fast-track disbursement tool, the poor and marginalized have only limited access to such projects. Governments often have an incentive to provide community-driven reconstruction resources selectively, in order to increase their political support and may be reluctant to extend such programs to areas that are less important politically, making it difficult to scale programs up.

The authors also find that community-level trust and reconciliation building is effective only if it is linked to a comparable process at the national level. They conclude that community-driven reconstruction projects should be viewed not just as humanitarian efforts but also as potential political tools. An understanding of existing political and social relations and reconciliation structures on the ground, as well as the establishment of community capacity, are thus necessary preconditions for the equitable distribution of resources in such projects.

> Overall, the evidence on the effectiveness of community-driven reconstruction projects as a means of delivering development aid or rebuilding civil society is weak.

> Community-level trust and reconciliation building is effective only if it is linked to a comparable process at the national level.

Pearce (2007), who studied civil society participation in Colombia and Guatemala, argues that civil society organizations can play a prominent role in building citizenship by confronting violent actors in all spaces and levels of socialization. By restoring plurality and opening "invisibly sealed boundaries," civil society organizations can curb violence by encouraging victims to understand violence.

A key metric of the success of community-driven reconstruction projects is the extent to which they improve state-society relations and build social cohesion and citizenship. This set of objectives can be difficult to evaluate, as the studies reviewed below illustrate. A second and perhaps equally important measure of success is the extent to which resources flow to activities and groups most targeted by such programs, usually the people most likely to be victimized by violence.

Barron, Woolcock, and Diprose (2011) examine a community-driven reconstruction project in Aceh, Indonesia (BRA–KDP) that built on the national Kecamatan Development Program by targeting resources to victims of the conflict.[12] Program targeting by the center worked well, as conflict-affected communities were included in the program. Targeting within communities was weak, however, with conflict victims generally faring no better than nonvictims, despite the explicit intended targeting of conflict victims. Conflict victims were also more likely to report that their preferred projects were not selected for implementation.

A postconflict reconstruction project in Indonesia may have reduced rather than increased conflict victims' acceptance of excombatants.

Project funds were also used to provide private transfers to beneficiaries rather than investments in public goods. Not surprisingly, survey responses revealed income gains in program communities (the survey was conducted while the program was still disbursing funds). The study finds little evidence for any improvement in social cohesion or trust in governmental institutions, however. In fact, there is evidence that BRA–KDP was associated with less acceptance of excombatants by conflict victims in project areas, though there is no evidence of a greater tendency for tensions to escalate into violence (possibly because excombatants received some of the funds that were meant for civilian conflict victims).

A potential solution to the problem of measuring social cohesion is to complement survey data with behavioral games, which provide clearer measures of political practice and cooperation. The Fearon, Humphreys, and Weinstein (2009) study cited earlier suggests that there is a greater propensity to contribute cash and labor in program villages, with much of the effect coming from contributions by excombatants. Survey evidence also suggests that individuals in communities with community-driven reconstruction projects report less social tension and exhibit greater acceptance of previously marginalized groups. There is no evidence, however, of any improvement in material well-being, though there is some evidence of improvement in local public goods. Fearon, Humphreys, and Weinstein do not see this improvement in public goods as unmixed evidence of the benefits of community-driven reconstruction in a conflict environment. In fact, they make the point that conflict usually occurs at levels that are higher than the "community" that such programs target. It is possible that strengthening cohesion at the local level could exacerbate conflict across communities. Their study finds no discernible effect on participants' beliefs in broader democratic principles or other measures of citizenship. Furthermore, there was little impact on measures of social inclusion of refugees or new migrants into the community, although respondents in treated communities report greater trust in their leaders (see also Beath, Christia, and Enikolopev 2011 on Afghanistan).

Bellows and Miguel (2006) estimate the effects of the civil war in Sierra Leone (1991–2002), using unique nationally representative household data on conflict experiences, postwar economic outcomes, and local politics and collective action. They find strong evidence that individuals whose households had been subjected to intense violence were much more likely to attend community meetings, vote, and contribute to local public goods; they were also more likely to be cognizant of local political dynamics. Several tests indicate that selection into victimization is not driving the results.[13] The relationship between conflict intensity and postwar outcomes is weaker at more aggregate levels, however, suggesting that the war's primary impact was on individual preferences rather than on institutions or local social norms.

The use of community-driven reconstruction in postconflict settings is deeply affected by the context. The limited evidence is mixed. In some settings (Afghanistan, Liberia), such projects may have a positive effect on social cohesion. In some settings, people with a more direct experience of war (excombatants in Liberia, people affected by violence in Sierra Leone) were more likely to contribute to their communities and to participate in community meetings; in other settings, this was not the case. There is also no evidence to suggest that community-based

There is no evidence that postconflict community-based interventions increase trust or cohesion beyond the community level, or improve material outcomes.

interventions in postconflict settings increased trust and cohesion, had an affect beyond the community level, or improved material outcomes.

Participatory Councils and Deliberative Spaces

Public deliberation envisions a world in which citizens engage in reasoned, thoughtful debate to come to a consensual decision.

Public deliberation envisions a world in which citizens engage in reasoned, thoughtful debate to come to a consensual decision. It is the ideal form of participation. Its goal is to aggregate preferences through conversation, to allow the diverse views of a community to be consolidated and presented as one representative view.

Public deliberation is expected to have a number of beneficial effects—mirroring but intensifying the effects of participation. At the intrinsic level, public deliberation is expected to give voice and create a sense of agency and community; at the instrumental level, it is expected to enhance the capacity for collective action and repair civic failures by bringing the interests of citizens to the attention of the state. Important are not only formal deliberative forums but also what Mansbridge (1999) calls "deliberative systems," where discussion and debate continue outside formal spaces as informal conversations between citizens and representatives, political activists, media, and other citizens. This everyday deliberation changes the nature of participation, making it more discursive and consensual than merely ritualistic. Mansbridge claims that "when a deliberative system works well, it filters out and discards the worst ideas available on public matters while it picks up, adopts, and applies the best ideas." If, however, "the deliberative system works badly, it distorts facts, portrays ideas in forms the originators would disown, and encourages citizens to adopt ways of thinking and acting that are good neither for them nor for the larger polity" (Mansbridge 1999, 211). Deliberation is also at the heart of what Fung and Wright (2003) call "empowered participatory governance," a system of governance that translates deliberative decision making into policy decisions and actions (see chapter 4).

Two sets of questions arise in considering the effectiveness of such a system. The first has to do with whether deliberation that empowers all participants is possible in highly unequal societies. The second has to do with whether deliberative capacity can be built and nurtured. Can policy interventions induce a system of empowered participatory governance? In what contexts does deliberation work well?

Africa

Deliberative democracy is not widespread in Africa, although indigenous traditions of deliberative decision making, particularly in rural communities, have carried over to public decision making to varying degrees (see chapter 1). In the island nation of São Tomé and Príncipe, all adults were invited to a national forum in 2004 to gather in facilitated groups to discuss policy issues related to the use of the newly discovered oil reserves. Local facilitators were randomly assigned throughout the country. Humphreys, Masters, and Sandbu (2006) find that leaders significantly influenced the outcomes of deliberation, with one-fifth to one-third of the variance in outcomes explained by leader fixed effects. They also find that groups led by women and older men tended to have different priorities and emphasize different processes than other groups.

A similar situation appears to prevail in Malawi, where evidence from more than a thousand ethnographic journals, in which field researchers capture the conversations of rural Malawians, shows a marked difference between the quality of deliberation in informal and formal settings (Swidler and Watkins 2011). The data, collected in conjunction with a study on the role of social networks in the HIV/AIDS epidemic, show that people in rural areas engage in deliberation "frequently, energetically, sometimes vociferously" in everyday settings—markets, village meetings, and chiefs' courts—and freely "assert a variety of claims and moral principles" (p. 4) In induced settings such as donor-funded projects with deliberative modalities, however, they behave more like students in a rote-learning environment. Such settings "invoke the hierarchical template of school, with its colonial remnants and its deference to the prestige of modern learning" (Swidler and Watkins 2011, 4). Both facilitators and participants treat such forums like classrooms, where deliberation must be taught, giving citizens neither voice nor agency, as they are not engaging in a debate over their interests but simply acting out the scripts written by facilitators who are, in turn, following the dictates of donors.

Can deliberative skills be transferred from the private sphere to formal democratic settings? Can deliberation be cultivated without active instruction? In many contexts, communications media promise to be a useful tool. Paluck and Green (2009) examine the effects of a radio program that attempted to promote independent thought and collective action while discouraging blind obedience and deference to authority in

Deliberative decision-making groups led by women and older men tend to have different priorities and emphasize different processes than other groups.

postgenocide Rwanda. The program was randomly assigned to pairs of communities matched on a vector of observable characteristics, with the control community receiving a comparable structured program about HIV/AIDS. The program encouraging independent thought improved people's willingness to express dissent and seek collective solutions to common problems, but it had little effect on their beliefs and attitudes.

Paluck (2010) tests the impact of a year-long radio talk show that was broadcast in tandem with a soap opera on randomly assigned communities in the Democratic Republic of Congo. Control communities heard only the soap opera. The talk show was designed to encourage tolerance and sharing of different perspectives; the soap opera promoted intergroup contact. Compared with individuals exposed only to the soap opera, talk show listeners were more likely to engage in discussion. However, they were also more intolerant, more focused on grievances, and less likely to aid members of the community whom they disliked.

These two media experiments demonstrate the potential and pitfalls of media-based strategies to promote deliberation in different post-conflict African contexts. Although deliberative skills are ubiquitous in informal forums, it is difficult to translate those skills to formal settings, which tend to be driven by leaders and follow predetermined scripts. The challenge for citizens is to develop appropriate political and cultural skills—what Swidler (1986) has called a cultural toolkit—to navigate the public sphere. The radio experiments in Rwanda and the Democratic Republic of Congo were structured precisely to develop this toolkit. They had mixed effects, helping build the capacity for deliberation and collective action in Rwanda while generating more noise than signal in collective discussions in the Democratic Republic of Congo. The radio experiments also raise the question of how long-lasting these effects are in the absence of active participation by a state that is committed to the idea of deliberation. Whether the effects will be sustained after the programs stop airing remains an open question.

Deliberative skills are ubiquitous in informal forums in Africa . . .

. . . but it is difficult to translate those skills to formal settings, which tend to be driven by leaders and follow predetermined scripts.

Asia

Gram sabhas (village assemblies) constitute the largest formal deliberative institution in human history, affecting more than 700 million rural Indian residents living in more than a million villages. Besley, Pande, and Rao (2005) analyze data on *gram sabhas* from 5,180 randomly selected households in 527 villages in South India to determine whether they yield instrumental (policy) benefits. They focus on a specific policy administered at the village level—access to a BPL card, which provides an array of public benefits. The authors estimate a regression that exploits within-village variation in individual characteristics to examine whether the targeting of BPL cards differs depending on whether the village held a *gram sabha* the previous year. They find that the targeting of landless and illiterate individuals was more intensive in villages that had held a *gram sabha*. Moreover, these effects were economically significant, raising the probability of receiving a BPL card from 8 percent to 10 percent. Some caution about these results is warranted, however, as it is possible that holding a *gram sabha* is correlated with other village characteristics that are important in shaping the way public resources are targeted.

Rao and Sanyal's (2010) qualitative analysis of 290 *gram sabha* transcripts from the same villages finds that the forums allow disadvantaged castes to gain voice and seek dignity and agency (see chapter 4). Ban, Jha, and Rao's (2012) quantitative analysis of coded versions of these transcripts emphasizes that these forums have characteristics that are consistent with an efficient democracy. Deriving hypotheses from models of group decision making under uncertainty, they analyze the transcript data to test two competing hypotheses of the types of equilibrium that could characterize *gram sabha* interactions: "cheap talk" (discussions are not substantive even though they may appear equitable) and "efficient democracy" (meetings follow patterns of good democratic practice). They find that in villages with high caste heterogeneity and less village-wide agreement on policy priorities, the priorities of the median "voter" (a reference individual whose expressed preferences track those of 50 percent of the population) are more likely to dominate the discourse, and landed elites have a negligible effect. Ban, Jha, and Rao conclude that *gram sabhas* are more than mere opportunities for cheap talk, that they more closely follow patterns observed in a well-functioning democracy.

Heller, Harilal, and Chaudhuri (2007) analyze qualitative and quantitative data from a survey of 72 *gram sabhas* in Kerala, where a "people's campaign" systematized and empowered deliberative systems in *gram sabhas*, which are considered exemplars of Fung and Wright's (2003) "empowered participatory governance." The authors find that civil society inputs strongly influenced the decisions of local and state

Gram sabhas are more than mere opportunities for cheap talk . . .

. . . discourse within them follows patterns observed in a well-functioning democracy.

governments and that the campaign had positive effects on social inclusion, giving both lower-caste groups and women a more active role in decision making.

The evidence from India highlights three main principles of effective participatory governance. First, *gram sabhas* work because they are constitutionally mandated, which gives them legitimacy and clout and ensures that they are seen as ongoing rituals that will not disappear. Regularity ensures that public interactions have to accommodate all citizens, regardless of class, caste, or gender and that all citizens can voice their opinions publicly in a way that holds local government accountable. If deliberative forums are temporary or ad hoc events, they can be much more easily ignored, manipulated, and rendered ineffective.

Second, the evidence suggests that in order to provide the right incentive for participation, deliberative forums must have clout. Third, embedding such forums within the context of electoral democracy is helpful, but providing voice and agency to all citizens in settings with low literacy is a challenge.

Indonesia has a long tradition of consensual decision making at the local level. The World Bank–supported Kecamatan Development Program (KDP) attempted to move these traditions into more formal, modern settings. Over its 10-year life (1998–2008), KDP provided block grants directly to rural communities to fund projects prepared and selected through a deliberative process. The aim was to create participatory structures that would be a permanent alternative to decision making led by elites. KDP has been the subject of much scholarship and has generated a large number of important research findings highlighted throughout this report. The focus here is on the findings on the efficacy of deliberative forums.

Olken (2010) presents the results of an experiment in which 49 KDP villages were randomly assigned to choose development projects through the standard KDP deliberative process or by plebiscite (direct vote). Two types of projects were chosen by these processes for each village—a general project and a women's project chosen exclusively by women. Olken finds that plebiscites resulted in dramatically higher satisfaction among villagers and increased their knowledge about the project, their perception of benefits, and their willingness to contribute. He finds that the type of projects selected did not change as a result of the plebiscite. For the women's project, the plebiscite resulted in projects being located in poorer areas of the village, suggesting that it shifted

Gram sabhas work because they are constitutionally mandated, which gives them legitimacy and clout and ensures that they are seen as ongoing rituals that will not disappear.

One study finds that deliberation may be less effective in equalizing decision making than plebiscites . . .

power toward poorer women, who may have been disenfranchised in more elite-dominated deliberative meetings. These results demonstrate that deliberation may be less effective in equalizing decision making than a direct election and that plebiscites may increase the legitimacy of and satisfaction with development interventions.

Olken's results are contradicted, to some degree, by an in-depth, large-sample qualitative study by Barron, Woolcock, and Diprose (2011), who take the unusual approach of combining a counterfactual design with qualitative analysis to study the mediating impact of KDP's deliberative spaces on local conflict. Their analysis investigates two central questions: how KDP interacted with prevailing social tensions and management of local conflict and, more generally, whether deliberative interventions such as KDP support progressive, nonviolent social change in a dynamic environment or make things worse.

The authors selected two districts in Indonesia considered to have high capacity in their ability to manage conflict and two considered to have low capacity. Within each district, three subdistricts (*kecamatans*) were chosen—three that had KDP matched with one that was a control. The treatment and control subdistricts were matched through propensity score analysis, with the scores reflecting various economic indicators, including poverty rates and the availability of infrastructure. Qualitative observations supplemented the propensity score matching method in order to eliminate poor matches. Data were collected from 41 villages in these matched *kecamatans* where conflicts were observed, and cases of conflict in the treatment and control *kecamatans* were matched to be similar in type. Data collection was conducted over a seven-month period by a team of researchers who conducted case studies of conflict, interviewed key informants, observed deliberative processes, and conducted focus group discussions. The researchers also culled data on other local conflicts from local newspapers.

The study finds that although KDP and other development projects frequently trigger conflict because of competition over resources, the deliberative spaces within KDP make those conflicts far less likely to escalate and turn violent, largely because decisions emerge from a consultative process that communities perceive as legitimate and equitable. The likelihood of violence is also mitigated by the fact that KDP has facilitators and other procedures to manage conflict as it arises. However, there is little evidence that KDP has a positive impact on conflict at an aggregate level or even a direct positive impact on nonproject-

> ... and that plebiscites may increase the legitimacy of and satisfaction with development interventions.

> In Indonesia, deliberative spaces made conflicts far less likely to escalate and turn violent, because decisions emerged from a consultative process.

271

related conflict at the local level. The project's main impacts, in fact, are on conflicts that emerge from the project itself. There are three main reasons for this finding: villages have other mechanisms to deal with nonproject-related conflicts, KDP facilitators are not perceived to have the legitimacy to mediate disputes outside KDP, and project facilitators do not have the capacity to deal with nonproject disputes.

KDP impacts are highly variable, though in both low- and high-capacity districts, program functionality matters more than the inherent capacity to manage conflict. There is also considerable variance over time, because KDP was not a standard project but had a considerable learning-by-doing component. This learning took place at different rates in different contexts, depending on the support the project received from government officials, the resistance of people whose interests were most threatened by KDP's transparency and accountability, and the quality of implementation. KDP is an assemblage of principles and procedures over which frontline facilitators have some modest discretion while interacting with villagers over many months. The quality of facilitators also varies, with some working tirelessly, beyond the call of duty; some merely doing what the job description requires; and some (though not many) capitulating to corruption.

Latin America

Latin America has witnessed several significant innovations, notably participatory budgeting. As described in chapter 1, participatory budgeting began as an organic innovation in the city of Porto Alegre, Brazil, where over time civic activists made the case for greater public deliberation in determining municipal budgets. When the party supported by activists (the Partido dos Trabalhadores [PT]) came into power, it implemented a deliberative process for budgetary decision making that came to be called "participatory budgeting" (Baiocchi 2011).

A series of studies tracking outcomes before and after the introduction of participatory budgeting (albeit without a counterfactual) finds substantial improvements. The budgeting process became substantially more transparent and responsive to citizens' needs (Souza 2001; Schneider and Baquero 2006; Zamboni 2007), it also empowered marginalized groups and made the budget more pro-poor (Souza 2001; Schneider and Goldfrank 2002; Serageldin and others 2003; Evans 2004). And the level of corruption decreased (Ackerman 2004;

> Participatory budgeting made the budgeting process more transparent and responsive to citizens' needs, empowered marginalized groups, made the budget more pro-poor, and reduced corruption.

Cabannes 2004). However, while accountability improved as a result of a more transparent and deliberative process, the forums' lack of legal authority resulted in power remaining with the mayor's office (Wampler 2004).

These studies are descriptive or tracking analyses of largely organic innovations. They say little about how participatory budgeting would work if induced by an intervention or how any changes that resulted would compare to a counterfactual in which participatory budgeting was not introduced.

One of the few counterfactual analyses of participatory budgeting is by Baiocchi, Heller, and Silva (2011), who use a discontinuity design. They match five municipalities in which the PT came to power with a small margin of victory in 1996 and subsequently implemented participatory budgeting with five municipalities in the same region and of similar size in which the PT lost by a small margin, resulting in the nonadoption of participatory budgeting. As the PT is very much a party born of civil society and Brazil's social movements of the 1980s, Baiocchi, Heller, and Silva (2011) assume that two municipalities in which the PT garnered similar vote shares will be similar in terms of their local tradition of political activism and the composition and strength of civil society. In matching municipalities in this manner, they also try to control for scale and geography.

The researchers selected five pairs of the best-matched municipalities (one pair in the South, two in the Southeast, one in the Northeast, and one in the North). Analyzing a mix of data from quantitative surveys and carefully collected in-depth interviews and group discussions, they find that, in general, participatory budgeting municipalities facilitated much more effective forms of engagement than their non–participatory budgeting counterparts. In all municipalities with participatory budgeting, the effect was to increase the flow of information about municipal governance, create a space for citizens to voice their demands and to scrutinize what were once highly insulated and discretionary decision-making processes. This allowed citizens to bargain from a position of greater strength with municipal authorities.

There was considerable variation across the municipalities in how these outcomes were achieved, however. One municipality, João Monlevade, combined direct participation with a range of planning and coordination functions. Another, Gravataí, fashioned a set of processes that were very direct and required little mediation but that also made it

Participatory budgeting facilitated much more effective forms of engagement . . .

much more difficult to coordinate at higher levels. A third, Camaragibe, built a system that went beyond the budget to encompass administration. Its participatory administration resulted in a highly complex institutional design that combined forums with a range of coordinating institutions. The Camaragibe model required a high degree of mediation, in the form of powerful delegates who were often closer to the state than to their communities. These differences reflected pragmatic adaptations of participatory budgeting to local realities, in particular to local civic capacity.

Participatory budgeting improved governance outcomes, but did it repair civil society failures? In three of the five cases studied, Baiocchi, Heller, and Silva find that changes in civil society–state relations brought about by participatory budgeting were in the direction of democratic deepening, with municipalities graduating from the status of simple representative democracies in which civil society had little power to communities with more deliberative systems. However, the introduction of participatory budgeting does not inevitably deepen democracy, as illustrated by one case (Mauá), in which an improvement in the mode of engagement came at the expense of civil society's autonomy, and the political party actually exercised more control over civic actors. Overall, institutional reform mattered mostly for changing the institutional setting—for creating more meaningful points of interface between the local state and civil society. Institutional reform did not have much of an impact on the self-organization of civil society.

> . . . it did not inevitably deepen democracy, however.

Summary

What the evidence from all these regions shows is that context—the degree of capacity of civic groups, their relationship with the state, the responsiveness of the state, and the quality of facilitation and implementation—affects the impact of deliberative processes. Geography matters, as does history, the literacy levels of the population, culture (especially the culture of deliberation), and the level of social and economic equality. It is possible to build deliberative capacity and to use that capacity to repair civil society failures in some contexts—but it does not happen quickly; doing so requires long-term and sustained engagement. There may be some role for interventions that focus on communications media, but questions remain as to how long-lasting such effects will be. The quality of facilitation matters, but facilitators may also lead

> Context—the capacity of civic groups, the responsiveness of the state, and the quality of facilitation—affects the impact of deliberative processes.

discussions that reflect their own preferences rather than the preferences of citizens. Most important, the degree to which the state is responsive to deliberative innovations makes a great deal of difference.

Conclusions

Collective civic action has two broad aspects. The first is cohesion—the ability of a community to coordinate and to manage its own affairs on matters that are relatively independent of states and markets. The second is the ability of a community to represent its collective interests to the agents of the state and persuade the state to be more responsive to its needs.

Can projects that attempt to induce participation and build "social capital" help repair civil society failures? The evidence on this important question is weak, for several reasons.

First, there is a problem of attribution. Because much of what induced participation does is get facilitators to work with communities, an important question is whether it is the facilitators who are causing the impact or the community's experience with managing collective activity. The few studies that have tried to measure facilitator effects find that facilitators strongly influence stated preferences. Participation also tends to be driven by project-related incentives—people get together to derive benefits from project funds. It is very difficult to know whether these effects will last beyond the tenure of the project, although the limited evidence on this issue indicates that it may not.

Respondents also tend to repeat project slogans in their responses, in the belief that this is what outsiders want to hear. As a result, simple survey questions on complex concepts like "trust" and "ability to cooperate" often tend to elicit answers that are more reflective of rhetoric than reality.

Keeping these important caveats in mind, there is some evidence, mainly from self-reports of participants, indicating a higher incidence of trust and cooperative activity in treatment than in control areas. Group formation, however, tends to be both parochial and unequal. Absent some kind of affirmative action program, groups that form under the aegis of interventions tend to systematically exclude disadvantaged and minority groups and women. Moreover, similar types of people tend to

Whether projects that attempt to induce participation and build "social capital" can help repair civil society failures remains unclear.

Facilitators strongly influence the preferences community members state.

Community members repeat project slogans in their responses, in the belief that outsiders want to hear them.

Absent affirmative action, groups that form under the aegis of interventions tend to exclude disadvantaged groups and women, sometimes reinforcing existing divisions.

Evidence from Africa seems to suggest that people emerging from civic conflict have a strong desire to participate. A well-designed and implemented project could draw on this inherent need.

Quotas for women and other disadvantaged groups in decision-making bodies must remain in place long enough to change perceptions and social norms.

Deliberative forums seem to work when they have teeth.

form groups with one another. As a result, projects rarely promote cross-group cohesion and may even reinforce existing divisions.

Participatory interventions are often also seen as a valuable tool in postconflict settings, where the need to get funds on the ground quickly is great. The limited evidence on the effectiveness of such projects in postconflict areas suggests that context matters a great deal, as does the quality of the intervention. Projects tend to have very limited impact on building social cohesion or rebuilding the state. They tend to exclude the poor and be dominated by elites. However, evidence from Africa seems to suggest that people emerging from civic conflict have a strong desire to participate. A well-designed and implemented project could effectively draw on this inherent need.

Repairing civic failures requires reducing social inequalities. One way of doing so is to mandate the inclusion of disadvantaged groups in the participatory process. Evaluations of community-driven development projects provide virtually no evidence on this important question. However, a growing body of evidence from village democracies in India indicates broadly positive impacts. Quotas in village councils and presidencies for disadvantaged groups and women tend to change political incentives in favor of the interests of the group favored by the quota. Mandated inclusion also appears to provide an incubator for new political leadership while changing the incentives for clientelism. Evidence indicates that women and other excluded groups are more likely to stand for office for nonmandated seats once they have had some experience in a mandated seat. Quotas can also weaken prevailing stereotypes that attribute low ability and poor performance to traditionally excluded groups. However, lasting change requires that the inclusion mandates remain in place long enough to change perceptions and social norms.

Do deliberative forums help improve voice? Forums in which citizens gather to make direct representations to civic authorities or are empowered to make decisions that have a direct bearing on their lives seem to work when they have teeth. In particular, when the central and local governments recognize the legitimacy of deliberative forums and are responsive to them, they can transform the nature of civil society and state interactions. The ability of citizens to engage in public discussions on policy questions is strongly related to literacy: deliberation is far more effective in literate settings. However, even in poor, unequal settings, there is evidence that deliberation may have intrinsic value by promoting dignity and giving voice to the disadvantaged. Perhaps the most consistent finding is that deliberative forums are more effective where they are an integral part of the policy-making process and where higher-tier governments are committed to ensuring greater citizen participation.

Deliberative forums are more effective where they are an integral part of the policy-making process and where higher-tier governments are committed to ensuring greater citizen participation.

Notes

1. The community reconstruction project was randomly implemented in 42 of 83 eligible communities (program villages were selected through a public lottery). The project aimed to improve the material well-being of resident households, reinforce democratic political attitudes, and increase social cohesion. To assess the impact of the program, the authors used survey data collected at baseline and follow-up as well as a study on behavioral outcomes. The survey data included the usual range of socioeconomic welfare measures as well as measures of social cohesion and trust.

2. The public goods game assessed the amount of funding a community could raise for a collective project. Each player started out with an "endowment" provided by the game implementer. Players were then offered an opportunity to invest their endowment in a common pool. Money added to the common pool was multiplied—typically doubled or tripled—by the game implementer and divided equally among all players, irrespective of individual contributions, which remained anonymous. If all players cooperate fully (that is, contribute the entire endowment), the common pool is maximized and each player gets a multiple of his or her initial endowment. With anonymous contributions, each player faces the temptation to free-ride on the contributions of others.

3. Village pairs were randomly allocated to treatment and control groups.

4. Because project resources were spent largely on local public goods that were under construction at the time of the survey, the welfare effects were not assessed.

5. The village development committees (VDCs) set up by the project were required to channel their village development plans through ward development committees (WDCs), which forwarded them to the district council for final approval.

6. The authors use matching techniques and national survey data collected before program implementation to select comparison communities. The social capital measures were obtained through qualitative work in the sample villages, following program implementation.

7. The comparison group is obtained by exploiting a pipeline setting. The program was introduced in phases. The second phase (Rural Poverty Reduction project [RPRP]) started three years after the first phrase (DPIP) and was introduced in different districts. At the time of the survey, DPIP had been available to survey villages for about three years and RPRP was just starting. A potential concern with the pipeline strategy is geographical variation across treatment and control areas. The study does not test for

parallel trends. Instead, it uses propensity score matching on observables over an area of common support at the village and household level.

8. The authors identify three subgroups of interest: people who joined new groups under the program (new participants), people who already participated in a self-help group before the program started but converted into a program group subsequently (converted participants), and people who did not join the program (nonparticipants). To control for household self-selection into a program's self-help group, they form control groups using households that were potentially new, converted, and nonparticipants in the control districts based on their participation status three years after the program became available.

9. The author attempts to deal with selection into DPIP by using a quasi-experimental evaluation design that exploits state borders as an exogenous source of variation in treatment assignment. The strategy involves selecting only treatment villages in Madhya Pradesh that are close to its border with Uttar Pradesh and then "pairing" each village with its neighbor in Uttar Pradesh, which did not have the option of being a DPIP village but is assumed to be similar to the treated village in all other respects. She uses a similar strategy for control villages, selected from villages in Madhya Pradesh that were also on the border but did not get DPIP, yielding "control pairs." This identification strategy rests on two crucial untested assumptions, namely, that (a) the treatment and control villages in Madhya Pradesh had the same baseline levels for the relevant response variables as the "paired" village in Uttar Pradesh and (b) any difference in the relevant baseline outcomes in Madhya Pradesh and Uttar Pradesh was the same in the control and treatment pairs. Only under these conditions could this approach reveal the treatment effect of DPIP. There is no prima facie reason to expect this set of assumptions to hold, and the author provides no evidence in support of them, other than a comparison based on village population, caste composition, and gender ratio before the program. It is unclear why these variables are the relevant ones for the outcomes of interest.

10. The IAT is an experimental method used in social psychology. It relies on the idea that respondents who more easily pair two concepts in a rapid categorization task associate those concepts more strongly. The taste IAT is a computer-based double-categorization task that examines the strength of respondents' association between images of (anonymous) male and female leaders and normative categories of good and bad. To measure gender occupation stereotypes, the authors use an IAT that examines the strength of association between male and female names on the one hand and leadership and domestic tasks on the other.

11. Scheduled Castes and Scheduled Tribes (SCs and STs) are groups mandated by Indian federal constitutional guarantees for affirmative action because of their former status as "untouchables." OBCs (Other Backward Classes) are castes listed by state governments in India as deserving of affirmative action because of a history of poverty or discrimination.

12. The study used propensity score matching to identify control villages that did not receive project funds. It used an instrumental variable approach to evaluate the effects of the program in treatment villages.

13. The authors acknowledge that they cannot rule out the possibility that omitted variable bias is playing some role—that is, that the types of people victimized tended to be the people who would have become postwar local leaders anyway. However, there is no strong evidence that more educated people or community leaders were targeted. Additional tests—demonstrating robustness in the youth subsample and in chiefdoms without permanent bases, where conflict-related violence victimization is likely to be more indiscriminate or random—argue against the hypothesis that the systematic targeting of community leaders is driving the results.

References

Ackerman, J. 2004. "Co-Governance for Accountability: Beyond 'Exit' and 'Voice'." *World Development* 32(3): 447–63.

Agarwal, B. 2001. "Participatory Exclusions, Community Forestry, and Gender: An Analysis for South Asia and a Conceptual Framework." *World Development* 29(10): 1623–48.

Arcand, J.-L., L. Bassole, G. Rota-Graziosi, and J. P. Tranchant. 2008. "The Making of a (Vice) President: Party Politics, Ethnicity, Village Loyalty and Community-Driven Development." CERDI Working Paper 200633, Centre d'Etudes et de Recherches sur le Développement International, Clermont-Ferrand, France.

Arcand, J.-L., and M. Fafchamps. 2012. "Matching in Community-Based Organizations." *Journal of Development Economics* 98(2): 203–19.

Baiocchi, G., P. Heller, and M. Silva. 2011. *Bootstrapping Democracy: Transforming Local Governance and Civil Society in Brazil*. Stanford, CA: Stanford University Press.

Ban, R., S. Jha, and V. Rao. 2012. "Who Has Voice in a Deliberative Democracy: Evidence from Transcripts of Village Parliaments in South Asia." *Journal of Development Economics* 99(2): 428–38.

Ban, R., and V. Rao. 2009. "Is Deliberation Equitable: Evidence from Transcripts of Village Meetings in India." Policy Research Working Paper 4928, World Bank, Washington, DC.

Bardhan, P., and D. Mookherjee. 2012. *Political Clientelism and Capture: Theory and Evidence from West Bengal*. Working Paper, Department of Economics, University of California, Berkeley.

Bardhan, P. K., D. Mookherjee, and M. P. Torrado. 2010. "Impact of Political Reservations in West Bengal Local Governments on Anti-Poverty Targeting." *Journal of Globalization and Development* 1(1): 1–34.

Barron, P., M. Woolcock, and R. Diprose. 2011. *Contesting Development: Participatory Projects and Local Conflict Dynamics in Indonesia*. New Haven, CT: Yale University Press.

Beaman, L., R. Chattopadhyay, E. Duflo, R. Pande, and P. Topalova. 2009. "Powerful Women: Does Exposure Reduce Bias?" *Quarterly Journal of Economics* 124(4): 1497–540.

Beaman, L., E. Duflo, R. Pande, and P. Topalova. 2012. "Female Leadership Raises Aspirations and Educational Attainment for Girls: A Policy Experiment in India." *Science* 335(6068): 582–86.

Beath, A., F. Christia, and R. Enikolopev. 2011. *Elite Capture of Local Institutions: Evidence from a Field Experiment in Afghanistan.* Working Paper, Department of Government, Harvard University, Cambridge, MA.

Bellows, J., and E. Miguel. 2006. "War and Institutions: New Evidence from Sierra Leone." *American Economic Review* 96(2): 394–99.

Besley, T., R. Pande, L. Rahman, and V. Rao. 2004. "The Politics of Public Good Provision: Evidence from Indian Local Governments." *Journal of the European Economics Association* 2(2–3): 416–26.

Besley, T., R. Pande, and V. Rao. 2005. "Participatory Democracy in Action: Survey Evidence from Rural India." *Journal of the European Economic Association* 3(2–3): 648–57.

Bhavnani, R. R. 2009. "Do Electoral Quotas Work after They Are Withdrawn? Evidence from a Natural Experiment in India." *American Political Science Review* 103(1): 23–35.

Cabannes, Y. 2004. "Participatory Budgeting: A Significant Contribution to Participatory Democracy." *Environment and Urbanization* 16(1): 27–46.

Casey, K., R. Glennerster, and E. Miguel. 2011. "Reshaping Institutions: "Evidence on Aid Impacts Using a Pre-Analysis Plan." Abdul Latif Jameel Poverty Action Lab Working Paper, MIT, Cambridge, MA.

Camacho, A., and E. Conover. 2011. "Manipulation of Social Program Eligibility." *American Economic Journal: Economic Policy* 3(2): 41–65.

Chase, R. S., R. N. Christensen, and M. Thongyou. 2006. *Picking Winners or Making Them? Evaluating the Social Capital Impact of CDD in Thailand.* World Bank, Social Development Department, Washington, DC.

Chattopadhyay, R., and E. Duflo. 2004a. "The Impact of Reservation in the Panchayati Raj: Evidence from a Nationwide Randomized Experiment." *Economic and Political Weekly* 39(9): 979–86.

———. 2004b. "Women as Policy Makers: Evidence from a Randomized Policy Experiment in India." *Econometrica* 72(5): 1409–33.

Chin, A., and N. Prakash. 2010. "The Redistributive Effects of Political Reservation for Minorities: Evidence from India." NBER Working Paper 16509, National Bureau of Economic Research, Cambridge, MA.

Cliffe, S., S. Guggenheim, and M. Kostner. 2003. "Community-Driven Reconstruction as an Instrument in War-to-Peace Transitions." Conflict Prevention and Reconstruction Working Paper 7, World Bank, Washington, DC.

Deininger, K., and Y. Liu. 2008. "Economic and Social Impacts of Self-Help Groups in India." World Bank, Development Economics Research Group, Washington, DC.

Duflo, E., and P. Topalova. 2004. "Unappreciated Service: Performance, Perceptions, and Women Leaders in India." Working Paper, Department of Economics, MIT, Cambridge, MA.

Dunning, T., and J. Nilekani. 2010. "When Formal Institutions Are Not Enough: Caste, Party Politics, and Distribution in Indian Village Councils." Working Paper, Department of Political Science, Yale University, New Haven, CT.

Evans, P. 2004. "Development as Institutional Change: The Pitfalls of Monocropping and the Potentials of Deliberation." *Studies in Comparative International Development* 38(4): 30–52.

Fearon, J. D., M. Humphreys, and J. M. Weinstein. 2009. "Can Development Aid Contribute to Social Cohesion after Civil War? Evidence from a Field Experiment in Post-Conflict Liberia." *American Economic Review* 99(2): 287–91.

Fung, A., and E. O. Wright. 2003. "Thinking about Empowered Participatory Governance." In *Deepening Democracy: Institutional Innovations in Empowered Participatory Governance*, ed. A. Fung, and E. O. Wright, 3–42. New York: Verso.

Galasso, E., and M. Ravallion. 2005. "Decentralized Targeting of an Antipoverty Program." *Journal of Public Economics* 89(4): 705–27.

Heller, P., K. N. Harilal, and S. Chaudhuri. 2007. "Building Local Democracy: Evaluating the Impact of Decentralization in Kerala, India." *World Development* 35(4): 626–48.

Houtzager, P., A. Acharya, and A. J. Lavalle. 2007. "Associations and the Exercise of Citizenship in New Democracies: Evidence from São Paulo and Mexico City." IDS Working Paper 285, Institute of Development Studies, Brighton, United Kingdom.

Humphreys, M., W. A. Masters, and M. E. Sandbu. 2006. "The Role of Leaders in Democratic Deliberations: Results from a Field Experiment in São Tomé and Príncipe." *World Politics* 58(4): 583–622.

Kumar, N. R. 2007. *Pro-Poor Targeting and Participatory Governance: Evidence from Central India*. Institute for Economic Development Working Paper, Department of Economics, Boston University, Boston, MA.

Labonne, J., and R. S. Chase. 2008. *Do Community-Driven Development Projects Enhance Social Capital? Evidence from the Philippines*. Policy Research Working Paper, World Bank, Washington, DC.

Leino, J. 2007. "Ladies First? Gender and the Community Management of Water Infrastructure in Kenya." Working Paper, Department of Economics, University of California, Berkeley.

Mansbridge, J. 1999. "Everyday Talk in the Deliberative System." In *Essays in Democracy and Disagreement*, ed. S. Macedo, 211–42. New York: Oxford University Press.

Mansuri, G. 2012. "Harnessing Community: Assortative Matching in Participatory Community Organizations." Poverty Reduction and Equity Group, World Bank, Washington DC.

Munshi, K., and M. Rosenzweig. 2009. "The Efficacy of Parochial Politics: Caste, Commitment, and Competence in Indian Local Governments." NBER Working Paper 14335, National Bureau of Economic Research, Cambridge, MA.

Olken, B. 2006. "Corruption and the Costs of Redistribution: Micro Evidence from Indonesia." *Journal of Public Economics* 90(4–5): 853–70.

———. 2010. "Direct Democracy and Local Public Goods: Evidence from a Field Experiment in Indonesia." *American Political Science Review* 104(2): 243–67.

Palaniswamy, N., and N. Krishnan. 2008. "Local Politics, Political Institutions and Public Resource Allocation." IFPRI Discussion Paper, International Food Policy Research Institute, Washington DC.

Paluck, E. L. 2010. "Is It Better Not to Talk? Group Polarization, Extended Contact, and Perspective Taking in Eastern Democratic Republic of Congo." *Personality and Social Psychology Bulletin* 36(9): 1170–85.

Paluck, E. L., and D. P. Green. 2009. "Deference, Dissent, and Dispute Resolution: An Experimental Intervention Using Mass Media to Change Norms and Behavior in Rwanda." *American Political Science Review* 103(4): 622–44.

Pearce, J. 2007. "Violence, Power and Participation: Building Citizenship in Contexts of Chronic Violence." IDS Working Paper 274, Institute of Development Studies, Brighton, United Kingdom.

Rao, V., and P. Sanyal. 2010. "Dignity Through Discourse: Poverty and the Culture of Deliberation in Indian Village Democracies." *Annals of the American Academy of Political and Social Science* 629(May): 146–72.

Schneider, A., and M. Baquero. 2006. "Get What You Want, Give What You Can: Embedded Public Finance in Porto Alegre." IDS Working Paper 22, Institute of Development Studies, Brighton, United Kingdom.

Schneider, A., and B. Goldfrank. 2002. "Budgets and Ballots in Brazil: Participatory Budgeting from the City to the State." IDS Working Paper 149, Institute of Development Studies, Brighton, United Kingdom.

Serageldin, M., J. Driscoll, L. M. S. Miguel, L. Valenzuela, C. Bravo, E. Solloso, C. Sola-Morales, and T. Watkin. 2003. "Assessment of Participatory Budgeting in Brazil." Paper prepared for the Inter-American Development Bank, Washington, DC.

Souza, C. 2001. "Participatory Budgeting in Brazilian Cities: Limits and Possibilities in Building Democratic Institutions." *Environment and Urbanization* 13(1): 159–84.

Strand, A., H. Toje, A. M. Jerve, and I. Samset. 2003. "Community-Driven Development in Contexts of Conflict." Case Study, Chr. Michelsen Institute, Bergen, Norway.

Swidler, A. 1986. "Culture in Action: Symbols and Strategies." *American Sociological Review* 51(2): 273–86.

Swidler, A., and S. Watkins. 2011. "Practices of Deliberation in Rural Malawi." Paper presented at the conference "Deliberation and Development: New Directions," World Bank, Washington, DC, November.

Wampler, B. 2004. "Expanding Accountability through Participatory Institutions: Mayors, Citizens, and Budgeting in Three Brazilian Municipalities." *Latin American Politics and Society* 46(2): 73–99.

World Bank. 2011. *World Development Report 2011: Conflict, Security, and Development.* Washington, DC: World Bank.

Zamboni, Y. 2007. "Participatory Budgeting and Local Governance: An Evidence-Based Evaluation of Participatory Budgeting Experiences in Brazil." University of Bristol, United Kingdom.

CHAPTER SEVEN

Conclusion: How Can Participatory Interventions Be Improved?

DEVELOPMENT IS MORE THAN A TECHNICAL UNDERTAKING THAT can be handled by experts. It is a complex and often contentious process that works better when citizens participate in decisions that shape their lives and allows them to monitor the people whose task it is to govern their destinies. Consequently, it may make sense to engage citizens in the process of development and to induce communities to act collectively to make governments more accountable. Involving citizens in decision making may also have intrinsic value, because training them in the everyday business of democratic governance may enhance their dignity and promote their quest for freedom. As recent popular movements have demonstrated, these values have wide resonance.

The value of participation is clear. What is far less clear is whether participation can be induced through the type of large-scale government and donor-funded participatory programs that have become a leitmotif of development policy. This question is at the heart of this report.

This report does not emphasize more organic forms of participation, in the form of trade unions, civic watchdog groups, producer and consumer cooperatives, or activist groups of various types. Such engagement has tremendous capacity to initiate positive change. Indeed, it has been a driving force in many societal transformations throughout history, including the anticolonial and civil rights movements of the last century, the growing environmental movements, and the many ongoing movements for political and human rights, including recent popular democracy movements in the Middle East.[1]

In practice, organic and induced forms of participation are often linked. Large-scale induced projects may scale up organic initiatives or develop in conjunction with organic activism. An initial

The value of participation is clear . . .

. . . less clear is whether it can be induced through the kind of programs that have become a leitmotif of development policy.

outside stimulus may spur the growth of more organic institutions or movements.

From the perspective of development policy, however, it is induced participation that is being fostered, and it is on this that much hope has been pinned and tremendous resources expended. Moreover, there is a particular challenge at the heart of attempts to induce participation. It is to harness the spirit of organic participation—which is driven by motivated agents, is contextually sensitive and long-term, and is constantly innovating in response to local realities—and to turn it into a large, state-driven, bureaucratically led enterprise. It is this challenge that is the focus of our report.

This report examines two major modalities for inducing local participation: community development and the decentralization of resources and authority to local governments. Community development supports efforts to bring villages, urban neighborhoods, or other groupings of people into the process of managing development resources through a project-based approach. Advocates for community development believe that it enhances the capacity for collective action, builds community cohesion or "social capital," and strengthens the ability of the poor and disenfranchised to obtain better public services from providers and greater responsiveness from governments. The most common justification for community-based development is that it empowers the powerless by increasing "voice."

Community development projects are sometimes implemented through formally constituted local governments, but often they operate quite independently, and in some cases, such as in postconflict environments, they effectively substitute for formal decentralization. Community development projects have been variously labeled as "social funds," "community-based development," and "community-driven development"—all terms coined within the World Bank over the past two decades. Within each of these categories, project designs can range from community-based targeting, in which only the selection of beneficiaries is decentralized, to projects in which communities are involved in all aspects, from design to implementation and resource management.

In recent years, as the effort to expand community engagement in service delivery has increased, participatory education and health projects have become more common. These projects have many of the same features as more traditional community-based development or community-driven development projects, which usually focus on infrastructure, skills training, private transfers, and credit, in addition to "community mobilization." Most recently, such projects have also morphed into community livelihood projects, which, as their name suggests, focus greater attention on expanding opportunities for sustainable livelihoods for the poor through the promotion of participatory mechanisms for expanding access to markets, investing in communal assets, and building market linkages.

Decentralization refers to efforts to strengthen village and municipal governments on both the demand and supply sides. On the demand side, decentralization strengthens citizens' participation in local government by, for example, instituting regular elections, improving access to information, and fostering mechanisms for deliberative decision making. On the supply side, decentralization aims to enhance the ability of local governments to provide services by increasing their financial resources, strengthening the capacity of local officials and streamlining and rationalizing their administrative functions. As this report is about participatory development, the decentralization evidence focuses on the demand side.[2]

This report builds a conceptual framework for thinking about when and how to induce participation that is structured around the idea of "civil society failure." Markets and governments are now widely recognized as subject to failure. Yet the policy literature, particularly at the local level, is rife with solutions to market and government failures that assume that groups of people (village communities, urban neighborhood associations, school councils, water user groups) will always work toward a common interest. Rarely is much thought explicitly given to the possibility of civil society failure—the possibility that communities, however constituted, may also face significant problems of coordination, asymmetric information, and inequality, which may limit their ability to respond to and resolve market and government failures.[3]

Development policy related to participatory processes needs to be informed by a thoughtful diagnosis of potential civil society failure and its interaction with market and government failures. Such an analysis is necessary for developing a clearer understanding of the tradeoffs involved in moving decisions to local communities, in each context. It is also necessary for identifying the avenues that any given project or policy provides to rectify or repair specific civil society failures.

The report reviews more than 500 empirical studies of participatory development interventions to address issues of central interest to policy makers. These issues include the following:

Markets and governments are now widely recognized as subject to failure . . .

. . . but civic groups are often (erroneously) assumed to always work toward a common interest.

- The viability of using participatory poverty reduction projects as a vehicle for improving important development outcomes, such as service delivery, livelihoods, infrastructure quality, or the management of common pool resources
- The potential for induced participatory projects to increase government accountability and reduce capture and corruption
- The efficacy of participatory projects versus programs implemented in parallel by local governments
- The feasibility of sustaining positive outcomes when projects go to scale
- Whether induced participation can create durable improvements in social cohesion, citizenship, "voice," or the capacity for collective action.

A growing body of literature allows for a better understanding of some of these questions. This newer literature, as well as a large body of case studies, was used to build an evidence base for these questions. In doing so, the report cast a relatively wide net, using well-executed studies by economists, sociologists, political scientists, and anthropologists. The report, does not, however, make any attempt to be exhaustive, particularly for the case study evidence.

On several important issues, the literature is thin. For these issues, the report relied on the few (often one or two) carefully executed studies that were available. Greater weight was placed on studies that had a valid comparison group. Without an adequate comparison group, it is difficult to attribute observed changes in beneficiary communities to the specific program or intervention being assessed. The wider process of development can alter outcomes over time through processes that operate independently of the intervention.

Generally speaking, the report's findings derive from econometric analysis. Ideally, this econometric work should be complemented by good qualitative work, which can help to illuminate the processes that resulted in the observed impact. There is an unfortunate dearth of such work.

Three lessons, drawn from the evidence, appear to be abundantly clear:

Context, both local and national, is extremely important.

- Context, both local and national, is extremely important. Outcomes from interventions are highly variable across communities. History; geography; and the nature of social interactions, networks, and political systems all have a strong influence. As a

286

result, a successful project designed for one context may fail miserably in another. Strong built-in systems of learning and monitoring, sensitivity to context, and the willingness and ability to adapt are therefore critical in implementing projects. As some of the evidence shows, carefully designed projects, whether they are implemented by governments or by donor-funded implementing agencies, are able to limit the negative impact of "bad" community characteristics, at least to a degree.

- The idea that all communities have a stock of "social capital" that can be readily harnessed is naive in the extreme. Building citizenship, engaging communities in monitoring service providers and governments, and supporting community-based management of natural resources or management of infrastructure requires a serious and sustained engagement in building local capacity.

- Both theory and evidence indicate that induced participatory interventions work best when they are supported by a responsive state. Although local actors may have an informational and locational advantage, they appear to use it to benefit the disadvantaged only where institutions and mechanisms to ensure local accountability are robust. In fact, local oversight is most effective when higher-level institutions of accountability function well and communities have the capacity to effectively monitor service providers and others in charge or public resources. Thus, induced participatory development appears to increase, rather than diminish, the need for functional and strong institutions at the center. It also implies that project implementing agencies for donor-funded projects need to have the capacity to exercise adequate oversight. However, there is little evidence that donors alone can substitute for a nonfunctional state as a higher-level accountability agent. When funds are parachuted into communities without any monitoring by a supportive state, decision making is captured by elites who control the local cooperative infrastructure, leading to a high risk of corruption. Reforms that enhance judicial oversight, allow for independent audit agencies, and protect and promote the right to information and a free media appear to be necessary for effective local participation.

These findings are consistent with the large body of case study evidence that Fox (1993) describes as a "sandwich movement" of

The idea that all communities have a stock of "social capital" that can be readily harnessed is naive in the extreme.

Induced participatory development appears to increase, rather than diminish, the need for functional and strong institutions at the center.

To effectively induce participation, enlightened state action from above has to interact with social mobilization from below.

In the local sphere, within which the intervention is conducted, the center has to ensure that local agents of the state are responsive to community demands.

enlightened state action from above interacting with social mobilization from below.[4] The state does not necessarily have to be democratic (although democratic states are more likely to support development). However, in the sphere in which the intervention is conducted—at the level of the community or the neighborhood—the state has to be responsive to community demands. For example, schools that incorporate parents into decision making will be more responsive to parental demands if parents have a measure of control over school budgets. Village governments will become more responsive to the needs of citizens when both function within an electoral democracy supplemented by deliberative interactions.

The Importance of Context

Inducing local participation is a difficult, often unpredictable, and potentially contentious undertaking.

Inducing local participation is a difficult, often unpredictable, and potentially contentious undertaking. The empirical evidence presented in this report must be viewed with this fact in mind. The heterogeneity in outcomes should not be surprising once the role played by local conditions and the precise contours of project design are understood. Given the increased (and sensible) emphasis on civic engagement for effective and equitable development, it is important to build a body of solid evidence on the effectiveness of specific modalities for inducing participation and to assess the cost-effectiveness of such efforts.

In view of the substantial reliance on evidence from quantitative evaluations of community-driven development projects and decentralization efforts, it is also important to reiterate that an effective evaluation must proceed with some understanding of a project's trajectory and the timeline over which an impact on specific project outcomes is likely to be observed. Predicting a trajectory of change is hard to do in participatory projects. Very few evaluations take this issue seriously or verify assumptions about long-term impacts by returning to the site of the project after a few years have passed. Moreover, some outcomes may be inherently difficult to measure. Most evaluations, for example, are likely to miss subtle shifts in perceptions or beliefs that could mature years later into effective civic activism or a more inclusive society.

Local development policy occurs at the intersection of market, government, and civil society failures; interactions are deeply conditioned by culture, politics, and social structure, and they vary from place to place. Context matters, at both the national and the local level (for more on context, see Goodin and Tilly 2006). At the national level, nationalist ideologies—the manner in which the (colonial and postcolonial) state has created and propagated identity—can create symbolic public goods that facilitate collective action by building a participatory ethic.

History matters. The way policies and institutions—land reforms, education systems, the judiciary, the media, and efforts at social inclusion—have evolved can influence the responsiveness of governments to civic mobilization, affecting the incentives for collective action. A history of organic participation matters greatly, for several reasons. Some countries have a long history of civic participation, developed in the process of struggles for independence from colonial rule or against the rule of entrenched elites. Such social movements help give legitimacy to civic activists and create a culture that facilitates civic mobilization. A history of organic participation creates a community of peer educators, who can train others on how to reach a consensus, engage in participatory planning, and hold governments accountable for their actions. In time, organic participation can make it easier to institute a cadre of trained facilitators who can spearhead scaled-up community-based interventions. A history of organic participation also creates an enabling environment within which social entrepreneurs can spark participatory innovations, the most effective of which can have important lessons for scaled-up induced interventions.

The social, economic, demographic, and cultural contexts matter. The nature and extent of social and economic inequality and the composition and diversity of groups affect both induced and organic participation. Inequality and heterogeneity strongly affect the cultures and norms of cooperation that evolve within a community. These norms have a bearing not only on the nature of collective action but also on the role of local leaders. Do local leaders act in ways that support or undermine the larger interests of the community they claim to represent? Do they maximize rents, or do they lead with the collective welfare of the community in mind?

Geography matters. Remoteness from more developed areas, difficult terrain, and harsh weather conditions can increase vulnerability, leading to weaker development outcomes. Both social heterogeneity and geography have a bearing on the local cooperative infrastructure—the community's capacity for collective action. If a village has a long history of successfully managing common property resources, that capacity

History matters.

The social, economic, demographic, and cultural contexts matter.

Geography matters.

could potentially translate into a collaboration to manage a school, for example. Urban migrant communities can consist of people from the same region (who therefore retain rural norms and customs) or different places (which could make cooperative behavior more challenging).

Politics matters.

Politics matters.[5] The nature of the local state and its relationship with local communities deeply affects the extent to which the "nexus of accommodation" hampers development. As described in chapter 3, in contexts with compound market, government, and civil society failures, local and national political leaders, bureaucrats, and strongmen are often embedded within an extractive equilibrium in which the interests of citizens are given the lowest priority. Breaking this nexus—changing the equilibrium in a manner that makes the state more responsive to the needs of citizens—is at the heart of effective participatory development.

Donors, Governments, and Trajectories of Change

Effective civic engagement does not develop along a predictable trajectory. It is likely to proceed along a "punctuated equilibrium," characterized by long periods of seeming quietude followed by intense and often turbulent change. The "quiet" periods are not inactive. They are full of nascent, covert action, during which civic activists slowly begin to influence their neighbors to think differently, act collectively, deliberate effectively, and develop the courage to take on powerful interests. Without such risk-taking, the nexus of accommodation is hard to break.

Donor-driven participatory projects often ignore the fact that effective civic engagement does not develop along a predictable trajectory.

When donor-driven induced participatory projects attempt to build civic capacity, they assume a far less contentious trajectory. Conditioned by bureaucratic imperatives, they often declare that clear, measurable, and usually wildly optimistic outcomes—including greater civic capacity—will be delivered within a specified timeframe. As most projects are sold as poverty reduction or local infrastructure projects, declared outcomes include declines in poverty and vulnerability, without much attention to the effort, resources, or time frame required to achieve a sustained increase in the incomes of the poor. Unrealistic expectations often set such projects up for failure.

Changing social and political systems is far less predictable than building dams, bridges, roads, schools, or clinics.

One important reason behind this overly ambitious approach, especially at the World Bank, is that it maintains a path-dependent institutional structure that continues to derive from a focus on capital-intensive development and reconstruction. Building dams, bridges, roads, or even schools and clinics is a much more predictable activity than changing social and political systems. Repairing civil society and addressing political failures requires a shift in the social equilibrium that derives from a change in the nature of social interactions and from modifying norms and local cultures.

These tasks are much harder to achieve than building infrastructure. They require a fundamentally different approach to development—one that is flexible, long term, self-critical, and strongly infused with the spirit of learning by doing. As demonstrated later in this chapter, the World Bank falls far short of adopting this kind of approach in its participatory projects. Other donors are probably not much different.

> A fundamentally different approach to development—one that is flexible, long term, self-critical, and strongly infused with the spirit of learning by doing—is needed.

Open Research Questions

The evidence on many participation-related issues is thin. More research is needed on several open questions.

What Is the Link between Local Civic Capacity and a National Civic Sphere?

Under what conditions will attempts to build local civic capacity help build a national civic sphere? This question goes at least as far back as John Stuart Mill, who believed that good citizenship is built at the local level. Many participatory interventions—particularly interventions that attempt to transform the nature of citizenship by improving the "demand side" of governance and "building trust" in postconflict situations—are premised on the belief that such interventions will lead to a more accountable and cohesive civic culture at the national level. Very little is known about whether these local interventions are effective, however, or whether they can coalesce into national civic movements. In fact, the evidence suggests that under some conditions, greater local cohesiveness can actually exacerbate communal tensions.

How Important Is the State?

A related set of questions refers to the incentives faced by central governments in devolving power to local communities. Under what conditions can devolution be sustained over the long term instead of being rolled back by central authorities? How does this possibility of policy reversal affect the design and implementation of such programs? If participatory projects require an effective central state, is participatory development inappropriate in countries with weak states? How can local development be promoted in communities in which the central state is not effective?

The evidence overwhelmingly suggests that effective community-based interventions have to be implemented in conjunction with a responsive state. Yet almost all econometric studies of participatory interventions focus on the communities themselves rather than the context within which they operate.

More generally, research is needed on how to make the state, and its agents, more responsive to communities. What is most important—incentives, better monitoring, or training?

There is also a debate over whether donors can substitute for a non-functional central government as a higher-level accountability agent. It is possible that they may help in the short term (by improving the performance of interventions) but be harmful in the long term (by hampering the evolution of an effective state). This largely theoretical debate should be complemented by better evidence.

How Important Is Democracy?

Credible elections within decentralized settings appear to provide a clearer mechanism than informal deliberation for punishing unpopular policy choices or excessive rent-seeking by incumbents. More research should be conducted on the conditions under which elections work, and—in particular—whether community-driven development projects that induce greater accountability with elections and mandated inclusion improve their effectiveness. Another important open question is the extent to which a shift toward democracy at the local level affects the allocation of resources, particularly if it shifts resources away from traditional elites and toward the less powerful in society.

How Do Top-down and Bottom-up Approaches Compare?

The evidence is very limited on how top-down approaches compare with bottom-up approaches in delivering goods and services to communities. Most evaluations of participatory approaches typically compare the intervention with the status quo—a counterfactual in which nothing is done. Such an approach says nothing about whether participatory interventions are better or worse than centrally administered interventions.

How Effective Are Local Interventions with "Soft Outcomes"?

Questions remain even about the efficacy of local interventions that seek to achieve "soft outcomes." Does participation build the capacity for collective action? Is it empowering? Do citizenship training programs work? Very few studies examine these questions, most of which do not lend themselves to easy generalization. Moreover, the literature tends to measure soft outcomes with responses to survey questions, which can be unreliable in measuring impact. Greater use of framed field experiments and behavioral games in conjunction with survey data could be beneficial.

What Is the Appropriate Role for Nongovernmental Organizations and Facilitators?

Very little is known about the efficacy of the widespread practice of hiring nongovernmental organizations (NGOs) to plan and implement projects and provide services at the local level. Is doing so more efficient than giving such authority directly to local governments or community bodies?

Facilitators are the lynchpins of induced participation, yet almost nothing is known about their incentives, their training, or the social and political constraints they face. Much more could be learned about how to improve their performance and even the extent to which basic factors such as experience, age, and gender affect performance.

How Should the Poor Be Targeted?

Too little evidence is available on whether targeting the poor with proxy means testing or other centralized "objective" metrics of household status is better or worse than community-based targeting.

How Important Is Corruption?

A few important studies of corruption have been conducted, and there is an increasing, and healthy, trend toward relying more on direct measures of corruption (for example, engineering assessments of road quality) rather than perception-based measures. This kind of research should become the norm, as improving the demand side of governance is often claimed as a cure for corruption and perception-based measures tend to map poorly to measured levels of corruption and capture.

How Well Have Livelihood Projects Worked?

Livelihood projects and other attempts to use community-based interventions to repair market failures, including community management of microcredit funds, remain largely unstudied. Very little is known about attempts to use community groups (artisans cooperatives, farmers cooperatives, and so forth) for income-generating activities. Some case study evidence exist on these issues, but little rigorous quantitative analysis has been conducted.

What Makes Deliberation Effective?

Another set of questions goes to the heart of the decision-making process within communities. What makes deliberation effective? Do facilitators contribute to the deliberative process? To what extent does deliberation influence the process of preference aggregation, building consensus among people with heterogeneous interests? How can the quality of deliberation be improved? Can deliberative spaces be made more effective and deliberative systems built?

What Kind of Research Should Be Conducted?

Most studies of large-scale participatory interventions ignore the processes that lead to an outcome (or the lack of one). Process is much better understood with the use of qualitative tools. Thus, more than most other development interventions, evaluations of participatory projects call for a mix of qualitative and quantitative methods—something that is almost never done well. A promising mode of enquiry is the use of qualitative data with research designs that are typically associated with quantitative studies—large samples, experimental designs, or the use of methods to generate credible counterfactuals such as matching.

Very few well-done, in-depth ethnographies of participatory projects have been conducted. Although some development anthropologists are

Very few well-done, in-depth ethnographies of participatory projects have been conducted.

beginning to do serious work in this area, much of the literature on the anthropology of participatory development seems to rely on thin data (a perfunctory reading of project literature, "touch the water buffalo" field visits that last a week or two). Some of these studies have received wide attention in the anthropological literature, but their appeal likely derives from their ability to tap into preexisting prejudices about "neoliberal" institutions rather than from the carefully grounded ethnographic insights that characterize the best anthropological work.

Monitoring, Evaluation, and Attention to Context: Results of a Survey of World Bank Projects

The variability in the local context and the uncertainty surrounding the trajectories of participatory development projects highlight the importance of developing effective monitoring and evaluation (M&E) systems. To be effective, participatory development projects require constant adjustment, learning in the field, and experimentation.

> To be effective, participatory development projects require constant adjustment, learning in the field, and experimentation.

A notable example of an effectively monitored induced community development project is the $1.3 billion Kecamatan Development Program (KDP) in Indonesia, which was active between 1998 and 2008. KDP provided block grants directly to rural community-based organizations to fund development plans prepared through a participatory process. In this regard, it was very similar to a large number of other community-based projects. Where it differed was in the extent to which it relied on context-specific design and attention to monitoring systems (Guggenheim 2006).

KDP's design was based on two key elements: a careful analysis of existing state and community capacity and cooperative infrastructure, drawn from a set of studies of local institutions, and a deep understanding of the history of community development in Indonesia. Implementation involved creating a tiered network of motivated and trained facilitators, who created a feedback loop to facilitate learning and worked with engineers to supervise construction. Villagers took control of expenditures and procured goods and services on a competitive basis. They formed monitoring teams that checked the delivery of material and the quality of construction, reporting their findings to the village forum. In addition to participatory monitoring, the project conducted audits at the subdistrict (*kecamatan*) level. In addition, independent NGOs and journalists were contracted to monitor and report on the quality of the project on a random basis. These innovations in monitoring were supplemented with more conventional quantitative tools, such as a carefully designed management information system (MIS), several qualitative and quantitative evaluations, and case studies (Wong 2003). Most important, the project emphasized an honest system of communication, which allowed observations, both critical and complimentary, to constantly inform innovations in design and implementation. KDP is among a small group of World Bank–funded participatory projects that have made an effort to build effective monitoring systems.

> Most World Bank–funded participatory projects have not made an effort to build effective monitoring and evaluation systems.

As part of the background work for this report, the authors conducted a review of M&E systems in World Bank–supported participatory projects, with a view to understanding the extent to which induced projects take learning by doing seriously.[6] The data come from the analysis of documents from 345 projects in operation between 1999 and 2007, all of which allocated more than a third of their budgets to participation. For a randomly selected subsample of 20 percent of these projects, the design of the M&E system was assessed by analyzing the project appraisal documents for each project. These documents—one of the main documents the Bank's Executive Board examines before approving a loan—should ideally include a detailed account of the monitoring system and of the manner in which the project will be evaluated.

The analysis also examined implementation status reports and implementation completion reports for the sampled projects, in order to assess the effectiveness of the M&E systems proposed in the project appraisal documents. Implementation status reports are typically prepared by the project manager after every supervision mission. Implementation completion reports are self-evaluations of projects screened by the Independent Evaluation Group.[7] The analysis also assessed information from project supervision documents, which synthesize the results of regular project visits by Bank operational task teams.

An important limitation of these data is that they exclude any kind of M&E activity that is not reported in project documents. A survey of managers of current and recently completed community development projects was conducted to fill this gap. The survey, conducted in 2010, was sent to all 165 managers of the 245 projects that were either active in 2009 or had closed the previous year.[8] Forty-one managers (25 percent) completed most of the survey questions (all figures reported in this chapter come from project managers who completed a significant portion of the survey). The responses suggest that the survey was more likely to be completed by project managers whose projects had some type of M&E system in place. The results therefore likely provide an upper bound on the presence and quality of monitoring and evaluation systems in place across all participatory projects at the World Bank.

Findings from Project Documents

One of the striking things about the project appraisal documents is how similar they are. It is almost as if there is a template for participatory projects. Not only the design but also the language often seems to be cut and pasted from one project to the next, suggesting a lack of attention to context in designing participatory projects.

Although all of the project appraisal documents surveyed mentioned M&E, only about 40 percent described it as an essential part of the project design. And although 80 percent of the implementing agencies engaged an M&E specialist, the quality of the specialist—like the quality of the implementation—was highly variable. Furthermore, only about 40 percent of the sample documents detailed the kind of monitoring information that was collected. One-third of the documents did not even state that an MIS—a key project monitoring tool—was part of the information collection system.

To improve the quality of project M&E, the Bank introduced a new results-based management framework in 2004. All project appraisal documents are now required to show how the project's monitoring indicators will make it possible to attribute outcomes to changes introduced by the project. In the past, indicators were so broadly defined— "reduction in the gap between rural and urban income inequalities," "improvement of GDP per capita"—that they may or may not have been an outcome of the project. The new results framework requires that relevant and easily measured indicators be included in the final matrix of outcomes, so that project impacts can be more easily tracked. Furthermore, the results framework must include data collection methods and measurable objectives, as well as implementation status reports based on monitoring data, to improve learning by doing.[9] The results-based framework was also expected to make M&E more useful as a planning and management tool.

Sampled projects from before and after 2004 were analyzed to determine whether the introduction of these new standards improved the quality of M&E systems. The results show that although the

> The design and even the language of World Bank project documents often seem to be cut and pasted from one project to the next.

> Introduction of the results-based framework in 2004 does not appear to have improved the quality of monitoring and evaluation of World Bank projects.

297

number of M&E indicators was reduced by nearly half, 40 percent of the indicators remained imprecisely formulated ("improved allocation of expenditures," "careful monitoring of effectiveness"). And although the number of indicators reported in implementation status reports rose (from a quarter to about two-thirds), only 22 percent of projects appeared to have collected data on the indicators that were supposed to measure intermediate progress. Most projects thus did not have access to timely monitoring data and could therefore not have been engaged in learning by doing based on real-time project performance data.

The monitoring systems used in these projects were also assessed based on aide-memoires, midterm reviews, and implementation completion reports, which provide a running picture of the Bank team's most important observations and recommendations over the life of the project.[10] Seventy-five percent of the assessments of monitoring systems tended to be negative. The most frequently observed deficiencies were the lack of a well-designed M&E system and poor implementation. These deficiencies were most often attributed to poor human and technical capacity and lack of sufficient funding. Other reasons included the lack of institutional capacity, the absence of a baseline (which made it impossible to track progress), and the formulation of outcome indicators that could not realistically be attributed to the impacts of the project.

Projects performed more or less similarly on evaluations. Although half the project documents explicitly mentioned that impacts were being evaluated and 70 percent of those mentioned some kind of impact evaluation with a comparison group, only 14 percent described the methods employed. Among the more credible methods mentioned were propensity score matching and randomized trials. But the majority used beneficiary assessments, participatory appraisals, and perception surveys, which are not well suited to making causal claims. In the remaining 30 percent of projects, it was not clear what was meant by an evaluation or how it was to be performed.

The degree to which M&E can help the project adapt through learning mechanisms depends on the attention it receives from project managers (that is, whether M&E is a management priority). The experience of project managers with participatory projects may also matter. Among all 374 managers of participatory projects, 44 percent were managing more than one project, and about a third of these managers were managing three or more projects. Project managers tended to be fairly inexperienced with participatory projects, with an average of

Having more than one manager over the life of a project—as half of the World Bank's participatory projects did—can be disruptive for effective management and learning systems.

1.85 years of experience in managing projects of this type and 4.3 years of experience managing projects of any kind. Half of all projects had two or more managers over their life, which can be disruptive for management and for effective learning systems.

An important aspect of learning by doing—and the satisfaction of beneficiaries—is the existence of an effective grievance and complaint mechanism. A third of all project appraisal documents from 1999 to 2007 mention some kind of grievance mechanism, and the average rose from a fifth of all projects before 2004 to half of all projects after 2004. Most project documents from both periods, however, provided very little information about the grievance mechanism. Only a quarter of documents that mentioned such a process explained how it worked, and only a third made provisions for documenting complaints. Complaints received through these mechanisms were sorted into three categories: poor quality of construction works, lack of transparent project selection criteria, and lack of community involvement in the selection process. This rather generalized complaint system raises questions about how well these processes are established in practice.

Complaints and grievance systems can be powerful tools for ensuring that difficulties experienced by various project partners are considered and addressed in a timely manner. If used correctly, these systems can not only enhance project effectiveness but also promote community ownership of the project. In contrast, using these mechanisms as decorative planning instruments may undermine the engagement of different stakeholders if their complaints are not acted on.

Half of all projects since 2004 have included grievance mechanisms . . .

. . . but few explained how the mechanism worked or indicated how complaints were to be documented.

Findings from a Survey of Project Managers

The group of managers who completed the survey had far more experience with participatory projects than the average project manager: only 5 percent had fewer than 2 years of experience, and almost 60 percent had more than 10 years of experience managing participatory projects (figure 7.1).

More than 60 percent of survey respondents reported that the project had an MIS system that collected and maintained data on both development objectives and intermediate outcomes. More than 60 percent reported that monitoring data were publically available in some form, and half of these managers indicated that this information was available on a website. Almost two-thirds reported that the project collected

Figure 7.1 World Bank project managers' years of experience working on community-driven development and local governance projects

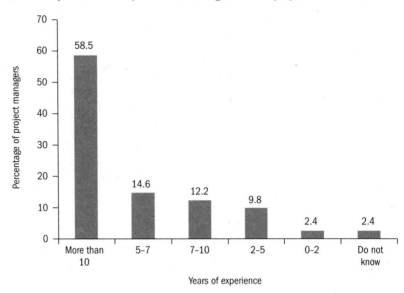

tracking data and that an impact evaluation was either underway or had been completed. A large share also listed other types of monitoring activities, including field missions, participatory assessments, and facilitator feedback.

In the survey, 88 percent of project managers stated that their project had a grievance mechanism in place, and 64 percent of these managers (54 percent overall) reported that a record of grievances was being maintained. The results presented below should therefore be viewed as the opinions of seasoned project managers who were engaged to some degree in building effective M&E systems into their projects.

Strikingly, the vast majority of project managers do not perceive M&E as a priority for Bank Senior Management (figure 7.2). They also believe that if the Bank did not require M&E, government counterparts would not engage in it (figure 7.3). A large majority (75 percent) also believe that the Bank's operational policies do not provide any incentives to engage in systematic M&E (figure 7.4).

Two-thirds of project managers believe that the Bank's M&E requirements and supervision budgets are not tailored to project size, project complexity, or country context (figure 7.5). Only a third believe that the standard timeframe for projects (an average of 5.5 years) is sufficient for realizing participatory objectives (figure 7.6).

> Eighty percent of project managers surveyed believe that if the Bank did not require monitoring and evaluation, government counterparts would not engage in it . . .
>
> . . . and 75 percent believe that the Bank's operational policies do not provide the right incentives to engage in systematic monitoring and evaluation.

Figure 7.2 Percentage of World Bank project managers who believe monitoring and evaluation is a priority for senior management

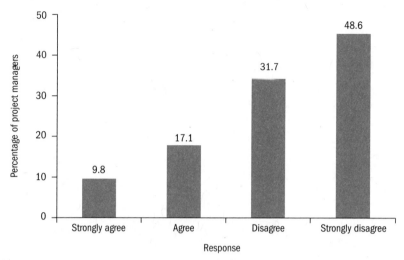

Figure 7.3 Percentage of World Bank project managers who believe government counterparts would engage in monitoring and evaluation if the Bank did not require it

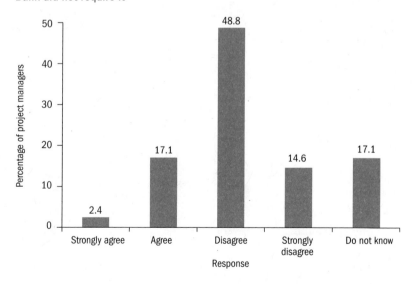

In the end, the measure of how well an M&E system performs is the extent to which data guide project implementation. In the sample review, only 14 percent of projects explicitly outlined procedures for revising the project if the M&E data indicated that it had gone off

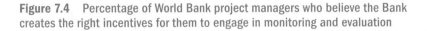

Figure 7.4   Percentage of World Bank project managers who believe the Bank creates the right incentives for them to engage in monitoring and evaluation

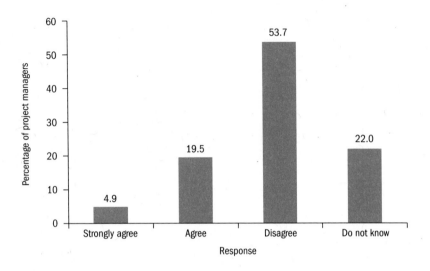

Figure 7.5   Percentage of World Bank project managers who believe that project supervision budgets are tailored to project size, project complexity, and country context

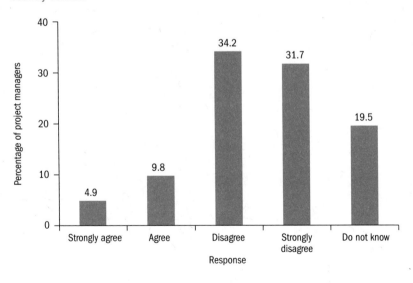

track. Surveyed managers report that important project design changes occurred in only a third of projects. In half of those cases, the changes were induced by internal learning mechanisms; external advice and exogenous changes in the country induced fewer changes. Most changes

Figure 7.6 Percentage of World Bank project managers who believe that participatory development projects are supported long enough to achieve sustainability in community processes

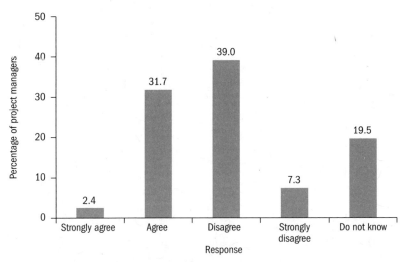

had to do with improvements to the M&E system itself (for example, refinement of indicators) or to the project's participatory mechanisms. These changes led to, among other things, more responsibility being granted to communities (for example, control over the project budget); increased inclusion of vulnerable groups in the participatory process; and closer collaboration with local authorities.

In sum, task managers who responded to the survey demonstrated a reasonable degree of awareness of what constitutes effective M&E design and practice in participatory projects. Many institutional barriers prevented them from translating this knowledge into action, however. An open and effective M&E system requires a tolerance for risk, flexible project design, and adequate resources, little of which was evident.

The survey highlights several problems, including along with lack of management support, the lack of an adequate project supervision budget, and the fact that most World Bank managers believe that governments see monitoring systems as a box to be checked off in order to qualify for a loan rather than as an instrument to help improve the effectiveness of projects. Given their sense that country counterparts have little incentive to implement good M&E systems, explicit support from the World Bank may be critical.

Given project managers' sense that country counterparts have little incentive to implement good monitoring and evaluation systems, explicit support from the World Bank may be critical.

303

The Need for Better Monitoring and Evaluation and Different Project Structures

A review of the literature on participatory development conducted in 2004 found a lack of attention to both monitoring and evaluation (Mansuri and Rao 2004). Eight years later, the gap in evaluation is beginning to be addressed, but there is still a very long way to go. The lack of attention to monitoring changed little over this period. Inflexible institutional rules that do not internalize the complexity inherent in engaging with civic-led development remain, and insufficient emphasis continues to be placed on the importance of context. Unless these conditions improve, participatory development projects will continue to struggle to make a difference.

The World Bank and other donor agencies need to take several steps to improve participatory projects. Projects need to be informed by high-quality political, social, and historical analysis in order to tailor design to context. Currently, most Bank projects include very poor political and social analysis. There is more of a tradition of economic analysis, but even this has not been done well for participatory interventions. Analytical work needs to better understand the intersection between market, government, and civil society failures—particularly at the local level—and how the intervention would address them.

Instead of focusing entirely on inducing participation, policy may also be well served by finding ways to ride the waves of organic participation—by, for example, inviting civic activists to help monitor participatory projects, creating an enabling environment in which civic activists can be agents of change, establishing spaces for public deliberation in local governments, and working with both citizens and governments to create incentives for greater government responsiveness to the needs of citizens. It is not at all clear, however, that directly funding organic activism—say, through a grant mechanism for NGOs—would induce participation. The implementation challenges that come with scale would still be present, without the accountability governments face. Long-term development requires a sustained effort to improve the quality of governance rather than attempts to bypass it by working through organizations outside government.[11]

Poor implementation is often the weakest link in inducing participation at the local level—and also the most difficult to fix—because implementation problems are deeply embedded within a country's social and political environment. Implementation must grapple with some

Poor implementation is often the weakest link in inducing participation at the local level.

of the most difficult challenges facing development policy, including deeply entrenched discrimination and inequality, a culture of corruption, and lack of accountability in government. Given the uncertain trajectories of change in local participatory development and the challenge of adapting to highly variable local contexts, it is critical to track funds, monitor and assess the performance of functionaries, and carefully assess changes in the lives of intended beneficiaries—all of which require effective monitoring systems and well-designed evaluations.

Strengthening Monitoring

Good monitoring data can support project supervision and implementation in real time, reveal potential roadblocks early, and allow for sensible midcourse corrections (shifts in design or implementation). A credible learning-by-doing approach depends on such data.

It would be useful to view impact evaluations not just as tools to be used to assess the total impact of an intervention but as tools that can be used to inform project design by scientifically testing the efficacy of

The use of new cost-effective technologies, such as short message service (SMS)–based reporting and mobile phone–based data collection, could assist greatly in this effort. But better data collection is of no use unless it is coupled with efforts to make the data useful for project managers and facilitators at every level of the project. Making data operationally useful requires developing methods and interfaces where data can be presented in a useful and simple manner for project implementers to understand. It should also include process monitoring, where qualitative data from carefully designed case studies are gathered and summarized to help project staff better understand and find solutions to implementation challenges. Attention also needs to be paid to "soft" monitoring. Grievance mechanisms must have teeth, and complaints about projects must be addressed. Community members should be given authority to shed light on local problems.

Improving Impact Evaluation

Although the impact evaluation of Bank projects has improved in the past eight years, there is much room for improvement. Most participatory projects remain unevaluated, and the projects that are evaluated tend to be the ones that are better designed and implemented, leading to a biased understanding of the effectiveness of such interventions.

It would be useful to view impact evaluations not just as tools to be used to assess the total impact of an intervention but as tools that can be used to inform project design by scientifically testing the efficacy of

The impact evaluation of World Bank–supported participatory projects has improved in the past eight years . . .

. . . but much room remains for improvement.

305

alternative designs in pilot projects, particularly in uncertain contexts, such as postconflict situations. In such contexts, a more experimental approach could be taken, in which carefully designed pilots are scientifically analyzed before being scaled up. Quantitative evaluations would also benefit from complementary qualitative work that sheds light on the processes and mechanisms that lead to change.

In order for M&E systems to be useful, there has to be tolerance for honest feedback to facilitate learning instead of a tendency to rush to judgment coupled with a pervasive fear of failure. The complexity of participatory development requires a higher tolerance for failure. Project managers must have the freedom to take risks and innovate without fear of reprisal if their innovations fail. Inculcating a culture of learning by doing requires a change in the mindset of management and clear incentives for project team leaders to investigate what does and does not work in their projects and to report on it.

Patience is a virtue. Project structures need to change to allow for flexible, long-term engagement with more realistic outcomes and timelines, leaving the door open for long-term and sustained engagement at the local level. Local participation does not contribute to development when it is nothing more than the ad hoc, myopic creation of projects. Local participation works when it has teeth, when it builds on organic movements, when it is facilitated by a responsive center, when it is adequately and sustainably funded, and when interventions are conditioned by a culture of learning by doing.

> If monitoring and evaluation systems are to be useful, there has to be tolerance for honest feedback to facilitate learning . . .
>
> . . . not a rush to judgment coupled with a pervasive fear of failure.

Notes

1. A review by Gaventa and Barrett (2010) focuses on more organic forms of participation at the local level. They review more than 100 case studies of participatory efforts, highlighting several examples in which civic activists in municipalities and villages around the world have bravely and effectively fought against injustice and poverty and for inclusion and accountability.
2. Supply-side aspects have been the focus of other reports and reviews by the World Bank (see Shah 2006a, 2006b; Broadway and Shah 2007).
3. Several project managers have informed the authors of this report, quite forcefully, that they do indeed pay close attention to community capacity in designing projects, which, in their view, take civil society failure into account. However, a careful reading of the World Bank's design documents for participatory projects (PADs) reveals, with a few notable exceptions, that project designs demonstrate a shallow and naive analysis of the ability

of communities to manage their affairs and tackle local government and market failures.

4. See Tendler's (1997) seminal work on decentralized development in Northeast Brazil. However, participatory engagement may make a difference even in the absence of a supportive state, usually when engagement is organic and thus outside of, and often in resistance to, the state (Gaventa and Barrett 2010).

5. Baiocchi, Heller, and Silva (2011) develop a useful typology of the relationship between civil society and the state that has broad applicability to understanding the context for failures in deliberation and participation.

6. The authors are very grateful to Catherine Gamper for conducting the analysis on which this section is based. They are also grateful to the Social Development Anchor for its help in sharing the data and facilitating the survey with task team leaders.

7. The Independent Evaluation Group (IEG) is charged with evaluating the activities of the World Bank Group. Its director-general reports directly to the World Bank's Executive Board. The goals of evaluation are to provide an objective assessment of the results of the Bank Group's work and to identify and disseminate lessons learned from experience.

8. The distribution of projects across regions was as follows (the first number represents the share of participatory projects surveyed in each region, the second represents the share of each region in total projects surveyed): Africa (43 percent, 31 percent); Latin America and the Caribbean (4 percent, 19 percent); South Asia (9 percent, 17 percent); Europe and Central Asia (13 percent, 13 percent); East Asia and Pacific (19 percent, 12 percent); Middle East and North Africa (11 percent, 7 percent).

9. In the past, data collection was often referred to as "general statistical data available," and targets were described in vague terms such as "improved," "increased," or "decreased."

10. On average, there were four aide-memoires per project, and 40 projects had midterm reviews. Aide-memoires and midterm reviews were collected based on the same stratified sample described earlier. The number of projects reviewed was 40 instead of 68, because 28 projects had no English aide-memoires or midterm reviews available.

11. NGOs can play an important role in periods of crisis, when there is a need to deliver emergency assistance quickly. They can also be useful in implementing carefully evaluated experimental pilot projects, which can inform new designs.

References

Baiocchi, G., P. Heller, and M. K. Silva. 2011. *Bootstrapping Democracy: Transforming Local Governance and Civil Society in Brazil.* Stanford, CA: Stanford University Press.

Broadway, R. and A. Shah. 2007. *Intergovernmental Fiscal Transfers: Principles and Practices.* Public Sector Governance and Accountability Series. Washington, DC: World Bank.

Fox, J. 1993. *The Politics of Food in Mexico.* Berkeley: University of California Press.

Gaventa, J., and G. Barrett. 2010. "So What Difference Does It Make? Mapping the Outcomes of Citizen Engagement." IDS Working Paper 347, Institute of Development Studies, Brighton, United Kingdom.

Goodin, R., and C. Tilly. 2006. "It Depends." In *The Oxford Handbook of Contextual Political Analysis,* ed. R. E. Goodin and C. Tilly, 3–32. New York: Oxford University Press.

Guggenheim, S. 2006. "Crises and Contradictions: Understanding the Origins of a Community Development Project in Indonesia." In *The Search for Empowerment: Social Capital as Idea and Practice at the World Bank,* ed. A. Bebbington, S. Guggenheim, E. Olson, and M. Woolcock, 111–44. Hartford, CT: Kumarian.

Mansuri, G., and V. Rao. 2004. "Community-Based and -Driven Development: A Critical Review." *World Bank Research Observer* 19(1): 1–39.

Shah, A. 2006a. *Local Governance in Developing Countries.* Public Sector Governance and Accountability Series. Washington, DC: World Bank.

———. 2006b. *Local Governance in Industrial Countries.* Public Sector Governance and Accountability Series. Washington, DC: World Bank.

Tendler, J. 1997. *Good Government in the Tropics.* Baltimore, MD: Johns Hopkins University Press.

Wong, S. 2003 "Indonesia Kecamatan Development Program: Building a Monitoring and Evaluation System for a Large-Scale Community-Driven Development Program." Discussion Paper, East Asia and Pacific Region, Environment and Social Development Unit, World Bank, Washington, DC.

Index

Figures, notes, and tables are indicated by *f*, *n*, and *t*, respectively.

E

F

G